EDUCATION in the PERSPECTIVE of HISTORY

EDUCATION

EDWARD D. MYERS

Professor of Philosophy, Washington and Lee University

HARPER & BROTHERS PUBLISHERS, NEW YORK

in the
PERSPECTIVE
of HISTORY

With a concluding chapter by

Arnold J. Toynbee

Foreword by Alvin C. Eurich

Contents

Foreword

by
Alvin C. Eurich

In this era of Sputniks, Jupiters, Able and Baker, education can no longer be provincial. Like society, it urgently needs a world view, but such a perspective can come, of course, only from those who have acquired it. This is the educational challenge. Whether or not one agrees with Arnold Toynbee's theory of history or conclusions, his perspicuity and perspective based on a great mosaic of history's intimate details are a matter of record; they stand irrefutable. As a world historian he has no peers.

After reading his *A Study of History* and noting the absence of any treatment of education, we approached him to ask whether he would consider writing a supplementary volume telling how the various civilizations handed down from one generation to the next the accumulated experience, knowledge, and wisdom of the human race. What was the role of education during the "period of growth," the "time of trouble," and the "universal state" of these civilizations? Would such an analysis yield new insights regarding education for our own time and circumstances?

Following some reflection, Professor Toynbee concluded that such a treatise would be eminently worth preparing and might prove to be exceedingly valuable. His world-wide commitments for travel, lecturing, and writing, however, prevented his personally undertaking the detailed study and investigation required for some years to come. Hence he agreed to help plan the study, read critically the text as it was prepared, and write the conclusions if a competent scholar thoroughly familiar with his work would collect the materials and

vii

prepare the text. At Dr. Toynbee's suggestion, Edward D. Myers, Chairman of the Department of Philosophy at Washington and Lee University, was asked to accept the major responsibility for preparing this book. He obtained a year's leave of absence and engaged Professor Albert L. Lancaster of the Virginia Military Institute as an associate. After a period of planning with Dr. Toynbee, they spent the year working in Munich, where the library resources for this type of study were outstanding. At all stages Professor Toynbee remained in close touch with the investigation and, after reading the completed text, he summarized in his conclusion the important implications for education.

The scope of this work is vast. It extends from the five primary civilizations (Andean, Egyptiac, Indus, Sumeric, and Shang) through three secondary (Sinic, Indic, Hellenic), and seven tertiary societies (Far Eastern and its Japanese offshoot, Orthodox Christian and its Russian offshoot, Hindu, Islamic, and early Western—the latter including the abortive Far Western Christian civilization and the arrested Spartan and Osmanli developments). Although the adequacy of historical materials varies greatly from one civilization to another, the authors found it more than sufficient to trace the persistence of the oral and apprenticeship methods in education.

In this rapidly changing world, when men say they would not trade an hour for months of yesteryear, new means of communication and transportation force startling and strange relationships between people who stand at vastly differing levels in the progression of civilization. Just as the "Quaker Oats box" crystal radio in the 1920's was a forerunner of immediate communication to people in a limited geographic area, so now television, videotape, and the relaying of the first voice, the President's message, from a satellite 400 miles beyond the earth foretell instantaneous visual and oral communication to all people on this planet. These developments, coupled with the explosive growth of factual knowledge and the perfecting of deadly instruments capable of destroying the human race, pose new problems for our civilization.

As Arnold Toynbee so aptly states in his conclusion: "Every man, woman, and child that is alive today is living in a world in which mankind is now faced with the extreme choice between learning to live together as one family and committing genocide on a planetary scale."

This book, for which all thinking men must be deeply indebted to Professors Toynbee and Myers, does not provide the answers. Instead, it gives rise to irrepressible questions about the goals, the substance, and the methods of education. Still more important, this penetrating analysis of the sweep of history offers a basic perspective essential to the intelligent solution of the difficult problems on which man's survival rests. It is for man—each one of us—to decide whether our civilization will go the way of all before us or whether, through education, we can break traditional patterns and attain new heights of achievement for all humanity.

Preface

In his Foreword Dr. Eurich has told how this book came to be written and has stated the idea that lay behind it. When he suggested the idea of attempting to make a comparative study of the means of transmitting and improving the cultural heritages in the several civilizations, of attempting to put "education" in as broad a perspective as possible, Dr. Lancaster and I were glad to undertake the task while, at the same time, we had misgivings about its magnitude. Our two institutions were kind enough to give us leaves of absence. The Fund for the Advancement of Education, through its Director, Dr. Eurich, gave us a grant that made it possible to do the work. In addition. Dr. Eurich made possible the several conferences with Professor Toynbee and was himself an unfailing source of encouragement and suggestions throughout the research for and the writing of the book. It is a pleasure here to record our indebtedness to Dr. Eurich and to the Fund, without whose material help and spiritual encouragement the study would not have been undertaken nor completed. The views and opinions expressed in the book, however, are solely those of the author, and for them the Fund for the Advancement of Education has no responsibility.

Dr. Albert L. Lancaster, with his knowledge of the languages in which the sources were found, his understanding of the Toynbee background, and his knack for extracting the gist of a document or a book, was an invaluable collaborator in the research, of which he did rather more than half. He also read, criticized, and helped to improve every page of the text in first and second draft. Without his help the book could not have been written, and it is a pleasure to record his large share in its making.

An unrepayable debt of gratitude is owed to Professor Arnold Toynbee for the perspective provided by his *A Study of History,* for his ready willingness to assist at all stages and, above all, for his concluding chapter.

It is pleasant also to record our hearty thanks to Dr. Gustav Hofmann, Director of the Staatsbibliothek in Munich, whose kindness in placing the services of the library at our disposal was very great and without which the research could not have been done; to Mr. Noel F. Sharp, Superintendent of the reading room of the British Museum, for similar services; to Professor Herbert Franke of the Ludwig-Maximilians-University in Munich for his invaluable assistance in the studies concerned with China; and to Professor Horst Hammitsch of the same university for his assistance in the studies concerned with Japan.

The Oxford University Press has graciously given permission for the use of Charts I and II and for the use of the several quotations from Arnold J. Toynbee's *A Study of History* and from his essay in *The Legacy of Greece.* I am very grateful to the Oxford University Press for these permissions.

Edward D. Myers

Bad Godesberg

June 1959

PART ONE

Introduction

1. *The Toynbee Background*

It is evident from the large and increasing number of books and articles on education that the problems confronting education in the Western World are enormous and pressing and that, so far, no generally accepted and acceptable solutions to the problems have been advanced. It is manifest also that not only those who are professionally concerned with education, but also, and to an increasing degree, the general public and leaders in fields other than education are becoming aware of the problems and are concerned to find solutions.

The idea of this book was advanced in the belief that many problems may more clearly be analysed and solutions thereto more readily found as they are viewed in a broader perspective. The purpose of the book is not to offer solutions to current educational problems nor even, for the most part, to formulate the problems, but only to provide that broader perspective. If experts or interested laymen find in the book clues or suggestions or insights that enable or assist them more clearly to formulate the problems and to work towards more adequate solutions, then the book will have served its purpose.

A more pressing necessity to consider education in a broader perspective arises from the fact that in the twentieth century, the Western World finds itself more intimately and inextricably linked with other parts of the planet than ever before. If therefore, education in the West is to help people to understand, communicate with, and live with the peoples of other cultures, it must provide some background for that understanding and communication and community. And it can do this only if it sees its own problems in terms not merely of its own history and cultural ethos but also of those of other societies.

The term education is here used not only in the sense of the training of youth, but also in the broader sense of the means whereby one generation transmits its cultural heritage to the next.

The historical background or framework in which education is treated is that of Arnold J. Toynbee's *A Study of History*.[1] It is therefore necessary to state the leading ideas of the book that will be found useful in the treatment of education.

Toynbee accepts, as a working definition, the suggestion that history is the nexus of events which issues from men's purposes and aspirations interacting with such natural forces and conditions as geography, climate, and resources. But he qualifies this by adding that written history is concerned not with all the events in the total nexus, but only with those events and actions on the common ground of the fields of action of the human beings concerned. That is, the true concern of history "is with the lives of societies in both their internal and external aspects."[2]

The question about what society is, or about the relation between the individual and the group is, of course, one of the stock questions of sociology, and there are two stock answers to it. The first answer is that the individual human being is a reality which is capable of existing and of being apprehended by itself and that society is an aggregate of such discrete individuals. Toynbee rejects this answer on the ground that man is essentially a social being who does not live to himself alone.

The second stock answer is that the reality is the society and not the individual; the society is a perfect and intelligible whole, while the individual is simply a part of this whole, who can neither exist nor be conceived as existing in any other capacity or in any other setting.[3] This, in turn, is rejected on the ground that the reality is the individual; society as an aggregate of human beings has no significance nor, indeed, existence.

Having rejected the two stock answers, Toynbee then offers his own: "A society . . . is a relation between individuals; and this relation of theirs consists in the coincidence of their individual fields of action; and this coincidence combines the individual fields into a common ground; and this common ground is what we call a society. . . . A field of action cannot be a source of action. . . . The source of social action can only be each or some or one of the individuals whose fields of action constitute a society on the ground where they coincide. . . . It is human individuals and not human societies that 'make' human history."[4]

This conception of society may readily be illustrated in the experience of ordinary people: a man may be the head of a family and at the same time a member of a political club, a sports club, a religious body, and a trade union. The society which is the political club is the common ground of those activities of the several members which coincide on that ground, and so with the other societies. If the local political club be affiliated with other local clubs so that it is a part of a larger national or international society, then it may be seen as the "vehicle of the impersonal relations" between the several members, and as such is, in Toynbee's definition, an institution. While the individual may have personal relations with all the other members of the local society, it is impossible for him to have such relations with all the members of the national or international organization. The society, as an institution, therefore, is the vehicle of the impersonal relations between him and all the other members in this field of their activities. A larger society, of which the individual is a member, is that institution which comprehends the lesser societies without being comprehended by them; for example, the larger society may be the nation. A still more comprehensive society is what Toynbee calls the "civilization."

In his treatment of history Toynbee tacitly leaves out of account all the lesser societies and concerns himself only with the larger ones—the civilizations, which are the most, or, as we shall see, the next most comprehensive institutions. These are the societies the lives of which are the true concern of history.

None of these smaller societies of which the individual is a member is, in itself and in isolation, an intelligible field of historical study. That is, if one were to study the history of the local political or sports club, one would find that, over a period of time, he would have to take into account forces and factors and influences other than those concerned only with the local society and operative only within it. Further examination would show that the history of no such society is or can be written in terms of the factors and forces operative solely within it. Thus no such society is, in itself, an intelligible field of study.

This conclusion follows *a priori* from Toynbee's definition, but it may be established also by sampling the history of a society taken as typical of its class. Toynbee examines a single test case: the national history of Great Britain. The evidence from this single case may be regarded as sufficient because if the history of any nation were in itself an intelligible field, Great Britain would be that nation. Her principal constituent, England, is as old as any nation in Europe, and she has been kept in isolation, both geographically and politically, to an exceptional degree. But an examination of her history shows that in none of the seven main chapters thereof has she been either isolated or self-sufficient: for example, the establishment of parliamentary government in England was the product of forces that were not peculiar to England but were operative on the continent as well. The industrial revolution in England was the product of forces that were operative elsewhere as well. And, as with England, so the history of neither Germany nor the United States nor any other national state is, in itself, an intelligible field.

Toynbee finds, by further investigation, that the intelligible field is a larger society which comprises a number of national states. This larger society he calls a "civilization"; it has a greater extension in both space and time than has any one of the single political communities into which it is articulated. So, if the history of England can be written only by taking into account forces operative also in Italy and Spain and the Netherlands, the history of France can be written only by taking into account forces operative also in Germany and Switzerland and Austria—and so on. An examination of those more widely influential forces and factors shows them to have been operative over an extent of space and period of time covered by the larger society of which all these separate national states are members. This larger society is the Western Civilization.

Toynbee's arguments on these points are coercive and conclusive, and they are applicable equally to the separate national states of other civilizations. By applying the criteria discovered in the examination of the Western Civilization he is able to identify some twenty-six other civilizations.[5]

Further, the conception of civilization as a society, in the sense of a common ground whereon the fields of action of individuals coincide, holds for these larger societies. For example, the actions of a person living in the fourteenth century in Western Europe—say, an Edward III or, at the very beginning of that century, a Boniface VIII —could, and did, through the prevailing institutions, have effects on the lives of many persons living then in Western Europe, but none on those persons living on Honshu, or in South Africa, or in the Central American jungle—and *vice versa*. It is thus clear that the Western Civilization in the fourteenth century is separate and distinct from the Japanese, Mexic, Hindu, Far Eastern, and Islamic contempory civilizations, and they from each other.

These conceptions of society and civilization may be summarized in a paragraph, as follows. The source of all social action is the individual human being, who is also the locus of all spiritual reality and value. The range of each person's activities coincides to some extent with the field or range of those of other persons. The common ground, or area of coincidence, of the different fields of activity is a society. In any society in which many persons are involved there are impersonal relations; institutions are the vehicles of these impersonal relations. Some societies are more extensive than others. The successive changes, in time, in any less extensive society can be understood and explained only by taking into account forces and factors that are operative not only in and on that society but also in a more extensive society. The society that is an intelligible field of study in itself is one which can be understood in terms of the forces and factors operative within it only—that is, without going outside it for explanatory factors. Such a society is called a "civilization" to distinguish it from the national states that have commonly been the fields of study of many historians.

The civilization must also be distinguished from the primitive society that, literally, has no history. A comparison of the characteristics of the two species of society shows that institutions, division of labor, and mimesis are all common to both. Institutions have already been defined. The fundamental division of labor is between the majority, who extend "the narrow radius of their personal lives by living vicariously through the representative activities" of the minority, and that minority whose activities are representative. Mimesis is the acquisition, through imitation, of such social assets as emotions or aptitudes or ideas which the majority have not originated for themselves, and which they might never have had if they had not imitated the minority who already possessed these assets.

We have seen that a society itself cannot be a source of action, and the number of individuals who are capable of initiating social action in any field is smaller than the number of those who are incapable of so doing. The individuals who are so capable constitute the creative minority and may be called the creative geniuses of the society.

In all societies there is a body of customs and rules, written and unwritten, some rigid and some more flexible, which controls the behavior of the individuals as members of the society. The society itself was founded as the result of the creative activity of some one man or small group of men in responding to a challenge offered to the whole group, and each custom and rule had its origin in similar individual activity. The total body of law and custom—what Bagehot calls the "cake of custom"—was created by the imitation by the mass of men of patterns of behavior, aptitudes, emotions, and ideas which had been originated by a few creative individuals; subsequent generations had, by hereditary social drill, fixed those patterns and aptitudes into the "cake of custom." In the primitive societies that we now know, mimesis is directed towards the older generation and towards the ancestors. And in a society where mimesis is thus directed backwards, custom rules and the society remains static, and this is the case with known primitive societies. In societies in process of civilization, on the other hand, "mimesis is directed towards creative personalities which command a following because they are pioneers. . . . In a society where mimesis is thus directed forward towards the future, the 'cake of custom' is broken and the Society is in dynamic motion along a course of change and growth. In this contrast between a dynamic movement and a static condition, we have at last come upon a point of difference between civilizations and primitive societies."[6]

This is a point of difference, however, only between civilizations and primitive societies as we now know the latter: it is not permanent or fundamental, since primitive societies, in order to have come into being and in order to have evolved Man out of Sub-Man, must once have been in dynamic movement and activity with mimesis directed forward. Toynbee suggests that primitive societies, as we see them today, are static because they are recuperating "from the strain of a successful effort to attain the state in which they now persist."[7] Further, in every civilization, even in the period when it is most lustily growing, the mass of its members is in the same stagnant, quiescent condition as the members of the primitive societies and are men of like passions, of identical human nature, with Primitive Man.

Thus, the contrast between a dynamic movement and a static condition is the point of difference between primitive societies and civilizations amidst the similarities between them.

The first problem connected with a study of civilizations is that of their origins: how and under what circumstances did they come into being? Two stock answers that have been offered give race and environment as the positive factors which account for the origins of civilizations. But an inspection of the several origins discloses the fact that of two or more nearly identical environments, one has produced a civilization and the other or others have failed to produce one, and that civilizations have emerged in environments that are utterly diverse. Environment, therefore, cannot account for the origins of civilizations. And a survey of all the evidence shows that the "so-called racial explanation of differences in human performance and achievement is either an ineptitude or a fraud."

From the evidence surveyed in examining the race and environment theses Toynbee concludes that "even if we were exactly acquainted with all the racial, environmental, or other data that are capable of being formulated scientifically, we should not be able to predict the outcome of the interaction between the forces which these data represent. . . . There is one thing which must remain an unknown quantity. . . . This unknown quantity is the reaction of the actors to the ordeal when it actually comes. . . . These psychological momenta, which are inherently impossible to weigh and measure and therefore to estimate scientifically in advance, are the very forces which actually decide the issue when the encounter takes place."[9]

Genesis is rather a function of interaction, and the phrase which most adequately expresses this idea is "challenge-and-response." All civilizations have come into being as responses on the part of individual human beings to the challenges offered to them by the physical environment or by the human social environment or by a combination of the two.[10]

The conception implied in the phrase "challenge-and-response" is applicable both to human individuals and to human societies. Indeed, the sources to which Toynbee turns for statements of the conception are the great myths—myths concerned primarily with the play of superhuman forces as they affect the individual human soul. The essence of the conception is that when the individual's equilibrium (or rest or contentment) or static condition is disturbed by any force, whether arising externally, as from the physical or social environment, or internally, as from the grasping of a new idea or from a spiritual experience or an increased awareness, then the effort towards a restoration of equilibrium is the response of the individual to the disturbing force. The emphasis in the phrase is in its implication that the response is unpredictable, "free," not scientifically determinable; the phrase is used deliberately in place of such possible labels as "cause-and-effect"—which would suggest that the effect is scientifically predictable—or "stimulus-response"—which would suggest an automatic reflex action arising mechanically (or physiochemically) from the disturbing force.

The human individual, as physical body, as organism, and as self-conscious, is always in a condition of somewhat unstable equilibrium: physical forces are unceasingly acting on him, biological forces are equally unintermittent in their impacts, and the social factors of his human environment are always present. Thus any "state of equilibrium" in the individual is always only relatively stable and any challenge is only one of a number of simultaneously presented disturbances, the one that is most impressive or most important to the individual at the time. His response to the challenge is an effort to restore the disturbed equilibrum—and, if successful, does restore it —but on a higher plane or level for the self-conscious human being. This abstract conception is concretely illustrated in the ordinary experience of Everyman: the challenge arising out of the human social environment of the home and family impinge on the individual; he responds in his own way to those challenges and, response by little response, begins to establish his place in the family and his character as an individual. After a while, he enters school or kindergarten and discovers—often with shock and dismay—that neither his teachers nor his schoolmates have the same attitudes towards him as do his parents and brothers. This strange new set of attitudes calls for response and "adjustment" on his part, and he makes these responses. And so on, similarly, through each stage of his career and, at some stages, almost daily.

The operation of challenge-and-response in a primitive society may be seen in the beginnings of the Egyptiac Civilization. When, perhaps seven or eight thousand years ago, the climate of North Africa began to change, the primitive peoples began to be confronted with a physical challenge of the first magnitude. The land in which they lived was gradually changing, because of the diminishing rainfall, from a parkland that supported game and provided sufficient means of subsistence for them, into the sandy waste it is at present. All their customs, habits, ways of life had, in the course of uncounted generations, been developed in response to the previously existing conditions and adapted to them. Those ways had become fixed in the "cake of custom."

Now that the physical environment was becoming different, the primitive peoples of the land were confronted with three possible alternatives: they could retain their age-old customs and habits, migrate southwards where the earlier climatic conditions continued to prevail, and so continue the kind of life lived by their ancestors. Some of the peoples seem to have adopted this alternative, thereby evading the challenge of desiccation.

The second alternative was to retain the customs of their ancestors and to remain in the land. Since those customs could not suffice to produce a livelihood under the changed and changing conditions, the peoples who followed this alternative paid the price of death for their failure to adapt.

The third alternative was to remain on the land and follow the lead of those creative geniuses who first conceived the possibility and ways of harnessing and impounding the waters of the Nile, irrigating and working the land, and making permanent settlements on the now fruitful land. This alternative required the shattering of the primitive "cake of custom," and the adoption of it set this people on the way of dynamic growth.

A survey of the environments which produced the civilizations that arose in response to physical challenges alone shows that civilizations arise, not in environments that offer easy conditions of life, but in difficult environments. This suggests the conclusion that in all cases the heavier blow produces the stronger stimulus. But a further comparative study shows that in some cases the stimulus may be so severe as to destroy the possibility of a response, and that a more accurate formula is that "the most stimulating challenge is to be found in a mean between a deficiency of severity and an excess of it."[11]

The three abortive civilizations discussed in this book are examples of the effects of excessively severe stimuli.[12]

The five arrested civilizations were all immobilized in consequence of having attempted and achieved a *tour de force:* they were responses to challenges that were on the very borderline between a degree of severity that still affords some stimulus and a degree that brings into operation the law of diminishing returns.[12]

Thus in order for a civilization to be called into being, there is required an optimum challenge that is a mean between deficiency of severity and an excess of it, plus the origination of a response to the challenge by a creative genius or creative geniuses. It is required also that the response worked out by the geniuses be so inspiring and their leadership of such high caliber that the apathy of the uncreative masses be overcome to such a point that the "cake of custom" is broken and their mimesis is directed towards these geniuses. It is further required that the responses be of such sort as not only to meet the present ordeal but also to put the society in a position favorable to meeting the next challenge when it comes, and that the response shall not be a *tour de force* which will immobilize the society—lest growth be arrested after the initial challenge has been surmounted.

Thus the geneses of all civilizations are transformations from a static condition to a dynamic activity as the result of a challenge offered to a society. And, if genesis is to be followed by growth, the single, finite movement from the disturbance caused by the stimulus to a restoration of equilibrium is not enough. "To convert the movement into a repetitive, recurrent rhythm there must be an *elan,* working through a series of overbalances," and this *elan* can be detected in the histories of every one of the civilizations that were not arrested or aborted.[13]

An analysis of the growth process in the several civilizations shows that it involves, in all cases, a progressive simplification of apparatus. This simplification entails a "transfer of energy, or shift of emphasis, from some lower sphere of being or sphere of action to a higher sphere" so that "perhaps we shall be describing the process in a more illuminating way if we call it, not 'simplification,' but 'etherialization.' "[14] The criterion of growth is therefore etherialization, or shifting of the scene of action out of a material field into another field in which the action of challenge-and-response may find an alternative arena. "In this other field, challenges do not impinge from outside but arise from within, and victorious responses to challenges do not take the form of surmounting an external obstacle or overcoming an external adversary but manifest themselves, instead, in an inward self-articulation or self-determination."[15]

This tendency of the action to shift from one field to another—and it is always a tendency only, for there is no case of challenge-and-response in which the entire action takes place on one or the other of the two fields exclusively—this tendency is growth, whether in a civilization or in an individual human soul.

An example of this shifting of the scene of action may be seen in two successive responses of Western Civilization: the challenge of the onslaught of the Scandinavians evoked the response which was the feudal system. The feudal system entailed a social, economic, and political differentiation between classes and this differentiation produced certain stresses and strains in the structure of Western Civilization. "These strains produced the next challenge with which the growing Society was confronted. Western Christendom had hardly rested from its labors in beating back the Vikings before it found its next task in the problem of replacing the Feudal System of relations between classes by a new system of relations between sovereign states and their individual citizens. In this example of two successive challenges in the history of our Western Civilization, the shift of the scene of action from the exterior to the interior field is plainly apparent."[16] All of the civilizations show a steady increase in self-determination from their beginnings to the time of their breakdowns.

It is clear that by "growth" Toynbee does not mean geographical expansion, population increase, larger accumulations of physical monuments, temples, amphitheatres, and viaducts, or even multiplication of encyclopedias or textbooks. Indeed these phenomena are not incompatible with the later stages of breakdown and universal state, and have indeed often accompanied those later stages, as we shall see. The largest temples ever built by the Romans, for example, were constructed during the empire; the period of greatest geographical expansion of the Greeks was after the society had broken down; the compilation of the vast Chinese encyclopedias was made after the growth period had ended.

At their breakdowns the several civilizations were confronted by a challenge to which they, or rather their creative minorities, were unable to work out an adequate response. The ultimate criterion and the fundamental cause of the breakdowns of civilizations is a loss of harmony between their parts, the outbreak of internal discord, and the consequent loss of self-determination. This discord partially reveals itself in social schism which appears in two different dimensions simultaneously: the schism between geographically segregated political communities or nations, and the schism between geographically intermingled but socially segregated classes. The articulation of the society into a number of separate nations "gives rise to an internecine warfare on a crescendo note between these nominal members of one and the same body social; and this warfare exhausts the energies of the society before it brings itself to an end through a 'knock-out-blow' in which a single surviving state is left staggering, half-dead, among the corpses of its fellow combatants."[17]

This period of internecine warfare may fittingly be called the "time of troubles" of the civilization in which it occurs. The time of troubles is followed by a universal state established by the surviving nation which happens to be able to muster the last ounce of energy required to dispose of its exhausted remaining opponents. And because the society is materially exhausted and spiritually enfeebled and war-weary, the universal state is able to enforce a kind of relative and uneasy peace between the separate conquered nations over which it exercises dominion and this "universal peace" is, in the histories of civilizations, the last rally before the final relapse into total disintegration.

The classes into which the civilization is reft at the breakdown are the dominant minority, the internal proletariat, and the external proletariat. The creative minority having failed, at the breakdown of the civilization, to work out an effective response to the challenge, and consequently having failed to evoke mimesis from the masses by persuasion, now attempts to hold by force the position of inherited privilege which it has ceased to merit. The erstwhile creative minority is thereby transformed into the dominant minority.

The internal proletariat is that mass of the people who are members of the civilization and who do not now eagerly follow the minority but are compelled to a sullen acquiescence by force or by the threat of force. The term proletariat is here used not in the Marxist sense of the urban laboring population, but to mean any social element or group which in some way is "in" but not "of" any given society. "A 'proletariat' is an element or group in a community which has no 'stake' in that community beyond the fact of its physical existence."[18]

"The true hallmark of the proletarian is neither poverty nor humble birth but a consciousness—and the resentment which this consciousness inspires—of being disinherited from his ancestral place in Society and being unwanted in a community which is his rightful home; and this subjective proletarianism is not incompatible with the possession of material assets."[19] Examples of the internal proletariat in Western Society in the twentieth century may be seen in the unemployed everywhere, in the "sharecroppers" of the middle western states of the United States, and in the vast majority of the total population of Europe under the Nazi regime.

The external proletariat consists of those members of alien civilizations or of primitive societies which have been recruited—in many cases, forcibly—into the body social of the civilization.

As disintegration proceeds further and further towards final dissolution, the proletariat becomes more and more estranged from the dominant minority and that minority is compelled progressively to increase the force with which it holds its position in the saddle. As the dominant minority increases the force it uses, the proletariat repays "injustice with resentment, fear with hate, and violence with violence"[20] until it finally executes its acts of withdrawal from under the now intolerable dominance of the minority.

The dominant minorities of the civilizations, however, have not been wholly uncreative. They have succeeded in producing, at the very end of the time of troubles, a universal state, and some of them have produced philosophies.[21] The external proletariats have produced a number of barbarian warbands. The internal proletariats have produced religions.[21]

An examination of the origins of the religions shows that they fall into two classes, the criteria of which depend on the source of inspiration of the religion. Christianity, for example, derived its inspiration not from indigenous Hellenic sources but from a proletariat which had been forcibly conscripted into the Hellenic society from the remnants of the Syriac society; its inspiration is therefore Syriac and alien to the Hellenic society. Hinduism, on the other hand, is a religion which arose from entirely indigenous sources during the time of troubles of the Indic society.[21]

In a number of cases, the religion created by the internal proletariat has developed into a universal church, and four of the universal churches have served as "chrysalises" for later-developing civilizations. For example, when the universal state of the Hellenic Civilization—the Roman Empire—finally fell and disintegrated, what followed the fall and disintegration was not a political and institutional vacuum. Politically, the Roman Empire was followed by a bevy of barbarian successor-states, and the institutions of the Christian Church persisted. That church with its institutions served as the chrysalis within which not only the Western Civilization but also the Orthodox Christian Civilization came into being. Similarly, when the Sinic Civilization collapsed, the universal church which was Mahayana Buddhism served as the chrysalis for the later Far Eastern Civilization. And when the Indic Civilization fell, Hinduism was the chrysalis for the Hindu Civilization; when the Syriac Civilization collapsed, Islam was the chrysalis for the Arabic and Iranic civilizations.

Toynbee's original comments[22] on the "chrysalis" phenomenon are, briefly, as follows. The Christian Church is, historically, as striking a phenomenon as is the Roman Empire, in the first place by reason of the universality it acquired from the empire by growing up within its framework and deliberately taking the empire's organization as the basis of its own. The Roman Empire, as the universal state of the Hellenic society, incorporated in itself the whole of that society, including the three great classes into which it had been reft:

the dominant minority which was maintaining itself on the surface, the internal proletariat which was pressing up from below, and the external proletariat which was pressing in from outside. The "Catholic Church" in its first phase conformed to the pattern of the Roman political universe by incorporating into itself the whole of the internal proletariat. In this phase, the universality of the Church fell short of that of the Empire inasmuch as it embraced only one of the three elements which the Empire in some sense held together. On the other hand, the Church's hold over the affections and allegiance of the internal proletariat was far greater than the Empire's hold over either portion of the proletarian underworld, because the Church had been established by the internal proletariat themselves out of their own spiritual and material resources in order to satisfy their own sense of their own needs, whereas the Empire presented itself to them as an alien institution imposed upon them by force. . . . Thus, while the Empire was a house built upon the sands . . . the Church proved to be a house founded upon the rock. . . . And so, when the moribund Empire fell, the ensuing "interregnum" gave the living Church an opportunity to perform an act of creation. The Church then played the part of a chrysalis out of which there emerged in the fullness of time a new society of the same species as the old society which had disappeared—but disappeared without carrying away the Church in its ruin as it carried away the Empire.

As early in the study as the fifth volume, Toynbee had remarked: "When we examine the universal churches we shall find ourselves led to raise the question whether churches can really be comprehended in their entirety in the framework of the histories of civilizations, within which they make their first historical appearance, or whether we have not to regard them as representatives of another species of society which is at least as distinct from the species 'Civilizations' as the civilizations are distinct from the primitive societies."[23] At the same time, however, he had used, throughout the studies of the earlier volumes, the conception of civilizations as intelligible fields and as self-contained units of social life on the whole—"at any rate by comparison with the relatively parochial and ephemeral political communities into which they are apt to articulate themselves in their growth stage."[24] He had continued to use the conception because it had proved to be a useful tool of thought.

But when he came to consider contacts between civilizations he found that an expansion of the field of study was required, and that "for a study of higher religions, the minimum intelligible field must be larger than the domain of any single civilization, since it must be a field in which two or more civilizations have encountered one another."[25] Thus the initial working hypothesis that the civilization is intelligible was found not to hold of civilizations in their disintegration phases. And thus Toynbee's initial hypothesis was discarded by him, unregretted and unmourned, in a characteristic empiricist temper.

He has been criticized for "brushing aside" the labor devoted to the first six volumes, but that criticism is quite unwarranted. He has not brushed aside that labor any more than has the astronomer when he drops the magnifying glass with which he has been studying his photographs and turns to his sighting telescope in order to find a larger field than any the photographs show. Toynbee has simply abandoned a conception that was discovered to be no longer adequate to account for another class of facts and has turned to a new and larger conception.

This is the interpretation of civilizations, not as intelligible fields in isolation, nor as self-contained units of social life, but in terms of their effects on the history of religion. If, he says, we apply this principle of interpretation, we are enabled to think of the second-generation[26] civilizations as having come into existence, not in order to perform achievements of their own, but in order to provide an opportunity for fully fledged higher religions to come to birth.

The primary, or first-generation, civilizations are those that were derived from primitive societies; the secondary, or second-generation, civilizations were derived from the primary civilizations. The higher religions have all arisen in the secondary civilizations. The third-generation civilizations were all derived from the preceding secondary civilization through a chrysalis church: thus the Western Civilization was derived from the Hellenic through Christianity, the Orthodox Christian and its Russian Offshoot also from the Hellenic through Christianity; the Hindu from the Indic through Hinduism; the Arabic and Iranic from the Syriac through Islam; the Far Eastern, in both China and Japan, from the Sinic through Mahayana Buddhism.[26]

With these terms in mind, and thinking of the civilizations in terms of their effects on the higher religions, the reader can follow Toynbee's thought when he writes: "On this showing the successive rises and falls of the primary and secondary civilizations are an example of a rhythm . . . in which the successive revolutions of a wheel carry a vehicle, not on the repetitive circular course that the revolving wheel itself describes, but in a progressive movement towards a goal. . . . The descending movement in the revolution of the wheel of Civilizations . . . is the sovereign means of carrying the chariot of Religion forward and upward."[27]

Thus the histories of civilizations appear as circular and repetitive —each originating, growing, breaking down, going through a time of troubles and, all except the currently extant ones, finally disintegrating. With the new and larger conception in mind it is possible to examine the universal states, as the penultimate stages of the civilizations, not as ends in themselves, but as means to something beyond them.

Coming, as they do, after the long and agonizing time of troubles of the civilizations, the universal states are "symptoms of social disintegrations, yet at the same time they are attempts to check this disintegration and to defy it."[28] The conscious purpose of the dominant minorities in establishing the universal states "in every case, is to preserve themselves by conserving the wasting energies of the society . . . and their intention in establishing a universal state is to use it as a means to this self-regarding end. This intention, however, is never fulfilled. A universal state, however long its life may be drawn out, always proves to have been the last phase of a society before its extinction."[29] Toynbee then asks who are the beneficiaries of the services of the universal states.

In order to find an answer to the question he makes a survey of the services and beneficiaries of the institutions of the universal states. The institutions include installations (which include communications, garrisons, colonies, provinces, and capital cities), currencies (which include official languages and scripts, legal systems, monies, weights and measures, and calendars), and corporations (which include armies, civil services, and citizen bodies). The survey is thorough: it covers all these institutions of all the universal states, so far as the data are known.

One example may be given: when the makers and masters of the Roman Empire constructed and maintained their impressive system of communications, they had a clear and precise idea of the purpose of that system. It was to defend and maintain the empire. Yet the system was utilized by other parties and for other purposes than the intended one: the highways certainly enabled and possibly inspired the barbarians to make straight for the heart of the Hellenic World; the highways facilitated the journeys of Saint Paul and other Christian missionaries and, thereby, the growth of the Christian Church. And, as it was with the Roman communications system, so it was with those of the other universal states: the beneficiaries were other than those intended by the builders and makers of the systems. And, as with communications, so also with the other institutions.

Toynbee's surveys, and the whole study of universal states, lead to two summary conclusions: "First that, in so far as their achievements bear fruit, the harvest is apt to be reaped, not by the sowers themselves, but by alien hands; and, second, that insofar as they become creative in this indirect, second-hand, vicarious way, through the creative acts of their alien beneficiaries, they are creators unintentionally and indeed against their will. Their own primary aim is, not to be creative, but to survive, and the experience of losing their lives in order to find them again in the lives of their beneficiaries does not reconcile them to their fate; it provokes them to recalcitrance and indignation. Our survey . . . has shown that the principal beneficiaries of universal states are universal churches."[30]

That the principal beneficiaries of the states are the higher religions may be taken as established. This fact, taken by itself and in isolation, "proves" nothing, but it does give empirical content to the conception of the secondary civilizations as providing opportunities for fully fledged higher religions to come to birth. And the accumulation of the scores of illustrations of the fact has the effect of suggesting that there is perhaps a purpose behind the series of phenomena.

Toynbee's conclusion is that the higher religions are other and more extensive "intelligible fields" and that the class of them is another species that stands to the species "civilizations" as the civilizations stand to the primitive societies.

The above are the leading ideas of Toynbee's book that give the perspective in which education may be considered, and provide the framework and background for a comparative study. Yet there are two other ideas that may be found to be useful and illuminating and should be briefly stated. These are his conceptions of the philosophical contemporaneity and the philosophical equivalence of the several civilizations.

Toynbee's view of the philosophical contemporaneity of the several civilizations may be simply stated: if the age of Mankind on Earth is perhaps 300,000 years, and if the age of civilizations is about 6,000 years, then the lives of all the civilizations of all three generations are concentrated within less than one-fiftieth part of the lifetime of Mankind; and this is the "philosophical contemporaneity." If a critic were to remark that *all* that is significant in the history of Mankind has, however, taken place in that fiftieth part, the reply might be that the transformation of Sub-Man into Man is surely significant; so is the development of language, whenever and however it took place; and so also were the discoveries of the use of fire and of the wheel.

But there is another, and perhaps more important, sense in which civilizations are contemporary.[31] This is expressed: "The experience that we were having in our world now [1914] had been experienced by Thucydides in his world already . . . Thucydides had been over this ground before. He and his generation had been ahead of me and mine in the stage of historical experience that we had respectively reached; in fact, his present had been my future. . . . Whatever chronology might say, Thucydides' world and my world had now proved to be philosophically contemporary. And, if this were the true relation between the Graeco-Roman and the Western civilizations, might not the relation between all the civilizations known to us turn out to be the same?"

From this suggestion it follows that if the Greeks of the time of Thucydides had lived through a stage that we are now living through, and if we took the same turning that they had taken, then we might expect to find ourselves in the same blind alley as they had found themselves. And if that blind alley were an undesirable place to be, then we perhaps could learn from the experience of the Greeks that we should, in order to escape that blind alley, take another turning.

The conception of the philosophical equivalence of the civilizations, is, in the earlier volumes, simply this: if we employ, not the subjective feeling by which each member of each civilization judges his own to be "superior" to others, but the criterion of the goal of all human endeavours, then it is clear that all civilizations have fallen short of that goal and are, in this sense, "equivalent."

This conception is, as has just been seen, modified but not rejected in the later volumes: some civilizations—those of the second generation—have provided opportunities for the higher religions to come to birth and, in so doing, have been more useful and therefore more valuable to Mankind than civilizations of the first generation, which produced only other civilizations, and than those of the third generation, which appear to be "vain repetitions."

These, then, are the leading ideas from Toynbee's *A Study of History* that provide the framework within which education is to be considered.

2. *The Apprenticeship Method*
and Oral Tradition

There are two phenomena that are so characteristic of education in all societies that preliminary mention of them is required. These are the apprenticeship method and oral tradition. The first is in universal use. The second seems to have been in use in the primary civilizations; it was certainly in use in the early phases of all the secondary civilizations, and continued in use in the later phases of some of them; it was, and is, in use in some of the third generation civilizations.

The Apprenticeship Method

By the "apprenticeship method" we mean learning, in any field, by observation and imitation from other persons who are more accomplished than the learner.

All persons learn their native language by this method: the child hears the speech sounds made by other members of his family and imitates them—at first, very often, meaninglessly—until he can reproduce them intelligibly. He may or may not be corrected by an older person when he mispronounces a sound or misuses a word, but, sooner or later, and after much trial and error, he corrects himself.

In similar fashion, by observation, he learns the attitudes of approbation or disapprobation of modes of behavior, attitudes towards things, ideas, and other attitudes—in short, the whole customary ethic of his family and social group. As he becomes older he learns, by the same method, all his early-acquired skills and habits and, still later, in his games, for example, he tries to imitate his elder's actions and behavior and work. The little girl tends to learn to do the tasks

23

performed by her mother; the little boy, those of his father.

Still later, the child is allowed to sit with the grown-ups and to listen to their talk about weather and crops, about the beasts and the fields, about man and good and bad—and thus he absorbs and grows into the whole body of lore possessed by his class in his society. He begins to do odd jobs in the house and field and goes along with the shepherd or farmer and watches and helps and is finally allowed to take over some of their tasks. It is by this method that all persons learn their native language, the customs, habits, ethics, and traditions of their society. It is by this method that the basis of the cultural heritage of the society is transmitted.

When intended instruction is given by the elder it is only an addition to the fundamentals of observation and imitation which constitute the essence of the method. This intended instruction is added by the elders in most cultures, as we shall see, when the child is at some age between four and seven years. Also, in most cultures, if the father is a specialist in some particular occupation, he later on trains his son in his specialty, and so develops the hereditary skills of the shepherd, hunter, farmer, fisher, and—perhaps later in the development of the culture—of the miller, painter, carpenter, smith, wheelwright, cooper, bowman, fletcher, thatcher, weaver, and others. As the division of labor among the specialists becomes narrower and more refined, the specialist takes as apprentices also the promising or interested sons of his neighbors. And so developes a formal "apprentice" system, as in the Western European medieval guilds, in formal instruction in the Indic educational scheme, and in many another time and place.

These later developments are only formalizations of the general apprenticeship method, the essence of which remains the same. The necessary ingredients are curiosity and imitativeness and the capacity for observation, and these are, happily, present in the human being at birth.

Oral Tradition

Not very long ago at one of the eastern colleges in the United States a student was accused of cheating on an examination because, in answer to a question, he had copied down, verbatim, a couple of pages from the textbook. When accused and confronted with the evidence the student replied that he had indeed copied down the two pages—however not from an open textbook, but from his memory. This reply was greeted with considerable scepticism: was he asserting that he had actually learned by heart those two particular pages in the book? He replied that he had, and proved his innocence by reciting, on the spot, not only the two pages in question, but also the pages immediately preceding and following. The charge against the student was dismissed and his feat of memorization was regarded —and correctly regarded—as most unusual in the twentieth century Western educational world.

This incident illustrates the fact that in our modern education, small—some would say, no—use is made of memorization. This small use is in large part derived from our almost complete dependence on books, notebooks, tape recorders and other memory aids in the sphere of education and on these and shorthand reports, memoranda in triplicate, and other devices in the spheres of business and government. The consequence of all this is that we are inclined to be sceptical of oral tradition and to forget that much has been achieved without writing by many peoples.

We forget that whole literatures have been created and transmitted for generations without the use of writing at all; that at least one civilization was, from beginning to end, wholly illiterate; that the art of writing had its origin in some civilizations, not in literary or creative, but in purely utilitarian motives; and that it is possible to regard the art of writing as a blessing not wholly unmitigated.

Our scepticism with regard to the reliability of oral tradition derives from the small use we now make of it and is legitimate with regard to our own culture. But this scepticism should not be applied as a matter of course to other cultures where the oral tradition was a living and creative force.

For example, the vast literature of the Indic Civilization[1] was created and transmitted entirely orally for, at the least, about twelve centuries, and probably about thirty centuries. Further, the transmission of that literature, and especially of the sacred writings, was perfectly accurate from beginning to end. This perhaps becomes comprehensible when we consider that the precise preservation of every word, every syllable, and every accent was believed to be of vital importance. There is a story, related by Piggott,[2] that stresses the importance. The story tells how a certain demon recited a spell against the god Indra. But the demon incorrectly used one accent with the result that the spell recoiled against himself, with fatal results.

We shall see, in the examination of the Indic and Hindu educational practices, that education was entirely oral even after writing had come into common use for other purposes. That the texts were, and still are, orally but accurately transmitted is agreed by all scholars in the field. This may be illustrated by another incident—this one historical—related by Piggott. He writes, "Not long ago in Benares an illiterate Hindu priest appeared who dictated a very long religious work in verse, until then unknown and unrecorded, which on internal evidence of style and language belonged at least to the Middle Ages, since when it had been passed on orally through a certain line of priests."[2] As we shall see, this kind of thing is just what would be expected from the Indic and Hindu systems of education and, where Piggott writes "unknown and unrecorded" it is implied that the work was unknown to European scholars and unrecorded in the literature that has been reduced to writing.

The invention of writing in at least two civilizations derived from purely utilitarian motives. In the Sumeric Civilization, writing first appears in the elaborate and complicated accounts of the towns and cities and temples. In the (possibly related) Indus Culture, writing and arithmetic appear shortly after the society had developed to the point of producing trade and traders, and Professor Speiser's summarizing phrase is that "writing was not a deliberate invention, but the incidental by-product of a strong sense of private property." In the Andean Civilization, on the other hand, complicated accounts were kept—and, we must presume, with reasonable accuracy—without the use of writing, although the Incas did have that remarkable mnemonic device, the quipu.

That writing may perhaps not be an unmixed blessing is indicated by the comment of an authority whose own education had been mainly oral, who was a teacher and author, who knew and used books, and who was in a position to observe both the merits and weaknesses of writing and oral tradition. Plato wrote:

Socrates.   The story goes that Thamus said many things to Theuth in praise or blame of the various arts, which it would take too long to repeat; but when they came to the letters, "This invention, O King," said Theuth, "will make the Egyptians wiser and will improve their memories; for it is an elixir of memory and wisdom that I have discovered." But Thamus replied, "Most ingenious Theuth, one man has the ability to beget arts, but the ability to judge of their usefulness or harmfulness to their users belongs to another; and now you, who are the father of letters, have been led by your affection to ascribe to them a power the opposite of that which they really possess. For this invention will produce forgetfulness in the minds of those who learn to use it, because they will not practice their memory. Their trust in writing, produced by external characters which are no part of themselves, will discourage the use of their own reminding; and you offer your pupils the appearance of wisdom, not true wisdom, for they will read many things without instruction and will therefore seem to know many things, when they are for the most part ignorant and hard to get along with, since they are not wise, but only appear wise.

Phaedrus.   Socrates, you easily make up stories of Egypt or any country you please. . . .

Socrates.   Writing, Phaedrus, has this strange quality, and is very like painting; for the creatures of painting stand like living beings, but if one asks them a question, they preserve a solemn silence. And so it is with written words; you might think they spoke as if they had intelligence, but if you question them, wishing to know about their sayings, they always say only one and the same thing. And every word, when once it is written, is bandied about, alike among those who understand and those who have no interest in it, and it knows not to whom to speak or not to speak; when ill-treated or unjustly reviled it always needs its father to help it; for it has no power to protect or help itself.[3]

It seems clear that in the Sumeric Civilization, in both its Sumeric and Semitic phases, learning by heart was always emphasized and that the "oral tradition was primary, creative, sustaining." This holds true also of the Babylonic Civilization, of the Syriac, of the Arabic and Iranic and the later Islamic, of the Indic and Hindu throughout all their phases, and of the Hellenic throughout its growth phase. It is true also of Hebrew education, at least down to the first century.

The assertion has often been made, and the idea more often implied, that the first genuinely literary treatments of poetry, history, myth, and other traditions appear with the reduction of the traditions to writing. The assertion and the implication can not be substantiated. It appears, rather, that the reduction to writing "means in the main only that a tradition in a more or less fortuitous form is fixed on paper."[4]

"And yet something new has happened . . . an impersonal intermediary link has been introduced between the bearer of the tradition and the receiver."[4] It was perhaps the impersonality of this intermediary link that induced the Brahmans of India, in both civilizations, vehemently to oppose the writing down of revealed literature; that caused Plato to say that he never had and never would write down the essence of his philosophy; that induced Muslims to transmit the Quran orally; that required the Hebrew rabbi to memorize the Talmud from a teacher; that made it, as Caesar reported, "against the principles of the Druids to commit their doctrines to writing."

The question of the reliability of oral tradition seems to have become acute in the special field of Old Testament criticism in recent years and a major controversy appears to have developed between two or more opposing schools.[5] Some consider that the appearance of writing in a tradition is a sign of cultural degeneration and link it with a "general crisis of confidence." Others declare that the "role of oral tradition and its trustworthiness has been greatly exaggerated"[6] and that where writing was common, the tradition was written and where not, it was not.

Happily, it does not fall within the purview of this note to decide the issue. It is sufficient to observe that, not only among the Hebrew wing of the Babylonic internal proletariat but also throughout other civilizations, the lack of a written tradition has not been incompatible with a very high degree of achievement in literature and in other arts.

This observation appears to be desirable, or necessary, in view of the indispensability of written and printed materials in all forms of our modern Western education.

PART TWO

Education in
Thirteen Civilizations

The surveys of education should, ideally, include all the civilizations of the three generations as well as the abortive and arrested ones. However, this is unfortunately impossible for the simple but sufficient reason that the necessary information is lacking. The little available information about the primary civilizations was not thought to be sufficient, or sufficiently illuminating, to be included in the text; but it is interesting enough to be included in Appendix I, p. 293. Of the nine secondary civilizations, only four are sufficiently well known to make it possible to give an account of education in them, and the information about one of these, the Babylonic, is so scanty that the account of its education has been relegated to Appendix II. This appendix also includes a note on the peculiarities of Jewish education. Of the eleven tertiary civilizations, only eight have left evidences sufficient to make possible an account of education, and one of these was abortive.

As will be seen, the chapters on the different societies are very uneven in length and unequal in content. This unevenness arises, not from any opinion that one was more important or significant than another, but from the fact that about some there is a great deal more information than about others.

There is, on the other hand, enough information about the thirteen or—to include those treated in the appendices—nineteen societies to enable us to see significant similarities amid the differences, to note trends that are characteristic of different stages of development, and to recognize some problems as perennial. Enough is known about education in these societies to provide a perspective and background against which some clues to more adequate solutions of the perennial problems may be found.

I.   In the Secondary Civilizations

Education in any society is inseparable from the social structure, the basic religious and philosophical beliefs, and the prevailing customs and manners. In an account of education in the secondary civilizations —so distant in time and place from our own—it is necessary to give a minimum statement of the fundamental beliefs and of the social structure in order for the educational system to be intelligible. The social and political implications of education are recognized by all who have written on the history of education and were perhaps best summarized by Milton in his definition of education. Milton wrote: "I call, therefore, a complete and generous education that which fits a man to perform justly, skilfully, and magnanimously all the offices, both private and public, of peace and war."

We have now to give an account of the education that prevailed in the Sinic, Indic, and Hellenic civilizations and that was thought to fit a man to perform private and public offices. The account will have to say enough about the nature of those offices in relation to the thought and social structure of the society to enable us to understand the nature and function of the education.

3.   The Sinic Civilization

Period of Growth

The Sinic Civilization had its origin in response to the challenge of the disintegrating Shang culture[1] and was therefore a secondary civilization. Its homeland was that of the earlier culture: the middle basin of the valley of the Yellow River in north China. Toynbee dates the origin of the Sinic society at about 800 B.C.; Fitzgerald gives the year 770 as the approximate date. Toynbee gives 634 B.C.—the date of the collision between the powerful Tsin and the later Chou—as the end of the growth period.

Creel[2] conjectures that, at some time prior to the emergence of the Sinic society, a "ruling, fighting class" had gradually separated itself out from the general population. This class consisted in, or originally included, the creative geniuses who gave the lead to the rest of the people in working out adequate responses to successive challenges. By the eighth century the whole society was being ruled and directed by the members of the noble clans, membership in which was obtained by birth only.

During the whole of the growth period the religion of the society was the cult of the noble clans: it was the worship of ancestors and of the gods of soil and crops. The total population of the society was divided into two classes,[3] between which there was an unbridgeable gulf. The noble was born into a family the names of whose ancestors were known for generations back; the peasant had no surname and no pedigree. The noble married with elaborate rites and ceremonies;

32

the peasant youths and maidens met in a spring festival in free association and a union was translated into formal marriage in the autumn only if the girl were with child. The noble inherited his land and the income from it; the peasant was landless. The peasant could not, therefore, participate in the cult of the nobility. On the other hand, the peasant was not excluded from the benefits of the sacrifices, for the aristocracy were as much priests as they were rulers and nobles. They performed the sacrifices and other rites for the benefit not only of themselves and their clan and their retainers, but also for "every living man." Fitzgerald suggests[4] that it was this priestly function of the nobles, and the attitude and conceptions which accompanied it, that prevented the rise of a purely priestly class in early Sinic society. There were priests, but they performed also non-priestly functions.

The political organization of the society during this period strongly resembled that of Western Europe during feudal times. In theory the "Son of Heaven" was the supreme lord of the land, but in practice he had ceased to have more than a formal primacy over the other feudal princes. The basis of the political organization was religious.

The term *chun tzu,* in this period, meant simply an aristocrat, any member of the limited number of hereditary, ruling, noble clans. It is important to notice the meaning of the term at this time, since later on it acquired another, derivative meaning. The *chun tzu* were not, however, unlettered nobles.[5] They were polished aristocrats who were counsellors, officers, governors, and courtiers in times of peace and, in war, were the generals, staff officers, and warriors.

There was an educational system for the nobility, and exclusively[6] for them. This education was entirely humanistic or "classical," including music, arithmetic, poetry and other literature, and, especially, training in etiquette and ceremonial. Creel[7] holds that "there is considerable indication" that every *chun tzu* was expected to be able to read and write. He suggests[8] that at this time there was also another, but small, class of educated officials, scholars, and teachers, who were dependents of the *chun tzu,* and who produced the books which, he says, "must have run into the tens or hundreds of thousands."[9]

The precise date of the origin of the official class cannot be given, but according to Creel,[10] "it goes into the misty background of Chinese history." Whether it was in existence at the beginnings of the Sinic society is doubtful, but that it was in existence, as a clearly defined class, by the end of the growth period, seems certain. Probably the class developed gradually during the entire period. The tradition of the official class is "by far the longest tradition of its sort in human history."[10] Throughout that tradition the educational emphasis was humanistic, or what would today be called "liberal" or "general" rather than technical or special or vocational.

The education of the peasants during the whole period of growth was never formal or systematic or official, with the single exception of the stated occasions when, in the villages, the laws were read and interpreted to them. The education that they received was—as with most peasants in most times and places—by the apprenticeship method.

Further, "the law was a system of penalties devised for, and applicable only to, the common people."[11] The noble clans were not subject to the rule of law, but only to their own code of chivalric morality as expressed fundamentally in the rites. A serious offense against the rites could be expiated only by the suicide of the offender. It is Fitzgerald's opinion that this system worked well during the height of the feudal period when the courts of the many lords were still intimate and local, but that as the greater nobles began to absorb the fiefs of the lesser and as the system began to disintegrate, the old chivalric code ceased to be a bulwark against the spread of lawlessness and disorder.

The theoretical supremacy of the king was based not on any "divine right" conception but on a mandate from "Heaven." This mandate was conferred only on a sage king whose virtue had entitled him to receive it. Therefore a king who was not virtuous, who misruled his kingdom, was deprived of Heaven's mandate and rebellion against him was not a crime.

The general world-view of the people of this early period is not easy to discern through the emptiness of the lack of records. But the view of a later time—the fourth or the third century B.C.—is not so obscured and that view, in all probability, was not radically different from the vague philosophy of the earlier period.

The general world-view was that there are in the universe two forces, symbolized by the Yin (negative, female, dark) and the Yang (positive, male, light). These control, or are, the universe, and all natural phenomena are the result of the interaction between them. The earliest Chinese cults were therefore "directed to maintaining, by magical forces, the harmonious"[12] balance between these two forces, in order that there might be sufficient rainfall for crops, that the cattle might be fertile, and so on.

Of man it was believed[13] that he has two souls. One of these, the animal soul, comes into existence at conception, and at death, goes into the tomb with the corpse, is nourished by the offerings to the dead, but gradually sinks down into a kind of vague underworld. (The parallel with the Homeric conception of the soul here is obvious.) The other, the higher spiritual soul, comes into existence at birth, and at death, ascends to heaven and lives the life of a nobleman.

Education through the whole of the period of growth of the Sinic Civilization was aristocratic, oral, private, humanistic or "classical," confined to the nobility, and tutorial in the sense of involving close personal relations between the teacher and the pupil. And that education was based on and required an ideal.

The Time of Troubles

Whether we reckon, with Toynbee, the time of troubles of the Sinic society from the last third of the seventh century B.C. or, with Fitzgerald, the "Period of Warring States" from the beginning of the fifth century, the period of anarchy and violence was well underway and, unless we suppose that it began suddenly and without prior historical causes, the beginnings may reasonably be dated from the late seventh century. It ended in 221 B.C.

The time of troubles in the Sinic Civilization was, as in others, a period of increasing loss of self-determination, manifested in schism between the several warring states, in an increasing violence in warfare, and in increasing general anarchy. It was a time when established institutions were overthrown, old loyalties destroyed, and provincial isolation broken down. The result in China, as in Greece at the same period, was that men began to question traditional beliefs about the world order and so philosophers appeared and philosophical schools began to arise.

The philosophers did not question the validity of monarchy as the proper form of political organization—that was taken for granted very nearly throughout the history of Chinese thought—but only the moral foundations on which the monarchy should be based.

At some time early in the time of troubles, or perhaps even late in the period of growth, there had appeared, in some parts of China, the beginnings of district schools for the sons of the nobility.[14] The number of the schools and the size of the school population are not known. But in a number of districts there were schools in which the boys lived from about age ten until they were twenty. The curriculum included dancing, music, archery, chariot-driving, writing, arithmetic, and perhaps most importantly, strict instruction in etiquette and in the rites and ceremonies. These subjects were taught in semester courses according to the seasons: the outdoor exercises in spring and summer, the indoor in fall and winter.

These district schools were for the younger sons; eldest sons were entitled to go to the royal college at the capital, where the heir apparent was educated. The best among the district school pupils were also sent there. The curriculum and training at the royal college were of the same type as those of the district schools.

The life of the students, who were confined within the school, retained traces of the time when the school was the house where the young boys were prepared for initiation into manhood without having any communication with the adult community. As another trace of the earlier institution, the school was located outside the village or urban community, and a semi-circular ditch (a complete circle for the royal college at the capital) marked its separation from the profane world. Even towards the end of this period it remained a place which was forbidden to women and to men other than the teachers.

When his studies were completed the young man went home to ready himself for the initiation ceremony. After he was initiated he was an adult, a warrior, was fit to receive a fief, to make public and private sacrifices, to enter the service of his feudal lord, and to marry.

It is just possible that there may have been also a school for girls; if there was, then they, like the boys, entered the school at the age of about ten and received instruction in their proper duties: above all, obedience, then weaving, the unwrapping of silk cocoons, and finally, in the religious rites in which they would have a role after they were married.

About the sixth century there grew up a class[15] of small landowners who were socially intermediate between the princes and enfieffed vassals on the one hand, and the landless peasants on the other. From this class of poor nobles came the intellectuals of the time. Some settled as tutors in populous centers to train boys for public service, others wandered from court to court seeking—and sometimes finding—appointments to feudal lords, some few gained reputations for learning and acquired large followings. Still others, disgusted at the chicanery and deceit of the charlatans, and unable or unwilling to make themselves heard above the clamor of conflicting opinions, retired to their homes or to some secluded spot to teach small bands of disciples. And some became village school teachers: they taught writing and the first elements of the rites, music, and archery to the noble children to prepare them for the district school.

Among these wandering scholars the most notable, and the first of whom definite records remain, was Confucius (551-479 B.C.), and among the so-called "Hundred Schools" of philosophy of the time (which can all be classified into a half-dozen broad categories) the Confucian School was, in the end, although not in the beginning, the most influential.

There were already in existence at this time the "Five Classics": The Books of Changes, of History, of Poetry, of Rites, and the Spring and Autumn Annals.

Confucius' first work was to collect, edit, and transmit at least the "Spring and Autumn Annals" and perhaps also the other four books as well. He, like the other philosophers of the time, was concerned to find a moral basis for human conduct and for the reorganization of society. His whole teaching was a reaction against the loose spirit, the anarchy, and the excesses of his time. He therefore insisted on the "rectification of terms" for, as Confucius wrote, "When words, or terms including names, no longer meant what they had been intended to mean, they lost their value. When an usurper was called Duke, or a parricide described as murder, then men could not distinguish the truth from falsity, their consciences were blurred, they lost their sense of shame, and they abandoned virtue and adopted vicious courses."[16] Confucius was here insisting on the correct use of terms only as a means to the great end of reforming morals, but his later followers, as we shall see, carried the doctrine of the necessity of the "rectification of terms" to such pedantic excesses that, at times, learning and philosophy were degraded almost to mere exercises in criticism and exegesis. Confucius himself sought to influence the course of political development by serving as adviser to one or another feudal lord, but he was successful primarily as an "educationalist." It was he whose influence helped to develop that class of gentleman in China who became so important in later times: the professional teacher and potential official;[17] his activities were in many ways similar to those of the Greek sophists who were his contemporaries. He, like Socrates, left no writings, and his teachings are to be found only in what his later disciples said he had taught. It is therefore necessary usually to refer, not to the teachings of Confucius himself, these being uncertain and subject to the interpretation of later disciples, but to the "Confucianism" of a given period or disciple.

Confucius appears[18] to have followed the framework of the instruction of the official schools. Omitting dancing, archery, and chariot-driving, he taught the rites, music, and literature. He had his students study the Books of History and of Poetry and gave real courses on the rites. It was a complete cycle of studies that he directed in his school and these studies had the traditional character. He seems to have taught no definite philosophical doctrine, to have denied that he had any originality of thought, and to have derived all his teaching from the old texts.

Others among the "hundred" rival schools were Taoism, the teaching of the book called the *Tao Te Ching,* attributed to the probably not historical Lao Tzu; Mohism, from the teaching of Mo Tzu, a younger contemporary of Confucius; and the school of Yang Chu, who erected pure selfishness into the cardinal virtue. The last school to arise was not, properly speaking, a philosophical school at all, but a system that rejected all philosophic systems and sought a new principle of authority in the recognized power of the sovereign state —a sort of Chinese "Leviathan" doctrine; this was the school of the Legists.

The Legists held that man was by nature evil, and they sought only to reorganize society for the purpose of carrying on successful war, of obtaining mastery for the lords they served. But they did believe that the law should be applicable to all, noble and serf alike; that the prince alone, supreme and autocratic, should have entire control. They disapproved of the rival schools to the extent of considering their very existence a danger, because the divergent views would lead to parties, intrigues, and even rebellion.

Education, then, during the time of troubles, was, for the masses of the people, by the apprenticeship method only. For the nobility there were the schools of the wandering scholars similar to the school of Confucius, and the continuing district schools. Although Confucius did say that "in education there are no distinctions of class," there is so much evidence to the contrary that his saying should be interpreted as affirming, not democracy in education, but only that a person might, by study and ability, rise from lowly origins to high rank among scholars.

By the time of Mencius (372-289 B.C.), and in large part as the result of his teaching and influence, the most generally accepted and influential Confucian doctrine about education was as follows.

That which Heaven confers on man, that with which he is endowed at birth, is his nature. By this hereditary nature men are nearly alike, although there are hereditary variations. That which educes the nature is the Way (*Tao*—way, truth, fundamental doctrine, word; cf. the Greek *logos*), and this Way is linked with and derived from the cosmic order as much as is the nature. The Way cannot be followed by man alone or unaided or of his own accord. There must be a cultivation, a putting in order, a building of the Way in human experience. And that which cultivates the Way is called "education" (*chiao*—education, cultivation, culture, *Kultur*). Not only teaching, but also civilization, government, religion, certain organizations, "may be expressed by the word *chiao* or the combinations into which it enters."[19] The purpose of all education is to produce the *chun tzu,* the "superior man." The superior man is one who is careful and cautious regarding things not yet seen or heard, who never departs from the Way, who has benevolence without anxiety, wisdom without perplexity, courage without fear, and develops what is good in others.

In the pursuit of knowledge there must be a clear distinction between what is known and what is not known. The powers of the mind must be concentrated in full attention; but since the mind does not function independently of the heart and emotions, they also must be rectified and purified. The pursuit of knowledge, to be successful, must be motivated by a deep desire for learning. The senses as instruments of learning are inferior to the mind, but must nevertheless be used, for, as Confucius is reported to have said, "Study without thought is vain, and thought without study is dangerous."[20]

One of the constant and pervasive characteristics of Chinese thought is that it does not draw any clear distinction between the individual human self and the rest of the universe.[21]

Not only has Chinese thought failed to draw the distinction, but certain thinkers have urged formally that there is no distinction. The doctrine has been called "mysticism"[22]—that is, "a belief in that state in which all things form one body." In such a state—the state is rare and has to be achieved by the individual—all distinction between the self and the not-self are obliterated, the individual self becomes one with the ground of its being, which *is* its being, which is the spirit of the universe. It was thought that the individual self had originally been one with this spirit, but had become separated therefrom through obstructions and divisions which arose later. The attainment of this state is the highest aim and the final achievement of individual self-cultivation and, so far from being self-obliteration, is the fullest self-realization.

This is certainly the doctrine of the later Sung Confucianists who based their doctrine on Mencius, and Fung Yu-Lan believes that it is probably the doctrine of Mencius himself.[23] It seems most likely that it was the doctrine of Mencius.

Mencius asserts that all things are complete within us, that we are fundamentally one with the universe, but that because of certain obstruction within us we appear to be separated from it. This is a state of not being "sincere." If, he says, "one finds sincerity when one has examined oneself, there is no greater delight"; that is, reunion with the universe is the final bliss. The way to achieve this end is to use the "work of love" as the method, for it is through the "human-heartedness" of love that one seeks and gains sincerity. This is because the qualities of altruism and "human-heartedness" lessen the division between the self and other.

During this period education was, gradually at first and then with increasing acceleration, opened more and more to members of classes other than the nobility. So schools began to be developed to take care of the increased numbers of students, although the old tutoring system continued for a long time alongside the new schools. The problems of dating and the lack of records on this point make it impossible to be certain, but what evidence there is seems to suggest that during this period there was one further development. This was the increase in the use of written materials with the tendency towards uniformity and stereotypes. There was no decrease in the intimacy of the personal relationship between the teacher and the student; indeed there was no such decrease throughout the history of the Sinic, and the later Far Eastern, Civilization. The teacher was always regarded almost as a "second father."

The Universal State

The Sinic time of troubles came to an end in 221 B.C. when Prince Cheng, the last feudal duke of Ch'in, the state which was able to administer the "knock-out blow" to its exhausted remaining opponents, consolidated the realm and took the title of Shih Huang Ti, or First Emperor.

Shih Huang Ti transported 120,000 noble families from all parts of China to Shensi[24] and, by thus removing them from their ancestral estates and uprooting them from their provinces, destroyed forever the power of the feudal aristocracy. By this action—and by other actions—he destroyed also in large measure the social and political system of ancient China. He disarmed the conquered populations, centralized the government, completed the building of the Great Wall, initiated and carried through the building of a system of trunk-roads, standardized the axle-length of carts, standardized weights and measures, and unified the customs of all the peoples within the Wall.

He also standardized the written language[25] and, in 213, caused the "Burning of the Books" and the persecution of the scholars. The positive effect of the first was to establish perhaps the most effective and enduring bond of unity among the Chinese peoples, while the negative effect of the latter was similar.

It was seen above that many rival schools of philosophy had developed during the time of troubles, that each of these was concerned to find a recipe or prescription for a good, stable, successful government, and that each had sought to have its own prescription adopted by one or another of the feudal states. The Legists believed that the very existence of the rival schools was a danger to the state, because their different views would lead to dissension and rebellion.

Under Shih Huang Ti the Legist school won out over all the others because it, and it alone, had a record of successful application to state policy: that is, its doctrine of the rule of law was the only one among the competing doctrines that had really built a strong state.

The purpose of the Edict of 213 was to secure uniformity of thought and opinion by suppression of rival doctrines. Fung Yu-Lan says[26] that the edict ordered the burning only of books in private possession, not those in libraries and official archives, and that it was aiming not to wipe out the learning of the time but only to standardize thought. He adds that the emperor encouraged scholars of wide learning and that these included men belonging to all the different schools. Fitzgerald, however, suggests[27] that the edict aimed at the extinction of the rival teachings and says that "no less than 460 scholars were put to death for concealing their books." In any case, the effects of the edict were to destroy a very large number of books, to break the power and influence of the aristocracy and, perhaps most importantly, to unite them as they had never before been united, in hatred and hostility to the imperial regime. Not only were the nobility united as never before, but, their ruin having exposed the peasantry to the full weight of the Ch'in despotism, with all its forced labor and increasing taxation, the peasants were now willing to listen when the ex-aristocrats preached revolt. Shih Huang Ti died in 210 B.C.; within a year there was a spontaneous revolt in all parts of the empire; in 207 Liu Pang, a common soldier, received the surrender of the Ch'in capital and established the Han Dynasty.

Liu Pang and his successors needed help in governing the vast empire; they sought—and obtained—that help from the dispossessed nobility. Obscure descendants of the old aristocratic families were sought out and made kings of the five states, all strictly subject to the emperor. In 191 B.C. the edict proscribing philosophy and the literature of the feudal period was formally repealed and the vast labor of restoring the ancient books was begun. The books were reconstructed in part from the scraps of writing that remained and in part from the capacious memories of the older scholars. In the process of reconstruction, the principles of higher criticism were developed and carried to a high level and were never thereafter lost to Chinese learning. Of all the scholars who participated in the work of restoration, the Confucians contributed most and this contribution was a major factor in giving to them the ultimate victory over the other schools.[28]

According to Fung Yu-Lan,[29] however, Confucianism won out because, despite all the great social changes, "the ancient patriarchal social system maintained itself without great deterioration, so that the ceremonial teaching and regulations of the past continued, in part at least, to find practical application." The changes were indeed very great: the government was no longer feudal, but centralized in the emperor; the great bulk of the population was no longer the agricultural serf, but the free peasant; the ancient ceremonial rites were no longer restricted to the nobility, but were now appropriated by the common people. But despite these changes, most of the people were still grouped in ancestral clans, and still wrung their living from the soil. As they appropriated the ceremonial teachings, it was necessary to employ those who knew the rites, and these were the Confucianists; similarly, as the Han Dynasty began to draw up in final form the new institutions that were to be used in government and society, they found it necessary to employ the services of the Confucian clerks and scholars.

Thus Confucianism, under the Han Universal State, became the dominant philosophy, indeed, for a long while, almost the only philosophy. But this dominant Confucianism was not that of Confucius.

Although the Legist school had practically disappeared under the Han, it had left one principle as a legacy to Confucianism: "The idea of a single orthodox doctrine which was alone deserving of government patronage and support."[30] This idea, which had been no part of the original Confucianism, was now, in the Imperial Age, used to give the doctrine a kind of sanctity it had neither enjoyed nor desired during the feudal period.

Further, the Han Dynasty had established itself without benefit of the theories of either the Confucianists or the Legists or any other school; vigorous and stable government was now a fact. Consequently, authority now had no obvious need of moral foundations, and so the questions that had given rise to the "Hundred Schools" were no longer being asked. As the Han rulers recruited scholars into the civil service, those scholars, on the whole, contented themselves with a monopoly of official positions and with their identification with polite society. "To be a scholar was to be a Confucian. The memory of the other schools faded away."[31] And so completely had the hereditary nobility lost caste and position in the revolution that under the Han, the memory that the ancient privileges of the scholar had been founded on birth rather than learning had also faded away from the minds of the conservatives. The *chun tzu* was now thought of as a "superior man," not because of any inherited superiority, but because of his acquired learning.

Orthodox Confucianism at this time reverted to what seems to have been the teaching of Mencius about man, namely, that he is by nature good, and falls into evil only through lack of instruction. This conception of man, according to Fitzgerald,[31] "has coloured the whole organization of Chinese society. The state was professedly based on a moral authority, not on military force or legal sanctions." The state certainly honored learning above birth (it will be recalled that the founder of the Han Dynasty was not a noble but a common—or uncommon—soldier), and certainly the affairs of state were carried on by men of letters; yet the legal system applied to the lower classes was based on fear as the deterrent and was enforced through cruel and barbarous penalties. Justice, benevolence, and goodness were the dominant ideas of the Confucian theory of government; force and severity were absent in the theory. But force and severity were the basis of the legal system, while justice and benevolence had little or no place.

It has been mentioned that an Imperial Decree of 191 B.C. had repealed the edict proscribing philosophy and literature. Already in 196 another edict had sought capable men to help the emperor rule. The appeal was for capable men from all social ranks and was, in effect, an effort to broaden the social basis of the civil services. It was an effort also to keep power in the hands of the emperor by keeping it away from the possessors of the few remaining fiefs.[32] It was one of the great achievements of the Han emperors that they succeeded in persuading the new scholar class of civil servants that the teachings of Confucius could be applied to their regime; that the Confucian ideal of loyalty to the prince was applicable to every servant of the state and that the prince could be none other than the emperor. The scholars having been so persuaded, they, as a class, became closely associated with the centralized state, and this interpretation of Confucian doctrine became one of the more enduring legacies of the Han State.

Although the Edict of 196 was renewed in 178, 165, and 142,

there were as yet no serious plans for a system of public education or for state schools, although private education continued as it had done during the two earlier phases of the Sinic society.[33]

The Emperor Wu-Ti issued, in 124, the Edict which laid the foundation of the system of state schools and state examinations.[33] By this edict, fifty young men were to be chosen from the most virtuous and scholarly provincial candidates, brought to the capital for a year's training and then retested. Those who survived the later test were to receive official appointments; those who did not were to be returned to their homes. New candidates were then selected to fill the vacancies. The measure of fitness of the candidates was determined by the examination, and the examination was based on the Confucian classics. The emperor was persuaded, as the scholars had been, that Confucian doctrine alone should be the core of Chinese culture and that it should permeate the nation. From this beginning, with the Edict of 124, gradually developed the unique and gigantic state examination system which survived the fall of the Han Dynasty and, with it, the Sinic Civilization itself; it survived the interregnum of barbarian successor-states, the growth and time of troubles and universal state of the later Far Eastern Civilization, to break down finally only in A.D. 1905. But before it broke down, it influenced the development of the examination system in the distant Western Civilization.

About 7 B.C. the number of students at the capital was raised to three thousand; during the first and second centuries there seem to have been some state-endowed district schools, but the details about these are few and unclear. Galt[34] is probably interpreting the scanty evidence more broadly than is justified in his suggestions that after 124 B.C., there was a continuous system that included universities, examinations, and district schools. The few extant edicts of the first and second centuries do give directions about the selection and examination of candidates, but they reveal, at the same time, that abuses had crept into the system, and that entrance into the civil service was obtained in many cases, not by knowledge of the classics, but through family connections and bribery. And one result was a stream of complaints about the constantly changing bureaucracy that had no concern for the needs or wants of the people. Goodrich thinks[35] there was actually no really effective system of public examinations and that most official positions were filled by appointments based on the recommendations of provincial authorities, the chief requisite for which was the prospect of a comfortable future for the candidate.

In A.D. 84 a college for Confucian doctors was established, with fifty students.[36] Three centuries later, it was said to have 30,000 students. The curriculum was strictly classical, including only:

1. Li-Chi "The Book of Rites"; the sources of this book go back probably to the period between the fourth and first centuries B.C., but it was compiled in its final form under the Han; it deals with the forms of initiation ceremonies and with court etiquette.

2. Shu-Ching "The Book of History"; dates from the period from the ninth to the sixth centuries B.C. and consists of speeches and documents.

3. Shih-Ching "The Odes"; this is as ancient as the Shu-Ching; it contains both religious and secular poetry; it consists in hymns in honor of the ancestral kings, hymns used during ritual feasts of the court, at receptions and at archery contests, in satirical odes against enemies, and in love poetry.

4. Ch'un-Ch'iu "The Spring and Autumn Annals"; the history of the feudal state of Lu from 722 to 481 B.C.; Lu was Confucius's state and the book was edited by him.

5. I-Ching "The Book of Changes"; the book is concerned with divination: the reading of oracles; it includes commentaries on the earlier writings.

A sixth classic, the "Book of Music," was added under the Han.

The desire to establish correct texts and to interpret them rightly dominated the work of the scholars, and in their zeal for the task, their labors sometimes degenerated into pedantic exercise in copying and memorizing, in exegesis and criticism. It was remarked above that the danger of this degeneration was inherent in Confucius' own insistence on the importance of the doctrine of the "rectification of terms."

At the same time that this bookish curriculum was being established, Confucianism as an ethical and etiquette cult was proliferating complicated prescriptions about conduct that extended even to details of dress and posture.[37]

The work of the scholars was notable: not only did they recover very nearly all of the lost books, but gave also an almost complete inventory of books in circulation at the beginning of the first Christian century.[38] Between A.D. 175 and 183, by imperial order, the complete texts of the classics were engraved in stone. The leading motive for this seems to have been the fixing of authentic texts rather than the mere preservation of texts that had already been authenticated.[39]

This engraving in stone was one of the indispensable steps in the long process that led to the final development of printing, for the next step, the making of rubbings from the engraved texts, was the direct predecessor of block prints. Other indispensable steps that had already been taken were the very early invention of the hair brush, which by the third century B.C. had been refined into the hair-pen, and the invention of paper at the beginning of the second century A.D.[40]

It has been mentioned that in the process of reconstructing the lost books, the Confucian scholars had developed the principles of textual criticism. It is the opinion of Gardner[41] that in this discipline, Chinese scholarship is easily the equal of the best of Western scholarship. He more precisely defines this discipline[42] as that "which is concerned with the authentication, establishment and meaning of texts, but not with their historical appraisal or utilization." The Han scholar was concerned to discover what the classic had actually said and meant, and he was in large measure motivated by the belief that the way to right government, to truth, and to the moral life was the way that had already been discovered and stated in the classics.

Another and more important reason for the training of officials in the classics was that the classical language was in process of becoming unintelligible. Hu Shih says[43] that already in the second century before Christ it had become unintelligible to the people and was gradually ceasing to be understood by the officials. Not only was the spoken language changing, but also different ways of writing the classical had appeared. This was why Shih Huang Ti was compelled to standardize the classical script. And it was why his Han successors were compelled to recruit their civil servants from among those who could read the script and, further, to found the schools and to take other measures to increase the numbers of those who could: when some officials could not understand the imperial orders that were sent out to the provinces it was necessary to see to it either that the officials learned the script or that office was conferred on those who could.

Thus already in China under the Han there was the divorce between the classical language of officialdom, of formal education, of philosophy, and of written literature, and the vernacular of the people. And thus the official, formally educated Chinese, on the whole, looked to the past.

Chiang writes[44] that the more important characteristic Chinese ideas of life and of institutions are those of duty, of the fulfillment of duties, and of the home. To live, it was thought, "is to fulfill the duties of life," and to attain the supreme good one must "perform to the utmost his duties of life"; the fulfillment of duties is the only way to happiness. Chiang holds that "all the institutions of China are permeated with the idea of happiness through, and in, duty." The home was conceived as the prototype of the state, for the state is based upon families; furthermore, the state exists for the people and not for the sovereign.

Under the Han Dynasty the school system became state controlled, and the curriculum fixed; bookish learning became the only, or almost the only, means of advancement in the civil service.

At the close of the second century A.D. the Han Empire fell (although it endured nominally until A.D. 221 when the last Han sovereign was compelled to abdicate). Its fall introduced an era of anarchic violence, barbarian intrusions, and petty successor states to the fallen empire.

4. *The Indic Civilization*

Period of Growth

The Indic Civilization had its origin in response to the twofold challenge of the disintegrating Indus Culture[1] and of the moist tropical forest environment of the Indus-Ganges River valleys, wherein lay its homeland. The time of origin may be tentatively dated in the fourteenth century B.C. and that of breakdown in the eighth, although the problems of chronology in this society are greater, perhaps, than in any other. The time of growth is roughly that of the "Vedic Age."

The people of the earlier Indus Culture were Dravidian; the immigrating Aryan peoples seem to have given the creative leadership in working out successful responses to the successive challenges. Our knowledge of the Aryan peoples, and of their customs and beliefs, is based on the Vedic literature.

The Vedas comprise four collections of writings: the Rigveda, Samaveda, Yajurveda and the Atharvaveda, of which the oldest is the Rigveda. The language of the Rigveda is the Sanskrit of a date generally conceded to be about 1000 B.C.,[2] but parts of the collection are certainly older, going back to, at latest, the 15th century B.C. It is a collection of hymns that were chanted or recited by the priests at the sacrifices. The Samaveda is a collection of melodies for the chants; the Yajurveda is a series of prescriptions or directions for performing the sacrifices; the Atharvaveda is essentially different from the other three, being a prayer book for the simple folk.

The Brahmanas are a vast literature consisting chiefly of ritual texts and speculation about the ritual practices. The Aranyakas are the concluding portions of, or appendices to, the Brahmanas, and are concerned with the symbolism and hidden meanings of the sacrifices and the rituals performed in connection therewith.

The Upanishads, which date from perhaps the beginning of the eighth century B.C., are philosophical speculations about the ultimate questions: the nature of the universe, man's relation to it, the meaning and purpose of life, the *summum bonum*.

It seems clear from studies of this literature that during the Rigvedic period, the Aryan tribes had spread over the whole country from the River Kābul to the Upper Ganges and had established themselves in small principalities under hereditary monarchs.[3] They succeeded not only in establishing themselves in the area but also in bringing the indigenous Dravidian peoples under their influence so that at the very beginnings, there was already a blend of Aryan and Dravidian cultural elements.[4] It appears also that, little by little, smaller and weaker principalities were absorbed by the larger and more powerful, so that a number of the princes or kings came into control of relatively large and compact kingdoms and that, in some of these, large, planned cities had begun to appear by the end of the Vedic Age. The geographical center of this Aryan-Indic world was the "firm middle country" from the Saravasti River to the Gangetic Doab; from here, during the later periods, the Indic Civilization spread over the rest of the Indian subcontinent.

The Rigveda consists of 1,017 hymns which were originally the possession of the priestly families and were passed on from father to son orally. Since the proper recitation of the hymn was necessary to the effective action of the sacrifice, the greatest care was taken to ensure that it was perfectly learned and perfectly intoned. Whether writing was known in the Vedic period is still an open question, but it is certain that writing was not used at all for the transmission of the Vedas during the whole history of the Indic society.

It seems that at the very beginnings there was teaching of the Rigveda by concerted recitation, that is, the teacher would recite a verse or hymn and the students would repeat it after him, over and over again, until all the students were perfect in the lesson. In some cases, the father was the teacher of his son and of the sons of some of his neighbors. But already in this early period instruction included not only the memorization of the hymns but also the preparation of youths for initiation into adulthood and preparation of the *Brahmacharin,* the "religious student" or "student of divinity."

Details of the preparation for initiation are not known. The training of the Brahmacharin aimed not only at imparting the Veda but also at the training of character and the sharpening of the intellect. The evidence is clear that the method of debates was used in instruction.

With the growth of the literature connected with the sacrifices, that is, with the gradual appearance of the other Vedas and later writings, the problem of the transmission of this growing body of literature became increasingly urgent.

The solution of the problem was the development of different kinds of priestly schools and different classes of teachers. One school would give instruction in the Rigveda, another in the Samaveda, and so on. It seems clear that, by the end of the period,[5] at latest, a candidate could not qualify as a priest unless he had passed through one of these schools, that the schools had become well developed institutions, and that many of them had well established reputations. There were also *gurus*—masters—of different grades; there were *Kshatriya* (warrior-class) teachers; and there were wandering teachers, comparable to the wandering scholars of the Sinic society and to the sophists of Greece. By the end of the period there were wandering teachers of all sorts going about the country, and public debates and disputations, both spontaneous and arranged, were common.[6]

Probably the majority of students were studying at one or another of the priestly schools or under a guru. The life of the student began only after he had formally requested acceptance by the master and the request had been formally granted.[7] After this, the student was ceremoniously admitted to the household of the guru; the ceremonies involved the student's assuming a number of obligations and taking a number of vows. He undertook the duties of tending the household fire and of daily alms-begging; he vowed always to be truthful and to observe his duties; he was to be devoted to the guru and to his parents; he was to practice hospitality and faith and generosity.

The daily alms-begging, obligatory on all students, had little or nothing to do with the financial status of either the master or pupil, but was for the purpose of the inculcation of "plain living and high thinking."[8] It seems clear that the guru was under no obligation to accept a student unless he was convinced of the moral excellence and sincerity of purpose of the candidate. The very core and backbone of the whole system was moral training, and it was dominated by the one ideal of the development of character.[9]

The elaboration of the ritual sacrifices led not only to the development of the other Vedas and later writings but also to the development of the rudiments of some of the sciences.[10] A necessary element in the sacrifice was the altar; the elaboration of the rules for the construction of altars gave birth to the beginnings of geometry and algebra. The desire to discover and establish the most propitious seasons and times for the sacrifices, as well as for other functions and purposes, led to astrology and, later, to astronomy. The extreme care taken to ensure the preservation and transmission of correct texts led to grammar, philology, and phonetics. Later on, in the Aranyakas, the concern about ultimate questions led to philosophy and the development of logic. As a consequence of these developments, already before the end of the growth period, there was a tradition of the necessity of six subjects for the proper reading, understanding, and use of the Vedas.

The six subjects were phonetics, meter, grammar, etymology, astronomy, and ceremonial practice. These constituted the minimum, basic curriculum, in addition to the perfect memorization of the Veda of the school. In addition to these subjects it seems that in most schools physical training was an integral part of the educational scheme and that, in some at least, military science was also taught.

The period of studentship seems normally to have been twelve years.

In the beginnings of the period of growth—and it is uncertain how long this condition lasted—women were trained in the Vedic lore and there are even references to some outstanding women teachers.

The teachers were mostly Brahmans, though the later characteristic Indian caste system had not yet developed.

It seems[11] that there were no primary schools in the early growth period, and that there were no fixed rules for the advancement of pupils from one course to the next higher. This was left entirely to the discretion of the teacher who advanced the pupil according to his capacity and ability.

The state had nothing whatever to do with education during this period. All education in this period was aristocratic in the sense that the Brahmans taught their own sons, the sons of other Brahmans and sons of the two other higher classes. But although the higher classes were hereditary, that to which most respect was paid by all was the class of Brahmans—the intellectual aristocracy—and the kings and princes were not necessarily of this class at all, but were rather usually of the kshatriya or warrior class.

In general terms it seems that the goal of education was religiously conceived—the goal was ultimate self-realization achieved through self-discipline.[12] And the individual was to discipline himself into self-realization through realizing his greatest powers and preparing himself for service to society in that direction. He was, above all, to perform his duty, regardless of his rights, in the community and class to which he belonged by birth and breeding. Society was conceived as an organic whole in which all individuals had a function, but their functions were different, and varied according to their innate abilites. The individual could achieve self-realization and perform his social function and discharge his social duties only by using his own innate powers to the full, and he could use them to the full only in his own class and station.

Thus in the period of growth Indic education was oral, private, tutorial, semi-aristocratic, basically religious, controlled by an ideal. All "practical" education was by the apprenticeship method.

Time of Troubles and Universal State

The Indic Civilization appears to have broken down and entered into its time of troubles in the eighth pre-Christian century. From this time on there was an increase in destructive wars among a multiplicity of local states and in the other social schisms characteristic of the time of troubles of other societies. The history of the period is far from clear because the record of events is incomplete; dates, when they can be given at all, are uncertain; the names of even the chief actors in the historical pageant are for the most part unknown. The sixteen great states and the four autonomous clans of the sixth century[13] had disappeared into the Mauryan Empire by the last quarter of the fourth century.

If we take the eighth century as the beginning of the Upanishadic teachings, and the time of the Buddha and Mahavira about 500 B.C. as the end thereof, then the Upanishadic era coincides approximately with the first two-thirds of the Indic time of troubles. It came to an end with the founding of the Mauryan Empire in 322 B.C. By the time of the great Buddhist Emperor Asoka in the third century, that empire embraced nearly the whole of the Indian sub-continent. It continued until the beginning of the Hellenic intrusion under the Bactrian king Demetrius in 185 B.C. (The raid of Alexander had been only an episode.) The Hellenic intrusion continued under the Kushan Empire until A.D. 390, when the Indic universal state was resumed by the Guptan Empire. The Guptan Empire lasted until about A.D. 475.

The evidence and data necessary to draw distinctions between the educational theories and practices and institutions of the time of troubles and those of the universal state simply do not exist. It is therefore necessary to treat education of both periods as if it were all of a piece, although some distinctions can reasonably be made, and the likenesses and differences between Upanishadic and Buddhist teachings can be made clear.

This lack of evidence and data is of course deplorable, but perhaps not so deplorable as would have been the case if there were so great a lack for the Sinic or Hellenic civilization. For, both with the Indic Civilization and its Hindu successor, the ethos of the society was religious and other-wordly to a greater extent than in any other civilization. There was never, in either society, the same interest in mundane affairs nor in the succession thereof that induced the Chinese, for example, to compile and keep their magnificent records and chronicles. Perhaps it was a consequence of this dominant ethos that the educational theories and practices in the Indic society seem to have undergone fewer fundamental changes from beginning to end than they did in the other civilizations.

The works called the Aranyakas and the Upanishads were, together, originally named the Vedanta, that is, the end of the Vedas.[14] The word Upanishad[15] came, in time, to mean the secret or restricted teachings that were, and could only be, transmitted orally by a guru to an advanced disciple. Still later, the word acquired the sense in which it is now used: the texts which incorporate such doctrines. Thus the very word itself indicates what was clearly the case with instruction in all the Vedic and Vedantic literature: it was regarded as revealed knowledge, which could be imparted only orally by a master to a pupil who had proved himself worthy to receive it. This last feature is strikingly recurrent in the Upanishads: the teacher refuses to give instruction to a pupil until he is fully satisfied about the student's competence, both mental and moral, to receive the instruction, and especially so when it is concerned with the deeper truths.

By the end of the Upanishadic period at latest, the art of writing was fully developed, and under the rule of Asoka, if not earlier, it was extensively used for administrative purposes. By the end of the same period the alphabet and writing were taught to all children who had been accepted by teachers. Yet, despite all this, the knowledge and use of writing seems to have made no difference at all in the method of teaching and learning.[16] The method continued to be oral and the study of manuscripts was even condemned. The evidence seems to show that the Buddhist sacred books, as well as the books of other sects and the Vedas, were not, during this period, written down, but were memorized, despite the monks' realization that parts of the canon might thus be lost.

Majundar finds it difficult to understand this preference for the oral transmission of literature.[17] In view of the vast mass of literature of the fifth and fourth centuries B.C., and the very extensive use of writing for administrative purposes, he conjectures that "books were much more extensively in use than is now commonly believed, or was admitted by priestly writers and monks." But when we recall the importance and persistence of the oral tradition in other cultures[18] we do not find this conjecture persuasive. However, Majundar rightly adds that the emphasis was clearly on the primacy of the role of the teacher in an educational system whose function was not only to impart knowledge but also and mainly to develop character—teachers, not books, were the important sources of instruction.

It seems clear that by the end of the Upanishadic era at latest, considerable attention was paid to the training of the child during its earliest years. According to the perhaps somewhat idealized picture drawn by Das,[19] the home education of the child began with the ceremony of tonsure at the age of three or five, the age of developing egotism in the individual. The parent took advantage of this growing egotism to establish regular habits in the child's daily life: the habits of early rising and cleanliness, especially of his eyes and teeth. He was taught that he was a brother to the animals, indeed to the whole of the natural order, and "was led from nature to nature's God. This was the foundation of his spiritual training."[20]

It seems clear also that primary education did not exist in Vedic times but did exist by the close of the Upanishadic age. What is not clear from the evidence is whether all or some—or, if some, which— of the Hindu children were given primary education. It is reasonable to suppose that it was given only to children of the three upper castes, and the caste system, which had been developing all the while, had reached a state of high rigidity by this time.

The primary schools, like other schools, were wholly private and consisted in the guru or master with those pupils whom he had accepted into his household. The child was apparently admitted at about the age of seven.

With the advent and development of Buddhism in India there seems to have spread among the people the desire for some elementary education which, in the Buddhist monasteries, included some secular education. The curriculum in these monasteries began with the alphabet and a primer and advanced to the study of grammar. Grammatical studies continued from the beginnings at the elementary level until the pupil was about twenty years of age. Grammar was regarded as preliminary to the study of higher subjects in the secondary and later stages of education. On the secondary level a study of arts and crafts was introduced, and in the more advanced stages, medicine, logic, and philosophy.

Venkateswara holds[21] that Buddhism and Jainism introduced only a few changes in the methods of teaching. He mentions especially their emphasis on the use of the vernacular and the Buddhist introduction of a new method of maintaining discipline. This was the device of public confession before an assembly of the brethren. He adds that "corporal punishment was sanctioned and came into common use."

By the end of the Upanishadic age the vague Vedic tradition and practices in education had become codified into something like a regular system. Education had developed its own rituals and ceremonies and most of these tended to emphasize the religious aspect of its character and its aim of educing personality and aiding self-fulfillment.

The first educational ceremony was performed by the pupil at the age of five (or seven?). It involved the offering of worship to certain deities, the learning of the alphabet and, according to one authority quoted by Majundar,[22] the learning of the rudiments of writing and arithmetic.

The next ceremony was that associated with the acceptance of a pupil by a guru. This marked a turning point in the student's life, for he now left his own home and family to enter the household of his teacher and become a member thereof. Admission to the guru's household was determined solely by his judgment of the applicant's moral and intellectual fitness to receive instruction. Residence in the teacher's household involved the begging of alms, tending the sacred fires, and serving the teacher by word and mind and deed. The regulations required the student to rise early, to pray and worship, to take regular daily baths, to wear simple dress and tonsure and to eat simple food, to sleep on the bare ground, to be celibate, and to observe a strict personal and moral discipline. There were also day students who attended the guru's classes but did not live in his household. Normally, the guru received no fees from the pupil, who, however, after the completion of the course, did give the master such presents as he could afford.

Nor did all students who were accepted complete the course: some few found the study too irksome and the discipline too strict, and deserted; some were dismissed by the teacher for an offense or for incompetence; some simply left for a life of ease and one who did so was branded as a *khatvarundha,* i.e., one who slept on a cot when he should have been sleeping on the ground.

There were three classes of teachers—the *guru,* the *āchārya,* and the *upādhyāya.* The guru was he who, having performed all the rites, gave instruction in the Vedas. The āchārya was one who taught the Vedas after having performed only one of the earlier ceremonies. The third was one who taught only a portion of the Vedas. Teaching was almost but not quite a monopoly of the Brahmans, and the teaching seems to have been for the most part excellent.

Another classification of teachers is given in the Mahabharata, the great epic of about the end of the time of troubles. There were two classes: the professional teachers who received fees for their work and taught only portions of the Veda or Vedanta; and there were those who taught the Vedas and Upanishads without receiving fees. The former were condemned as not worthy of an invitation to certain important social ceremonies. In addition to these two classes of teachers there seem to have been also experts in "education" or pedagogy.

That considerable thought was given to the process and theory of learning is indicated by the following steps of study given in one of the authorities:[23] (1) eagerness on the part of the pupil to listen to the words of the teacher, (2) grasping the lessons of the teacher, (3) apprehension and understanding of the teacher's words, (4) retention of what had been heard and understood, (5 and 6) discussion, both with the teacher and with other pupils, (7) full knowledge and understanding of the meaning of the teacher's lessons, and, finally, (8) a comprehension of the deeper truths that lie beneath and behind those given in the lessons. A stray verse of the time sums up the process as follows: "A student learns a fourth from his teacher, a fourth by his own intelligence by himself, a fourth from his fellow pupils, and the remaining fourth in course of time by experience."

The subjects of study included not only the entire Vedic literature but also economics and related subjects, dialectics and politics, lexicography, prosody, phonology, grammar, etymology, astrology and astronomy, omens, auspicious marks on the body, and interpretations of dreams and signs. It is not clear just where a division was drawn between the instruction given by a guru and that given in one of the higher schools, but probably there was no division. It is clear that there was no system of annual "classes" or of examinations. Advancement of the pupil was by achievement, and the rate and degree of achievement was determined by the master.

The Brahman teachers gave instruction not only in all academic subjects but also in archery, military science, and arts and crafts. The Mahabharata contains the singular injunction that persons of all four castes should listen to recitations of and discourses about the Vedas.

By about the end of the fifth century B.C. special schools had begun to appear, and by the Guptan age they were fully developed. Of these special centers of higher learning there were two kinds. The first kind included those run by a single teacher who admitted to his household as many pupils as he could manage. The other kind developed out of the Parisads and hermitages.

The Parisads were assemblies of learned Brahmins who gave decisions on all points connected with the Brahmanic religion and learning. These assemblies were like both judicial assemblies and ecclesiastical synods, with some of the functions of each, and were also similar to the associations of masters or teachers of the European Middle Ages. The hermitages, as the name implies, were places to which several or many learned men had retired from the world in their old age. Many of them included in their personnel teachers whose fame had spread far and wide and to whom, consequently, students came from all over the land.

The very large centers of higher education—they could perhaps be called universities—consisted of several departments. A passage in the Mahabharata lists these as follows: a large common hall for prayer and worship, a school of Vedic studies (or "department of divinity"), a military science school, and departments of botany, economics, and transportation. The greatest of these universities was at Taxila, although Banares was another and hardly less important center. The fame of Taxila seems to have reached its height under the Emperor Asoka, and that fame was due to the eminence of its teachers. It was exclusively a center of higher, not elementary, education; its students were drawn from all castes and social ranks, and the king's son, while at the university, was as poor as the peasant's. Studies were chosen by the student out of the very wide variety of offerings and were not specifically assigned according to the caste of the student.

In the Guptan age there were at least one or two medical schools in connection with the great centers.[23] The medical education was for a prescribed period of seven years after a general program of studies and, for this school alone, the student was required to stand an examination before graduation. The surgery of the time was advanced enough for the graduates to be able to perform successful appendectomies.

By the time of the Guptas or earlier the caste system in India had become fixed. Vedic study was binding on members of the three "twice-born" castes, but an intellectual career was reserved for the Brahman (the highest caste, the intellectual aristocracy), while the Kshatriya (warrior or ruling caste) was destined for a political and military career and the Vaisya (commercial or trading caste) for an economic career. The studies and schools sketched above were intended primarily, although not exclusively, for the highest caste, and seem to have been sufficiently comprehensive. But the course of studies prescribed for the other castes was not less so.[24]

Even in the late Upanishadic age the Vaisya was expected to have knowledge of "the value of gems, pearls, corals, metals, cloth, perfumes and condiments, of the manner of sowing seeds and the qualities of soils, of weights and measures, of the varieties of merchandise . . . of different languages and different countries."[25]

The data about the education of a prince is very scanty, but it seems that he had, in addition to the usual Vedic lore, special training in history, in military science, and in the different elements of the army, such as elephants, horses, chariots and specialized weapons.

With the advent and spread of Buddhism over India went the gradual founding and growth of numbers of Buddhist monasteries. By the Mauryan period many of these had become famous, and, under the Guptas, one or two became outstanding.

Buddhist education was not based on Vedic study, and its teachers were not Brahmans, except for those who had been converted to Buddhism. Further, the Buddhist monasteries were open to men of all castes and not only to those of the three upper castes. Apart from these differences, the methods of education used in the great Buddhist monastery-universities remained about the same as those in the Brahmanic centers. For the first ten years or so, the student lived in absolute dependence upon his teacher, and the method of teaching was exclusively oral; great store was set on memorizing, although memorizing for constant pondering over the meaning, rather than mere learning by rote; there was a long course of grammatical studies preliminary to the higher studies of logic, yoga, and metaphysics; and great importance was attached to the methods of discussion and debate.

By the Guptan period several of the Buddhist centers were admitting advanced students who were, and intended to remain, laymen. In these institutions especially there was a high ideal of academic catholicity so that they welcomed knowledge from all quarters and from all sects and creeds.

The most famous of the Buddhist universities was the monastery of Nalanda in Mahadha. It owed its foundation to six successive generations of Guptan kings and was renowned not only for the magnificence of its establishment but also for the intellectual and moral superiority of its monks. Its total population numbered several thousands; they were maintained out of the revenues of a hundred villages endowed for the upkeep of the monastery. By its excellence it attracted students in such numbers that only two or three out of ten applicants succeeded in gaining admission. The monks at Nalanda devoted themselves entirely to study and debates. There seems to have been a system of ranking the monks according to ability and experience. Students of all castes and classes were admitted. Nalanda's only rival was Valabhi in Kathiawar.

Of the fundamental beliefs and principles underlying the Indic educational methods and practices, one of the more important was the belief that each man is born a debtor with a threefold obligation to the founders of his religion and culture, to the gods, and to his parents. In the earlier Vedic period it was thought that he repaid the first debt as a student by his study of the Vedas, the second as a householder by the performance of sacrifices, the third by offerings to the manes and by himself becoming the father of children. After these debts were all paid, the individual was then free to devote himself to the meditation by which he might achieve salvation. Education was seen as a process that continued throughout the life of man, but as divided into four stages in such a way that the performance of the duties of one stage prepared him for the next.

With the development of the Upanishadic philosophy greater importance came to be attached to the fourth stage, and so the conception of the true function of education at each stage was subtly influenced and altered. Despite the very great variety and multiplicity of philosophical views, arguments, positions, insights, and problems in the Upanishads, there is one pervasive idea or principle that dominates it all and that may be taken as summing up the Upanishadic philosophy.

This is the idea that behind or beneath the multiplicity and change and matter of the phenomenal world, behind even the polytheistic pantheon, there lies Brahma. Brahma is spiritual, is a unity. And the individual self, the Atman, is somehow identical with Brahma. The idea is summed up in the lapidary formula "That art Thou," which may be slightly expanded to read: "The Universe is Brahma, but the Brahma is the Atman." To put this in slightly different terms: there is a unity of all spirit in the one supreme spirit which is also Ultimate Reality. The Atman—the essence which is the spirit of the individual human being—is Brahma, the universal spirit. This unity of all spirit is a unity among all living things.

This Indic assertion that the essential human being is one with the spirit of the universe is likely to strike the modern Western reader, with his almost unquestioned assumption that man is an entity separate and isolated not only from other men but also from Nature and God, as unintelligible or absurd. But it would perhaps be hasty and unwarranted to dismiss as nonsense any important belief about fundamental human experiences that has been widely held, critically examined, and asserted on the basis of the actual experiences of large numbers of thoughtful persons who have lived in widely separated times and places. We have seen already[26] that a characteristic of Chinese thought is that it does not draw any clear distinction between the individual human self and the rest of the universe, and that some Chinese thinkers asserted the possibility and reality of an experience in which the individual becomes aware of his identity with the universe. We shall see[27] that in early Egyptian thought the nature of the individual human being was grounded in cosmic forces.

Since these beliefs are alien to most Western thought and therefore strange to most Western readers, it is perhaps not superfluous to add here some remarks about Indic philosophy that may make it seem a little less strange and alien.

Perhaps the general characteristic of these long and strongly held beliefs is that in addition to the everyday sensible and sense-apprehended world of stocks and stones and flesh and blood, there is another world, a spiritual realm, that is different from the sensible world which, instead of being external to it, is radiating through it and interpenetrating it always and everywhere. We can see a clue to this idea in the ordinary experiences of Everyman: we suffer "pangs" of toothache and "pangs" of conscience; we call both experiences by the same name, yet we recognize, as soon as our attention is called to it, that the two experiences are different in kind. The one can be localized in a nerve, can be treated with a knife or with drugs; its rate of propagation over the nerve can be measured in feet per second, it is physical and chemical, it is material. The other cannot be localized in space, cannot be probed for with knife or dentist's pick, is not physical or chemical, is not material. We recognize similarly the radical distinction in kind between the "pleasure" of scratching an itch—as Socrates elegantly put it—and the "pleasure" of solving a difficult problem or of reading poetry or of listening to music, between the "satisfaction" of dining well and that of having overcome an ignoble impulse.

To focus the attention on this difference and its radical character, and to attempt systematically to work out an explanation of it, commonly results—as it has clearly resulted in Western philosophy, notably since Descartes—in a metaphysical dualism: that is, a rational account of the nature of things in terms of two fundamentally different and mutually irreducible principles.

But to focus the attention exclusively on this difference between these two kinds of experience is to ignore other aspects or kinds of human experience that may be, for all we know, equally or more important. One of these kinds of experience is that suggested by Browning's lines in *Paracelsus;*

> Truth is within ourselves: it takes no rise
> From outward things, whate'er you may believe,
> There is an inmost centre in us all,
> Where truth abides in fulness; and around,
> Wall upon wall, the gross flesh hems it in,
> This perfect, clear perception—which is truth.
>
> A baffling and perverting carnal mesh
> Binds it, and makes all error; and to *know,*
> Rather consists in opening out a way
> Whence the imprisoned splendour may escape,
> Than in effecting entry for a light
> Supposed to be without.

These lines seem to suggest that it is an inner, self-authenticating, immediate awareness of Truth itself; that Truth is within; that it is within all men; that this awareness does not require either the complex apparatus of the senses and nerves or the classifying, symbolizing action of the conceptualizing mind.

Another kind of human experience is that recorded by William James[28] in which the subject stated that, in a brief moment, "The whole of my life passed before me, including each little meaningless piece of distress, and I *understood* them. *This* was what it had all meant, *this* was the piece of work it had all been contributing to do. I did not see God's purpose, I only saw his intentness and his entire relentlessness towards his means . . . I wondered why, since I had gone so deep, I had seen nothing of what the saints call the *love* of God, nothing but his relentlessness. And then I heard an answer, which I could only catch, saying, 'Knowledge and Love are One, and the measure is suffering.' "

Examples of experiences of these other kinds—from the poets and the mystics and ordinary people—might be multiplied endlessly,[29] but reflection on them all suggests the conclusion that a sharp metaphysical dualism does not give an adequate account of the whole of human experience, and this partly for the reason that it does not begin by taking into account all the kinds of experiences.

That all the kinds of human experiences must be taken into account is based on the reasonable assumption or presupposition that the universe is "an indivisible whole, but the intellect cannot handle it except by abstracting selections of specimens of it. This selection is bound to be both arbitrary and imperfect to some extent"[30] and the arbitrariness is increased as the number of the kinds of specimens is decreased.

Thus to start from and to take account only of the everyday experiences of ordinary people has led, in the West, to certain conclusions which are commonly—almost universally—accepted and which Professor Broad has formulated as "Basic Limiting Principles."[31] Among these are the principles that "It is impossible for *A* to know what experiences *B* is having or has had except by hearing and understanding sentences descriptive of that experience, or by hearing and interpreting cries or gestures that *B* makes, or by seeing and making inferences from material records"; that "it is impossible for an event in a person's mind to produce directly any change in the material world except certain changes in his own brain"; that "it is self-evidently impossible that an event should begin to have any effects before it has happened"; that "it is impossible for a person to perceive a physical event or a material thing except by means of sensations which that event or thing produces in his mind." Broad then demonstrates that each of these four basic limiting principles (as well as the other five that he formulated) is refuted by phenomena the evidence for which is as unassailable as is the evidence for basic facts in the natural sciences.

For example, the two long series of experiments in telepathy carried out by Professor Gilbert Murray[33] demonstrated that ideas were communicated from one mind to another independently of the complex apparatus of the senses and nerves and of the physical stimuli of light rays or sound waves. This is a refutation of the first of the limiting principles mentioned above; the evidence for the phenomena refuting the other principles is established by as great weight of observation and experiment as is the evidence for telepathy—or for phenomena in the natural sciences.

Now it may be objected that "psi" phenomena are relatively rare, or are beyond the capacities of ordinary men, that we are concerned only to give an account of the ordinary experiences of mankind, and that therefore such experiences may be left to one side as insignificant or trivial. The objection may be answered by the observation that the experiences of the rare creative poet or painter or musician or mathematician, while not so rare as returns of Halley's comet, are yet not so common as blackberries,[34] but that we do not, for this reason, ignore or discount the poet's experience. It may be noted, too, that the objection that ordinary men are incapable of telepathic and similar experiences is perhaps not well founded, for there is a tradition in India that every man has these capacities—though in different degrees—and that there are ways of developing them; indeed, there is little evidence that the ordinary man in the West does not have the capacities, though there is evidence aplenty that he has not developed them.

Thus if we bring into our purview not only the differences in our everyday experiences, but also these other, less commonplace, kinds of experience, then we perhaps find our minds more open to the suggestion that the easy classification of all human experiences into material or spiritual (physical or mental, of the body or of the mind) is not and cannot be finally satisfactory. And perhaps our minds are also more open to the suggestion that the self of which we have become aware by learning to discriminate it from other selves in our

social environments, is only a superficial manifestation of a deeper—
or higher—Self, that is, Brahman.

If we take into account all the experiences of the mystics—in all
religions and in all ages—we find the suggestion of the Unity of
all in a supreme Spirit that is substantial to lives and minds and
spirits and matter: "He who experiences the unity of life, sees the
Self abiding in all beings and all beings in the Self; everywhere he
sees the same. . . . He who sees Me everywhere, and sees all in Me; I
am not lost to him nor is he lost to me."[35] "Hereby know that we
dwell in Him and He in us, because He hath given us of His Spirit."[36]

For the mystic himself, who has had the illuminating experience of
the Spirit that is substantial to all, that experience seems to be as
coercive and immediate as, and more coherent than, any experience
on any other level. For the rest of us, who have not had the experience for ourselves, so great a weight of evidence from so many witnesses almost compels the adoption of an hypothesis of an underlying
Reality that manifests itself through and in all.

The essence of the Indic conception is perhaps that there is a Unity
among all living things. This can be, and has been, expressed in a
variety of ways: "The Atman is the Brahma," "That art Thou"; one
of the Buddhist (and in this respect Buddhism was characteristically
Indic) poetic statements of what happens when the individual
achieves Nirvana: "The dewdrop slips into the shining sea"; and
perhaps a similar conception is suggested in such statements of Jesus
as, "I am in the Father, and the Father in me"; "Ye shall know that I
am in my Father, and the Father in me"; "Ye shall know that I am
in my Father, and ye in me, and I in you"; "Inasmuch as ye did it
not to one of the least of these, ye did it not to me"; "I and the Father
are one."[37] Expressions of this sort may be found in very many of the
poets and in nearly all the mystics.

These expressions all seem to suggest a numerical identity of the
Atman and the Brahma—that is, they seem to suggest this if, and
only if, they are taken literally and out of context. In the larger context in which they appear are to be found other expressions that offset the suggestion of an equation or numerical identity. The other
statements suggest, not a numerical identity, but an otherness: God
is transcendent as well as immanent. Above all, God is other than
the individual. It is not clear that in the Upanishads, or in the Bhaga-

vadgita, God is identified with the self, whether individual or collective.

There have been Indic sages—as there have been mystics in Christianity and Islam and other religions—who have fallen into the error of identifying God with the self, but this identification, taken literally as a numerical identification, does not seem to be the teaching of either the Upanishads, the Vedanta, the Gita, nor of Buddhism.

If, now, we raise a question about the credibility of this hypothesis of a spiritual reality substantial to all things, to which the soul is akin, and immediate knowledge of which is man's end and goal, there are at least two major considerations that must be reckoned with. The first is that, for very many persons, what is here being described as an hypothesis or belief is neither, but is, rather, an immediately experienced certainty. The second is that the hypothesis is, and has been, for perhaps the greater part of Mankind throughout its history, no hypothesis at all, but rather a fundamental presupposition recognized as self-evidently true.

As to the first consideration, we have already seen that for the mystic himself, his experience of Reality is as coercive and immediate and coherent as any experience on any other level. It is true that his attempts to communicate that experience are, on the whole, unsuccessful, that in the attempt he employs metaphors that are often mixed, and analogies that are often confused and confusing, and that the statements of one mystic often seem to contradict those of others. But this, of course, is just what would be expected: his effort to tell about his experience is like that of the man who attempts to describe the world of light and color to one blind from birth. And it is like that of Plato's philosopher who, after having been liberated from the cave and seen the sun itself, attempts to describe the sun to the prisoners who, all their lives, have seen only the flickering shadows cast by an uncertain flame.

For the mystic, the knowledge that is his as a result of his experience is as certain and irreducible as knowledge can be. It is as certain as the knowledge that something *is,* the knowledge of being. And among those reputable and sensible men who have reported such experiences there have been members of all the several civilizations, not of one or two only.[38]

On the whole, however, the hypothesis of a spiritual Reality substantial to all things has not been the generally accepted assumption in the West and, in the West, there have been perhaps fewer persons who have had the coercive experience of that Reality than in India or China. In very general terms: in the West, Man has experienced himself as sundered from the world, as a discrete individual separate both from other individuals and from the rest of the world. This is perhaps one of the most fundamental and basic of the presuppositions of the thought of the West.[39] It is so fundamental and so basic that any view that runs counter to it has, in the past, not even been considered or, if considered, has been rejected without adequate examination or even partial comprehension. There are, of course, many exceptions to this general statement.

There now seems to be, however, in addition to the continuing minority tradition, an increase in the number of Western thinkers in different fields who take seriously the conception of a non-dualist underlying Reality.[40] But, apart from these exceptions, the main currents of Western thought run counter to, rather than with, the conception. In much of non-Western thought, on the other hand, "the fundamental presupposition of all philosophy and all religion is that Man is a part of the totality of Being. The nerve of philosophical thought is the actual experience of the unity of the Real."[41] This is also characteristic of the beliefs of the "ancients" of the whole of the Near East of the third and second millennia before Christ; it is characteristic of the beliefs of our remote ancestors of the Ice Age.[42] On the whole, the main currents of Western thought seem, in this respect, to be eddies running counter to the main stream of human thought.

Perhaps this excursus into philosophy has served to render the fundamental Upanishadic belief that the self of the individual human being is somehow at one with the spirit of the universe a little more intelligible and, possibly, a little more acceptable.

This fundamental belief entails or includes, of course, the further belief that the individual human being can have—and that very many human beings have had—the immediate experience of unity with Brahma. As Sir Charles Eliot says,[43] "The possibility and truth of this experience is hardly questioned in India and the task of religion is to bring it about, not to promote the welfare of tribes and states, but to effect the enlightenment and salvation of souls." It might similarly be said that the task of education is, ultimately, to prepare the individual for the experience of unity with the supreme spiritual Reality. The development of character in the individual—the underlying aim of Indic education—found its culmination in the self-realization of the Atman in the Brahma. The child's lesson that he is a brother to the whole of the natural order was predicated on this belief that the Atman is the Brahma. The last stage of the individual's life-education sought to achieve the recognition and immediate awareness of the true and intimate relation between himself and the eternal self. This awareness, this experience, is the ultimate bliss, the highest happiness, the *summum bonum,* the end of life.

This fundamental belief entails or includes also the belief in trans-migration, that is, that the spiritual principle of the individual human being appears and reappears in a succession of tenements, and that the character of the successive tenements is determined by the quality of his life in the preceding tenement—in short, as a man acts now, so shall he be in the next life; as he acted in the latest, so is he in this life.

To an extraordinary degree, greater than in any other civilization, the ethos of the Indic and Hindu civilizations was religious. Sir Charles Eliot comments[44] that in India more than in any other land the mind of the people finds "its favourite occupation and full expression" in religion, that this is true of Dravidians as well as Aryans, and that most Indians of all classes and castes, have an interest in theology and "often a passion for it."

In the content and methods of formal education in the Indic Civilization there was a tendency towards formalism and the fixing of stereotypes that was noticeable during the time of troubles, became marked at the beginning of the universal state period, and dominant at the end thereof. For example, in the important science of grammar, Panini produced his great work under the Mauryan Empire. This book on grammar has been hailed even by Western scholars as the most complete and systematic compendium that has been produced in any language. The book was adopted as final and definitive by Indic scholars and, although many books on grammar were written after Panini, it was always accepted that his authority must not be departed from.[45]

As with the science of grammar, so it was also, the evidence suggests, with the methods of teaching, clearly with the content of the curriculum, and to a certain extent, even with philosophy.

We have seen that throughout the growth period of the Indic Civilization education was oral, tutorial, private, semi-aristocratic, basically religious, and controlled by an ideal. Except for the fact that at the great university centers, both Brahman and Buddhist, students of all classes were admitted, thus "democratizing" education, the same characteristics seem to have been true of Indic education during the time of troubles and the period of the universal state.

The end of the Guptan Empire and of the Indic Civilization came in the last quarter of the fifth century A.D. Already, about A.D. 455, the Hunas (Huns) had begun to filter into northwest India. With the death of the last emperor, Skandagupta, A.D. 467, there was an outbreak of wars of succession which further weakened an empire already threatened by the barbarian hordes. These hordes, having passed through Persia and having destroyed the Kushan Empire, now poured into India. The following three centuries in India present the classic picture of barbarian intrusions and of a bevy of successor states to the now defunct universal state.

5. *The Hellenic Civilization*

Period of Growth

The Hellenic Civilization came into being towards the end of the twelfth century B.C. as a response chiefly to the physical challenge of the barren land of the Aegean Islands and coast, but partly also to the social challenge of the disintegrating Minoan Civilization. The growth period of the society lasted from the beginnings to the breakdown at the outbreak of the Atheno-Peloponnesian Wars in 431 B.C.

It is in Homer that the first expression in literary form of the Greek character appears and that the first clues to the nature of Greek education are found.

Education, in Homer, is education of the aristocrat. The social organization of the society was, in many ways, similar to that of the Western society during the period from the Merovingians to about A.D. 1000, and it was similar to that of the Sinic Society during its early period. At the apex of the social pyramid was the king. Beneath the king were the nobility, the aristocracy. Of these, the older men were the counsellors and advisers, while the younger were the warriors, the chevaliers, the attendants at court. The hewers of wood and the drawers of water, the laborers and fishermen and traders, were the base of the social pyramid. We must assume that all education of the lower class was by the apprenticeship method, for Homer mentions only the education of aristocrats.

This Hellenic aristocracy had originated in pre-Homeric times as the ruling, fighting, thinking, creative class that had gradually separated itself out from the general population. This class consisted of the creative geniuses who worked out adequate responses to successive challenges and whose lead was followed by the rest of the people.

The content of the education of the young aristocrat was both moral and practical. The distinction between the two in early Hellenic society is drawn by Jaeger and Marrou and others, but it may be doubted whether the Greeks themselves would have made the distinction or even recognized it. It is probable, rather, that they—as well as the members of the early Sinic and Indic societies—would have felt it to be unreal, forced, artificial. They would have thought that the morally cultivated man, the ideal man, was cultivated in his behavior as well as in his inner nature; that his behavior was somehow an expression of his inner nature and not separable from it. Yet the distinction can be drawn, especially for the purposes of presentation and analysis.

The practical content of the education of the young aristocrat included training in those arts and skills necessary to him in his station in society. These included courtly manners and etiquette; "music," that is, singing, lyre-playing and dancing; oratory; sports and games: horsemanship, wrestling, jousting, boxing, archery, javelin-throwing, weight-putting, foot-racing, and perhaps above all, chariot-racing.

As a result of his training in courtly manners and etiquette and oratory, the young noble was expected to know how to conduct himself in the court and among the people, how to speak well on all occasions and what were appropriate subjects for discourse, and how to respond to unforeseen circumstances. As a result of his training in games and sports, he was expected to be able to do well in all of them but not to "specialize" in any one to the exclusion of the others. Later on in Greek education, the "gentleman" would have felt it beneath him to excel in a sport or game—that was left to the professional who, for his particular proficiency, paid the price of being deficient in other games or in manners or in readiness of wit.

The moral content of the training of the young aristocrat included maxims of practical wisdom and external morality, and it included the presentation of an ideal of existence. This ideal dominated the other aspects of early Hellenic education, and the one word that sums up the value in the ideal is the Greek *arete*. The word means "excellent in its kind or way," and the "excellence" of the ideal involved more than one aspect or facet.

There is first the aspect personified in Odysseus of "the many devices or stratagems"—a kind of cunning, the ability to get out of awkward situations. But more fundamental than this is the ideal embodied in Achilles, an ideal that can be expressed in a single phrase: "an heroic morality of honor,"[1] and that had its basis in a fundamental pessimism. The Greek warrior of this time could look forward to a short life and a sudden death, and he had small hope of any consolation in the shadowy existence beyond the grave. Yet despite his pagan love of life, so short and precarious, he was ready to sacrifice his life for something higher. And that something higher was honor or glory. The *arete* of the Homeric hero was a proud morality combined with warlike valor[2] or, more simply, valor in the chivalric sense of the word.[3]

The one concern of the Homeric hero is with his own personal honor; he is always striving to be the best and to get ahead of all others, to dazzle and to be victor in competition. Marrou[4] holds that this concern and this striving are not expressions of a mere egocentrism but are, rather, striving after an Absolute Beauty and Perfect Valor that far transcend any actual heroic deed or heroic life. Certainly the ideal of Greek education of a later date was transcendent.

The method of Homeric education, as distinguished from the content, was that of setting forth the pattern or example. The counsellors or teachers were always holding up for emulation by youth the heroic example, the idealized models of perfect *arete*: the hero who was both warrior and orator, who could serve equally well on the battlefield and at court.

The teacher, in Homeric education, was an older man to whom the young noble was entrusted and from whom he received counsel and whose example he followed. The tutor tried always not merely to teach the youth but also to mould his character. The relationship between the tutor and his charge was personal, intimate, and long lasting, and the companionship between the two extended not only to the court, the market place and the battlefield but also into all aspects of daily life. The tutor strove always to stand out in the eyes of the younger man, and the younger strove always to show himself worthy of the friendship of his tutor. Thus the education of the young man was furthered by daily association, personal example, conversation, and gradual initiation into all the activities of the older

—in the club, the gymnasium, and the banquet. Public opinion—and, later, in Sparta, the law—held the tutor morally responsible for the development of the youth who had been entrusted to him.

The social position of women in Greece towards the close of the Homeric period was higher than at any later date. She had a fairly constant status, both social and, apparently, legal, as mistress of the household. As such, her *arete* included sober domestic morality and prudence, although the real *arete* of woman was beauty.

If we accept the century between 850 and 750 B.C.[6] as approximately the time of the composition of the *Iliad,* and a somewhat later date for the *Odyssey,* it seems that within another century Homer had become the standard educational treatise of Greece. He was learned and recited not only by the bards but also, in part at least, by all cultivated men. He was the "classic" of Greece to a much greater extent than Dante ever became for Italy or Shakespeare for England, and remained the educational classic throughout the whole time span of the Hellenic Civilization.

But succeeding periods of course added their own "classics" and made their own contributions to the Hellenic moral and educational ideal. Hesiod (c. 700 B.C.) began his career as a bard, reciting Homer. But he was from Boeotia, a region at that date still wholly peasant, and in his own poems, he added to the Homeric ideal elements derived from his own experiences in his own time and place. It was Hesiod who introduced the conceptions of Right and Justice and Truth as founded in the eternal laws of the universe itself.

In Hesiod the statement of these conceptions is put in symbolic, mythological language, but through him the general ideas entered into Hellenic thought and so were a part of the background against which the later, more clearly and precisely formulated, conceptions developed. His conception of abstract Justice was an object of faith, not a provable hypothesis, and Justice was, for him, grounded in the very nature of the universe, not dependent upon the caprices of Olympian gods. His conception of *arete* was derived not from the aristocratic training of the Homeric hero but from that of the ordinary man who had to work for his living. Righteousness and work are the foundations of *arete,* and man can win or develop it only by the sweat of his brow. Thus Hesiod added to, and in so doing modified, the Hellenic ideal that had first been stated in Homer.

There exist few details about Greek education from the time of Hesiod to the fifth century, but the poems of Theognis of the second half of the sixth century throw some light on his time. The poems were elegies to be sung or recited at banquets at the aristocratic clubs, and some of them are instructions to his young friend and pupil. The content of the teaching is the traditional wisdom of the noble class and suggests that the upper-class education of the time was primarily moral in the sense that it was concerned with character-building and the development of personality against a background of polite and leisured society. It is clear that the close personal relation between tutor and pupil still held.

Marrou convincingly argues[7] that, throughout the whole of early Greek educational history down to the time when proper educational *institutions* were established, only one type of thorough education was possible, and this was education by the tutor-disciple method in which there was a close personal bond. Throughout this early period the pupil was chosen by the tutor and had to show that he was worthy of being chosen and retained as disciple. This was in large part the ground of the opinion that the tutor who taught for money, who made a business out of teaching, who offered his learning to the first customer who could pay, was to be despised. This general opinion persisted throughout the growth period of the Hellenic society and, in parts of Greece, well into the time of troubles. It reflected an awareness of the dignity of culture and a conviction that only the few were worthy of it. It perhaps reflected also the Platonic belief[8] in the superiority of oral teaching and direct communication over the impersonality of the written word.

All instruction in Greece from the earliest times down to the breakdown was oral. It is perhaps possible, as Kenyon has suggested,[9] that the Homeric epics were composed in writing and that written copies of them existed from the earliest times. But the earliest copies were certainly owned exclusively by the professional bards, and Homer was taught orally to the young aristocrats. Even during the fifth century, when Greek literary creativeness reached its peak, book production was on a very limited scale, and there is no evidence that serious education was other than oral.

When the teacher of letters—the *grammatistes*—made his appearance, and when letters began systematically and generally to be taught to children, is difficult to say. The institution of ostracism, that is, the banishment of a citizen by vote of his fellows, which votes were written on bits of pottery and cast into a box, was introduced in 508-507 B.C. It has been argued that this required a knowledge of writing, as to be sure it did. But that it did not require a knowledge of writing on the part of all voting citizens is shown by the fact that several series of ballots with the writing in the same hand have been recovered.[10] The evidence shows that from the beginning of the fifth century there did exist some kind of systematic instruction in reading and writing. It also shows that this instruction was only a minor part of education and that to be possessed of this knowledge alone was not sufficient to enable a man to be called "educated."

We have seen that in the very beginnings of the Hellenic society, the Homeric hero was striving to realize in his own life and deeds an Absolute Beauty and Perfect Valor that was somehow greater than and beyond any actual life or deed. And we have seen that Hesiod had grasped the conception of an Absolute Justice and Absolute Right that were somehow independent of particular right actions and just laws and were grounded in the nature of things. After Hesiod the general Greek conception of *arete* had begun to change from that of valor, in the chivalric sense, to include the idea that *arete* must be won or developed.

The word *arete* is derived from the same root as the word *aristos*— "best"—which shows superlative ability or superiority, and which was used in the plural form—*aristoi*—as the regular term for the nobility. Thus in the beginnings the *aristoi*, the nobles, were simply the members of the limited number of hereditary ruling families. But as the general conception of *arete* underwent a change, so the conception of the *aristoi* as the "best," the most "excellent," began to refer a little less exclusively to inherited position. This is not to say that after Hesiod the term was used at once to refer to "excellence" that was not inherited—the aristocratic tradition in Greece persisted until very late; rather, there was a slow and very gradual development of the idea that some men, who were not born into the noble class, might achieve the highest human excellence, and that some, who were born into it, might not.

It was during the growth period that the Hellenic society gradually realized and developed its characteristic conceptions of man, the ideal, and the universal laws underlying particular phenomena, although the final philosophical formulation of these conceptions did not take place until after the breakdown.

Jaeger[11] presents the view that Greek thought was, from the outset, anthropocentric in the sense that its chief concern was with man, not with gods or kings or spirits. However, man was conceived not as an autonomous individual and not even as primarily a member of the social group, but as an ideal. The ideal dominates the conception of man as an individual and as a social being. If we ask "What is the ideal man?" the answer in Greek thought, according to Jaeger,[12] is that "it is the universally valid model of humanity which all individuals are bound to imitate." This model was not to be finally defined or fixed in a formula by any human mind; it was believed to be real, to be itself, to be the guide and criterion according to which the human character and personality is to be shaped. It was to this ideal that not only the Greek philosophers but also the educators, poets, and artists looked.

An illustration of this tendency to seek to understand the universal rather than to master a multitude of particulars may be seen in the superlative works of the sculptors. Their representations of the human body in so great a variety of free motions and postures and attitudes were derived not from mere copying of a number of observed actual positions and motions but from having learned the general laws of physiological structure and of balance and movement. Another illustration may be seen in the efforts of the earliest philosophers to discover and formulate some single principle in terms of which all the manifold variety and apparent differences of the phenomenal world could be understood and accounted for. The degree of their achievement in this line is shown by the fact that by the end of the fifth century, they had formulated an atomic theory to account for the variety of motions and differences among physical substances in terms of irreducibly small, uniform, material particles—thus anticipating the Newtonian physics, in this respect, by nearly twenty-one centuries.

Another illustration is seen in the forms of oratory, drama, and literary style—forms first discovered and formulated by the Greeks, but remaining still in canons now taught (or taught until yesterday) in the textbooks of our Western society. A final illustration may be taken from a time of about a century and a half after the breakdown of the society: Euclid's presentation of the axioms, postulates, problems, and solutions in plane geometry was successful enough to be used throughout antiquity and down to the present century in the West.

All these are illustrations of the Greek ability to recognize the existence of, then to detect, and finally to formulate, the general laws that underlie particulars. Geometry, for example, was invented by the Egyptians, not by the Greeks; but it was the Greeks who reduced what had originally been an empirical science, devised for the purpose of measuring land and fixing boundaries after flood waters had subsided, to a set of universal rules that held for all plane figures.

Similarly, the Greek anthropocentrism was not concerned primarily with the subjective self of the individual, but with the general principles (laws) of the human nature in every man. The Greeks recognized that there are comprehensible natural principles to which the life of the human body is subject, and, in like manner, inherent or immanent principles of the mind and spirit. And they believed that these principles are "given" in the nature of things, not invented by man, nor imposed arbitrarily by gods, but eternally present, awaiting discovery by man.

These principles are, in a sense, "ideal." In geometry, for example, it is possible to draw on the blackboard, or perhaps, to find in nature, an infinite number of triangles each one of which may differ in length of sides or size of angles from every other. But every triangle conforms to the rules about triangles, so that the geometer can make correct statements about *the* triangle even though *the* mathematical triangle may never have been found in nature and may never have been drawn in sand or on a blackboard. This ideal triangle is of such sort that conceptions of it and statements about it are correct even though it may never have been embodied in the world of things at all. Or, the physicist may formulate a rule or "law" that freely falling bodies fall with an acceleration of thirty-two feet per second. This rule is only ideally correct, for no actual falling body whose rate of acceleration has been measured, and none whose rate ever will be measured, has fallen or will fall at the mathematically precise rate stated in the formula. Yet the physicist states the rate given in the formula as correct or "true." Thus the general principle or law states an "ideal" which particulars, whether they be triangles or falling bodies, can only approximate. The ideal is never wholly or fully embodied in any concrete particular thing or movement.

Similarly, the ideal Valor that appeared in the deeds and character of the Homeric Achilles did not fully or completely appear in him or his deeds, for he and they were only approximations to the ideal. And the ideal Justice conceived by Hesiod did not—and indeed, in its very nature, could not—be fully embodied in any just act or just law. Nor could the ideal Beauty be fully embodied in any particular statue or person or any other thing.

The obvious criticism of this kind of thinking is that these so-called ideals are nonexistent, unreal, and only the products of human thinking—and many Greeks made the criticism. Indeed, the question of the reality of the ideal has been one of the perennial problems of Western philosophy from Socrates and Plato to Bertrand Russell. But as Plato himself pointed out, if there be no such reality as Beauty independent of the opinions of observers and of particular beautiful things, then there can be no rational discourse about beautiful objects. For when a man says that a thing is beautiful, he is asserting either that there is an independent quality of beauty present in it or that he, privately and subjectively, likes it. If he is asserting the latter, then there can be no dispute, for only he can know directly about his likes. If he is asserting the former, then he is asserting that the thing really has a quality that is independent of both him and his interlocutor, and the thing could not have the quality unless it were already there to be had.

These ideal qualities are quite independent of human observers and of particular things and of time and place. Propositions about triangles, for example, would still be true whether Euclid had ever discovered or formulated them or not. They were true, the Greeks would have argued, even when the Egyptians were dealing only empirically with actual angles and lines. They are, in an important sense, eternally true, if "eternally" be taken to mean independent of time rather than everlasting.

The general set of beliefs about these ideals or standards or models was formulated and presented by Plato in the first half of the fourth century; but according to Jaeger and others, Plato was giving the clearest expression to a general characteristic of Greek thought as a whole: the awareness of general, permanent principles that underlie events and changes both in nature and in human life. More will be said about Plato below; this brief sketch is of one of the more important developments in Greek thought during the period of growth.

It was during this period also that the Hellenic Civilization developed, and became aware that it was developing, its idea of culture. The word culture in the West is now generally used in the sense made current chiefly by the anthropologists: the sense of the total complex of the customs, ways of life, and expressions of thought and feeling of any society, with no reference to any value or ideal. For the Greeks, culture was this total complex, and education as culture was the work of the whole community, but it was culture inspired by and directed towards an ideal. The purpose of culture as education was to produce a higher type of human being; it was the shaping of character in accordance with an ideal. The ideal was consciously pursued, and education was conceived as the work of the entire community in all its aspects both in shaping the character of the individual and in transmitting the character of the community. This is the Greek *paideia,* a conception which includes more than is suggested by either "culture" or "education"; it includes the humanistic ideal of an ethical-political culture.

If, in the development of this ideal, the aristocratic *arete* and pattern was the first vital stage, the early *polis,* the city-state, was the second. From the sixth century the historical developments in the Hellenic society produced the *polis* as a type of community conceived as a spiritual entity and as itself an ideal. What the *polis* was, and what it meant to its citizens at the peak of its development, is suggested in the funeral oration put into Pericles' mouth by Thucydides at the end of the Atheno-Pelopennesian War, towards the end of the fifth century. Athens, says Pericles, is the education of Greece, the school of Hellas.

Athens is the education of Greece because, among other reasons, "We [Athenians] lead a life of freedom not only in our politics but in our mutual tolerance of private conduct. We do not resent our neighbor doing what he pleases, nor subject him to those marks of disapproval which poison pleasure though they may inflict no formal injury. . . . We cultivate the arts without extravagance and the intellect without effeminacy. . . . Our politicians do not neglect their private affairs and the rest of us devote ourselves to business without losing touch with politics. . . . The individual Athenian will never meet his equal for self-reliance, versatility, and gallantry, in whatever situation he may find himself."[13]

Versatility, individual initiative, freedom, self-reliance and self-sufficiency, the cultivation of the arts and the intellect, concern with political affairs—these are some of the marks of the citizen of the *polis,* which is the sum of the lives of its citizens in all their aspects. The *polis,* by virtue of its power, its history, its constitution and civic life, its politics and its principles, is a unity, a whole, complete in itself. By making its citizens the bearers and supporters of this unity and participants in the whole, it gives to them its own characteristics. The *polis* is at once the educator and the goal of education. The freedom and self-sufficiency of the *polis* is the foundation of the freedom and self-sufficiency of its citizens, and, at the same time, rests on the educable nature of its citizens to be able to take over the functions of the whole.[14]

The development, from the sixth century onwards, of the political community as an ideal had been accompanied by the suggestions, by scattered thinkers, of other types of ideal communities. The Pythagoreans had formed a kind of missionary community to create a new type of man who would free himself through knowledge. Heraclitus had turned to humanity as a whole to try to form a sort of union of all men through reason, although without the mediation of schools or a school. The Hippocratean guild, which was bound together by the Hippocratic oath, was a sort of hereditary class, but full membership in it demanded a noble humanitarian ethic. But none of these communities made anything like so influential a contribution to the educational ideals of Greece as did the political community, the *polis.*[15]

The concern with the development of political *arete* (that is, *arete* arising out of participation in the *polis*) is the starting point for the sophists, for Isocrates, and for much of the thought of Plato. It was chiefly these who, in the latter half of the fifth century and the first half of the fourth, shaped the educational ideals that endured, with some later modifications, throughout the life of the Hellenic Civilization, and were in part transmitted to the West as a permanent part of the legacy of Greece.

What was the education current in Athens during the first half of the fifth century, the education that produced, or was thought to produce, the political *arete,* the education that Marrou, following Aristophanes,[16] calls the "old education"? To begin with, education was in no way the official concern of the state: the state did not recruit or select teachers, or set the curriculum or furnish endowments. The community as a whole did, to be sure, educate its citizens by using the athletic and musical competitions that were held during the great festivals; but this was not the official state, the government.

The Athenians, says Thucydides,[17] were the first among the Greeks to give up the practice of going about armed and, in so doing, to adopt a less violent way of life. This occurred at the same time that Athens first came forward as a cultural leader, and may have been in part the cause. By the beginning of the fifth century, life and culture and education in Athens, and perhaps in much of the rest of Greece, had become predominantly civilian. But education had remained the privilege of the leisured artistocracy; it was still not for the peasant or artisan or shopkeeper or trader.

With the change to a predominantly civilian life, the older ideal of valor in war, emulation of the warrior-hero, and the great deed in battle had changed to that of valor and the great deed in sports competitions. The odes of Pindar, for example, in the first half of the century, celebrate the deeds of the Pan-Hellenic athletic champion as Homer had celebrated the deeds of the earlier warriors. This belief in the fundamental value of athletic ability as a sign of *arete* persisted for a long time as the ideal of the free man.

But, in the fifth century, changes were taking place: the population of Athens was increasing, and as it increased, more and more persons were becoming financially able to give their sons an education. As the pressure of numbers increased, so gradually the older system of strictly private tutorial training became inadequate to meet the needs of the time. Simultaneously the city-state itself was becoming increasingly democratized, so that it was no longer universally or even generally believed that only aristocrats were entitled to an education. The result was the development of a new type of collective education, and the creation of the school. The old, private, tutorial education of course persisted for a long time alongside the newer schools, and there was a considerable reaction against this new trend in education. Some of the poems of Pindar (d. 466 B.C.) reflect this reaction. For him, race is a necessary if not a sufficient condition of *arete;* the really wise man is one who knows by nature, while those "who know only because they have had lessons" are to be scorned. Yet despite the scorn of the aristocrats, it seems probable that by the end of the century—that is, within a generation of the breakdown of the society —many children were being educated in the schools.

There were three teachers in these schools: the teacher of athletics, the teacher of music, and the teacher of letters. The first was the most important, for although education was becoming increasingly democratized, it retained the stamp of its aristocratic origin. The athletic teacher taught the child to run, to throw the javelin and discus, to wrestle and box, to jump, and to prepare himself for the athletic games.

The music master taught both vocal and instrumental music and dancing, and he was nearly as important in the educational scheme as was the teacher of athletics. Marrou rightly emphasizes[18] the fact that the Greeks of the fifth century and later looked upon themselves, as educated persons, primarily as musicians. Plato, in the first half of the fourth century, remarked[19] that anyone who could not take his place in a choir, as both singer and dancer, is not truly educated. The music master seems also to have taught the literary element in education.

The cultivated man was expected to know and to be able to recite not only a certain amount of Homer, but also a number of lyric poems. The recitation and singing took place at the banquets or symposia that were regularly held at the clubs, but the learning of poems had not only an entertainment and literary value. Many of the songs did have a moral content and were deemed of value as a part of moral training.

The third teacher, the teacher of letters, was third not only in order of origin but also in importance. It seems that by the end of the century all educated persons were expected to be able to read and write but also that the mere knowledge was not sufficient to entitle a man to be called educated.

Thus this "old" Athenian education of the end of the period of growth was rather more athletic than intellectual, artistic or "musical" than literary. None of it was designed to train a man primarily either for war or for politics or for business—it was not technical or vocational in any sense. It was still dominated by an ideal and the ideal was to produce a man both beautiful and good—an ethical ideal. It must always be remembered that much of what the Athenian learned was still by the apprenticeship method. He was accustomed to spending time in the marketplace in conversation with his fellow citizens, to sitting in on the citizen-assemblies and to listen carefully to the great orators and statesmen, to serving in the army or navy, to observing the work of the architects and engineers and sculptors and painters, to listening with eagerness to the plays of the great dramatists, to participating in the life of the *polis* as a whole. And it was these "liberally" or "generally" educated men who were the generals in the army, the commanders in the navy, the architects of the policy of the city-state, the audience for the plays of the dramatists, and it was out of their ranks that the dramatists and poets and philosophers emerged.

It has been noted above that Pindar reflects the old belief in the aristocracy of race; Plato (428-347 B.C.) believed in an aristocracy of spirit and intelligence. We have seen above that Hesiod made a contribution to this change, and must now add that fifth century tragedy contributes also, even as it records the process of change. The dramas of Aeschylus (d. 456 B.C.) and Sophocles (d. 405 B.C.), especially, embody the new conception of human character that was developing in their time, and record the dramatists' own struggles with the spiritual problems arising out of the new developments.

The *polis* in Aeschylus' time was already much more than the official government; it was the collective effort of all its citizens. It had become a political cosmos—a unity with order—through the intellectual and moral efforts of men, united in the *polis,* to escape the political chaos of the previous century. Aeschylus used the old myth of Zeus conquering the primitive Titans to develop the theme that despite attacks and disorder, order constantly re-establishes itself against disorder—cosmos triumphs over chaos. But there is a price to be paid: the individual human soul learns, and cosmos is re-established, through suffering.

Sophocles seems to assume the existence of a society whose highest ideal is culture and the formation of the ideal human character. He shows clearly, for the first time in Greek literature, a vast interest in the spiritual principle that informs—or is—the being of man. By placing the spiritual principle at the center of man's life he was raising the ideal of *arete* to a higher power; he was discovering that the springs of action in man's life and being are spiritual. As, much earlier, the sculptors had discovered and made use of the general principles—the "laws"—of the body and of motion and balance, so now Sophocles was groping towards the discovery of the general principles of the spiritual realm in which lies the center of man's being.

This development in Greek thought as manifest in the drama was paralleled by the development in philosophy. The earliest Greek philosophers of the sixth century—Thales, Anaximander, Anaximenes—had sought to discover the single principle of order and harmony in terms of which the variety among physical phenomena could be understood. Their main interest had been in the physical world, the natural order. Their success had been very great. When Socrates (470-399 B.C.) was a young man[20] he heard that the philosopher Anaxagoras had written a book which expounded the causes of things, including human actions and the disposition of all things "for the best." Yet he was disappointed when he took up the book. To be sure, Anaxagoras had, at the outset, said something to the effect that mind was the principle that built up and arranged the universe, but as he went on, he referred everything to mechanical and physical causes, as all the other physicists had done. And this was as if he had accounted for Socrates' own search for the book and subsequent reading of it by saying that he did so because the bones and muscles of his body had arranged themselves in such and such a way and had performed such and such movements.[21] But this kind of account leaves no place for Socrates' own *decision* to secure the book or for his *curiosity* about what it might have to say. And so Socrates found the merely physical, mechanical "explanations" inadequate—as he would find biophysical, or physico-chemical-mechanical explanations inadequate. He therefore turned away from these philosophers and began his search for an understanding both of the springs of human action and of the ordering of the universe in terms of a spiritual principle. This was the great Socratic "revolution" in Greek philosophy: the shift from philosophical inquiry primarily into the nature of the physical world into the realm of ethics, mind, spirit. And after Socrates came Plato.

But contemporary with Socrates were the great sophists whose work was one of the important factors that produced the pedagogic revolution of the second half of the fifth century.[22]

The increasing democratization of culture, and above all, the establishment of political democracy in Athens and other city-states demanded a new kind of education and entailed a new stage in the development of the conception of *arete*. A new kind of education was needed for the leaders of the people.

With the rise of the democratic city-state and the sharply increasing numbers of citizens whose origins were middle class rather than aristocratic, the state now found itself confronted with the problem of finding and educating young men who could serve as the leaders. As Jaeger observes,[23] the middle class *polis* was at a disadvantage compared with the old aristocracy for, although it had a new ideal of manhood and of citizenship, it had no means of deliberately educating the young to attain that ideal.

The new conception of *arete* was of political *arete*—that is, the excellence of the individual human being in relation not only to a transcendent ideal, but as having his existence in a political community. And so the question was, What type of education will develop political *arete* and will train the leaders of the people? The citizen was still eager to excel, to be superior, but now that excellence was to be manifest not in sport but in political leadership.

The sophists sought an answer to the question and devised a solution to the problem—a solution that, in the opinion of many, was successful.

The sophists did not open schools but gathered around themselves groups of young men—many of whom came from aristocratic families—for training. The training was designed for the art of politics. The period of training seems to have lasted, for most of the students, for three or four years. Since they had no ready-made clientele, and since they charged fees, they had to solicit customers by word-of-mouth advertising and by demonstrations of their skill. The demonstrations took three forms: the delivery of a carefully prepared lecture, an extemporized lecture on some subject suggested by a member of the audience, or a free debate with another sophist or some other person, also on a subject chosen by the audience. And so began the public lecture.

Having found clients by these means, the sophists then undertook the entire training of the youths entrusted to them. It seems that, with most of them, a contractual arrangement was entered into and some of the most famous demanded, and received, a considerable fee.[24] Having got students and made the contract, the sophists taught them by a modified tutorial system. It was no longer a relationship between a tutor and his one disciple, but between the teacher and a group of pupils, although probably not more than ten at most.

The sophists undertook to teach the art of politics and to develop political *arete*. This *arete*, for them, consisted primarily in intellectual power and oratorical ability, eloquence. With this emphasis, ethical qualities took an inferior place to intellectual qualities and to skills in the formulation and delivery of persuasive addresses. The education which was to teach this *arete* was regarded as a special art or skill. This was only one example of the tendency of the time to divide life into a number of special activities, each with its own purpose, its own theory, and its own body of knowledge, and each of which could be transmitted by education.

Another distinction was also drawn during the time of the sophists, and this has been best put by Jaeger:[25] "Before the sophists, there was none of the modern distinction between culture and religion in ancient Greek education: it was deeply rooted in religious faith. The rift between the two first opened in the age of the sophists."

The content of the sophistic education was nothing less than dialectic, rhetoric, and grammar. Again to quote Jaeger:[26] the new skill "is clearly the systematic expression of the principle of shaping the intellect, because it begins by instruction in the form of language, the form of oratory, and the form of thought. This educational technique is one of the greatest discoveries which the mind of man has ever made: it was not until it explored these three of its activities that the mind apprehended the hidden law of its own structure. . . . Rhetoric was the principal form of cultural education in later classical antiquity. It suited the Greek passion for form so well that it actually ruined the nation by overgrowing everything else like a creeping plant. . . . Together with grammar and dialectic, rhetoric became the basis of formal education throughout Europe. These three were called the Trivium in late antiquity, and blended with the Quadrivium to form the system of the seven liberal arts . . ."

Words were weapons in the new political skill, and political events are the results of the actions of this weapon since words give the speaker power over his auditors. Therefore the sophists developed grammar as the linguistic knowledge of these weapons, dialectics as the sport or gymnastics with the weapon to bring flexibility and suppleness to the mind, and rhetoric as its skillful employment.

In order to appreciate the importance of the art of speaking in the city-state we must recall that, geographically, it was small enough so that a citizen could walk from any point on its boundary to the marketplace in the city between sunrise and sunset and that, consequently, when important questions concerning the state were to be debated, *all* citizens could be present—and usually were. Also, the democracy of the time was direct, so that the citizen who was able to impose his own point of view on the assembly or on one of the councils by his power of speech was held in the highest esteem. And finally, there was a good deal of both public and private litigation in the *polis,* and the successful man was he who could get the better of his opponent before a panel of judges. Thus, in both public and private life, words were weapons, and the mastery of rhetoric was of crucial importance. In this field the sophists developed a technique for condensing and teaching the best lessons that had been learned from practical experience. Its aim was entirely practical: to win cases, or to persuade the assembly to a course of action deemed desirable by the speaker. It was practical, utilitarian, not concerned with ultimate philosophical questions at all.

Dialectic was, essentially, the art of winning an argument—any argument. The method was to take points conceded by an opponent and to use them as the basis for further argument. The method was vastly refined, and in the process, the logical structure of argument was laid bare. The advanced student was taught how effectively to argue for or against any proposition. So skillful did some of the sophists become and so effective were their teachings that it was not until the time of Aristotle that false could be distinguished from valid inferences. The effect of the dialectic on the later developments in Greek thought was enormous. However, at the same time, the success of the sophistic technique served to confuse convincing rational argument with mere tactical tricks that are, Marrou remarks, "sometimes little better than low cunning (we are, after all, in the country of Ulysses)." This has been remembered about these great teachers so that our own terms "sophistry" and "sophistic" are pejorative.

Grammar, rhetoric, and dialectic were not, however, the only subjects of study in the sophists' curriculum. They gave instruction also in the four subjects that were later to make up the medieval Western Quadrivium: arithmetic, geometry, astronomy, and the study of the numerical structure of musical intervals and rhythm. And, finally, they began the kind of study and investigation that is now called literary criticism: in their hands it was largely a way of investigating the relationship between thought and language.

It was remarked above that the sophists' study of rhetoric was entirely practical and utilitarian. So also were all their studies. Some of them even included philosophy in their course as a desirable subject—provided it were not taken too far. It was a useful subject so far as it served as a training for the mind and led to proper education.

This limitation of the study of philosophy was typical of the sophists' solution of a difficult educational problem, for, as Marrou comments:[27] "There is a fundamental antinomy between scientific research and education. If a young mind is made a slave to science and treated merely as an instrument in furthering scientific progress, its education suffers, becomes narrow and short-sighted. But if on the other hand too much emphasis is laid on the open mind, on a purely humanistic culture, there is a danger of superficiality and unreality. This problem has still not been settled: it was certainly not settled in the fifth century B.C. when against the solution offered by the Sophists there arose the stubborn opposition of Socrates."

As against the sophists, although he was in his own time numbered among them, Socrates appeared as the "gadfly" of Athens. Continually questioning those who laid claim to knowledge—poets, dramatists, statesmen, sophists themselves—he exposed the lack of foundation in the mere humanism of much of the thought of his time. He went about insisting that all merely human knowledge was of little or no account and demonstrating, by questioning, that those who claimed to know often did not. Along with this intellectual scepticism[28] he asserted that the only concern of man is the "tendance of the soul," the care of the spiritual principle that is his essential being.[29] This spiritual principle is grounded in ultimate reality and Socrates seems to have held the view that it is only through knowledge of the ultimate reality that genuine human *arete* can be achieved.

This knowledge is not a knowledge of facts that may be discovered by scientific research, nor is it knowledge of formal principles of the sort the sophists were expounding; it is, rather, a kind of direct awareness of the ultimate nature of the Good as it is in itself. To go further into the question of what exactly Socrates did teach would involve the whole difficult question of where exactly his thought ends and that of Plato begins in the writings of Plato, who is the chief source of our knowledge about the teachings of his master. This has been a matter of controversy among the commentators from the time of Aristotle to the present.

In very general terms, it seems fairly clear that Socrates' main opposition to the sophists was in his insistence on the primary importance of the discovery of the ultimate Truth and the Good itself as against their practical utilitarianism, and on the primacy of the spiritual nature of man as against his participation in the political community. He seems also to have held that the main work of the educational process was that of discovering and then developing the aptitudes of the student—always in the direction of spiritual perfection.

With the work of the sophists, Greek education went over from a primarily athletic and "musical" emphasis to a primarily intellectual emphasis. Athletics continued, for a long time, to be important and to be included in school curricula. But after the fifth century, as competition grew even more keen, athletics became, little by little, more and more professionalized and specialized, while the champions came more and more to be recruited from the rural and uncultivated parts of Greece, and from among those who had no interest in learning, nor in the old aristocratic *arete,* nor in "music."

This brief sketch of the sophistic revolution in Hellenic education has been included under the growth period of the society. If we date the breakdown and the beginning of the time of troubles at 431 B.C., then the sophistic revolution overlaps the end of the growth period and the beginning of the following period. But the breakdown of any civilization is, of course, a process that continues over a period of time, rather than a single definite historical event. And while the account of the sophists could perhaps as properly have been given under the later period, the greatest of the sophists had done their work by the outbreak of the Atheno-Peloponnesian wars and, more importantly, the historical forces that had produced them were forces that were operative in the growth period rather than later.

We have now seen that during the period of growth of the Hellenic society education began as aristocratic and as the privilege exclusively of the nobility. The content of the earliest education was moral and practical, although the Greeks themselves would probably have drawn no such distinction. The method held up for emulation the model, the example, the ideal pattern. The ideal governed both the method and the content of education.

The only method used was the tutorial, and this involved a close personal relation between the teacher and the pupil. It required also that the pupil prove himself worthy of the instruction that was to be given to him by the tutor. This tutorial method was purely oral from beginning to end of the period, although during the last century thereof, writing was taught at the primary level and a knowledge of reading and writing was, at the end, expected of educated persons.

Education was, throughout the period, wholly private: the state as such in no way interfered, or even concerned itself, with education. Education was also "general" or "liberal" in the sense that it was not specialized or vocational or technical: it did not aim at producing specialists in any field. Those who were specialists seem to have got their training by an advanced apprenticeship method.

Throughout the period there was a gradual shift in emphasis from the warlike and chivalric to the athletic and "musical" and, finally, with the sophists, to the intellectual. With the sophists came also the distinction between culture and religion. There was, however, with the Greeks no such distinction as is now, and has been throughout its history, commonplace in the West: the distinction between politics on the one hand, and on the other, ethics or morality. If the origin of the distinction in the West lies in the fact that our ethics derive from Christianity and our political theories from the Hellenic conception of the state, the Greeks had no such double source. Man lived in a political community and right action was therefore action inside that community; indeed, ethics were regarded by some Greeks as a branch or subdivision of politics.

The Time of Troubles

The time of troubles of the Hellenic Civilization lasted the four centuries from 431 B.C. to the accession of Augustus and the establishment of the Roman Empire as universal state in 31 B.C. It was during the first quarter of the fourth century that Greek education finally achieved its definitive form, and it did so largely as the result of the work of two great teachers, Plato (427-348 B.C.) and Isocrates (436-338 B.C.). This is not to say that there were no other teachers; there were, and they were many and able. But the historical importance of the schools of Plato and Isocrates is far greater than that of all the others together, for it was these two that established the program, the content, and the ideal of Hellenic education. Isocrates opened his schools in 393; Plato founded the Academy in 387.

It was Plato who developed and gave final form to the doctrine of Ideas as ideal forms or patterns or archetypes, eternal, immutable, and wholly independent of human thought about them.[30] It was his belief that genuine knowledge is knowledge of these Ideas as the unchanging principles of things, and that the highest knowledge is knowledge of the supreme Idea—the Good.

If the teaching of the sophists was utilitarian in seeking immediate practical results, that of Plato was founded on his belief in unchanging truth, in the Ideas as the only objects of genuine knowledge. And if the sophists' criterion was success in winning cases and influencing people, Plato's was truth.

And so Plato founded the Academy as a kind of combination "Institute for Advanced Study," graduate school, and upper-class college. It was not an institution open to all applicants but a sort of intellectual fraternity, all the members of which were in close association with each other and with the master, linked by common interests and by the bonds of friendship. Plato seems to have given lectures and to have used the old form of discussion as at banquets or symposia. The structure of the dialogues suggests that he did not give his disciple-students his own answers to philosophical questions but rather encouraged them to work out for themselves a correct statement of the problem, then the line of attack on it, and finally the solution, if one could be found—all under the guidance of the teacher. The primary purpose, however, of the Academy—as of all education, in Plato's view—was not instruction in philosophy nor the solution of philosophical problems; it was not even the production of statesmen who could serve as councillors and law-givers for the Greek states; it was the self-realization of the individual human being. The highest virtue of the soul was the harmonious working together of all the faculties under the dominance of reason in pursuit of the Good. The highest achievement was the apprehension or vision of the Good.

Plato was successful, though, in the secondary aims of the Academy: pupils of his occupied positions of trust and influence all over the Hellenic world; and the philosophy that he worked out during his years as head of the Academy was so enduring and so influential that a leading twentieth-century Western philosopher—Whitehead—was moved to remark that the whole history of Western philosophy had been but a series of footnotes to Plato. Whether any of his pupils, or even Plato himself attained complete apprehension of the Good is not known: he wrote[31] that he had never and would never set down in writing the heart of his own teaching, thus until the last retaining that distrust of the written, as against the spoken, word that has been noticed above.[32]

Even so, it was not chiefly through the Academy, but through the whole body of his written works that Plato exerted his enormous influence on his contemporaries and on posterity. The two books, the *Republic* and the *Laws,* contain most of his educational program, although all his other writings must be considered in connection with these two.[33]

If the whole body of his works be taken into account, Plato gives a complete program of education. Before sketching that program it should be mentioned that he advocates two innovations that were subsequently adopted in the Hellenic society: state control of education in the form of official selection and supervision of the teachers with salaries paid by the state, and equal education of boys and girls. It will be recalled that since the earliest beginnings in Homer, Greek education had been exclusively for boys, and that throughout the growth period it had been wholly private. Plato advocated these two changes and, as we shall see, they were in large measure adopted after his time.

His program of primary or elementary education was basically that of the "old" Athenian education: it was to include gymnastics and music and was to begin for the child at the age of seven, after a three-year period of supervised kindergarten. The physical education was to be given in gymnasiums or public stadiums by professional teachers who were to be paid by the state; it was to include such "new" sports as fencing. And, under the influence of a recent development of the concept of preventive as well as merely curative medicine, Plato urged that physical education should include the teaching of rules about diet and hygiene.

The "music" of the curriculum was also that of the old education, but with the addition of the requirement that the child should learn to read and write and begin the study of the classics. There was also to be a kind of test or examination for the literary studies, in the form of competitions and games.[34]

Into the "music" of the primary education Plato introduces mathematics. The children were to learn numbers, as they had done under the old education, but now they were to do practical exercises in arithmetic and geometry as well. This training in applied mathematics was an innovation that was borrowed from the Egyptians and was important; but in Plato's view, the chief importance of the study of mathematics lay in its unique value as mind training. And it was valuable, he said, for all students whatsoever, for whoever can reason —and all human beings can—can "do" mathematics. That is, all persons can learn mathematics, and profit from learning, on this elementary level. But Plato did not think that all could go on to the more advanced study; the few who could go on were to be carefully chosen.[35]

The stages of the schooling period were the kindergarten, ages three to six; the primary, from six to ten; the secondary, from ten to eighteen. The formal schooling was then to be interrupted for the two-year compulsory military service. From each stage to the next there was a kind of screening or testing of the students by means of competitive games and recitations (there is no hint yet of a formal, written examination), and those who had been able to stay the course were to do "higher" or "graduate" studies from twenty to thirty. The basic discipline in these graduate studies was to be mathematics although advanced studies in all the sciences were also included. The purpose of the whole course was to teach the student to see the inter-relationships between all studies and to detect those clues in each of them that pointed to the fundamental reality that underlay them all.

Those sudents who survived this arduous training—and they would be only a small percentage—were now ready for a five-year course that would lead them into the higher truths of philosophy. But even this was not the end. That very small intellectual elite who survived this course were now, for fifteen years, to enter into active political life in order to gain practical experience and to develop moral character. At the end of this time, at the age of fifty, they were ready to begin that final philosophical study which was the contemplation and understanding of the Idea of the Good.[36]

Isocrates,[37] like Plato, accepted the "old" Athenian primary and secondary education as the early, basic training, but his emphasis was on grammar and literary studies rather than on the other aspects of "musical" training. He included mathematics, and for the same reasons that Plato had; and he added history. But, and by way of contrast to Plato, he included dialectics, or the study of philosophical problems, in the secondary training and limited the amount of time that might be given to it, so that the study might be "not in excess." All this was education before the student entered the school of Isocrates.

His school gave a course lasting three or four years; the tuition fee was one thousand drachmas for the course; it seems to have been successful, for he became rich from the fees and gifts from students. His purpose was to train leaders of the people and the one proper, basic subject for this purpose was rhetoric. He seems not to have accepted all applicants, but only those who could show innate talents for the kind of training they were to receive: memory, voice, poise, industry, and imagination. He seems never to have had more than nine pupils at any one time, and on an average, only five or six.

In his course, the theoretical material was given at the very beginning and was kept to a minimum. He almost immediately set the students to work making outlines for and composing speeches after the manner of models that he supplied. He used his own prepared speeches as the models, and trained his pupils to collaborate with him in the preparation of still other model speeches, in this way leading them to see for themselves the principles of structure and the ideals that lay behind the models.

He taught that oratory and ethics were indissolubly linked, that form and content were inseparable, as were the speaker and his speech. If the orator is seeking to move his hearers, then he must choose an important and profound subject that is, at the same time, in conformity with virtue; the genuine orator will embody the virtue of his words in his life as, conversely, the personality of the orator is embodied in his discourse. Thus as the orator applies his thought to his subject he is tending towards the development of character and towards greatness of soul, and thus, for Isocrates, rhetoric is insensibly transformed into ethics, literature into life.

As against Plato and the basis of his teaching, Isocrates held that "knowledge," in Plato's strict sense of the term, is not possible; that the best that man can achieve is "right opinion." And since the Platonic knowledge cannot be achieved, there can therefore be no complete theory that is at the same time precise and detailed enough to dictate the course of action that ought to be followed in concrete situations in the complex of actual affairs. In actual situations men must act, not philosophize; and they can act only on the basis of right opinion; hence the educated man is he who has right opinion and the knack of using it to hit on the right—or at least the less harmful —solution of particular concrete problems. The education in rhetoric was intended to develop in the student that ability to make decisions, to perceive those imponderables that so often guide public opinion, to use what was thus perceived in forming opinion. This training in using the relation of form and content in literature and speech, in finding the right expression, in developing a feeling for the nuances of thought, resulted in the development of what we would now perhaps call "judgment," a quality no successful man of affairs or administrator or leader can be without. It is perhaps a kind of knack, and it does appear to depend upon a grasp of or a feeling for situations that is as much intuitive as it is logical and theoretical.

Both through his example and his teaching Isocrates contributed largely to the creation of an ideal of literary (i.e. "oratorical") personal culture. In working to produce leaders of the people Isocrates succeeded in this primary aim to an astonishing degree, but he succeeded also in shaping the educational ideal that dominated Hellenic society for the generations that came after him.

The ideal that Isocrates left as a legacy was oratorical or literary; that of Plato was, as we have seen, philosophical. Both remained ideals of Hellenic education throughout the rest of the life of that society: the tension between them was never resolved. Plato and Isocrates formulated not only the educational ideal of antiquity but also, as Marrou puts it[38] the main categories of advanced culture and the main principles of education.[39]

We have noticed, on the one hand, Plato's dependence on oral instruction and discussion for communication of the higher truths of his philosophy, and, on the other, the fact that by his time, the habit of reading was growing up and so was the habit of consulting books in libraries.[40] Plato's attitude seems to have reflected the general opinion. But Plato's pupil Aristotle (384-322 B.C.) wrote[41] that reading and writing are of first importance in education not only because of their usefulness but also because "they are the means of acquiring many other types of knowledge." And Aristotle's view seems to have reflected the general opinion of his generation: the Greek world now had the habit of reading, and oral instruction was no longer the characteristic and dominant feature of education.[42]

One consequence of this change of habit was the foundation of great libraries. The first of these was the museum and library at Alexandria, a city established by Aristotle's most famous pupil in 331 B.C. This was followed by the foundation of many another library at other cities, and the trade of book making began to flourish. The output of books of learning of all kinds, and of minor literary pieces, was enormous: popularizers, anthologists, and commentators turned out books in quantity so that by the third century, the habit of reading was firmly established throughout the Greek world. Under the successors of Alexander, Greek culture spread all over the areas that had once been under his political control, and during the third and second centuries, all of the great centers—Alexandria, Antioch, Pergamum and the others—became the seats of large libraries and the homes of scholars and of learning.

It was during the last third of the fourth century that education—the education that was to spread all over the Hellenic world and was to be adopted by the Romans—received its final form. In that form it became increasingly literary and bookish, although retaining its moral character; it became increasingly institutionalized and formal; and it became increasingly a municipal concern. These are all general tendencies and the tendencies did not develop at an even pace in all parts of the then expanding Greek world.[43] Throughout that vast territory, wherever there was a Greek foundation there was also a Greek primary school and a gymnasium.[44]

In this Greek world there grew up a kind of cultural unity—political unity had not survived Alexander's death and did not reappear until the Roman conquests—a unity that the Greeks themselves recognized as deriving not from a single race but from a single cultural ideal. This was the ideal of the Greek *paideia:* an ideal that by the third century was of a developed mind, of man who had realized his human potential, who had become perfected. It was this ideal of personal development towards the idea of man that was shared by those who pursued and enjoyed and perpetuated the Greek *paideia.* It was essentially and truly *human,* so that when the Romans translated the word into Latin they used their word *humanitas.*

The man whose thought was dominated by this ideal thought of himself as a citizen primarily of the world rather than of the particular local kingdom or empire of which he was politically a member. The *polis* still existed, indeed the Seleucids and Antigonids established and developed urban centers on the model of the *polis* so that there were more Greek cities than ever before, and the *polis* remained for a long time the chief administrative unit of the Hellenistic kingdoms —but the cultivated Greek no longer regarded his home town as the norm of thought and culture. Plato, as we have seen, and Aristotle after him, thought of ethics and education as necessarily within the framework of the *polis;* now the Greek citizen of the *oikoumene*— the inhabited world—thought of both, as the later philosophers treated both, as governed only by the ideal, the Idea of man. This ideal and the *paideia* that was thought to cultivate men so as to realize it, became almost a secular religion for many.

During the period following Alexander the Great, education became less and less a matter of private initiative and more and more subject to official control, until by the time of the appearance of republican Rome on the Greek scene, legislation on school affairs had become the normal thing. But we are misled if we think of this as state education of the same sort as that of present day Western Germany, for example, of even that of state education in the United States. The municipality was retained as the administrative unit by the Greek kings whenever possible; the state government was decentralized as far as possible, with the administrative machinery kept to a minimum, and with the public services, especially education, left to the municipalities.[45] These municipalities, which were now more numerous than they had been in the fifth and fourth centuries, were not uniform in their governments nor their currencies nor their calendars nor their school systems. The following statements about the school systems are therefore generalizations only: exceptions to most of the generalizations might be found in one or another of the Hellenistic cities.

By the end of the time of troubles the state—in the form of the municipality—everywhere was legislating about education and was concerned with it, but not everywhere to the same extent nor in the same aspects.

The general plan of education during the last half of the time of troubles was as follows. The child remained at home under the care of the women of the household until he was seven. There seem to have been no kindergartens, either private or public, for children under seven and the Greeks had little or no interest in the younger child. At seven the child entered the elementary school and remained there until he was fourteen. From fourteen to eighteen, he attended the secondary school; from eighteen to twenty, the ephebia—about which, more below. Along with the ephebic training, the apter students received a technically very good higher education which held possibilities of specialization in such subjects as rhetoric and philosophy and medicine. Finally, at a few great centers, there were schools, like those earlier ones of Plato and Isocrates, of advanced studies. There was a screening of students throughout the whole program so that only the best (and, of the best, only those who were financially able) could attend the higher schools.

In most of the Hellenistic cities only the ephebia were established and maintained by the state. It was the most official of all the schools. It was extremely widespread: we know about some hundred of them, scattered from Marseilles to the Black Sea.[46] The ephebia was under the control of a magistrate who was appointed to administer its affairs —perhaps we could think of him as a college president who was appointed by the city rather than by trustees or alumni. He was chosen from among the most influential and important persons of the city.

Of the primary and secondary schools there were two kinds: public and private. The latter were commercial in the sense that the teacher, or the head of the school and the few teachers associated with him, received fees directly from the parents of the pupils. In many cities, however, these private schools were under the supervision of an inspector of schools. How extensive was the authority of this functionary is not known. The public schools were supported by the city in only a very few instances; the financial structure was too precarious and the income too uncertain to permit it. They were supported, instead, by "benefactors."

Benefactors had for long existed in the Greek cities. In the fifth century they had been the wealthier citizens who, out of their own pockets, paid for putting on plays for the public, or for the upkeep of a navy vessel, or for some other public enterprise or spectacle. It was a kind of substitute for the graduated tax on incomes. The wealthy citizen might give money not only for the upkeep of monuments or the expenses of religious ceremonies, but also for the establishment and endowment of primary and secondary schools. The details of four such foundations are known, and it may reasonably be supposed that there were others.[47]

The ephebia reached its final form just after the middle of the fourth century—after the Macedonian conquests and so after its chief reason for existence had disappeared. Each year the list of eighteen-year-olds was submitted to the city council for checking; after the names had been checked those youths who were entitled to full civic rights were enrolled and began their two-year (later shortened to a year) term of military duty. Their instructors during the first year were especially chosen officers who were civil servants; the year was spent in barracks; the class was given physical and military instruction. The recruits wore uniforms. They were supported by the state.

The complete training of the youths in the ephebia was designed not only to prepare them for service in the army but also for full citizenship in the city. The registers were public documents that were kept in the state archives. In the fourth century all citizens seem to have been enrolled, but after the Macedonian rule some citizens were never admitted, some aliens were, and the term was shortened. At the end of the first year, the recruits took an oath of allegiance and so became full-fledged soldiers.

With the final loss of independence under the successors of Alexander, the Greek city no longer needed a civic army and so the ephebia gradually ceased to be a military college. It became a civil school serving the interests of a few, with a main emphasis on athletics but with courses in literature and rhetoric and philosophy.

The Greek taste for sport continued throughout the time of troubles and into the universal state period: wherever there was a Greek foundation there was to be found a gymnasium and a stadium. Physical education was taught in the schools and, as Plato had suggested, it came to include not only instruction in the particular sports but also rules of diet and hygiene as a kind of preventive medicine. But the particular sports came to be more and more specialized and professionalized and finally came to be spectator sports.

The inclusion of the "musical" elements of the "old" education also continued: children were taught to sing, to play the lyre, to participate in choruses, and to dance. But at the same time, the techniques of all these arts were developing apace so that specialization and professionalism here too became dominant. The many-sided amateur gave way to the professional who could dance or sing or play or compose much better than the amateur. The professionals were admired for their skill but despised because they performed or composed for money and so these arts also came to be largely spectator affairs.

The inclusion of so large an element of "music" and athletics in the school program after literary studies had attained first importance may be another example of the conservatism that seems to be inherent in pedagogic systems.

The Greek child's education began in the primary school at the age of seven. The Greeks had no infant schools or kindergartens and would have been amused and mystified at the modern Western studies of the "educational value" of elementary games. Of course the child was learning, by what we have called the "apprenticeship method," the language, the ways of his parents, and the habits of his family during the preschool period—but none of this was regarded by the Greeks as "education" in any proper sense of the term.

The primary schools existed all over the Greek world. It was communal, not tutorial, education, and both boys and girls attended. The one private element that still existed was the "pedagogue." He had, in earlier times, been only the servant whose duty it was to lead the child to school. He still performed this duty, but now he actually educated the child in morals and manners, coached him in his homework, and continued to watch over the child until he had reached adolescence or was ready for the ephebia. It was during this period that the word "pedagogue" began to bear the sense that it still retains: someone who is an educator. The pedagogue, however, remained distinct from the "master," whose duty it was to impart learning.

The primary school building was usually very simple: a small bare room with a chair for the teacher and backless stools or benches for the pupils. The teacher in the school was poorly paid and his position was close to the bottom of the social ladder. He was not expected to educate the child, but only to teach him to read and write; except in the municipally owned school, the teacher had to run after customers. To be sure, he was paid—but poorly: the average wage earned seems to have been only slightly better than that of a skilled workman. But the real reason[48] for the low status of a teacher was that he needed no special qualification for his job: if he himself could read and write and if his character and conduct were acceptable, then he could teach.

Thus the schoolmaster was responsible for only one aspect of the child's education: the mental side. The other sides were still given in the family and by the pedagogue, who was usually a member of the family although he might be a slave. And thus the educational problems of the Hellenic society at this time—a time perhaps "contemporary," in the Toynbee sense, with our own—were different from modern Western educational problems which, for the most part, are connected with the schools. The Greeks felt their problems to be concerned chiefly with the moral atmosphere, the character-building factors, that should surround education, and the school itself was of secondary importance in providing this atmosphere or these factors.

In the actual teaching of reading and writing in the school, the process was, briefly, as follows. In reading, the pupil was first taught to recite the alphabet, then to recognize syllables of two sounds, then of three, and so on, all taken in rigid alphabetic order. Next he learned words of one syllable, then of two—with the syllables separated—then of three, and so on. Next he learned to read short sentences, again with words divided into syllables. After a great deal of drill in this kind of exercise he was set to work on short passages from Homer and the tragedians. These passages were read aloud individually and recited in chorus, still syllable by syllable.

After the pupil had learned, somewhat, to read, he was taught to write. The master drew a model letter on the child's wax tablet; the child then copied the letter a great many times—and so on until he could write all the letters of the alphabet to the master's satisfaction. He next wrote syllables, then words, and finally short sentences in which all the letters of the alphabet were employed.

In primary school the children learned also the names of the cardinal and ordinal numbers and how to count on their fingers, that is, how to indicate any whole number from one to one million with the fingers of the two hands. The four operations of arithmetic seem to have been beyond the scope of primary education.

Discipline was summary and brutal. Corporal punishment seems to have been the only method for overcoming indocility: education and corporal punishment were as inseparable to the Hellenistic Greek as to the Egyptian scribe. Considering this fact and what appears to have been, from our point of view at least, psychologically defective teaching methods, it is scarcely surprising to read of children of ten or even thirteen who are said to be still "learning their letters."

It was said above that the child remained in the primary school until he was fourteen. This was an average age, not a fixed one. It seems to have been the average age by which most children had learned to read and write fluently—and "fluently" is a term that is open to interpretation and was differently interpreted by different masters. In general, the child who wanted to, or whose parents wanted him to, go on to secondary school, did so when his master considered that he was fluent in reading and writing. In secondary school, the literary "master" was no longer the "teacher of letters" but was the grammarian. The chief subject matter of the secondary school was classical literature—"classical" in the sense that an already existing collection of masterpieces was the basis of study and of the scale of values. It was, so to speak, a capital fund of masterpieces that needed only to be appreciated, not added to. The creativity of the growth period had dwindled almost to the vanishing point.

That collection of masterpieces, and the various kinds of studies of them, had become large and unwieldy. As a consequence, the same kind of thing happened in Hellenic education as happens in any society that enjoys a long cultural development. As each generation added something to the cultural heritage, the additions to the curriculum were usually added to the advanced studies; as more additions were made, the older one tended to sink to the secondary level and, in some cases, even to the primary, with the result that the lower curricula tended to expand unconscionably. Marrou[49] calls this "a general law" in education. We can see it in operation in American secondary curricula at the present time; it was in operation in Greece in the later centuries of the time of troubles.

Another consequence of the growth of the body of classics and of its having become unwieldy was the need to organize and systematize it. So the official educational canonization of the classics was carried to considerable lengths. By about the middle of the second century B.C. the canon was more or less fixed: lists of the great men in all fields were established, anthologies of the great works of the writers were made.[50]

The method of study of the classics was as follows. The child was first given a simplified summary of the story. He was also shown mural tablets and bas-reliefs illustrating the story and was asked to identify scenes and persons. Then the child was given a text of the classic and a good deal of time was spent correcting his text against that of the master. Then he was taught to read the text properly, that is, to separate the words and phrases and sentences and to read into it the proper punctuation (Greek manuscripts lacked such divisions). At this stage the goal was for the student to be able to declaim the text with expression, taking into account the sense, meter, and general tone of the work. Recitation from memory followed after the reading, and in the scholastic contests (which were often a sort of examination) prizes were awarded for recitations of poetry.

The explication of the text was the next stage, and this made up the major part of the work of the grammarian-teacher. The explication was both literal and literary: archaic and poetic words and forms had to be translated and explained, etymologies given, grammar and morphology treated at length. Then came the analysis of the work into parts, divisions, subdivisions, with lists of persons, times, places, events, and so on almost endlessly. This kind of exercise provided almost unlimited scope for the pedantic and uninspired teacher, and many of them took advantage of the opportunity. As the centuries passed, the accumulation of erudition had become so great, and so much ingenuity had gone into displaying it, that with very many teachers the scholarly apparatus over-shadowed the reasons for scholarship; the reasons for studying the poets and historians and philosophers were forgotten and only the minutiae of the studies remained. This is strongly reminiscent of the pedanticism that over-came the study of Confucian philosophy in China—and of some graduate courses in American universities.

In addition to the literary studies the secondary school curriculum included mathematics: the advice of Plato and Isocrates had been followed. The first and most important of the mathematical sciences was geometry. After Euclid (c. 330–275 B.C.) produced his *Elements,* it was adopted as the textbook and continued in use throughout the rest of the life of the Hellenic Civilization. The second study was arithmetic, the third was the study of the numerical laws governing musical intervals and rhythm. The fourth was astronomy. The text-books before Ptolemy (second century A.D.) were written by Aris-tarchus (310–250 B.C.) and Hipparchus (late second century B.C.). These four mathematical sciences were the Quadrivium as finally formulated about the middle of the first century.

The Quadrivium and the Trivium—grammar, rhetoric, dialectic—together were the "general education" of Hellenic and Roman times, that is, the usual everyday education received by the many.

It seems clear that in this general education the literary studies gradually became more and more important until, during the first century or so of the universal state, most mathematical studies were to be found in the education for specialists rather than in the secondary education.

After the secondary education the student went on to the higher education. The forms thereof were more varied than those of any lower stage and many possibilities were open to the able and industri-ous student.

The higher schools that had the greater number of pupils were of course the various ephebia. We have seen that the training given in these was both military and civil. The military was under the control of civil servants appointed by the state. The sports program was also usually under the control of state officers and, as in the secondary education, included much more than merely training in physical exer-cises. But the civil education, which was also an integral part of ephebic training and was given usually in the gymnasium, was con-ducted by civilians not officially connected with the college—by visiting lecturers, as it were. These lecturers were philosophers, rhetors, grammarians, and others. There were usually lectures, lessons, and even homework. In some cases, the philosopher or rhetor or poet was simply visiting in the town and was asked to give a lecture or two; in others, a famous teacher might be invited to remain in residence and give a whole course of lectures. Both the courses and the occasional lectures were genuine higher education in the sense that they presupposed the grounding of the primary and secondary training and went beyond anything included in the latter. However, since by the end of the period the term ephebic instruction had been reduced to one year, and since in this year military, athletic, and civil intruction had to be included, it is apparent that the degree of learning could not have been high. The student could, at best, have acquired only a smattering of the many subjects to which he had been exposed. Other types of higher schools were the museums, the medical schools, the philosophical schools, and the school of rhetoric.[51] For training of the professional man—the lawyer, jurist, engineer, general, navigator, physician, and other—there seem to have been no schools at all (except in medicine, as has been seen). The training of the professional was by the advanced apprenticeship and tutorial method exclusively.

Roman education,[52] down to the third century when it was first influenced, and later revolutionized, by Greek education, was peasant and apprentice. In origin it was not education primarily for a military aristocracy, as early Greek education had been, but for farmers who farmed the land themselves.

The educational unit was the family; the child's early education, as elsewhere, was entirely within the family. But in Rome, from the age of six or seven to sixteen or seventeen, the boy was the constant companion of his father. The father had complete authority over his children, he was his son's mentor and tutor. The son accompanied the father about the farm, observing and being instructed—in short, everywhere. The father taught the son what little book learning he had to have. And the daughter was the constant companion of her mother, learning to do the housework and spin and weave.

The fundamental basis of this Roman education was respect for the traditions of the city and of the family. The object was to develop in the youth the spirit of filial submission and self-restraint and an austerely moral character. The intellectual part of the training—reading, writing, geometry—was not emphasized but, rather, kept to a minimum: the boy should learn only so much as would be useful to him in keeping accounts and measuring land. The attitude was one of conservative utilitarianism.

At sixteen or seventeen the boy became a man and a citizen: he exchanged his childhood toga for the *toga virilis,* that of a man, and was given into the charge of a tutor. The tutor was usually a friend of the family and always a distinguished citizen or, if the boy was destined for a military career, a general. The tutor assumed the role of father and kept the young man by him constantly. So did the pupil learn, by the apprenticeship method, lessons of business, statecraft, oratory, and civic affairs.

During the development of Roman society from the sixth century to the third some families had of course become more rich and powerful than others. These patrician families became the aristocracy—a landed aristocracy—of Rome. In them the family tradition was especially strong. And as the family traditions became stronger, so the separate families developed their own distinctive traditions: one family was particularly proud, another inflexible, another democratic, another austere, and so on, so that the successive generations of these families were expected to, and did, manifest pride or austerity or inflexibility to an exceptional degree. But for all the aristocratic families, what had originally been peasant virtues—frugality and severity and industriousness—were still cultivated intensively.

For the aristocratic families also, as for all Romans, the traditions of Rome itself were fundamental. What was required of all citizens was sacrifice and renunciation for, and devotion to, the state. The Roman hero was always the man who had done something great for the state in time of danger: he had sacrificed himself to the public good. But there was a strict check on what the hero or the ordinary citizen might do for the state: the check of justice and of law. It was not thought that the end of public safety justified means that ran counter to justice or morality.

The Roman child seems to have made an early acquaintance with the law; in addition to becoming familiar with the traditions of the state and of the family he memorized the Law of the Twelve Tables. Later on, under his tutor, he learned a great number of precedents and the complex system of prescriptions that characterized Roman law. Many Romans seem to have received, after they had served their term with the tutor, a kind of professional and advanced training in law under an experienced barrister, again by the apprenticeship method.

These, in very brief, are the highlights of the old education that prevailed while Rome was still only the chief among a small group of Italian towns.

But Rome became more than this: towards the beginning of the third century she absorbed the Greek towns in southern Italy, and was influenced by Greek culture; towards the end of the century she conquered Sicily, and was influenced by Greek culture; in 168 B.C. she conquered Macedonia and, in 146, Greece itself. From this time on Rome was a bilingual state including many provinces in which Greek was the language. And this was by no means all: about 272 B.C. a Greek whose Latin name was Livius Andronicus came to Rome, started writing in the Latin language, and set himself up as a teacher. Needing a textbook, he translated the *Odyssey* into Latin; this served as a classic text for the Romans until the Christian era, and it was the beginning of Latin literature. About 168 B.C. the teacher Crates came to Rome as an ambassador from Pergamon. He fell into one of the Roman drains, broke his leg, and was so forced to remain in Rome for some time. During his convalesence he whiled away the time by giving lectures on Greek literature and grammar to all comers. Very many persons came. The effect of these lectures was so great that Suetonius dates Roman interest in these subjects from this time. During the second century more rhetoricians and philosophers found their way to Rome, and they all taught and lectured. The result was that by the end of the century, the Greek ideal of a culture based on literature and rhetoric and philosophy was widely, if not fully, accepted in Rome.

The enthusiasm for everything Greek was very great: Plutarch says "it was like a wind sweeping through the city so that people could talk of nothing else." And this enthusiasm was met with opposition from the old Roman conservatives: on at least three occasions the Senate passed decrees against philosophers and rhetors. But Greek culture and language had come to stay: the educated Roman spoke Greek and took pride in being able to. The one characteristic Greek aspect that was not adopted by the Romans was the sports program. Another that was adopted but very extensively modified was Greek art.

The Roman schools of the second century and after were simply copied from the Greek in all respects but two; the Romans pursued the study of law in addition to the Greek curriculum, and until the empire, education was left entirely to private initiative.

All educated Romans learned the Greek language and the Greek classics. On the other hand, few Greeks troubled to learn Latin. Officially, Rome contented herself with making Latin the exclusive language of military command for units of the army and the principal language for the municipal administration for colonies of Italian origin on Greek or Oriental ground. Otherwise, where Greek was the mother tongue or the established *lingua franca,* Latin was not imposed. Indeed, Rome went further and employed Greek for official use in Greek-speaking lands, even giving it an equal place with Latin in the central administration. At Rome itself, under the universal state during the Principate, the Chancery was organized in duplicate.

We have seen that the time of troubles of the Hellenic Civilization witnessed the foundation of the schools of Plato and of Isocrates. Plato was the great advocate of a "philosophical" education that was based on truth and on the grasp of universal principles. Plato had advocated two measures that were later adopted, with modifications, by the society as a whole: equal education for girls and boys, and state control over education. Isocrates was the great advocate of a rhetorical education with a literary emphasis. On the whole, it was he rather than Plato who was the greater influence in education.

By the generation after Aristotle, and partly as a result of his influence, the habit of reading was firmly established in the Greek world, the making of books had increased enormously, and collections of them in both public and private libraries were very numerous. Education became more and more bookish as the number of books increased and it became simultaneously, although for other reasons too, more and more literary. It was becoming also more institutionalized and formal. But, even so, Greek education during this period never quite lost its moral character nor its vision of the ideal.

With the loss of independence and self-sufficiency by the *polis,* after the Macedonian conquests, it gradually ceased to be thought of as the unit to which the educated man owed his ultimate allegiance. So the educated man began to think of himself as a citizen, not of the *polis,* but of the "inhabited world"—the *oikoumene.* This world was inhabited, he thought, by those men who aimed at the same ideals and were educated in the same *paideia* as he himself was.

During this period education became increasingly a matter of "state,"—that is, municipal—concern, until at the end of the period, municipal legislation about schools was the normal thing. There seems to have been three main reasons for this. The first was the general awareness that the educational needs of the population had grown so that private tutors and schools could no longer satisfy them. Consequently education, like many another service, was now seen to be a *public* service and, as such, could be given only by the whole community. A second reason seems to have been the influence of Plato's suggestion. The third reason was perhaps the influence of the ephebia. It was a state affair, both originally and as it continued; yet it did not take students who had not had the primary and secondary education. The state therefore had to supply, as far as possible, the preparatory education that was required for entrance into the required ephebic training.

We have seen also that during this period the list of "classics" had become fixed, as had the methods of teaching, and that the curriculum also had settled into those subjects that the Romans were to call the Trivium and Quadrivium.

And, finally, we have seen that Rome adopted the Greek educational system, the Greek classics, and the Greek language as a second tongue.

The Universal State

In 31 B.C. the wars that had wracked the whole of the Hellenic Civilization for four centuries were brought to an end. With the accession of Augustus, Rome was established as the universal state of the whole society and the *Pax Romana* was imposed on the war-weary, materially exhausted, and spiritually enfeebled hitherto separate states.

For education, the historic and successfully performed mission of Rome was to spread and establish the Hellenistic culture throughout the length and breadth of the empire. She imposed not only a political unity on the previously existing multiplicity of local states but also, in so doing, became the means whereby a unified culture could establish itself.

That culture did establish itself throughout the empire, but not equally in all parts nor among all classes. In the provinces, it was the towns that were Romanized while the rural areas were relatively neglected and, in the towns, the schools were always in the first instance for the governing classes whether they were composed chiefly of local persons or of Italians. But, wherever established, the schools were in all respects like those of the latter end of the time of troubles.

Beginning with this period the state came gradually to pursue an active policy of intervention in the affairs of the schools and of support of them. Towards the end of the first century the state, that is, the imperial government, granted to teachers certain financial favors, including exemption from taxation. At first these exemptions applied to all teachers of the secondary and higher schools, but only at Rome itself, and were clearly a device for attracting Greek teachers to the imperial city. But gradually the financial favors were extended to teachers in other cities. Indeed, every important city seems to have had its own schools. Most of them were financed out of municipal funds but some, apparently, privately. Even when schools were privately financed (as by the older "benefactor" system) they were supervised by the city. By the fourth Christian century every city of any importance was supervising the public school and was providing the salary for at least one teacher. The governing body of the city selected and appointed the teachers from a list of competitors. It is not surprising that in Athens there was stiff competition for appointments, while in other cities the town council had to resort to all manner of devices to secure competent teachers.

As the central government began to tighten its hold on all aspects of public life and to centralize administration more and more, so the autonomy of the cities in educational as in all other affairs diminished. An example of the tendency may be seen in the imperial foundation, in the first quarter of the fifth century, of the state university at Constantinople. The university was given a monopoly of all higher education in the city. The faculty included thirty members, almost equally divided between Greek and Latin, of whom one was a professor of philosophy, two were professors of law, and the others of grammar and rhetoric.

It was noticed above that the study of law was the one really new element added by the Romans when they adopted the Greek educational system. A knowledge of law was very nearly indispensable to

one who would participate in public affairs and it provided opportunities for a career even greater perhaps than those open to an
accomplished orator. At first all training in the law was by the apprenticeship method, but as the demand for instruction increased,
theory was developed and official institutions came into being. By the
second century there were some law schools and the standard texts
had become fixed, so that the teaching of law could now be organized
around recognized authorities. By the beginning of the third century
the greatest law school in the East had been established in Beirut.
At about the same time the imperial laws and constitutions began to
be collected. The first collections (called codes) seem to have been
made to facilitate the study of law in the schools. In A.D. 438 the
great Theodosian Code was promulgated.

The course of study in the law schools usually lasted four years,
although after the codes appeared, a fifth year was added at some
schools. The method of instruction was by reading, explaining, and
commenting on the basic texts.

Even before Diocletian (d. A.D. 305) the state had become increasingly bureaucratized and therefore in greater and greater need of
competent civil servants. After the Diocletianic reforms, the numbers of bureaus and of civil servants increased, so that the needs of
the state also increased. Thus a great part of the state's interest
in the schools arose from its need for civil servants. It recruited, now,
from all social classes; it recruited very many of the graduates from
the schools scattered all over the empire. The student who was
proficient in either eloquence or the law could be almost certain of
appointment to, and advancement in, the civil service. Towards the
end of the fourth century one of the duties of the city prefect in
Rome was to keep an eye on the students there and annually to list
the outstanding ones so that they might be recruited into the service.

The tradition of rhetorical or literary education continued under the
Roman Empire so that, to the end, persons with no legal or administrative training at all, but with competence in literature and
oratory, were appointed to the highest posts. As bureaucracies go, the
Roman Empire was an extraordinarily efficient machine, and it was
manned, at the top, by orators and barristers. It was thought that the
old classical education did induce mental flexibility and clarity and
that anyone whose mind had been developed in this way could, by

on-the-job experience, learn all he needed to know about the manage-ment of practical affairs.

With the increased bureaucratization of the administration there was also an increased need for secretaries, persons who could take notes quickly and accurately. There was available a system of short-hand for both Greek and Latin. As the need for shorthand increased, so teachers of the art were found to meet the need. And as the secretaries came to be indispensable so, in many cases, they were given greater responsibilities and authority, and by the end of the fourth century they were grouped, in the official lists, with the higher officials. As a consequence, a knowledge of shorthand very nearly guaranteed a career in the civil service and persons with a knowledge of both it and literature were quite certain of advancement. The use of shorthand was not confined to the civil services: it soon spread also into general use.

Marrou writes:[53] "To sum up this complex development in a single formula, it might be said that the history of ancient education reflects the progressive transition from a 'noble warrior' culture to a 'scribe' culture." This is a striking and convenient and easily remembered formula with the great merit of brevity. But, being brief, it does not suggest features of first importance that had emerged in the course of that long progressive transition.

One striking feature was the character of popular entertainment in the fifth century B.C. The Greek citizen controlled that entertain-ment, so it may be supposed that he got what he wanted: if he had not liked what was served up, he would have changed the bill. And what was served up was the most austere and uncompromising, the noblest and deepest drama that has been written. As an offset to the drama he was served also with the comedies of Aristophanes. And, what is perhaps most remarkable to a twentieth century West-erner, this drama was the Athenian counterpart of our movies and radio and television. It was, literally, the "popular" entertain-ment. We have noticed the development of thought in Aeschylus and Sophocles; but it should be added that the whole of the drama, since it was popular entertainment, was an educational factor of high importance, although an imponderable one. It was selections from this drama that remained, until the end, a part of the staple of the literary education of the Hellenic society.

Another feature that was remarked but perhaps not sufficiently emphasized was the education that the Athenian citizen of the sixth and fifth centuries received by conversation and observation. He was accustomed to spend time in the marketplace in conversation with his fellow citizens and in observing the work of the artisans. Those fellow citizens included the statesmen Themistocles, Aristeides and, Pericles; the dramatists Aeschylus, Sophocles, Euripedes, Aristophanes, and Menander; the orator Demosthenes; the historian Thucydides; the "artisans" included the architects of the Acropolis, Mnesicles and Ictinus; the sculptors Phidias and Praxiteles; the host of unknown vase painters and makers; the private small contractors who made the fluted columns of the temples and supplied the cut stones for lintels and pediments.

And not only did the citizen learn through observation of the work of these men and conversation with them, but he himself, having come to know the law as a kind of creative and formative agent—not, as the Romans conceived it, primarily a codification of practice—participated directly in the creative work of the law as he sat in the Assembly, heard cases, and helped to decide policy. And this tradition of direct participation and observation was not lost until after the city had lost its independence and after policy had become the affair of kings and emperors rather than of the citizen.

The most important of the developments in late Hellenic education was that of Christian education.

Christianity had appeared first as a "way" within the Jewish community—the first Christians were all Jews. As a consequence, Christian education followed Jewish education[54] in assigning the fundamental part of education to the family. The parents were to exemplify and to instruct their children in Christian morals and to assist them in the development of the Christian consciousness. Thus the first educational agency was the family.

The second was the church. Only the church could teach the fundamental truths—which became codified in the creeds and dogmas—of the Christian faith. From about the end of the first century the church carefully instructed the would-be Christian in the fundamental articles of the faith before he was admitted to baptism and to the sacraments. Those who instructed the applicants themselves received a considerable instruction before they were allowed to undertake this important task, and by the end of the second century, systematic teaching seems to have been developed.

Christianity from the beginning had had a Book—the Law, the Prophets and the Writings of the Jews; from the middle of the first century it began to enlarge that Book with its own writings: first the Apocalypse, then the letters of Paul and others, then the Acts of the Apostles, and finally, at the end of the first century and the beginning of the second, the Gospels. It was therefore from the beginning a literate religion and so in the distinctive Christian culture the literary side was of first importance. But this literary side did not give rise to special Christian schools.[55] Christians used the schools that were already established and added on to the instruction received therein the further instruction from church and family. And this in spite of the opposition of Christianity to the pagan cultural ideals.

The first distinctively Christian school to appear was the monastic school, in Egypt in the fourth century and somewhat later in Europe. It was for young monks only; it was devoted wholly to the Christian religion and so departed altogether from the classical Hellenic curriculum. In the West, learning to read and write was required of all students. The next Christian school to appear was the episcopal school. After the Roman Empire collapsed—and the classical school with it—it became necessary for the bishops to educate those who would become priests (in the sixth and seventh centuries some bishops themselves gave elementary schooling to children). Out of some of these episcopal schools arose some of the medieval Western universities. The third type of Christian school appeared in the sixth and seventh centuries in the parish schools, in which the local priest in a rural community gave lessons to the children of his parishioners. This school was the beginning of the ordinary village school of later times. Neither of these schools retained any part of the classical curriculum.

All these Christian schools belong properly to the later Western civilization, not to the Hellenic. They have been mentioned here simply to show the continuity or, perhaps more properly, the lack of continuity between education in the Hellenic world and in the Western.

With the collapse of the central administration of the Roman Empire at the end of the fourth century all the social services, including the schools, began the long process of disintegration. They did not of course disappear immediately nor at the same time everywhere. They persisted longer in the great towns in those lands that are now called France and Spain than they did in the smaller towns, and longer in Italy than elsewhere in the West. In the East, which had its capital at Constantinople, they did not disappear, but continued and underwent a slow transformation as the schools of the Byzantine or Orthodox Christian Civilization.

Thus education under the universal state of the Hellenic Civilization differed from that at the end of the time of troubles chiefly in two respects. First, the system of education included the great Roman law schools as a result of the importance of a knowledge of Roman law under Roman rule. Secondly, the concern of the state in educational matters had greatly increased, and this as a result of the state's need for civil servants.

II.　In the Tertiary Civilizations

The tertiary civilizations differ from the secondary in that they were all (except the abortive Scandinavian) derived from a preceding secondary civilization through a chrysalis church. Having arisen with chrysalis churches, they began their careers either already in possession of an alphabet and writing or very soon had both provided for them by the church. In this they were markedly different from all the secondary civilizations except the Sinic and the Babylonic. And being in possession of writing at the outset or in a very early stage, they had literature of a sort, thus differing from every one of the secondary societies except the Babylonic.

Having arisen as they did, they all began their careers also in possession of ethics, goals, ideals, and a set of beliefs. The "higher" religions may be distinguished from the primitive in that the former have arisen in civilizations, not in primitive societies, and in that they all have—originally had—missions to all mankind, not merely to the local tribe or nation or city. Further, they all taught the truths that the way of salvation is open to Everyman, that there is a brotherhood of all men, and that each man is, spiritually, of infinite value.

The heritage of the tertiary civilizations being thus different from that of the secondary we shall expect to find their educational theories and practices different also, at least in most cases. The education of the early period, for example, will not be found to be aristocratic

117

in the sense that it was so in the Sinic and Hellenic societies; nor will it be oral and tutorial to the same extent, nor private.

The tertiary civilizations that will be treated in this section are the Main Body of the Far Eastern, the Japanese Offshoot of the Far Eastern, the Orthodox Christian and its Russian Offshoot, the Hindu, the Islamic, and the beginning of the Western.

6. *The Main Body of the Far Eastern Civilization*

The Interregnum Between the Sinic and the Far Eastern Civilizations

Towards the close of the second century A.D. the Sinic Civilization had begun to collapse. With its collapse there began a period of anarchic violence in which a series of petty successor states sought political and military power, always fighting with each other and with the barbarian intruders who were sweeping into China from the north. If the beginnings of the growth period of the Far Eastern Civilization be dated at the last quarter of the fifth century, the interregnum between the end of the one civilization and the beginning of its successor lasted about three centuries. This interregnum is identical in some respects, and similar in many others, to the interregnum between the collapse of the Hellenic Civilization and the beginning of the Western, and to that between the fall of the Indic and the beginning of the Hindu. In all three there were petty successor states to the now defunct universal state, there were barbarian intrusions, and there were the universal churches serving as chrysalises for the new societies. All three were characterized by violence and anarchy that severely damaged, but did not totally destroy, the heritage from the earlier society.

In China the universal church that served as the chrysalis for the Far Eastern Civilization was Mahayana Buddhism. Buddhism had been introduced into China about A.D. 65 and had at once found favor at the Han Court. But it remained a curiosity of the capital without any influence on the society as a whole until after the Sinic society had collapsed. During the Han period some Buddhist scriptures had been translated into Chinese and the faith had been spread outside the capital to a few centers, but this work had been done almost entirely by foreigners. During the following interregnum Buddhism had spread throughout China rapidly and effectively, so that by the beginning of the fifth century, Chinese historians were asserting that nine out of ten families in the north were Buddhist, and by the beginning of the sixth, the whole of China was.[1] The spread of Buddhism had not gone on everywhere at an even pace or unopposed. There were intermittent persecutions of Buddhists everywhere in China (instigated for the most part by Taoists), but the persecutions were in no way like those that disfigure the pages of Western church history. The worst that was done by the authorities was to close or destroy some monasteries and require the monks and nuns to return to family life: there were no inquisitorial tortures or burnings of people.

The assertion that the influence of Buddhism upon the whole of China was so vast and so important that it may be rightly regarded as a "chrysalis" may be supported by statements from many authorities, of which two will perhaps be sufficient. Fitzgerald writes[2] that Buddhism was "by far the most important cultural influence of foreign origin" introduced into China before the nineteenth century; and that "the effect of Buddhism upon Chinese thought, art, and the customs of daily life is comparable to the influence of Christianity upon the nations of the West." And Carter demonstrates[3] that the widespread use of seal printing, and the first use of block printing, with all its enormous cultural effects, resulted from the introduction of Buddhism. The evidence could be multiplied. But there was no Buddhist influence on the state or government.

One of the reasons for the growth of Buddhism in China during the interregnum was that it offered a way of escape from the turmoil and distress of the time, a way that the conservative virtues of the Confucian system did not offer. Furthermore, the continuous wars resulted in the widespread destruction or disruption of schools, libraries, and places of worship so that the opportunities for Confucian learning diminished and the examination system for scholars virtually collapsed. Thus the influence of Confucianism upon the best brains of the people was diminished while Buddhism as a cultural influence was extending its sway.

Another reason for the steady growth of Buddhism during this time and during the whole of the growth period was the flow into China of missionaries from India and other countries of central and southern Asia, and a comparable flow of Chinese pilgrims to India. Both the missionaries and the returning pilgrims (of whom the most famous was the celebrated Fa Hsien, who made the long round trip A.D. 399–414) were strongly influential in the spread of Buddhism and in the collection and creation of a Chinese Buddhist literature. Through their joint labors a vast body of writings, consisting chiefly of the sacred Buddhist texts (sutras), was translated from Sanskrit into Chinese, and in the process, thousands of new terms were taken into the Chinese language. The sacred texts were not only translated, they were also studied; and this learning, together with the elaboration of the doctrines of the Chinese version of Buddhism, absorbed most of the best energies of the intellectual Chinese.[4]

This is not to say or suggest that Confucianism was dead or dying: it remained a living force. But during the interregnum Buddhism became also a force in the Far Eastern Civilization.

During the interregnum the collapse of the older institutions and practices was not complete. For example, here and there in China in the third century, examinations in the Confucian classics and for the civil services were held. But they were held only here and there and only sporadically as one local prince or another sought vainly to stabilize his rule. In the third and fourth centuries various princes founded state schools in their capitals, ordered instruction in the five classics to be given, and secured student bodies.[5] Outside of the capital, however, schools hardly existed at all and secular education dwindled to a very low point. At the same time, in the Buddhist monasteries, learning was kept alive among the monks, and the learning was concerned chiefly with the Buddhist scriptures, not the Confucian classics.

Period of Growth

Towards the end of the fifth century A.D. the turmoil of the interregnum began somewhat to subside and, in various parts of the land, order began to reassert itself. Toynbee dates the beginning of the growth period of the Far Eastern Civilization from this time. It may be suggested, as a point of reference, that the comparable "contemporary" date in the emergence of the Western Civilization out of the interregnum after the fall of Rome would be about the beginning of the eighth century. In China, from the end of the fifth until the end of the sixth century, there were various "dynasties" in various parts of the country. Then, in the last two decades of the sixth century, a native Chinese dynasty, the Sui, brought about a temporary unification of the land. Fitzgerald compares[6] the achievement of the Sui to that of Charlemagne: both achieved a sort of political unification of hitherto separate and diverse political units. But, whereas Charlemagne's empire withered after his death "and became an empty name," the work of the Sui was continued and completed by the T'ang dynasty, which was established A.D. 618 and which endured to 906. The actual power of the T'ang ceased a few years earlier than the latter date, c. A.D. 880, and this is the date of the breakdown and therefore of the end of the growth period.

As early as A.D. 466 the first beginnings of a system of public education were made in one of the northern kingdoms. An edict ordered the establishment of provincial schools that were to vary in size with the size of the province. The smaller were designed for forty students and were to have one professor with one assistant; the middle-sized were to have sixty students with one professor and two assistants; the larger, one hundred students, with two professors and two assistants. These figures are an interestingly close parallel to the Talmudic faculty-student ratio.[7]

In this kingdom the large provinces were said to have about fifty thousand families; thus the provincial school for a hundred students could accommodate only a very small fraction of the school-age population. The edict specified that the children of noble families were to be given first preference; so it is clear that those of middle- and lower-class families had practically no educational opportunity, although legally, and apparently by custom, they were not forbidden entry to the schools. The schools so established were not elementary and the student must have required private tutoring before he became eligible for admission to them; the expense of this tutoring was a further barrier for poor families.

But these early edicts were only rudimentary beginnings. With the foundation of the T'ang dynasty and the establishment once more of stable government throughout the empire, there began the most brilliant and creative period in the history of the Far Eastern society.

The poetry of the time was never surpassed, the art was as good as any produced earlier or later, the civil service was highly organized, the population of the state increased, civil and political affairs were well ordered, and very considerable provision was made for higher education.

Buddhism continued to flourish and grow, but, under the T'ang, so did Taoism and Confucianism. This phenomenon of the friendly co-existence of different sets of beliefs, which would seem so odd or impossible to a Christian or Jew or Muslim, was, and until very recently continued to be, characteristic of the Chinese receptivity and gift for compromise. The Chinese layman seems to have felt no sense of incompatibility in honoring Confucius and worshipping the Buddha and using Taoist rites at one and the same time. (This tolerance, both of Chinese thought and of the three doctrines, was not characteristic of Chinese converts to Islam or to Christianity, both of these religions being exclusivist and intolerant to a degree, and both derivative from Judaism.) And so when, late in the T'ang period, the Imperial Court favored Buddhism to the extent of endowing many monasteries and temples, Buddhism never acquired political power in China as did the Christian Church in the medieval West or as did Confucianism in the Far Eastern society at the same time. Political power remained in the hands of laymen who had had the Confucian training and were committed to Confucian doctrines although many of them were Buddhists in sympathy and in the practices of daily life.[8]

The T'ang emperors introduced the examination system for entry into the civil services. This was a necessary step because the need of the administration for trained personnel had grown far beyond what could be supplied by an hereditary officialdom. With the introduction of examinations of a large scale, schools were required to prepare applicants for the examinations, and they were established. As early as A.D. 631 the National Academy at the T'ang capital had over three thousand students[9] and, somewhat later, about eight thousand, drawn from all over China and a few even from Korea, Japan, and Tibet. At their peak, the T'ang schools altogether had an enrollment of over sixty thousand;[10] this indicates that there must have been a number of provincial schools in addition to the chief one at the capital.

In A.D. 754 an Academy of Letters, a kind of advanced institute, was founded. Here were gathered the most competent scholars of the time. Their duties were to write the official edicts and state papers and official prayers. This institute seems to have had a large influence in strengthening Confucianism as the official state doctrine. At about the same time, the scholars compiled three encyclopedias primarily as aids to the students who were to take examinations. The subject matter of these encyclopedias ranged all the way from state policy and official doctrine to particulars about the various crafts. All this was essentially knowledge that had been gleaned and winnowed by the preceding Sinic Civilization and had not been lost during the interregnum.

By the end of the seventh century the examination for the highest degree—the examination was conducted two hundred sixty-two times during the period of the T'ang regime—included: "(1) five essays on current events, (2) essays on the Confucian classics and history, (3) an original poem and a composition in rhythmic prose, and (4) special tests in such topics as Mathematics and Law."[11] The essentially literary character of such an examination is obvious. It seems that in the later T'ang period form, style, and recognized turns of phrase became rather more important than genuine comprehension of the subject matter and that the sections of the examination dealing with law, mathematics, and history became less important than the formally literary aspects.[12]

This increasing emphasis on form and decreasing emphasis on content is paralleled in Hellenic education only towards the end of the time of troubles and in the period of the universal state. But it will be recalled that in the Hellenic society, the literature had been created during its growth period while the T'ang "classics" had been inherited from the preceding Sinic society.

Confucian learning and Confucian scholars had become, at first useful, and then indispensable, to the T'ang rulers for about the same reasons that they had been to the earlier Han rulers:[13] it was the Confucian scholars who were clerically trained, and the bureaucracy had to have those who were so trained; it was the Confucian scholars who knew the rites, and the people demanded the rites—and so on.

Thus the T'ang rulers, even when they were Buddhists and were contributing largely to the support of Buddhist monasteries, were also supporting Confucianism as the official doctrine. They were, in a sense, compelled to encourage Confucian education because it was only the Confucian education that produced the scholars required as officials in the administration. By their training, these men could be counted upon loyally to perform their duties and to be ever ready with sound advice: the emperor did count on them, and they gave useful service. Their great disservice, and the flaw in the whole training, lay of course in the conservative perpetuation of a tradition that had arisen in an earlier society. The remarkable thing is that these officials who had only a purely literary training were able to perform their duties as efficiently as they did. The parallel with the training of the high officials of the Roman Empire in its latter days is obvious. In the Roman Empire and under the T'ang, on the other hand, the course of training was long enough and arduous enough so that only the more intelligent and industrious students could stay the course. As a consequence, it was the intelligent and industrious who passed the T'ang examinations and completed the rhetorical or law courses under Rome, and persons with these faculties could be expected to be successful in any line of endeavor. The educational and cultural traditions in both societies required the "literary" training for "educated" persons. At the same time, it is remarkable that the civil services of these two great empires—and the Han, as a third that we have noticed—required persons with literary training, and left it to their native wit and experience to devise solutions to practical problems.

Another flaw in T'ang officialdom derived in large part from the very length and rigor of the training: only the sons of the well-to-do could afford the time and energy and money for it. Hence, both under the T'ang and later, the civil servants constituted a class that lived on rents from inherited land and tended to despise and oppress the poor.

Information about primary and secondary education in this period is lacking. It appears that although the state established and maintained the higher schools that prepared candidates for the official examinations, it made no provision at all for the lower schools. The individual student, or his parents, had to find or provide the elementary schooling. The most likely guess is that there were tutors, with a few or several pupils each, who served the small towns and the less well-to-do families in those towns. It seems that the families who were financially able provided private tutors for their sons. The curriculum must have included writing and reading and arithmetic. But information is lacking about all details of lower education.

A little more is known about the student who had somehow acquired his elementary and secondary schooling. If he were the son of a noble or of an official who lived in the capital, he could go to the capital school, get his training, and take the state examinations. If he were the son of a middle-class family or of a provincial official, he could either continue his private tutoring or attend a provincial school. Such students then took qualifying examinations and, if they passed, were recommended to certain administrative boards for the examination at the capital. The boards passed on these recommendations, and approved candidates were then sent on to the capital. Yet another possibility existed in the occasional qualifying examinations that were given with imperial approval. Students who had, in one way or another, come to the attention of the authorities as having shown unusual talent were permitted to take these examinations. Franke conjectures[14] that "many" students got their learning otherwise than in the official schools, for an edict of A.D. 753 admitting to the examinations only students trained in the schools was revoked two years later. Some of these students who had received their training outside the schools managed to attract attention in the capital by the form and vigor of their writings, and so were allowed to take the examinations and to qualify for high office.

The taking and passing of the scholarly examinations was not, however, the only avenue to official appointment. There was a privilege given to the sons of officials whereby they could apply for, and receive appointment to, certain offices. The privilege did not give to the son the position that the father had held, and the number of appointments by privilege seems to have been limited, and much more limited for the higher ranks than for the lower.

It was during this period that printing was invented. In the West, the invention of printing is generally dated from the first use of movable type; in China, it is dated from the first block printing, and movable type is considered rather as an unimportant later addition. The steps that were necessarily prerequisite to printing had already been taken in China before the T'ang dynasty was established:

paper was invented under the Han about the end of the first century
A.D.—the earliest extant samples of Chinese paper date from the
middle of the second century. About A.D. 175 the Confucian classics
had been cut in stone, and twenty-five years later, rubbings on paper
had been made from them. Shortly afterwards, silk had been printed
with designs. Then, about the beginning of the fifth century, true ink
was first made from lamp-black ("India" ink; earlier inks had been
"lacquer" inks, made from tree gums). Then, finally, came the true
block print on paper with ink. The earliest block print extant dates
from A.D. 770 and was made in Japan; the earliest printed book extant—the Buddhist *Diamond Sutra*—was made in China A.D. 868.
But it is certain that true block printing was done in China as early
as the first part of the seventh century, and that books were being
printed, and used, in quantity long before the end of the T'ang
regime. And the art and its products were being exported to Korea
and Japan. Carter holds that "the dynamic force that created the
demand for printing" was "the advance of Buddhism."[15] However,
after printing had been developed in the Buddhist monasteries it
spread outward from these centers into the whole of the Far Eastern
Civilization and to its offshoot in Japan. It spread also, though slowly,
over the great silk route westwards to the Arabs and then to Europe.
About A.D. 1041 movable type was invented and used in China.

It was during this period also that fresh and free contacts with
other lands were made in plenty. Japan, as we shall see below, was
borrowing the culture, the political organization, and the religion
of the Far Eastern society. From the West, priests of various faiths,
traders, and travellers were being welcomed. During the last half of
the seventh century and the first two decades of the eighth there were
four embassies from Byzantium to the T'ang Court. In A.D. 638 the
first news of the rise of Islam was brought to the same court. In the
seventh and eighth centuries there were Zoroastrian, Manichaean,
and Nestorian Christian missionaries and churches. But A.D. 845, the
then reigning emperor suffered a change of heart, suppressed all alien
creeds (including Buddhism) and persecuted their followers.[16]
Buddhism suffered no permanent damage in numbers or influence, but
both Zoroastrianism and Christianity collapsed. It seems clear that
at the time the T'ang court library was well stocked with information
about the western religions and Fitzgerald is of the opinion that the

emperor "was perfectly familiar with the leading events and characters of western religious lore."[17]

Fitzgerald calls this period "the golden age of poetry"[18] and remarks that there are some three thousand names in the list of T'ang poets. The poets were, all of them, of course, members of the scholar class—although not all were employed in the public service—because only the scholars could write the ideographic script. Being members of the scholar class, and using the literary idiom that had for long not been the vernacular, the poets of the time were producing a literature that was not a literature of the people, but of a class. The classical language of poetry, of the "classics," of the examinations, of government edicts and official documents, was not the spoken language of the people. The vernacular had gone on changing and developing, as all spoken languages do, and was beginning to produce a literature of its own in the form of folk poetry.[19]

With the loss of real power by the T'ang, A.D. 878, and the final extinction of the dynasty, A.D. 907, the growth period of the Far Eastern Civilization came to an end and the time of troubles began.

Time of Troubles

The time of troubles, in Toynbee's reckoning, lasted the four centuries from A.D. 878 to the foundation of the Mongol Empire as universal state, A.D. 1280.

The three-quarters of a century following the collapse of the T'ang power was filled with turmoil and anarchy, with political power being assumed here and there by a series of ephemeral military dictatorships. In northeastern China, and Manchuria, A.D. 907, a pastoral nomadic people, the Ch'i-tan, established the Liao Empire and a certain order over that area. Their empire endured to A.D. 1125. In China proper, A.D. 960, the Sung Dynasty was established with the consent of a whole people weary of war and disunity and now conscious of their cultural unity. The policy of the Sung was pacifism; the dynasty endured to A.D. 1127.

It has usually been assumed by historians of China that the Chinese have always absorbed their conquerors. Wittfogel and Feng,[20] however, deem it "advisable to make a Copernican turn and say: Did the Chinese ever absorb their conquerors as long as the conditions of conquest and political separation persisted? . . . For China as well as for other civilizations, conquest not only stimulated culture transfer, but in certain important areas retarded and frustrated it. . . . Full cultural amalgamation occurred only when the disappearance of the social divide permitted the cultural divide to disappear also—that is, after the period of conquest had come to an end." These authors, in their magnificently scholarly study, seem to have established their point with regard to the Liao who, A.D. 1075, were boasting that their civilization was not inferior to that of the Chinese. They eagerly embraced Chinese Buddhism and accepted Taoism and Confucianism. But they retained at the same time the tribal religion of the Ch'i-tan, which was a sort of shamanism.

Buddhism was eagerly embraced: by the end of the tenth century, the number of Buddhist monks and nuns had grown so that membership in the monasteries and nunneries had to be restricted. The rulers made enormous gifts to the temples; they provided meals in honor of the Buddhist clergy: it was said that at the monster entertainments given A.D. 942 and 1078, fifty thousand and three hundred sixty thousand monks and nuns were fed. Yet the rulers retained their own tribal religion.[21]

In the organization and administration of their empire the Liao staffed the higher offices with native Ch'i-tan hereditary officials. Of the education of these persons nothing is known, but it must be supposed that it was by the apprenticeship method. The largest and most important group of non-tribal officials, however, were Chinese. These were selected by an examination system that had been adopted from the T'ang system, with appointments being made both to persons who had successfully passed the state examinations and by "privilege" to a few who appear to have taken a kind of simplified examination. The education of these civil officials was the same as that given to the corresponding class under the T'ang—an essentially literary training. It was these Chinese masters of script and number and the "classics" who administered most of the civil affairs of the Liao government. Military affairs remained in the hands of the Ch'i-tan tribal officers.

Under the Sung there was a clearly discernible rally of the creative forces of the Far Eastern Civilization. This rally declares itself in the rise of a school of painting which was perhaps the finest that the society ever produced.[22] In invention, the Sung period put to practical use what had been conceived under the T'ang: "The magnetic needle, used in the main in earlier times either as a toy or for the location of graves, was applied to navigation. Gunpowder, already known and used for fireworks, was . . . applied to war. Porcelain was so developed as to become an article of export to Syria and Egypt."[23] There was a vast increase in the number of printed books. The printing of the classical books was finally completed A.D. 953 and, A.D. 1041, movable type was invented. In the field of abstract thought the rally declared itself in the work of the Neo-Confucian scholars (completed by the last and greatest of them, Chu Hsi, at the end of the twelfth century), who reinterpreted Confucianism in the light of Chinese Buddhism—as, in the contemporary West, the scholastics were reading Aristotle into Christian theology.[24] Chu Hsi, and all orthodox Confucians, would have insisted that Neo-Confucianism added nothing new to the true doctrines of Confucius, that it was only bringing out the true meaning of the ancient texts which previous commentators had failed to grasp. In social theory and practice the rally is manifested in the reforms of the great Wang An-shih.

But the rally was only a rally: the creativity manifested in the achievements just noted was, on the whole, archaistic and conservative, nationalistic, and introspective.[25] The genuinely creative proposals of the reformer Wang An-shih were, in the end, rejected by the society they were intended to benefit. Under the Sung, the creative poetry of the T'ang period gave way to learned prose, and religious faith to philosophical speculation, both being dominated by a spirit of secularism and nationalism.

The reign of the sixth Sung emperor, Shen Tsung, A.D. 1068-1085, is memorable chiefly, or only, for the ministry of Wang An-shih and the revolutionary economic policy he conceived and instituted and, in part, enforced.[26]

Wang An-shih had interested himself not only in social and economic matters, but also in the educational policy of the state. In a memorial addressed to the emperor A.D. 1071 he wrote: "It is admitted that the present examination system has produced a number of good men, but that is because it is the sole avenue to official preferment. But I deny that the system is a good one. For any system which compels a man in the robust strength of his youth, when he ought to be studying the fundamental principles of philosophy and government, to shut himself up in his room and devote all his time and energies to the making of poetry and the composition of rhyming couplets is of necessity injurious. For such a man entering upon the duties of official life will have been denied all chance of gaining that knowledge which would be of practical value to him in that work."[27] He advocated, instead, the study of law, government, and political economy; he drafted sample questions for the final examinations and introduced improvements in the existing colleges of law, medicine, and military affairs. He was also instrumental in starting public schools in the districts throughout the empire. His proposed reforms in the school system were not adopted, and for the same reasons that his political and economic measures did not become permanent laws of the land: they were innovations that the conservative society could not accept.

In abstract thought, the great achievement of the Sung period was Neo-Confucianism. The Confucianism of all subsequent Chinese thought was this Neo-Confucianism. It became, in the twelfth century, the basis of the state examinations and remained so. Fitzgerald characterizes[28] Sung thought as "a retrospective return to purely Chinese sources, a conscious archaism, and a kind of cultural introspection." It was national, conservative, and pacifist. The long term result of the fixing of the doctrine by Chu Hsi was an increase in pedanticism and dogmatism and a general stereotyping and petrifaction of intellectual life.[29]

During the eleventh century and the early part of the twelfth, the Sung administration had developed the competitive examination system to a high point. The dissatisfaction with the strictly classical studies required of candidates and with the emphasis on memorizing that had been expressed by Wang An-shih was not peculiar to him alone—the dissatisfaction was rather more widespread. But it does not appear that the desire for change was able to prevail against the entrenched conservatism of the system and the increasing conservatism of Sung thought and attitudes as a whole.

Yet the level of education under the Sung was higher than at any earlier time. We have seen that Wang An-shih established district schools pretty well throughout the empire. In addition to these state schools, private education was flourishing. Buddhist, Taoist, and Confucian scholars offered their services as tutors; at least one hundred twenty-four private academies, with able scholars as teachers, were founded; many of the academies had libraries and printeries and appear to have been completely free of any governmental control or interference.[30]

Although the Sung had developed the competitive examination system to a high point and the state schools were turning out graduates in large numbers, at the same time they increased the number of "privilege" appointments until those who were appointed in this way equalled, or nearly equalled, the number of those who were appointed because they had successfully passed the examinations. It must be supposed that many of those who were appointed by "privilege" had been educated privately. This large and increasing number of civil service appointments indicates an increasingly large bureaucratization of the administration and an increasing dominance of the "clerkly" element in the government.

The core of the curriculum in the state schools and private Confucian academies was the Confucian classics; the great burden of the teaching in the lower schools was reading and writing and arithmetic, with most of the time necessarily being spent on the first two subjects.

One of the main philosophical principles agreed on by Buddhists and Confucianists alike was that man is innately good and perfectible. For the Confucianist, this meant that every man can become a sage and, for the Buddhist, that every man can achieve Buddhahood. Both were of course quite well aware that neither ideal is achieved in actual life, but both held that the ideal can be achieved by every human being. Since the ideal is not very often achieved, and since human beings vary greatly in their intellectual and physical capacities, society, for the Confucian, is an organization of unequal individuals each one of whom is expected to play his part, according to his abilities, in the whole. The universe was conceived as a harmony, and society as a part of the universal harmony, with man's nature being the link between the natural and the social orders. If it is a principle of Western democratic thought that men are somehow equal, then Confucian thought is not and never was democratic in this sense. The fact that men have different capacities and abilities requires them to occupy different stations in life and to perform different duties in society, and these stations and duties are no more "equal" than the differing abilities of men are. But it does not follow from this that there is or should be conflicts between either individuals or classes; rather, the

welfare of society as a whole depends upon the harmonious cooperation of the different classes and individuals. This general view of man
as good and of society as an ordered cooperation of unequal individuals seems to have been the characteristic Chinese view from the time
of the Sung to the late nineteenth or early twentieth century.[31]

In A.D. 1125 the Liao Empire fell and was supplanted in north
China by the Kin barbarians from Manchuria; two years later the
Sung Dynasty fell and was continued by the Southern Sung Dynasty,
and the time of troubles continued with increased severity as the
Mongol tribes from the north sought, with ever-increasing success, to
impose their power, by war, on the distressed civilization. The Mongols were finally successful in establishing their empire as universal
state over the whole of the Far Eastern Civilization A.D. 1280.

The Universal State

This last period in the history of the Far Eastern Civilization falls
into three phases. In the first phase, the rule was in the hands of an
alien people, the Mongols. The Mongols imposed their rule on China
effectively from A.D. 1280 to about A.D. 1351, being finally expelled
from all authority A.D. 1368. They were followed by a Chinese dynasty, the Ming, who ruled effectively from this date to A.D. 1644. They,
in turn, were followed by another alien people, the Manchus, who
ruled from A.D. 1644 to the foundation of the Chinese Republic, A.D.
1911.

Under the Mongols, whose vast empire extended from the shores
of the Pacific to Europe and Mesopotamia, China was only one administrative district among others. The Mongol rulers did not give
independent political leadership, and hence no positions of great
authority, to Chinese officials. They were compelled, however, to use
Chinese for almost all of the subordinate offices. Kubilai Khan had
tried,[32] early in the Mongol rule, to educate his tribesmen by founding special schools for them and promoting a Mongol script. But the
tribesmen showed little talent or desire for learning and the effort
amounted to little. The consequence was that educated Chinese filled
most of the minor offices.

The Mongols used the examination system for the selection of some
Chinese officials, but others were selected because they were deemed
trustworthy or especially able. The old examination system had fallen

into disuse at the very end of the time of troubles, but was revived, on a very limited scale, by the Mongols A.D. 1315 and continued in use until the end of their power. The examinations were given triennially but the average number of successful candidates was only about seventy.[33]

The Chinese school system under the Mongols seems to have continued, although on a small scale; the education given to candidates for the examinations was what it had been under the Sung. Taoism was persecuted by Kubilai, but Buddhism was favored by him and his successors. Confucianism continued its hold on the educated class and did produce, towards the end of the Mongol rule, a textbook that became a foundation stone in later Chinese education. It was a sort of elementary guide to knowledge, arranged in three hundred fifty-six alternately rhyming lines of three characters each and containing about five hundred different characters in all.[34]

The subordinate role played by the Chinese under the Mongol administration is shown by the fact that even the bureau of historiography, whose responsibility it was to compile the histories of the Sung, Liao, and Kin Dynasties, was nominally headed by a Mongol.

With the expulsion of the Mongols and the establishment of the native Chinese Ming Dynasty, there was a restoration of Chinese culture and learning and a new effort to compile all previous learning of the Sinic and Far Eastern cultures in one massive encyclopedia. The third Ming emperor had his scholars produce such a compilation in a vast work that required 22,877 books without the table of contents (or 22,937 with it) filling 11,095 volumes—the work of some 2,180 scholars.[35] This work was completed A.D. 1407.

The examination system for the selection of officials was extended and the examinations became more and more exacting. But, also, more and more candidates took and passed them. They were given about every three years with an average of two hundred eighty candidates passing each time. Goodrich estimates[36] that by A.D. 1469 there were about one hundred thousand civil officials of all grades in the Ming Empire. It is clear, by simple arithmetic, that not all of these officials had passed the examinations: only those of the highest rank had done so. Officials of the lower three ranks could still obtain appointments by "privilege" but those so appointed could not, under the Ming, progress up the official ladder to the top.

One innovation that was introduced A.D. 1487 was the requirement that in the examination essays, each theme was to be treated under eight headings. This remained a requirement until A.D. 1898. It is an indication of the stereotyped formalism and rigidity that now encased Chinese learning. Another indication is the assertion of a Ming scholar[37] that in the Neo-Confucian teachings of Chu Hsi "the Truth has been made manifest to the world; no more writing is needed: what is left to us is practice." This sterile and formalized rigidity characterized Confucian learning to the end.

Towards the end of the Ming Dynasty its increasing weakness was manifested in a series of rebellions among the people, increasingly frequent famines in one province and another, increasing corruption at the court and among provincial officials, increasing personal wealth of officials and poverty among the peasants. The question[38] was whether a new dynasty was to arise within China proper or was to come from the marches. The only border power ready to move in was the Manchu.[39]

The period of Ming decline had been the period of Manchu growth: from the beginning of the seventeenth century the Manchu power had grown steadily and, A.D. 1644, it established itself as the continuation of the universal state of the Far Eastern Civilization.[40]

Under the Ming Empire there were, in practice, two areas of government: the region of China proper in which the officials were directly responsible to the central government, and the areas further removed from the capital which were connected with the central government through a kind of vassal relationship and which were the seats of small feudal or quasi-feudal states. One of these small vassal states was under the control of the tribe that came later to be known as the Manchus. In this tribe there were the nobles and the serfs and also a class of free men who could—and some of them did—own property and serfs.

As the holdings of the nobility and of the free landowners increased they began to need the services of clerks. The Manchus tried to train their own people for administration and bureaucratic tasks in imitation of the familiar Chinese system, but soon found it easier to employ Chinese clerks. As early as the very beginning of the seventeenth century the Manchu ruler was insisting that neither kinship nor social position was to be taken as a sufficient condition for appointment to state office—that talent and ability were required. And the Manchus found that talent in Chinese officials. Scholar-serfs were early given appointments, and later, free Chinese were. These Chinese officials assured themselves of rights similar or equal to those they had enjoyed under Ming rule, and as the Manchu sway was gradually extended into Ming territories, more and more officials found it more advantageous to accept Manchu rule than to fight and die for a power that was clearly on the way out. Thus, concludes Michael,[41] "it was the Chinese system, Chinese officials and Chinese ideas that enabled the Manchus to conquer China." And so it is not surprising that the Chinese educational system was simply continued under the Manchu Empire.

The Manchus still retained, however, many of their old tribal ways and beliefs: even in the twentieth century the Manchu nobles still worshipped the old tribal deities[42] and still felt themselves apart from and superior to the Chinese.

Under the universal state of the Far Eastern Civilization the only change in the education that had been finally systematized during the time of troubles, was in the direction of increasing petrifaction and increasing literary emphasis. Yet, as Wang An-shih had noted long before, the system did produce many able administrators, learned scholars, and practical men of affairs. Under the Manchus, as under the Romans, persons with a "classical" and literary training showed themselves capable of holding the higher administrative posts and of taking decisions in practical matters.

All the while, underneath this formalized Confucian education, a popular literature in the vernacular was growing, a popular theater was developing, and at least one scholar has asserted that the novel and theater "were far more influential organs of education than the schools and the literary examination."[43]

We have seen that as early as the second century B.C. the classical language had already become unintelligible to the people and to many officials, and that the government had solved the problem of making its orders intelligible to the provincial officials by appointing to office those who had had an education in the classical language. After this system was fixed with the establishment of the examination system the supremacy of the classical language was assured, and it remained supreme until the twentieth century. But the spoken language continued to change, as all living languages do, and the changes went on unimpeded and untouched by the literary classics. Of the branches of vernacular literature that developed, it was the novels that were the most effective teachers of the living language. The living language had been the vehicle for folk songs and drama since the thirteenth century and for novels in the late sixteenth and succeeding centuries.

In this popular, vernacular literature[44] a distinction must be drawn between those works intended for the literate scholar gentry and those intended for the middle and lower classes. Some of the stories belong to the former class and their origins go all the way back to the fifth-century collections of anecdotes. The best of those early collections included stories from the Han and Tsin eras and was interesting to its audience because the stories were about the direct ancestors of the readers—as stories about our own grandfathers and great-grandfathers would be interesting to us. These stories were written solely by the gentry for the gentry about the gentry: no peasant or middle-class character appears in them, and of the gentry who appear, the full name, the kin, and the social position are carefully given. The ostensible motive of the stories is moral, but the moral is not labored. These early collections had many successors from the fifth century to the Manchu era, and out of them arose also the popular novels addressed to the lower classes.

This creation of a literary form out of a popular or quasi-popular vernacular literature was, of course, not the first in China: one of the Five Classics, the *Odes* or *Book of Poetry,* consisted chiefly of the anonymous folk songs of the earliest period of the Sinic society. Nor was it the last.

Out of the early collections of stories arose also the so-called "brush-drawings," which consisted of anecdotes, remarks on passages from the classics and on poems, descriptions of pictures and temples and of odd natural phenomena. This "brush-drawing genre" began to appear under the T'ang and reached its highest development under the Sung, but continued to be written to the twentieth century.

The novels proper were written by members of the scholar gentry in the colloquial language and addressed to the middle and lower classes. They were of course published anonymously or under *noms de plume,* for the scholar could not admit to authorship of works in the vulgar colloquial language. The novels can be roughly classified into four groups. The historical novels dealt with basic themes derived from official histories, although the better ones add episodes not found in the chronicles and used local traditions and legends. The second class of novels were a sort of "Robin Hood" genre; they were about gentleman-bandits who were always the "good" men, while conniving officials were the "bad" men. These enjoyed great popularity and continue to do so even today. The third class consisted of erotic stories; the small fourth class was mythological and satiric.

The novels of all four classes were at least partly didactic; they all show some moral element and all aimed at some instruction as well as much entertainment. They were addressed to the middle class that was literate in the colloquial language, but were communicated on a wide scale to the lower classes by professional storytellers.

In addition to the novels proper there were short stories. A typical seventeenth-century collection included stories that were designed to be read aloud or recited by the professional storyteller to lower class or peasant audiences. They contained idioms of popular speech, current proverbs, and fairy tale motifs. All the stories point a plain moral which is made very clear and the moral is aimed primarily at the peasants: the dividing of an inheritance by brothers is condemned, farm life is idealized, and so on. The purpose of these stories is stated by Eberhard[44] as follows: "The false idealization of the life, especially of the lower classes, the constant emphasis upon the Buddhist morality of rewards and punishments and the seductive presentation of the possibility of social climbing clearly show that a man of the gentry wrote these stories for the people in order to improve them morally. He hoped that his stories, just like the novels, would be presented by the story-teller before peasants and petty merchants or artisans in the tea rooms and thus exert on these auditors an 'improving' influence."

The potency of the vernacular literature in China is attested by the fact that within ten years of the abolition of the literary examinations in 1905 the despised spoken language had become firmly established as the language of education and of literary composition.

7. *The Japanese Offshoot of the Far Eastern Civilization*

As early as the first century B.C. there were some relations between the peoples of the islands of the Japanese Archipelago and those living on the mainland in China and Korea. From the first century A.D. these relations became increasingly frequent and close until, in the fifth and sixth centuries, "men of Ts'in and Han" crossed over. In A.D. 552 an image of the Buddha together with a number of volumes of Buddhist texts were brought to Japan from Korea and, A.D. 554, certain Buddhist monks as well as men learned in medicine and divination, the Confucian classics, music and calendar making, came to the islands. The latter date may conveniently be taken as marking the beginning of the Japanese Civilization. Within a quarter of a century after its introduction Buddhism had gained a firm footing in Japan.

Period of Growth

The indigenous peoples of the islands had not been without a culture of their own before the introduction of culture elements from the Far Eastern Civilization. They were already Shintoists. Early Shinto was in essence a nature worship with the idea of fertility constituting the core of its belief, and the idea of purity constituting the core of all its rituals and ceremonials.[1] They already had a tradition that they were a superior people ruled by one whose superior lineage reached back to the most remote antiquity and whose authority was at once paternal and divine. The tradition included the belief that the people were all of one race, indeed almost of one large family, so that the individual's welfare was subordinate to that of the nation as a whole:

the basis of individual morality was the belief in the importance of self-sacrifice for the good of the whole people. Since all were members of the whole nation, no special reverence was accorded the tribal chieftain beyond what he merited by his own deeds. And they already had traditions of filial piety, ceremonial etiquette, domestic arts, and music and dancing, in which the young were educated by the apprenticeship method.[2]

During the last half of the sixth century and the early years of the seventh there was a constant and increasingly large stream of Chinese scholars going to Japan and of Japanese men going to China to study and then, after a period of some years, returning to Japan with their acquired learning. As early as A.D. 668-671 a school was opened at the Japanese capital and, A.D. 681, a state school of advanced students, a "university," was founded. A code issued A.D. 701 provided that schools of two grades were to be established, chiefly for the purpose of training officials for the government. In the capital the already established higher school was given state support and to it were admitted children of all families of the fifth rank or higher, and upon petition, children of families of the next two lower ranks. The second grade of school was to be established in the provinces. The provincial schools were to be modeled after that at the capital, and each was to have one teacher. Children of provincial officials were to be admitted to these schools. All the schools, both in the capital and in the provinces, were staffed either by Chinese or by Japanese who had been trained in China.[3]

The curriculum of the capital school included calligraphy and reading,[31] the five Confucian classics, mathematics, Japanese literature, and law. That of the provincial schools included calligraphy and only three of the five classics. Students seem to have been admitted at about the age of fourteen and usually to have been provided with food and with their few books at government expense. They were exempted from all military services, public labor, and taxation during the period of studentship.

The Code of 701 fixed the number of students in the Confucian classics at four hundred, in calligraphy at twenty and in mathematics at thirty. These must have been the maximum figures and it seems clear that the quota, in the classics at least, was hardly ever filled. With the enrollments limited as they were to the children of officials of the higher ranks, it seems certain also that the schools could not provide all the officials needed to fill the offices, and all the more so since in Japan, as in contemporary China, the sons of the higher class officials felt little inclination to pursue the long and arduous course of studies which, when successfully completed, would entitle them to no higher rank than they had inherited.

In consequence of the dearth of officials with university training, an imperial order was issued requiring the sons of certain officials to attend the capital school, and requiring the successful completion of the course for appointment to certain ranks. But these measures were of little or no avail, for there were simply not enough graduates to fill the posts. The code had also required that teachers in the provincial schools should be graduates of the university; but since there were not enough graduates, there were cases of undergraduates being appointed to the provincial teaching posts and of single teachers being named for three or four provinces.[4]

These provisions of the Code of 701 remained for some time an ideal that was not achieved in practice. They were, however, the real beginnings of a system of state education that was, as we shall see later, amplified and improved. They are also a clear indication of the extent to which Japan borrowed from the contemporary system and curriculum of the Far Eastern Civilization.

Japan had also borrowed Chinese Buddhism. By about the middle of the seventh century Buddhism was the avowed faith of the court and hence, though perhaps less fervently, of the people. There was no question of its harmony with the original Japanese religion. This harmony derived, in part, from the tradition of compatibility between Buddhism and other faiths, and in part from the fact that the Japanese Buddhist leaders as a whole showed themselves to be patriotic Japanese. Perhaps the chief reason, however, was that the Buddhist ideal of social service in deeds of mercy for the benefit of all—not merely for the individual or his family—in order that all might be brought closer to Buddhahood, fitted so well with the early Japanese ideal of individual service and sacrifice for the good of all. The influence of Buddhism in extending the spiritual and intellectual horizons of the Japanese was very great; it was very great also in private education and in the monasteries. But it seems to have had little or no influence in the sphere of government education.[5]

In the sphere of government education the dominant, indeed the sole, philosophy that was regarded as essential was the Confucianism that had been borrowed from China.

In A.D. 710 the new city of Nara was laid out, on the model of the Chinese capital, and it became the first fixed capital of the Japanese Empire. Among the aristocracy who lived at the capital the chief intellectual employment was the study of Chinese language and literature. So great was the prestige of the Chinese script and language that, except for ordinary colloquial purposes, the native language was driven into disuse. "No scholar, no clerk, no courtier, and indeed no ordinary clerk or accountant, could get on without being able to read a Chinese text and to write a Chinese sentence."[6] At the beginning of the eighth century the university was reorganized. Appropriations were made from public funds for its support, although the appropriations seem to have been deficit appropriations that varied according to the amounts of the grants made to it by the families whose sons were students. With few exceptions, the students were all from aristocratic families and there is no indication of any effort to spread the borrowed Chinese education beyond the aristocratic circle.

It is Sansom's opinion[6] that the borrowing by Japan of the Chinese political system was a minor factor; the two major factors were the borrowing of Chinese writing and education, "which opened to the Japanese a new world of thought," and the borrowing of Chinese Buddhism, "which in time wrought essential changes in Japanese life and enriched it in almost every direction." And of these two major factors "by far the most profound and lasting in its effects was the vital impulse of Buddhism."

These comments of one of the great authorities on Japan, together with the brief account of the origins of the Japanese Civilization, are perhaps sufficient to show the justice and appropriateness of naming that civilization an "offshoot" of the Far Eastern.

In A.D. 794 the capital was removed from Nara to Kyoto and the university was again reorganized. The curriculum in the university seems to have become fixed during the next half century. It included the following:

1. The Chinese classics, especially a primer of ethics and the Analects of Confucius.

2. Texts of Chinese history; a Japanese chronicle, the *Kojiki*,[31] had

been compiled A.D. 712 but it was in colloquial, not classical, style and therefore was not deemed worthy of inclusion.

3. The law Code of 701.

4. Mathematics; the texts were a Chinese text on military science and another on mathematics as such, said to have included conic sections.

5. Calligraphy.

6. Composition in Chinese characters, with attention given to nothing but Chinese style.

7. Chinese phonetics.

At the end of the course, students were examined orally in reading and exposition of the texts by their teacher. Students answering two-thirds of the requirements were graded excellent, those answering half were graded fair; those answering less than half were graded poor and were not allowed to advance.[7]

The earlier practice of granting student aid seems to have become general during the ninth century and to have continued for the next hundred years or so; by the eleventh century, however, the state had lost interest in education.

During the ninth century a number of private schools were founded by the more powerful noble families, primarily for the education of members of their own clan. Some of these schools achieved imperial recognition as separate institutions of higher learning and as equal in rank to the university at the capital. Their graduates were exempt from the state university examinations, the examinations being given by the professors of the local school.

One consequence was that the clans who founded and supported these private schools could supply more and more of their own members for state offices; another was that, as these private schools produced more and more graduates, the state schools declined in importance.[8] There seem to have been at least six of these private universities that were founded in the ninth century and that continued to the breakdown of the civilization. The first instruction given in the schools was in the pronunciation of Chinese characters without regard to their meaning. The student was then advanced to writing the characters, and the curriculum for the most advanced students seems to have been about the same as that offered at the capital university.

It was the custom for the entering student to give presents to his teacher. This gift was in no way remuneration: it was a token of respect and reverence. The teachers were appointed and supported by the clan.

One of the Confucian works that was most widely studied was the classic of Filial Piety. By the end of the eighth century it was a part of the curriculum of every school, and it remained a part; every child who learned his letters memorized the commandments of this classic. There can be no doubt that it was a most important factor in the growth of the Japanese respect for elders and worship of ancestors.

One other ninth-century educational foundation must be mentioned: this was the private school founded in the capital A.D. 828 by the Buddhist monk Kobo Daishi. This monk had spent two years in China, and his school was modeled on the private village schools that he had seen there; it was open to students of all social ranks and was the first attempt to provide education for persons not of noble rank. The curriculum of the school included Buddhist texts, the Confucian classics, traditional Japanese ethics, calligraphy and composition; the teachers included Buddhist priests, Confucian scholars, and laymen. One of the teaching devices that was used was a syllabary[31] which was said to have been perfected if not actually invented by the founder of the school, and which remained long in general use as a primary instruction tool.

At first, and throughout the lifetime of the founder, the school enjoyed great popularity; but none of the later headmasters had either the influence or prestige of the founder, so that after his death the school deteriorated rapidly and appears to have closed in the tenth century.[9]

In addition to the schools already mentioned, there were a very few professional or technical schools. The school of medicine taught massage, divination, and pharmacy; that of music gave instruction in Japanese, Korean, and Chinese music and pantomimes; the school of divination seems to have taught astrology and the mechanics of almanac compilation. Nothing is known about further details of the curricula or about the numbers of students who attended these schools.

All of the schools during this period gave instruction on a level that presupposed elementary and secondary training. There were no elementary schools as such, and the student had to get his elementary training on his own—as did the student in then contemporary China.

It seems obvious that private families, or perhaps groups of families, employed tutors for this purpose. And this of course meant that elementary education was confined to those families who could afford the expense of a tutor.

During the very early period in Japan, before the introduction of the culture of the Far Eastern society, the social position of women seems to have been equal to that of men; with the introduction of Confucian and Buddhist beliefs her position became subordinate and there was no place for her in formal education. It appears, however, that in many instances brothers taught their sisters what they learned in school, and private home instruction was given to them in the use of the syllabary, although they were not expected to learn the Chinese ideographs. It appears also that after the removal of the court to Kyoto, A.D. 794, literature and music occupied the first place in the education of aristocratic ladies, and it is certain that the ladies participated in the great poem parties given by the emperor.

The art of poetic composition had existed in Japan from prehistoric times as an accomplishment of those who had the leisure to cultivate it. With the beginnings of the civilization in the sixth century it seems to have been even more assiduously cultivated and to have passed from being an accomplishment to being a socially necessary skill. Under the influence of Chinese customs, it was almost as if skill in making dainty couplets were taken to be evidence of ability in more important matters. Competition in couplet-making was a common game among the aristocracy; the emperor organized poem parties on a grand scale. These were genuine contests of literary skill; the ladies did participate—and occasionally won.

In A.D. 905 the emperor ordered the best poems of the previous century and a half to be collected. The collection was completed seventeen years later. It was known as the *Kokinshu* and included some eleven hundred poems. During the latter part of the tenth and earthy eleventh centuries a lady's education seems to have consisted of the *Kokinshu* and writing and music.

The great Fujiwara family gave a great deal of attention to the education of its daughters, for it had a monopoly on providing royal consorts—and so considerable control over the throne. A daughter of a family distantly related to the Fujiwara wrote the book that is perhaps the best known piece of early Japanese literature in the West.

This is the *Tale of Genji,* written by the Lady Murasaki probably at the close of the tenth century. It was written in classical Japanese and consists of a series of sketches that appear to have been drawn from observation.

The year A.D. 1185 may be said to mark the end of the growth period of the Japanese Civilization and the beginning of the time of troubles. The revolution of this date had had precursors in earlier revolutions A.D. 1160 and A.D. 1156, but the beginnings of troubles had shown still earlier symptoms: the minting of coins had ceased A.D. 958 and was not resumed for six centuries; the first infliction of the death penalty at the Imperial Court in three and a half centuries occurred A.D. 1156; the first recorded case of hara-kiri dates from A.D. 1170;[10] schools ceased to have the interest or support of the state in the eleventh century.

Time of Troubles

The Japanese warlords who wrested power from the unmilitary and cultivated Imperial Court were backwoodsmen who had developed their military prowess by extending the geographical frontiers of the society at the expense of the barbarian Ainu. In the process of developing their military prowess they had lost their hold on the culture so carefully nurtured by the society during its period of growth. They had also failed to develop any kind of centralized political or military control: it was each warlord for himself—so that the political map of Japan during the time of troubles shows a multiplicity of small states, each of which was defending its own independence against its neighbors and, sporadically, when it felt strong enough, attempting to enlarge its territory at the expense of the neighbors. The time of troubles was a period of anarchy and internecine warfare. The warlords were dominant militarily and socially and politically, although they theoretically owed an allegiance to the now shadow-figure of the emperor. They created a new warrior caste and within this caste there grew up a remarkable code.

Education other than that provided for the warrior flourished only in the temples and monasteries where Buddhist priests and monks made it their business carefully to preserve the books that would otherwise have been lost and to keep alive the learning that was now confined to so few. At some of the temples the priests instructed sons of both warriors and middle-class families, but we have no information about either the number of such temple schools or the number of pupils in attendance. State schools ceased to exist.

In place of the literary education that had been so eagerly sought by the nobility during the growth period, now, at the very beginning of the time of troubles, there began a new kind of training and developed a new kind of code. The training was the training of the warrior-knight, and the code was his code. The code was developed over decades and centuries from its first beginnings in the late twelfth century and came to be known as Bushido ("Bu-shi-do," "military-knight-ways"). It was the unwritten code of moral principles that the knights were instructed in and were required to observe; the knights *par excellence* came to be known as the *samurai* ("guards, attendants") and were a privileged class.

The sources of Bushido[11] were Buddhism, Shintoism, and Confucianism. From Buddhism were derived a sense of submission to the inevitable, composure in the face of danger or calamity, disdain of life and friendliness with death. It appears that even in the teaching of swordsmanship, advanced instruction in the art and in its theory included instruction in Buddhism. From Shintoism were derived loyalty, reverence and filial piety, and submission. From Confucianism were derived the desire for high character and the knowledge that would lead to its development.

The code that was developed emphasized the following virtues:

1. Rectitude or justice as the most important. These terms are inadequate expressions of the idea of the virtue which a bushi defined as a "power of resolution"—the power of deciding on a course of action in accordance with reason and of holding to that course without wavering. The virtue includes also the sense of duty.

2. Courage, as "the spirit of daring and bearing." Courage was not deemed a virtue unless it were exercised in a righteous cause. The spiritual aspect of the physical virtue was composure: "tranquillity is courage in repose."

3. Benevolence, a peculiarly Buddhist virtue. It included love, magnanimity, sympathy, and pity for all others, but especially for the weak and the vanquished. This benevolence was regarded as especially becoming to the samurai.

4. Politeness, as an outward manifestation of the feeling of benevo-

lence toward others. It included courtesy, urbanity, and modesty—far more than merely socially acceptable "manners."

5. Truthfulness.

6. Honor, as a deep consciousness of personal dignity and worth.

7. Loyalty.

The first aim of the education of the samurai was to build character, and character was built by developing in him these virtues. The second aim was to give training in the arts of the warrior: swordsmanship and the use of the spear, archery, military tactics, horsemanship, jiujutsu—and as much calligraphy, reading, ethics, literature, and history as would become a warrior. The method of training seems to have been by the tutorial-apprenticeship method, with one tutor having only one or a very few students.

The following assertion by an avowed apologist for the samurai and Bushido appears to be something of an exaggeration, but it does suggest that the enormous prestige enjoyed by the samurai did contribute to the moral education of the population as a whole. "What Japan was she owed to the samurai. They were not only the flower of the nation but its root as well. All the gracious gifts of heaven flowed through them. Though they kept themselves socially aloof from the populace, they set a moral standard for them and guided them by their teachings."[12]

The education of the samurai emphasized the development of character as of first importance, the skills of the warrior as second, and mere knowledge as third. Self-discipline was one important means used in the development of character, and perfection in etiquette and ceremonial was considered a part of this discipline. Several social arts were developing during this period and, of these, some were highly cultivated among the samurai. All seem to have been cultivated to some extent among the people as a whole. These arts were those of flower arrangement, gardening, the tea ceremony, and incense smelling.

The art of flower arrangement, Ikebana, had originated during the earliest period, developed steadily through Japanese history, and seems to have reached its height during the universal state period. It was regarded not merely as a decorative art, but as a means of cultivating gentleness of character and disinterested attention to things of the spirit by using common objects to produce aesthetic effects. Linear effects were primary, and in some arrangements, there were no flowers at all, only the bowl or vase and twigs. Later on, the art was taught in schools and there gradually grew up a recognized set of rules and classifications.

The tea ceremony—an elaborate, almost ritualistic refinement of the smallest act and gesture in the preparation, serving, and drinking of tea—was a grace of culture among both men and women. It was regarded as a soul-calming art and was used as such by the samurai. The incense smelling art was similarly regarded and similarly used.

The art of gardening was practiced only by men, and the garden was regarded almost as the expression of a philosophy or the embodiment of a quasi-spiritual ideal. The attention to and refinement of detail in all of these arts were carried to very great extremes—extremes that the Westerner would perhaps find ridiculous. But this refinement seems to have been characteristic of the best in Japanese education of this and the later period.

Something like this refinement was to be found in the apprenticeship education of the child into the ways and manners and customs of his family. He learned not only how to do the ordinary everyday things but also that there is a *right* way—the way of grace—of doing them. This education was extended to the rules of polite behavior and social etiquette that obtained both among the members of the family and among friends and strangers. These rules were so thoroughly learned by the child that they became a sort of second nature to him.

There is evidence that two of the great feudal families established schools of their own during the time of troubles, and one of these continued until the beginning of the sixteenth century as a center of Confucian studies.[13]

Several small Christian schools were established in the latter half of the sixteenth century but closed under the dictator Hideyoshi at the very end of the period.[13]

There is evidence also of the existence of a few private primary schools during this period. In some cases the teachers were *ronin,* the soldiers of fortune who temporarily found themselves without feudal allegiance. These home schools were, in some cases at least, coeducational; the number of pupils in each was never very great, perhaps eight or ten. The children were admitted at the age of six or seven; the school hours seem to have been from eight until two in winter and from seven until twelve in summer. The teaching was to very small groups: while one group of two or three was being taught, the other students read or wrote in copybooks, or otherwise took care of themselves. Most of the school time seems to have been taken up with exercises in the use of the brush pen, that is, in the practice of calligraphy.

In some of these private schools the girls were taught the household arts, but for the most part girls went to some other private home for lessons in all things that were not taught also to boys. The teacher in these schools was held in very high regard and there are isolated instances of grown men returning in later years to the teachers of their youth for advice and counsel. It may be concluded that, in some cases at least, the teacher was a moral preceptor and counsellor as well as a teacher of writing and arithmetic.

The time of troubles came to and end with the establishment by Ieyasu of the Tokugawa Shogunate as universal state, A.D. 1597.

The Universal State

The shoguns were dictators, ruling in the name of the emperor, and the shogunate was hereditary. The shoguns succeeded in bringing order and tranquillity to a land distressed by four centuries of civil war, and one of the first acts of Ieyasu, after he had set up a constitution to ensure order and establish his power, was to issue an edict concerned with promoting learning and re-establishing schools. The Edict of A.D. 1603 asserts: "If there were no higher humanity, society would disintegrate and unrest would never cease. To prevent such there is no better means than to influence the people by books. The publication of good books is the most valuable work of a beneficent government."[14]

Books and types were imported, intercourse with European traders and missionaries increased, and there appeared great promise of a cultural and literary and educational awakening. Ieyasu was an admirer of the scholar Seigwa, who had turned from Buddhism to the Neo-Confucianism of Chu Hsi; and to Seigwa was entrusted the task of establishing the first schools. In the schools so established by Seigwa and his influential disciples, Neo-Confucianism became the basis of all studies.[15]

The establishment of this orthodox conservatism in the schools was followed immediately by the "closing" of Japan to the Western nations. The expulsion of the Portuguese and Spaniards, and the official suppression of Roman Catholicism, was accomplished between A.D. 1614 and 1638. The Dutch alone were allowed to continue to do business with Japan, but they were confined in a ghetto on the tiny island Deshima, just off Nagasaki, and were allowed to trade only under conditions of extreme servility and at the price of periodic self-abasement.[16]

During the seventeenth century other schools and libraries were built and, towards the close of the century, the school at the capital was reorganized, under the direct supervision of the shogunate, as a sort of university for Chinese literature. After a still later reorganization of the school, A.D. 1795, only the sons of the immediate vassals of the ruling house, the Tokugawa, were admitted to it, and we may reasonably suppose that during the earlier period only very high ranking nobles were admitted. In the seventeenth century the shoguns greatly encouraged—indeed, almost required—the feudal nobles to maintain scholars at their courts and to open schools for their sons and for the sons of their vassals. By the end of the shogunate some three hundred forty of these clan schools had been opened;[17] attendance at them was the exclusive, or almost exclusive, privilege of the sons of the samurai and the nobles. The clan schools were modeled after that at the capital; in them all, the two chief subjects of study were the Confucian classics and the military arts. All state education —that is, education in the capital and the clan schools—was under the control of the conservative Neo-Confucians.

At some time during the late seventeenth or early eighteenth century the Tokugawa appointed a minister of education; the office became hereditary. It was the duty of this official to "exercise authority" over all intellectual activity, to check any that might endanger the shogunate and foster all that might strengthen it, and constantly "to occupy in harmless ways the minds and bodies of the Court circle and the military retainers." Students in the schools were forbidden to discuss current affairs or to consider heretical philosophical theories. In the annual examinations they were required to read and explain selected passages before university and certain other state officials. In A.D. 1666 a "non-approved" teacher was banished, and a little later, some unorthodox teaching was persecuted.[18]

One of the clan schools may be selected as typical of the kind of educational institution open to the young samurai or noble. This was the school in the province of Aizu.[19] The school was established about the middle of the seventeenth century and extensively rebuilt and enlarged at the end of the eighteenth.

The young samurai entered school at the age of nine, after two years of private family or tutorial training. Of some eight thousand houses in the city, about ten per cent belonged to samurai families. The city was divided into eight blocks; the young samurai of each block formed an independent and separate group and led a life separate from that of the other children. In the mornings, during the two years from age seven to nine, they went singly or in small groups to the teacher or to the temple school where the priest gave elementary instruction. In the afternoons, the children of the same group gathered in the home of one of its members. The oldest child present presided over the others, who seated themselves around him in a circle. He read or recited rules of conduct, e.g., "When you fight you must always be victorious"; "You must always be obedient to your elders." At each reading or recitation the members of the group bowed so low as to touch their heads to the mats on which they were seated. This reading of the rules of conduct was repeated daily, year in and year out. After the reading of the commands, each boy gave an account of what he had done the previous day. The deeds and words of each were criticized by the group as a whole and the presiding boy passed judgment and imposed punishments for improper conduct or speech. If the case were a difficult one, the opinion of an adult was sought. The latter half of the afternoon was spent in games.

The entrance into the school, at age nine, was the beginning of the second period of the group life of the boys. The school continued the stern discipline that had been begun in the preschool groups, and on the same basis. The school age-classes were subdivided into groups of eight or nine boys. These small groups showed a remarkable solidarity: they walked to school in a body, they had lessons in a body, they greeted other groups with bows and salutations in unison; upon arriving at the school each day a prefect took the swords of all the boys of a group and hung them together.

Studies continued from early morning until early afternoon, with only a short pause for a meagre lunch.

During the years from ages nine to thirteen the boys studied reading. This seems to have been nothing more than rote memorization of Chinese texts without comprehension. Beginning at age thirteen, and after the texts had been memorized, the student was instructed in the meaning of the texts. Beginning at the same age, formal instruction in archery and swordsmanship was given. From the ages ten to fourteen, and if the student elected it, further instruction in the classics already learned, and in other texts of Chinese literature, was given. Group instruction ceased when the boys were sixteen; from then on all instruction was tutorial, with one student to one tutor, for each subject.

From the ages eighteen to twenty-two the young samurai was taught the Confucian classics and the various branches of military science by special tutors. At the end of this period, the student graduated from the school.

The high points of the school year seem to have been the many rites and ceremonies that were conducted with a great deal of impressive pomp. These ceremonies were expressions of the spirit of Bushido and revealed the rigid social distinction that marked off the samurai from the rest of the population.

The ablest among the graduates of this clan school were sent on to the capital school for further study. Some of them received "scholarships" and travelled from school to school in the several clan districts; on their final return to the capital school or to their own clan school, they made written reports on their progress and achievements.

But neither these "wandering scholars" nor any other samurai pursued learning for its own sake: they studied the Chinese classics not as literature with a value of its own, but in order to get practical, moral guidance in the affairs of life. The chief educational aim of the young samurai of this period was to learn how properly to conduct himself as an individual, as a member of a family, as a member of the government of his lord's territory, or, possibly, as a member of the national government. Further, and as we have seen, even the instruction that he received in swordsmanship and the other military arts was designed to produce not only skill in the use of arms but also, and perhaps chiefly in this period, a certain kind of character.

A hint of the kind of atmosphere that prevailed in the clan schools may perhaps be seen in the rules that were posted in another school, and may be presumed to be similar to the rules of all the clan schools. The posted rules were:

1. The textbook shall be the . . . [with the names].
2. The standard of interpretation shall be that of the Chinese sage, Teishu.
3. Students shall not argue, placing their own interpretation against the accepted interpretation of the school.
4. Students shall be polite and diligent in study, avoiding frivolity.
5. Students shall consult upon questions of difficulty but yield to recognized explanation. They shall not debate concerning ancient teachings and the opinions of the sages.
6. Ability shall be honored, not jealously treated.
7. Even the poor, if earnest in study, shall be admitted to the school.
8. Respect shall be paid to all paper bearing the written character, and care shall be taken against fire.[20]

For children of other than the samurai, that is, the children of artisans, peasants, and merchants, there existed private or communal elementary schools. These had, for the greater part, developed out of the temple schools conducted by Buddhist priests during the time of troubles. Tuition fees at these schools were very low; they seem to have existed wherever there was sufficient population to support them. The children were taught reading, writing, and numbers: as in the other schools, great stress was laid on the development of character, on obedience to the state, and on industry and modesty in relations with others.

The spread of education among the people increased rapidly from about the middle of the eighteenth century onwards. It has already been noticed that from the beginnings of the universal state to the Meiji Revolution A.D. 1868 there was a total of about three hundred forty clan schools, most of them founded during the first half of the Tokugawa regime. In addition, some thirteen thousand other schools were founded for commoners. For a total population of about twenty millions, this is a considerable number of schools, even though the enrollment in any one school, and the average enrollment in them all, was less than in the average school of today.

The second half of the seventeenth century witnessed the beginning of the movement to make education available to the commoners. As we have seen, most of the formal education in Japan during the first two periods of its history, and all in the school established during the first years of the shogunate, was for the sons of the nobility and the samurai. In the seventeenth century there appeared a teacher named Kaibara-Ekken. He established a school, or schools, for the children of the common people, tried to include girls in the primary schools (and was, in a measure, successful), sought to give to the children an understanding of all that they read, and sought to emphasize the practical aspects of the moral discipline inculcated by the Confucian classics.

Even in Kaibara's schools and teachings, however, the Confucian classics were studied in Chinese, as they were in all other schools. Chinese had never become in any way the spoken language of the people, but it was the written language of the graduates of the various schools, and the literary language of the more highly educated.

In the Japanese language, the professional storytellers exercised a considerable educational influence. They made appearances in the streets, in public halls, and in private homes, and they had developed their art to a high point. The stories were for the most part about heroes of the feudal period, and were told with a wealth of gesture and pantomime. The pedagogic value of the story had been early recognized, and a serious intention to teach ethics and morals is manifest in many of the stories. By the beginning of the shogunate, a number of storytellers of wide reputation seemed to have been influential among the masses of the people.[22]

Another development of stories that were popular led to the production of the *No* plays. The themes of most of these plays, of which about two hundred are extant, were for the most part historical. The mask was used in the presentation of the plays, the treatment was solemn, the language was classical Japanese, and their influence was felt by the more highly educated among the people.

All professional and occupational training was by the advanced apprenticeship method. For the most part, the trades were also hereditary, being handed down from father to son, or to another child who was adopted into the trade.[23]

One of the clan schools that had been founded in the seventeenth century developed in such a way as to become prominent in the nineteenth. This was the school in Mito.[24] It had been founded in the same way and for the same purposes as had the other clan schools, that is, by the lord of the district in order to train the samurai and nobles. But at the very outset, this school seems to have selected from the classic texts in a way and with a critical sensitivity that the other schools had not. It was seeking a fusion of Confucian and Shinto thought, it emphasized historical studies, and it became more and more concerned with politics. This concern was not merely theoretical: the teachers and scholars of the Mito school not only theorized about government and politics, but participated in political activity. As dissatisfaction with the policies of the shoguns began to mount, so increased the demands that the emperor be restored to his rightful place as actual ruler of Japan. The scholars of the Mito school had a part in the agitation that led to the Meiji Restoration of A.D. 1868.

A larger role in the pre-Meiji reform agitation was played by the people's schools as a whole. As has been seen already, the capital school and the clan schools had, under the influence of Seigwa and the patronage of Ieyasu, the first shogun, made the classics of Neo-Confucianism the basis of studies. But Ieyasu had, at the beginning of his reign, zealously promoted learning of all kinds. The seeds of learning that had been nurtured thus early in the shogunate slowly germinated and produced the later reaction against both the imported alien Chinese thought and the ruling house, with its supporting warrior class, that was so closely associated with that alien thought.

The thought of the teachers in the people's schools, and consequently the thought of increasing numbers of the pupils and graduates of the schools, turned more and more away from the Sinified teachings of the capital school and the majority of the clan schools. That thought turned to native Japanese ideas and ideals and religion. As it did so, it insisted on a return to Shinto as the one valid Way for true Japanese people. During the later part of the seventeenth century the resuscitation of Shinto had been set in train by a Buddhist monk named Keichu. Keichu had been followed in the eighteenth century by a scholar who was interested in reconstructing the ancestral faith. The labors of these two men, and others of similar persuasion, were signs of a general romantic revival of interest among the people in their country's past, and with this interest grew a revulsion against everything foreign. In the movement against everything foreign and the increasing demand for the restoration of the emperor to his inherited and sacred power, these people's schools were a very great influence.[25] The movement that had begun in the literary studies of scholars had germinated and finally flowered in social and political criticism and in active political agitation for the abdication of the shoguns and the restoration of the emperor. In A.D. 1868 the effective power of the shoguns came to an end and the imperial power was restored under the Emperor Meiji.

The final blow that shattered the power of the shoguns was the impact of the West on Japan; in responding to that blow, the authors of the restoration set themselves the task of Westernizing their nation. This effort at Westernization was manifest in all parts of the national life (except religion) and perhaps especially in the schools.

On the 14th March, 1868, the Emperor Meiji offered the "Charter Oath of Five Principles" before the national shrine. These principles became the basis of the new Japan. The fifth principle reads, in part, as follows: "Wisdom and ability should be sought after in all quarters of the world for the purpose of firmly establishing the foundations of the Empire."[26] This became the educational principle of Japan. Wisdom was sought—perhaps not in all quarters of the world, but especially in the Western quarter. In July 1871, a Department of Education was established and under it a completely unified educational system was made uniform throughout the country. In 1886 the educational regulations were revised so that the entire system approximated that of then contemporary Germany.[27]

On the 30th October, 1890, an Imperial Rescript was issued; it set the fundamental educational policy of the country and it was read annually in all the schools. The rescript provided that all subjects of the emperor were to be modest and moderate; that they were to be affectionate towards their brothers and harmonious with and benevolent towards all; that they were to pursue learning and the arts and to observe the laws; that they were to offer themselves to the state in times of emergency "and thus guard and maintain the prosperity of Our Imperial Throne coeval with heaven and earth." The rescript concluded with the statement that "the Way here set forth . . . is . . . infallible for all ages and true in all places."

All schools were placed under direct supervision and control of the national government, which selected and appointed and, in the schools, trained the teachers. There were three divisions in the school system: the elementary schools, covering the first six years of the student's school life, beginning at age six; the secondary schools; and the higher schools and universities. The secondary schools were of various kinds, including technical schools, and covered from two to five years. The compulsory school ages were from six to fourteen years. The normal schools, which were numbered among the higher schools, were of two types: one for the training of teachers for the elementary schools, the other for teachers in the higher schools. In addition to these, there were schools for adult education. The function of the Bureau of Education and Learning was defined as that of "taking such measures as are necessary to lead the thoughts of the students into proper channels."[28]

The elementary school curriculum included courses in morals, the Japanese language, arithmetic, Japanese history, geography, science, drawing, singing, gymnastics, and (for girls) sewing. Uniform textbooks were used throughout the school system; the books were edited and published by the Bureau of Education. The schools were coeducational. In 1935 the attendance in the elementary schools was, according to Japanese government figures, a little better than ninety-nine per cent of of the school-age population.

The secondary schools were not coeducational. They were divided into the boy's schools, the girl's, and the technical, also for boy's. The curriculum of the boy's schools included morals, civics, the Japanese language, the Chinese classics, Japanese history, geography, a foreign (Western) language, mathematics, science, technical studies, drawing, music, practical work, and gymnastics; in the appropriate courses, special emphasis was laid on the "development of national character." In the fourth and fifth years the course was divided into terminal and preparatory for the higher schools. In the latter course, the emphasis was on the foreign language and mathematics.

The Westernization of Japanese education and techniques was accompanied by a growth in an intensely nationalistic feeling, which seems to have been deliberately fostered by the government. A Bureau of Thought Control had been established soon after the restoration and had published, or caused to be published, a series of documents that established the ideological norm for the Japanese people. Perhaps the most important of these documents was the "Kokutai No Hongi" —"Cardinal Principles of the National Entity of Japan"[29]—at any rate, this book was singled out and forbidden governmental circulation by a MacArthur Directive of the 15th December, 1945.

The book was an interpretation[30] of the educational philosophy of the Imperial Rescript of 1890 and served "as the norm by which was measured compliance with the ideological demands of the Bureau of Thought Control." As such, it was an official statement of internal policy; it was obvious, blatant, official propaganda. Its foundation was "the belief in the divine origin of Japan, its people and its ruling family." It was published in enormous quantities, yet was written in a prose so difficult[31] that few of those to whom it was directed were able to read it with understanding. This was the outcome of that revival of Shintoism and national feeling which had begun as an academic matter. And it was, as Hall says, a milestone in Japan's march to military conquest, to collapse, to total defeat.

8. The Main Body of the Orthodox Christian Civilization

It was remarked above[1] that the Roman Empire, as universal state of the Hellenic Civilization, collapsed at the end of the fourth century. The statement of course referred only to the Roman Empire in the West, where within a generation after the death of Theodosius the Great, A.D. 395, Africa, Spain, France, and Britain fell into barbarian hands. And under his two sons, Arcadius and Honorius, the two halves of the empire were divided, although in theory they remained one. They were in fact never after united. Earlier, when Constantine had founded his new capital in the East, he had created a second Rome, but the new Rome soon came to differ radically from the old in that she was not only the keystone of the defense of the Eastern and Danubian frontiers, but also a distinctively Christian capital— thus with a different character from the old pagan Rome.

The period after Constantine (d. A.D. 337) in the East was a formative period[2] during which the connections between the East and the West were gradually dissolving. During the fifth century, the controversies over heresies resulted in the ecclesiastical primacy of Constantinople, which was now not only the administrative center of the Eastern Empire, but also the center for Christian othodoxy and Greek culture. During the last half of the sixth century the Roman Empire in the Greek and Eastern provinces broke up. With the rise of Islam in the seventh century and its impact on all the areas and peoples with which it came in contact, the Byzantine Empire centered at Constantinople underwent further changes in its internal structure and, towards the end of the century, the Orthodox Christian Civiliza-

160

tion emerged as a society distinct both from the parent Hellenic Civilization and from its sister civilization, the Western.

The growth period of the society continued to its breakdown in the last quarter of the tenth century: the date of the outbreak of the great Bulgaro-Roman War, A.D. 977, is a convenient fixed point. The time of troubles of the society continued until the Osmanlis established their empire as the universal state of the civilization, A.D. 1372.[3]

Although the stages in the history of the Orthodox Christian Civilization can be identified and dated, the scanty materials about education do not permit a comparable division in the development thereof. There were scholars in plenty in the society at many different stages, but education is rarely described either by them or by the historians, and the allusions to curricula, methods, and personnel are for the most part vague and ambiguous. There is little direct evidence about schools; what indirect evidence there is must be derived almost entirely from biographies of a relatively few individuals.[4]

One of the distinguishing characteristics of the Orthodox Christian Civilization was the close relationship between church and state, in antithesis to the separation of church and state in the Western world. Indeed, Grégoire holds[5] that the Byzantine Empire was "by definition" the "Roman Empire in its Christian form" and that since this was the case, the church dominated the political, social, artistic, and literary life of the society just as much as it dominated the specifically religious life. And Hussey insists[6] that the whole outlook and orientation of the society was grounded in religion so that the church, as the official institution of religion, exerted an incalculably great influence on all aspects of life including the "secular every-day education" and the affairs of the state supported university.

At the same time, however, public education in the society was predominantly secular and independent of the church. Little is known about primary and secondary education after Constantine, but it is Marrou's opinion[7] that in the East, there was a "direct continuation" of the classical education that prevailed under the Roman Empire. Certainly the basis continued to be grammar and the classics, and the same textbooks and commentaries continued to be used and copied. In higher education, the dominant institution was the university at Constantinople, which had been founded A.D. 425 by Theodosius II,[8] and the curriculum in it remained entirely classical.

The program of studies in the university during the interregnum before the emergence of the Orthodox Christian society did not even include theology, and some—or many, at different times—of the faculty were notorious pagans. In the sixth century Justinian forbade both heretics and pagans to teach in the university, but the classical tradition was so strong that theology was never introduced as a department or even as a course, and there were attempts at pagan revivals as late as the ninth and eleventh and even the fifteenth century.[9] The university remained to its last days, A.D. 1453, a purely lay institution, giving a purely secular education.

We have seen[8] that at the time of its founding, the professorships in the university were about equally divided between Greek and Latin. But as time wore on and the rift between East and West widened, and as Greek came more and more to supersede Latin, the latter language gradually dropped out of use. By the eleventh century there was no more spoken Latin in Orthodox Christendom, not even in the university.[10] The "island" of Latin in the encroaching "sea" of Greek in the sixth century was the great law school at Beirut—until the destruction of the city A.D. 551 by an earthquake forced its closing. And in the sixth century, Justinian, who had published his Code, Digest and Institutes of Roman Law in Latin, "yet issued his later constitutions in the Greek language that they might the more readily be understood."[10]

Thus by the time of the emergence of the civilization, the education and culture were Greek and the lay, secular education was classical, but behind the Greek culture and the secular education the influence of religion and of the orthodox church were extremely powerful.

There were three types of education, or, rather, three types of schools: the classical, secular, lay schools which included the university and its preparatory schools, in which there was a predominantly secular secondary training; the monastic school; and the special patriarchal schools.[11] Each of the three, and the preparation for it, will be treated in turn.

The Orthodox Christian child was, it seems, very early taught by his parents, especially the mother, the distinction between true Christian learning and the classical, pagan culture.[12] He was brought up in the "nurture and admonition of the Lord" and listened at night to stories from the Bible, was made to learn some of it by heart, particularly the Psalms, and was trained in correct (Greek) pronunciation. The child was later on to be taught from pagan textbooks and was to read pagan literature, especially Homer, as a matter of course; at home he learned that "our"—that is, the Christian—learning was the true and that the pagan literature, if not actually false, was only in praise of virtue disguised as verse or story.

At the age of six or seven or eight the boy (although there were a few highly educated women, it appears that the girls did not go to school)[12] went to an elementary school. Most towns of size had at least one school with a fairly competent teacher or teachers, and children of all social classes could attend the schools; it seems that tuition fees were charged and that the schools were privately operated. The main subject of study in the elementary school was reading and writing. When the boy was ten or twelve he began the study of "grammar."

This study of grammar appears to have been a thorough grounding in classical Greek language and literature, especially in the form and matter of poetry, chiefly Homer. Homer was probably still learned by heart, and explained word by word.

After the student had mastered "grammar" he was ready to go on to a university. The curriculum at the university, seems to have been, again, still classical in method and content.[13] For rhetoric, the student would read and memorize Greek masterpieces, and compose speeches according to classical rules and in imitation of the older style. For philosophy he used chiefly Aristotle, Plato, and the Neo-Platonists. He seems to have got, somewhere in his education, a knowledge of mathematics and astronomy, and of the natural sciences, although it is not clear at what stage they were introduced nor how extensively or intensively taught. When he was considered sufficiently advanced in his philosophical studies he would try to apply his knowledge of Plato's doctrine to the sciences and mathematics in order to elicit the universal principles contained therein. The university curriculum was organized, more or less, into the classical Trivium and Quadrivium.

But "neither the names nor the sequence of different branches of Byzantine education are very clear."[12] School and university subjects appear to have overlapped; some study of medicine appears to have figured in both, as did some study of the law.

During the interregnum before the emergence of Orthodox Christendom as a separate society, there had been important centers of higher learning at Athens, Alexandria, Caesarea, Gaza, Antioch, Ephesus, Nicaea, Edessa and, of course, the law school at Beirut. Most of these were destroyed by the Muslim conquests, but culture was still alive in Athens in the twelfth century, Nicaea remained an important center of learning throughout the growth period and through most of the time of troubles of the civilization, and Edessa in the ninth century still supported a public teacher of grammar, rhetoric, and philosophy.

But the most fruitful center of study and the main pillar of the classical tradition was the university at Constantinople. During the dark and culturally barren period of the seventh century, before the emergence of the society as a separate civilization, the university was in eclipse, perhaps even closed. By the end of the first half of the eighth century it seems to have been temporarily in operation again if it had been closed.[14] Whether it was in operation during the Iconoclastic controversy (c. A.D. 726-842) is uncertain. The fact is that the records leave a gap for the period from A.D. 627 to the end of the eighth century—not only in the history of the university, but in the history of the society as a whole.[15]

In any case, A.D. 864 Bardas, the uncle of the then emperor, established within the precincts of the Imperial palace in Constantinople an academy for the training of imperial civil servants.[16] (The education of military officers was provided for in the discipline and technique of the army itself, which appears to have been of a highly cultivated and scientific character.)[17] The head of the school was a mathematician who had at one time lectured on philosophy and later became an archbishop. The school was, nevertheless, organized on strictly secular lines; it did not offer work in theology.[18] Dvornik[19] shows that there was a renaissance in the Orthodox Christian society that began before the close of the eighth century and continued through the ninth. This revival was twofold: on the one hand there was a return to the classical Hellenic culture and education, and this secularist movement emanated from the court; on the other hand, there was a pious cultural movement that emanated from one of the monasteries. Dvornik also holds that one of the conscious purposes that led to the founding of the academy was to take higher education out of the hands of the monks.

The secular renaissance was a deliberate revival of Hellenism—or, rather, what Toynbee calls a "resuscitation of the ghost" of Hellenism. About a century after the founding of the academy there were at least four professorships—in rhetoric, philosophy, geometry, and astronomy—and additional studies in grammar, arithmetic, music, medicine, and the law.[18] This curriculum was clearly that of the later Hellenic higher schools. The chief function of the academy was to produce civil servants. It was successful in fulfilling this function, for most of the officials who held high administrative office seem to have been trained in the academy.[20] In addition, several patriarchs and a large number of bishops were graduates, as were the highest jurists.

Professors in the academy seem to have been well paid and to have enjoyed a very high social status; they were appointed by the state. Tuition was free for the students and they may even have had subsistence scholarships.

With the beginning of the time of troubles in the last half of the tenth century education sank to a low ebb. The academy appears to have closed about A.D. 959.[20]

In A.D. 1045 the Emperor Constantine IX Monomachus founded (or refounded)[16] the university. The purpose, again, was to train imperial civil servants. The university was organized into two faculties, philosophy and law; students were chosen on the basis of merit, not birth or social rank; tuition was free; the curriculum was the same as before—the Trivium and the Quadrivium—and it remained so fixed until the end.

And all had to be "orthodox": the celebrated scholar Psellus was head of the school of philosophy, and he was compelled to make a "public profession of the orthodox faith"; his successor, having taught, or having been suspected of teaching, heresy, fell into disgrace with the emperor.

Toynbee[21] writes that "these two East Roman institutions of an educated hierarchy of professional lay civil servants were important not merely in themselves but because they made it possible for the resuscitated ghost of the Roman Empire in Orthodox Christendom to achieve its most remarkable and unfortunate triumph, the effective subordination of the Church to the State. It is in the relations between Church and State that the histories of Orthodox Christendom and Western Christendom show the widest and the most momentous divergence; and here we can locate the parting of the ways that respectively led the Western society forward along the path of growth and the Orthodox Christian society away along a path that was to end in destruction." Yet the church could, through the emperor, impose its orthodoxy on the education of state officials and so on the state itself.

About halfway through the time of troubles, the university had sunk to another low ebb, and with the capture and sack of Constantinople by the Fourth Crusade, A.D. 1204, all that was left of it moved to Nicaea. Some sixty years later there was again a Greek emperor on the throne and the school of philosophy was refounded at Constantinople, with the same curriculum, the same government support, and the same purpose. The university was, for the last time, again reorganized or refounded at the beginning of the fifteenth century.[20] The only change seems to have been a somewhat greater emphasis on medical studies. The university finally came to an end A.D. 1453 with the capture of Constantinople by the Osmanlis.

Brehier thinks[20] that the fifteenth century Orthodox Christian humanists had begun to regard the study of Greek literature as more than a sort of intellectual exercise that would train the mind and enrich the memory and enable the scholar to write well: they had come to love the Greek life and character as manifested in that literature so that they regarded the Greece of Themistocles and Pericles as their spiritual home.

It appears that in the fourteenth and fifteenth centuries there was some increase in private education, both on the secondary and higher levels,[18] but the extent of the increase is unknown.

The second type of school in Orthodox Christendom was the monastic school. It was exclusively for those who had dedicated themselves to the religious life, or those whose parents had dedicated them to it, for children were admitted at a very early age. From the beginning of Orthodox Christendom as a separate society until the thirteenth century the ban on lay children in the monastery schools was in force.[22] The teaching in these schools was narrowly confined to the Scriptures (illiterate novices learned the Psalms by ear and by heart), orthodox commentaries thereon, lives of saints, and a few patristic works. The children were taught to read and write but the instruction seems not to have been taken beyond the elementary stage. The monastic schools did not provide the counter to the highly secular education of the lay secondary schools and the university.

The counter to the secular education was offered by the third type of school in Orthodox Christendom: the patriarchal school or schools in Constantinople.[23] The very scanty sources suggest that these schools taught about the same subjects as did the secular schools, but with a different emphasis: all studies led up to the study of theology. The purpose and function of the school was to train clerics and to combat heresy. The professors were ordained deacons and the rector was invested by the Patriarch of Constantinople.

The curriculum seems to have been organized into two divisions: the one including grammar, rhetoric, some philosophy, and probably the other classical studies, the other including chiefly the study and exegesis of the Scriptures. The rector of the school taught the Gospels, there was another professor for the Epistles, and another for the Psalms. It appears that the professors of theology sometimes gave lectures in literature and philosophy in addition to their exegetical courses. It is known that one twelfth-century rector gave courses in mathematics and classical literature and philosophy which the students were required to take before they were introduced to the study of the Gospels.

After Orthodox Christendom came under Osmanli rule it found itself in the same predicament as Merovingian Gaul had found itself, and the church found itself confronted with a lack of schools that actually endangered the supply of priests and hence the continuity and maintenance of the Christian life. The orthodox church responded to this challenge in the same way that the Gallic church had responded in the sixth century: in every village the local priest gathered the children around him and undertook to teach them to read—chiefly the Psalter and other books used in the liturgy—and he taught some of the more apt to write.

Marrou[24] comments on the remarkable fact that even in the eighteenth century, the little Greek children could be heard chanting the tongue-twisting exercises in declension that had been used in the classical Greek school, so deeply was the classical tradition in teaching rooted in the Greek East.

This necessarily scrappy account of Orthodox Christian education gives no hint of the mass of literature produced by the society's writers. These writers were either ecclesiastics or officials, and the centers of literary productivity were the monasteries and the court.

The literature was not a great literature;[25] it included a great deal of theology, and history and chronicles, of which the late twelfth-century Princess Anna Comnena's account of her emperor-father's activities is outstanding. The princess was well versed both in classical literature and in the Bible, had a high standard of truth and accuracy, and her *Alexiad* is a remarkable story. The literature included also a great deal of hagiography and biography, and a single novel: *Barlaam and Iosaph,* of Indian origin, being a life of the Buddha transformed into an Orthodox Christian story; very many hymns were produced during the eighth and ninth centuries; some "romantic" poetry, one epic poem, and a great many moral didactic poems were also produced. One result of the eighth- and nine-century renaissance was the early tenth-century production, under the Emperor Constantine Porphyrogenitus, of an enormous anthology or collection of the best of the then extant classic Hellenic literature; a commoner and namesake of Constantine's of about the same time produced an anthology of Hellenic elegiac verse, and, at the turn of the thirteenth and fourteenth centuries, another private scholar, Maximos Planoudhis, produced still another, and independent, anthology.

These Orthodox Christian compilations of the literature of its parent civilization are parallels to the Far Eastern compilations of the literature of its parent society that have already been noticed.[26]

Not only were some of the monasteries centers of literary productivity, but the place of monasteries in general in the life of the society was both high and important. Those who were not monks —ordinary citizens, emperor, secular clergy, rich and poor—seem genuinely to have reverenced the monks whom they could recognize as holy men. The purpose of the monastery was to produce saints, and it was to a remarkable degree successful. The ordinary citizen reverenced also the life of the monastery as the highest type of life and it was therefore to the monastery that he looked for the solution of his problems. The Orthodox Christian monastery was consequently "an integral part of the life" of the society and was the concern "both of those who had a vocation for the holy life and those who had not";[27] it did perform public services, and the monks did—though often reluctantly—participate in public affairs.

A single story may illustrate the effect and the influence of monks and anchorites; although it is selected from the period of the interregnum before the emergence of Orthodox Christendom as a separate society, it is typical though an extreme example both of the participation of the monks in secular affairs and of the public attitude towards them.

Thus in A.D. 475-6 Saint Daniel the Stylite, at the instance of the emissaries of the Orthodox Patriarch of Constantinople, consented to descend from his pillar at Anaplus, up the Bosphorus, in order to save Orthodoxy from the Monophysite proclivities of the usurping Emperor Basiliscus. The mere news of the holy man's epiphany in the cathedral church of the Apostles in the Imperial City frightened the Emperor into evacuating his own capital and retreating to the imperial palace at the seventh milestone. It was indeed a crushing indictment of his conduct of public affairs that the report of his people's affliction should have moved the saint to reemerge from a physical isolation in which, by that time, he had been living already for twenty-four years and which was to have lasted unbroken till his death. Working spiritual acts of psychical and physical healing on his way, Saint Daniel led the clergy and people of Constantinople to beard the truant prince in his suburban asylum; and, when the guards refused the crowd admission to the imperial presence, the Saint directed the people to follow him in the scriptural symbolic act of shaking the dust of the palace precincts off their garments—which they did with such a thunderous reverberation that most of the guards on duty were moved to desert their imperial master and follow in the stylite's train. In vain the Emperor sent messages after the departing Saint to beg him to return to the Hebdomon; in vain he returned to Constantinople himself and besought Daniel to visit him in his palace there. In the end the Emperor was constrained to present himself before the Saint in the Cathedral and prostrate himself at his feet; and a public profession of Orthodoxy was the price that he eventually had to pay in order to save his throne by setting Daniel at liberty to resume his station on his pillar-top.[28]

The monks not only participated in public affairs on crucial occasions but also wrote histories and theology and supplied "some intellectual food for the masses, who would otherwise have been in danger of mental starvation" and, in writing the histories, supplied the only extant sources for some periods of Orthodox Christian history.[25] The monks played also a large role in spreading the faith, doctrine, and culture of Orthodox Christianity among the Slavs.

The first appearance of Slavs in East Roman history was about the middle of the sixth century in the region to the north of the Danube. By the middle of the seventh century they had occupied most of the Balkan Peninsula except the Albanian mountains, the coast, and Thrace. During the latter part of the eighth century the Bulgars, a Finno-Ugrian tribe, appeared and began to organize and control the Balkan Slavs; by the beginning of the ninth century Bulgaria, as an organized polity of Bulgars and Slavs, was firmly established in the peninsula. After a series of wars between the imperial power in Constantinople and Bulgaria a peace was concluded A.D. 831; Bulgarian and Slav merchants traded with and visited Constantinople, and Greek merchants and missionaries entered Bulgaria. Orthodox Christianity began slowly to spread in Bulgaria, especially among the Slavs, and about the same time the Bulgars adopted the Slav language.[29] Meanwhile, a new power had arisen.

This new power was Moravia; it had established itself in the area now approximately occupied by Austria, Hungary, and Czechoslovakia. Bulgaria and Moravia were the two ninth-century powers that stood between the Carolingian Empire of the West and Orthodox Christendom. Moravia already had fairly extensive trade relations with Constantinople and, A.D. 863, sent an embassy to the Greeks to ask "for a teacher who could preach Christianity to the Moravians in their own tongue. . . . [This] was one of the greatest turning-points in the history of the Slavs."[29]

There was a teacher available: the monk Cyril. He had already worked in Slavonic studies, had probably already developed an alphabet for Slavic, and was interested in both philology and religion. With his brother Methodius he had translated the Bible and some liturgical works into the langauge of the Macedonian Slavs, a language that could be understood by the Moravians and is still the liturgical language of the Slavonic churches. So Cyril and Methodius went to Moravia. The mission was initially successful but after their deaths the Cyrillic church collapsed and Moravia came under German influence.

At about the same time Bulgaria was induced to accept the Christianity of Constantinople, and so bound herself to the Orthodox Christian Civilization; early tenth-century Bulgaria was "an attempt to translate Byzantium into Slavonic terms. . . . As yet the civilization did not penetrate far below the surface, but the Church was slowly spreading it amongst the people."[29]

By about A.D. 1018 Constantinople had subdued Bulgaria and was in control of the whole of the Balkan Peninsula as far as Belgrade, except Dalmatia; but she did not introduce changes in local customs or taxation rates, and she allowed the Balkan Slavs to keep their Slavonic church as it had been, and the Cyrillic liturgy intact. Both politically and culturally, Orthodox Christian influence was dominant.

Orthodox Christian influence was also dominant among the Slavs of Russia.

9. *The Russian Offshoot of the*

Orthodox Christian Civilization

As the Bulgars had come into the Balkan Peninsula and organized and controlled the Slavs who were already there, so Northmen from Scanindavia came into the land that was later to be called Russia and organized and controlled the Slavs who were already there. These Northmen were kinsmen of those who raided far and wide on the coasts of Europe and were part of the same migratory wave out of the north. They were warrior-traders who, in the course of the ninth century, established posts—which were also camps— first at Novgorod, and then at Kiev, which became the capital of a principality. These Northmen were called Varangians or Rus. They did not themselves establish Novgorod or Kiev or any of the other early towns, but took over already existing Slav towns as bases. They were few in number in comparison with the Slavs of the land, and served as the organizers and leaders of the indigenous peoples, becoming, in course of time, assimilated by them. The early towns were organized on a feudal basis: each was the seat of some prince or lord who drew levies from it, and each lord was a vassal of the Grand Duke of Kiev. The local lords were also the chief merchants in their domains and the main business of the towns was trade.

In the course of the tenth century a series of at least four "treaties" with Constantinople regulated trade with the Imperial City; there was a quarter in the city reserved for the Russians; there seems to have been an annual large trading expedition to the city over a regular route.

But the Russians did not always go to Constantinople as peaceful visitors: the wealth of the city was so great and so tempting that, with slight provocation or with none, they assaulted it with force of arms. The first such attack occurred A.D. 860, and it was followed by others in the ninth and tenth centuries. The Russians were thus a menace and a problem, and the Constantinopolitan statesmen conceived a solution: the Russians should be converted to Orthodox Christianity.[1]

Already in the middle of the ninth century there had been a few Orthodox Christian missionaries in Kiev, but their initial successes had declined with the conquest of the city by the Russians. In the middle of the tenth century the missionary efforts were renewed and, A.D. 954, the Dowager Grand Duchess Olga of Kiev was converted and was received at Constantinople by the emperor. This conversion and reception did something to popularize Orthodox Christian culture in Russia, but most of the people remained heathen until the conversion of the Grand Duke Vladimir, A.D. 989. This was followed by the wholesale conversion and baptism of the Russian people.

The Russia to which Orthodox Christianity thus came was a primitive and barbarous land. Hence it was the Orthodox Christian Church that gave to the land all its culture: the Cyrillic alphabet was adopted as the medium of writing and Cyril's translations became the basis of the native literature; the already fixed dogma of the church was taken over in its entirety, so that there were no disputes concerning fundamental issues of faith and practice; the liturgical forms were similarly adopted; religious pictures furnished the model for Russian iconography; and Orthodox Christian ideas were everywhere influential in daily life. Thus the date of the conversion of Vladimir may conveniently be taken as that of the beginning of the Russian Offshoot of the Orthodox Christian Civilization. That this society was an offshoot not identical with the main body is as clear in the case of Russia as in that of Japan: despite the very large cultural and religious heritage from the main body, the language was different, the land was different, the culture became different, and the religious domination of Constantinople lasted only so long as the Imperial City remained powerful and inviolable.

At the outset Russian Christianity was an alien religion imposed on Slav and Northman alike, so that the church was in a measure dependent upon, and always closely allied with, the Grand Dukes of Kiev. She was given a tithe from the revenues of the state; the dukes founded monasteries and built churches, and sometimes put the state powers of compulsion at the service of the bishops. The church reciprocated by placing the advice of bishops and monks at the service of the state, by mediating between princes when they were feuding, by consecrating the dukes and blessing their campaigns, by looking after the poor and needy. And, as the state built a few schools, the church supplied the teachers.

Milioukov suggests[3] that after Vladimir's conversion, education in Kiev was compulsory. Certainly both dukes and clergy worked strenuously to create schools and to collect and copy books.[3] The efforts bore fruit, for by the beginning of the twelfth century Russia had priests in sufficient numbers to serve the people, and she had the beginnings of a native literature. The literature produced by Russia in the early periods was predominantly, almost wholly, religious and monastic: of the two hundred forty Russian writers known to have lived before A.D. 1600, only thirty were laymen and twenty secular clergy, the other one hundred ninety being monks.[4]

It is known that c. A.D. 1030 the Grand Duke founded an academy[5] in Novgorod for three hundred children to be instructed in "book-learning"; that he bade the parish priests "teach the people"; and that he established a library in connection with the cathedral in Kiev and gathered there scribes and scholars to translate books from Greek into Slavonic. Other dukes founded schools in two other cities.

Little or nothing is known of the curriculum in elementary and higher schools in Kievan Russia although it is known that both existed. A prayer book called the *Book of the Hours* was used as the first reader and was followed by the Psalter. It seems certain that some of the children of noble families were sent to Constantinople for their education. Vernadsky[5] believes that during this period, there was a fair number of schools and that the percentage of literacy, "at least in the upper classes, was high"; he believes also that a few of the more highly educated were perhaps as well trained as their Byzantine contemporaries.[5]

Among these more highly educated were, for example,[6] Hilarion of Kiev (c. A.D. 1050), who wrote discourses on the Scriptures and on the saints, and who shows in his writings how thoroughly and quickly some Russians had assimilated the Greek culture and, at the same time, had modified it in an original way; the author of the twelfth-century *Chronicle of Kiev* shows an enormous erudition as well as a consciousness of the unity of the Slavic peoples and their common origins; the monk Daniel of the same time wrote an account of his travels to the Holy Land; the letters of the contemporary Metropolitan Clement give references to Homer, Aristotle, and Plato and show other indications of a knowledge of the Greek classical writings, while the Bishop Cyril evidences a familiarity with the works of the Greek Fathers and imitates them intelligently. In addition to these writers and their works there appeared in the latter part of the eleventh century a juridical treatise, *Greek and Russian Ecclesiastical Rule,* and the original form of the *Russkaya Pravda,* the first codification of Russian customary law. Vernadsky concludes[7] that the "intellectual level" of the Russian educated elite was as high as that in contemporary Byzantium and the West, while Dvornik holds[8] that Kiev in the tenth to twelfth centuries was, as a center of culture, "far ahead" of anything in the contemporary West.

These scraps of information are all that is known of education in Russia during the period of growth, and this early bloom of culture wilted with the beginning of the time of troubles. If we date the beginnings of the society at the last quarter of the tenth century, then its growth period lasted only a little more than a century and a half. By the last quarter of the eleventh century the "center of gravity" had shifted north to the town of Vladimir, by the beginning of the twelfth century internecine warfare among the contending principalities had begun, and by the latter half of the century Kiev and the other towns of the Dnepr Basin had fallen into decadence. The internal troubles of the society were aggravated and other troubles were added by struggles with the Lithuanians and, beginning about the fourth decade of the thirteenth century, by the invasions of the Mongols.

During the four-centuries-long struggles among the multiplicity of contending principalities and the more than two-centuries-long struggle of all the principalities against the Mongols, education in Russia sank to an abysmally low ebb. During the same period one of the states, Muscovy, gradually rose to a position of importance, later took the lead in the struggle against the Mongol domination, and finally, at its union with the state of Novgorod, A.D. 1478, established itself as the universal state of the Russian Civilization.

It must be assumed that during this time, some priests taught some children and that there was some higher education for the few, since the continuity of education was not wholly broken and there were some scholars at the end of the period; but there is no evidence for the existence of any widespread education among the people nor even of systematic or higher education of the clergy.

The first great victory of the Russians over the Mongols took place A.D. 1380. Nearly a century later, A.D. 1472, Ivan III, Prince of Moscow, married the niece of the last East Roman emperor; A.D. 1489 he rejected all claims of the Mongols and assumed the title of tsar or autocrat: he was now no longer subject to any foreign power; Russia was an independent and sovereign state. And the Russian Church now became independent and sovereign—indeed, universal. Moscow was the successor of Constantinople, which, in Eastern theory, had been the successor of Rome. This idea seems to have been borrowed from Bulgaria.

During the fourteenth-century struggles of the second Bulgarian Empire with Constantinople, Bulgarian literature had, for a time, flourished. At the court at Trnovo there was something of a literary revival during which a Greek verse chronicle was translated into Bulgarian. This chronicle describes the decline of Roman power in Europe and the rise of the young and vigorous Constantinople to take its place. In the Bulgarian translation, Constantinople was replaced by Trnovo. At the close of the fourteenth century the Bulgarian Empire fell to the Turks and some of the Bulgarian scholars fled to Moscow; a Bulgarian became the Metropolitan of Moscow. Then, A.D. 1438–1439, was held the Council of Florence which resulted in the so-called "Union" of the Eastern and Western Churches. The Russian view of this action was that orthodoxy had been betrayed by the Greeks; so, in the fall of Constantinople A.D. 1453, they saw God's just punishment for betrayal. The Greek Church now being proved heretical, only the Russian Church remained true.

And so it was that at the turn of the fifteenth and sixteenth centuries, Muscovite scholars adopted and adapted the Bulgarian idea[9] and claimed for Moscow the primacy that had been Constantinople's after it had been Rome's. A chronicler of A.D. 1512 wrote: "Constantine's city is fallen, but our Russian land through the help of the Mother of God and the saints grows and is young and exalted."[10] In A.D. 1492 the Metropolitan Zosimus wrote: "Two Romes have fallen, the third will be Moscow, and there will be no fourth."[11] And finally, in the first quarter of the sixteenth century, the monk Philotheus wrote in a letter: "I wish to add a few words on the present orthodox Empire of our ruler: he is on earth sole Emperor (Tsar) of the Christians, the leader of the Apostolic Church which stands no longer in Rome or in Constantinople, but in the blessed city of Moscow. She alone shines in the whole world brighter than the sun. . . . All Christian Empires are fallen and in their stead stands alone the Empire of our ruler in accordance with the prophetical books. Two Romes have fallen, but the third stands and fourth there will not be."[10]

And so the Grand Prince of Moscow became, in Russian theory, the independent successor of the Byzantine emperor, and the Russian Orthodox Church the independent successor of the Greek Orthodox Church: Russia was now "Holy Russia." This assumption of imperial and ecclesiastical mantles was accompanied by changes in the manner of life of the tsars and in the organization of the palace: new imperial insignia were adopted, pomp and circumstance added into the life at the palace. But little was done for education.

Boris Godunov in A.D. 1598 tried the experiment of sending young Russians to Western Europe for study.[12] This was a break with tradition, for Muscovites previously had been allowed abroad only to Eastern Orthodox Christian countries and only on embassies or pilgrimages or for theological studies. The experiment was a failure: of the fifteen students sent abroad, only one returned. Boris also proposed the establishment of a university, but this was opposed by the church on the ground that "it was not wise to entrust the teaching of youth to Catholics and Lutherans."[13]

It appears that until the second half of the seventeenth century what little elementary education there was was given by the priests. A somber but apparently accurate statement is given by Milioukov:[14] "The ignorance of the Russian people is the source of its devotion. It knows neither schools nor universities. Only the priests teach the youth reading and writing; however, few bother with it."

The few elementary schools that existed in Muscovy from the beginning of the universal state until the late seventeeth century were chiefly for the purpose of training the clergy and a few government clerks. The teachers were local clergy, and the number of children taught very few. The subjects taught were reading, writing, and a little arithmetic.[15]

In Ukraine a quite different situation obtained. There the Russian Orthodox Church was confronted with Roman Catholicism and consequently found itself compelled to organize its education so as to be able to compete on intellectually equal terms for the allegiance of the people. There appears to have been a kind of organization of the elementary schools, and A.D. 1631, a higher school of theology was established at Kiev. This academy became the center of learning in Ukraine. Within a generation of its founding, a number of its scholars were called to Moscow and so Kievan learning became an important factor in advancing the intellectual life of late seventeenth-century Muscovy. In A.D. 1687 a Moscow academy, modeled on the one at Kiev but with more emphasis on Greek, was founded. Vernadsky[15] sums up the seventeenth-century development by saying that by the end of the century, "a thin layer of Westernized cultural elite had formed" and that this elite could serve as a "connecting link between Russia and the West" and also as "a center for the spread of new ideas" within Russia.

During the same century Russia had been subject to strong and increasing pressures from the West—Moscow had been occupied by a Polish army for the two years A.D. 1610–1612, and soon after Sweden commanded the whole eastern coastline of the Baltic Sea; the great response to this challenge was made under—it might almost be said, "by"—Peter the Great. The response was the forcible Westernization of Russia.

Toynbee points out[16] that Peter was by nature a modern Westerner born (A.D. 1672) two centuries before his time. He was ruthless and impatient of pomp; he delighted in manual skill and always took the initiative in his various projects by doing the hard work himself; he had mastered fourteen trades before he was thirty; he learned the use of all kinds of tools and mechanical apparatus; he seems to have had boundless energy. In A.D. 1697 he went to Europe on an eighteen-month trip. Of these months he spent nine learning the technique of ship building, spending five working with his own hands on the building of a frigate in Amsterdam and then going on to England to learn more. His whole interest was in technical, not social nor political, matters. In his entourage were a number of noble cadets; they were given precise instructions to master certain techniques; if they did not return with satisfactory evidence that they had done so, their estates were forfeit. During the trip he engaged more than a thousand Dutch, English, Scotch, and other experts, on long-term contracts, for service in Russia. On his return he even forbade any nobleman to marry until he had passed examinations in geometry and arithmetic and navigation, and he conscripted them all for compulsory public service—at the same time admitting to the public service men of ability from all social classes. All this was revolutionary.

His war against old Russian social tradition was equally revolutionary and was signalized by his shaving off, with his own hands, the beards of the nobles who came to congratulate him on his return in 1698; two years later he made the wearing of Western dress compulsory.

It seems clear[17] that the original motive of Peter, and the first need of Russia at the time, was to "catch up" with the West in military and economic affairs. The way to do this, as Peter clearly saw, was to Westernize the Russian armed services and techniques; to man these services and to use the techniques required a trained and educated personnel that was not to be found in the Russia of the time. Thence arose the necessity for Peter's drastic measures for the education of Russians and the importation of foreign experts in various fields. Prince Obolensky points out[17] that there was also in Russia in the seventeenth century a minority of the educated elite who genuinely believed in the superiority of Western to Russian culture and of Western to Russian institutions and wanted to see them adopted in their native land.

That Peter himself conceived education as primarily technical and narrowly utilitarian is clear.[18] Before Peter, men learned trades and professions by the apprenticeship method, and at the outset, Peter continued the use of the same method. The end of education, in his view, was not to develop the aptitudes or the personality of the individual human being, but to prepare him for a useful career; the navigator still learned on the ship, the functionary in his office, the doctor in the hospital and so on: the revolutionary change introduced by Peter was the acquisition of new techniques and skills and enough knowledge to use them. However, since one thing leads to another, it became manifest that the new techniques and accompanying new knowledge required a new kind of training and education—an education that was secular rather than religious, utilitarian rather than humanistic.

In 1701[19] he opened in Moscow a school for the training of officers for the armed forces; the school was under the direction of a Scottish mathematician; the pupils were from all social classes. In 1714[20] he forced some technical education on all male members of the Russian nobility by imposing the already remarked extraordinary penalty of forbidding marriage to them until they had passed some elementary examinations. Peter died in 1725, but he had already made provision for the founding of the Academy of Science which was opened by his wife the following year; it was "to become one of the greatest promoters of learning in Russia."[21]

The impetus given by Peter led to the founding, in 1730,[20] of a corps of pages, in 1731 a cadet corps, and in 1732 garrison schools. In 1736 compulsory education was imposed on all the male nobility between the ages of seven and twenty. Schools for non-Christian Russian subjects were founded at Astrakhan in 1732 and at Kazan in 1735. The University of Moscow was founded in 1755 with two gymnasia as adjuncts: one for noble children and the other for children of all other classes; and a commission for general elementary education was appointed in 1778. The school that had been opened in 1701 in Moscow was transferred in 1715 to the new capital, St. Petersburg, and renamed the Naval Academy; graduates and pupils of the academy became teachers in schools of mathematics that were founded in the chief cities of Russia. At the close of Peter's reign there were about forty such schools with a total of about two thousand students.[22]

The first hospital in Russia was a military hospital established by Peter;[21] a Medical Chancery was established in the last year of his life.

It may be repeated that education, in Peter's view, was always practical and utilitarian: "if men went abroad to learn economics, it was for the sake of his new tariff; if they were trained in languages, it was in order to act as translators or to serve as diplomatists . . . the Russians whom he sent to the West were assigned almost exclusively to technical training."[23]

It is clear from the mention of the studies and schools and programs established by Peter that he contributed a great deal more to the furtherance of mathematics and the sciences than he did to that of literature and culture. Indeed, even in the former his schemes "bore all the earmarks of the improvisor whose main interests lay elsewhere"[21]—yet they "jolted" Russians towards new ideas and new knowledge. For example, under Peter, Arabic numerals for the first time came into regular use, logarithms and the Copernican system were introduced, cartography and geographical knowledge were extended, and astronomy and preventive medicine actively encouraged. And printing and the creation of libraries—with all their inevitable consequences—were encouraged. In Peter's time all printing and presses belonged either to the church or to the state (there were no private presses in Russia until half a century after his death); during the whole of the seventeenth century up to his return from Europe, 374 books were published of which 19 were non-religious; during the twenty-seven years from then to his death 700 books were published, of which 400 were non-religious.

The narrow utilitarianism of Peter's view of education has been twice remarked: it now must be emphasized that the schemes he did introduce produced consequences far beyond what he foresaw or perhaps even desired, and this on the general principle of cultural diffusion that Toynbee calls[24] the principle or "law" that "one thing leads to another." As Summer puts it:

In his own lifetime . . . going to school in the West . . . neither led to the results he desired nor had much immediate effect upon Russian culture. His own intensely practical bent and his coarse heavy-handedness caused him to treat his subjects far too much like inanimate objects upon which could be rapidly imposed a new impress or novel tasks . . . [yet] this . . . aspect of his Westernization . . . was perhaps in its ultimate influence the most far-reaching of his innovations . . . [for] within the next two generations . . . very different results began to flow from Peter's peremptory insistence on training abroad. Among many of the upper class a taste for foreign travel rapidly developed, once it was no longer obligatory and no longer to be spent in antipathetic apprenticeship to navigation or gunnery. From such travel, and from Peter's opening of the door to foreign books and foreign ideas, modern Russian literature and culture were born.[25]

Further, modern Russian literature, which dates from the reign of Elizabeth (1742–1762), could not have been born had Peter "not opened so many doors that previously had been closed or at least only ajar."[26]

It must be emphasized also that when death removed Peter's iron hand there was a very large-scale backsliding to the pre-Petrine state of affairs: we have seen that at his death there were some forty secondary schools with about two thousand students. Of these, a little less than half were children of priests, about a fifth were the sons of soldiers, a little less than a fifth the sons of lesser officials, one-twentieth were the sons of urban families, and only 2.5 per cent were the sons of nobles.[27] Within two or three years of Peter's death the urban parents demanded that their sons be exempted from this compulsory training so that they could learn their trades in stores and shops, and the priests demanded that their sons be enrolled in diocesan schools, instead of the state schools, in order that they might be trained for the priesthood. These demands were met, with the result that fourteen of the schools closed. Of the remaining students some either ran away or were sent back to their parents and another fraction was composed of idiots, illiterates, and backward children.[27] Only three hundred of the remaining students finished the course. An attempt was made to combine these schools with the diocesan schools, but the synod refused, and the state secondary schools continued in existence only until 1744, when they were combined with the garrison schools that had been founded in 1732.[27]

Peter's efforts to improve primary education had almost no effect. On the occasion of the census of 1710 Peter's efforts to establish primary schools were summarized by the Archbishop of Novgorod as follows: "Census takers force priests to build schools in every parish and to teach various subjects in them. But they cannot say where to get the resources necessary to build these schools, nor who are to be the teachers, nor what subjects are to be taught nor where to get the supplies and the necessary material. All they say is that there will be a ukase about this."[27]

The diocesan schools of the seventeenth and eighteenth centuries were much more "going concerns," although whether any particular school was successful depended entirely on the vigor and interest of the local bishop. Some bishops neglected their schools until they dwindled and were closed; others enlarged the program of studies in their schools and attracted more and more students. The curricula of the better diocesan schools included reading, grammar, rhetoric, philosophy, and theology. In 1727 there were forty-seven such schools with about three thousand pupils among them.[27] Half of these were in the three Ukrainian dioceses: the cultural level of Ukraine was still much higher than that of the rest of Russia.

In A.D. 1782 Catherine II appointed a Commission for the Creation of Public Schools. The commission adopted the plan offered by a Serb who had been sent to Russia by Joseph II of Austria; the plan followed the Austrian school plan of A.D. 1774. The recommendation of the commission was followed by the empress and A.D. 1786 the first Russian general education act that covered the whole country was issued. The act provided that there was to be a major school in every major town and a minor school in every district town; the curriculum in the minor school was to include religion, Russian, Latin, a Western foreign language, and morals; that of the major school was to include these subjects as well as geography, history, science, mathematics, physics, and drawing. Private schools were ordered to be closed on the ground that education was the state's task and that the interference of amateurs could bring only harm; the public schools were to be for the children of all classes.[28]

The purpose of the act had been in part achieved by 1800. At that time there were three hundred fifteen schools in Russia[29] but about half the towns were still without them; there were some twenty thousand students in all the schools. There were no schools in the country for the peasants, but some or many of them succeeded in attending the town schools. But the ideal of the Act of 1786 of democratic education with children of all classes attending the same school was rejected by the nobility who refused to permit their children to associate with commoners in the school. The government was consequently compelled to give up the strict application of the principle of a common school for all, and a few boarding schools for aristocratic children only were established.

A new school act was issued A.D. 1802. According to it, Russia was divided into six educational districts. Each district was to have a university, each provincial capital a gymnasium, and each county a school. By the end of the reign of Alexander I, A.D. 1825, this program had been substantially realized: there were six universities, forty-eight gymnasia with about fifty-five hundred students, and three hundred thirty-seven schools with about thirty thousand students.[30]

Under Nicholas I (1825–1855) the number of gymnasia was increased from forty-eight to seventy-four and their organization and curricula modified. Latin remained an obligatory subject, but logic and statistics were dropped and the number of mathematics courses was reduced. Nicholas had seen in the revolt of the Decabrists a proof that the educational system was not what it ought to be and he began changing it by breaking the links between the several educational institutions. The parish and district schools were separated from the gymnasia and made independent. Admission to the universities, gymnasia, and higher schools was limited to free men, with serfs and household servants being admitted only to primary parish and district schools and to vocational and agricultural schools —of which there were very few. Many noble families employed private tutors for their children; on these tutors the state imposed restrictions and stipulated that children between the ages of ten and eighteen could be educated only in Russia.[30]

Russian educational policy after Peter had wavered between two contradictory ideals: one, of a democratic system, the other, of a class system with separation of students into different schools or different classes according to social rank. Under Nicholas the three leading ideas of autocracy, orthodoxy, and nationality were dominant,[31] and the class system idea seems to have prevailed. This perhaps was inevitable: already under Peter the secondary schools differed according to the social category of the students and even in his cherished Naval Academy there were class distinctions. Middle-class youths, after having learned to read, write, and count—that is, after two years in the mathematics and Russian language classes— were designated to fill positions of various kinds, as scribes, functionaries in the admiralty, assistant architects, assistant engineers, druggists, and so on. The sons of the nobility, on the other hand, continued their studies in higher classes and were prepared for careers in the navy. After the Naval Academy was moved to St.

Petersburg, A.D. 1715, most of its students came from the aristocracy, and especially from the wealthy aristocracy. The engineering school also, after it was moved to the new capital, drew its students exclusively from the aristocracy. The artillery school had students from the lower classes—chiefly the sons of artillerymen—but these children could not go beyond the lower grades—the higher grades, again, being reserved for the nobility. Milioukov summarizes[32] the effect of all this by saying that there was some elementary education for the lower social classes, professional (in the narrow sense) education for the higher classes, and a military education for the aristocracy.

These class divisions persisted in Russian education. The University of Moscow, for example, had been granted almost complete autonomy in the Act of 1803, but the state had violated that autonomy on several occasions. The new University Statute of 1835 under Nicholas required—in effect, though not absolutely—that the student body be drawn from sons of the nobility. The university was deprived of all control over the secondary schools, the minister of education was empowered to appoint professors, and the chief administrative authority was the "curator" of the school district. Students in all faculties were required to attend one course in theology and, A.D. 1849, the number of students in all faculties except those of law and medicine was limited to three hundred. Discussion by professors of the relation between land owners and peasants was forbidden and the teaching of constitutional law was suspended. Despite all these restrictive regulations students from the "inferior classes"—sons of tradesmen and petty officials—continued somehow to attend the university, and the ferment of ideas continued to work. Also, the study and teaching of science had somehow escaped government control and scientists remained in touch with the West through foreign residence and study. Out of the socially inferior but intellectually able students and teachers developed the cadre of intelligentsia, which, as Milioukov remarks,[33] stood outside of all other castes and classes. The role of the intelligentsia will be noted below.

Under Alexander II's liberal and energetic minister of education, Golovnin (1861-1866), the University Statute of 1835 was rescinded and the university regained its academic freedom and lost autonomy. Scientific missions abroad were encouraged and the organization of instruction was left to the separate faculties. Each faculty was headed by a dean, elected for a three-year term. The rector of the university was elected for a four-year term by all the full professors, and he, together with the academic assembly of full and assistant professors, administered all university affairs. Only a particular few of the assembly's decisions now needed ratification by the curator of the school district. Thanks to these measures, progress was rapid, and the period from 1863 to 1880 is the most brilliant in the history of the Russian universities.[33]

The great weakness of the Russian school system of this time lay in the almost total lack of primary schools. To fill this need Golovnin drew up a four-point plan:

1. The establishment of two categories of primary schools: normal or model schools to be organized by the Ministry of Education, and schools to be founded by private citizens or societies. The organization and programs of the schools were to vary to meet local needs.

2. These primary schools were to be under local school boards, and the boards were to be composed of representatives of various administrative bodies.

3. Attendance was not to be compulsory.

4. In regions where the language was not Great Russian, teaching was at first to be in the local language or dialect and only later in Great Russian.

A regulation of 1864 put this plan into effect and authorized the town administrative councils (Zemstvos) to concern themselves with primary education as much as with other public and private educational institutions. However, the competence of the councils was limited to financial control, while the control of teaching was left with the school boards of the provinces and districts. The councils succeeded in creating a special type of lay, primary school, which became a norm or model and which gave instruction to peasants. Of the nearly twenty-three thousand primary schools in existence in 1880 nearly eighteen thousand were founded as a result of the Regulation of 1864 and by the work of the administrative councils and peasant communities. The confessional schools, directed by the synod and supported by the state, tried to compete, but they could not rival the organization of the lay schools, whose number increased while the confessional schools decreased.

The Regulation of 1864 also introduced reforms in secondary education: social class was no longer a requirement for entrance; the only requirement became the successful passing of an examination. Three types of gymnasia on the German model were created: the humanistic gymnasium, in which Latin and Greek were taught, the "Realgymnasium" which did not require Greek, and the "Realschule" which required no classical language. Salaries of secondary teachers were increased and the Ministry of Education undertook a program of procuring and publishing suitable textbooks.

When, in 1881, Alexander II was assassinated and Alexander III succeeded to the throne, there began a program of despotic reaction marked by pogroms, religious persecutions, and restriction of civil liberties. The effective agents in this program were the procurator general of the Holy Synod who was, *ex officio,* a member of the cabinet, and the minister of education.

In 1884 a law was passed that put under the control of the synod— and, thereby, under the control of the procurator general—all primary village schools of the most elementary type, the so-called "ABC-schools." Two years earlier, the procurator had undertaken to combat the influence of the town councils by creating primary schools of the next grade above the "ABC-schools." These were called parochial schools and the work that they were supposed to give duplicated that of the primary schools that were founded and controlled by the town and village administrative councils. They were administered by the local clergy and supported by state funds. A law was passed which forbade the local councils to establish schools of their own where a parochial school existed or was planned. As a consequence, during the two years after 1882 the number of parochial schools—actual or on paper—increased from 4,500 to about 32,000.

The level of instruction in these schools was miserably low and could not sustain comparison with that in the schools of the local councils; the clergy that were supposed to administer them had no interest in academic work and most of them had no talent for it; the result was a setback for elementary education despite the increase in the number of schools. The goal of the teaching in these schools was no higher than reading and writing, both on an elementary level.[37]

The minister of education sought to limit the numbers of students attending the secondary schools—especially the classical gymnasia, which served as preparatory schools for the universities—to the upper social classes. In order to keep out of the gymnasia those students whose parents had no funds for home tutoring, he ordered the abolition of all preparatory classes for the gymnasia. Thus the secondary schools became, in large measure, schools for members of the upper social classes only.

In 1884 the autonomy of the universities were abolished by legislative act: university councils and faculty were put under the direct control of the Ministry of Education, deans and rectors and professors were now no longer chosen by the faculties but by the ministry, special inspectors were appointed to keep strict surveillance over students and faculty alike, control over the state examinations was taken from the faculties and given to government-named special juries. Older professors who displayed any independence were forced to resign and younger ones who did show the proper docility found their careers blocked. Despite severe penalties imposed upon them, the students repeatedly protested and rioted against these repressive measures.

Along with these restrictions upon academic freedom went equally severe restrictions on all religious and civil liberties, censorship of the press, and control over books permitted in the popular lending libraries: of some twelve thousand books in print in Russia in 1896 only about eleven hundred were authorized for circulation in these libraries.

Under Nicholas II, who succeeded Alexander III in 1894, the same laws remained in effect and nothing of consequence was done to remove the causes of the growing discontent and opposition to the government. As a result, the tensions continued to mount until they found their own relief in the explosions of 1917.

In 1914 there were about eight millions of pupils in the primary schools and, of these, many who succeeded in struggling higher on the educational ladder added to the number of intelligentsia.

Toynbee's general remarks[34] about intelligentsias apply to the Russian intelligentsia specifically. The very term itself—a Latin root and a Western idea with a Slavonic ending—suggests its meaning: "the intelligentsia is a class of liaison-officers who have learnt the tricks of an intrusive civilization's trade so far as may be necessary to enable their own community, through their agency, just to hold its own in an environment in which life is ceasing to be lived in accordance with the local tradition and is coming more and more to be lived in the style that is imposed by the intrusive civilization upon the aliens who fall under its dominion."[35]

The first recruits to the intelligentsia are officers in the armed forces, and these learn just enough of the alien society's skills and techniques to enable their own armies and navies to hold their own; the next recruits are the diplomatists; finally the intelligentsia develops its most characteristic types: "the schoolmaster who has learnt the trick of teaching Western subjects; the civil servant who has picked up the practice of conducting the public administration according to Western forms; the lawgiver . . . ,"[35] and, of course, the students of the schoolmaster and the apprentices to the lawyer and the civil servant. And the process of creating an intelligentsia is more difficult to stop than it is to start, for its prestige in the eyes of those who are eligible for enrollment in it is great, and eventually the "competition becomes so keen that the number of candidates rapidly increases out of all proportion to the number of opportunities for employing them. When this stage is reached, the original nucleus of an intelligentsia which is consoled by being employed becomes swamped by the adventitious mass of an 'intellectual proletariat' which is idle and destitute as well as outcast. The handful of chinovniks is reinforced by a legion of 'Nihilists' . . ."[35]

The chief characteristic of a member of the intelligentsia—whether in Russia or Japan or the Islamic world or the Hindu world—is that he is a "proletarian"[36] in the sense that he is conscious of being "in" but not "of" his society, of being "disinherited from his ancestral place in society and being unwanted in a community which is his rightful home." And, with the other members of the proletariat, as the disintegration of his society proceeds further and further towards final dissolution, he becomes more and more estranged from the dominant minority so that the minority is compelled progressively to increase the force with which it holds its position in the saddle. And as the dominant minority increases the force it uses, the proletariat repays "injustice with resentment, fear with hate, and violence with violence" until it finally executes its act of withdrawal from under the now intolerable dominance of the minority. The Russian proletariat did this A.D. 1917.

10. *The Hindu Civilization*

We have seen[1] that the Guptan Empire as the universal state of the Indic Civilization came to an end in the last quarter of the fifth century A.D. and was succeeded by a bevy of successor states, most of which were created by the barbarian Huns and Gurjaras who had swarmed into the derelict territories of the now defunct empire. About the last quarter of the eighth century, according to Toynbee's reckoning, the Hindu Civilization began to emerge. The break in continuity between the earlier Indic and later Hindu Civilizations is clear:[2] by the end of the eighth century the Indic rituals of the Vedic sacrifices had become extinct throughout most of India, Hinduism had replaced Buddhism as the religion of both the rulers and the masses, and the Indic vernaculars had been replaced by the vernaculars that are still spoken. The processes which were completed by this date had of course begun much earlier: the effacement of Buddhism by Hinduism —which had reacted against and adopted and adapted the philosophy of the earlier religion—had begun perhaps as early as the first century B.C., and the transformation of the Vedic religion into the later Hinduism had begun at about the same time; and Hinduism had become the "universal"—although not yet universally adopted—religion of and under the Guptan Empire. The replacement of the early vernaculars by the modern Hindi, Bengali, Maratti, Gujarati, and others is of course impossible to date precisely since language changes always proceed at an uneven pace and at different rates in different parts of a land, but must have been under way before the end of the Indic universal state.

Thus Hinduism had come into being at the end of the time of

troubles or during the early stages of the universal state period of the Indic society. It served as the chrysalis within which, during the interregnum, the Hindu originated.

During the growth period of the civilization the central figures were the numerous clans of a race calling themselves Rajputs ("Sons of Kings"). The Rajputs claimed descent from ancient Indian Kshatriyas, but were actually descendants of the Gurjaras, Huns, and other Central Asian tribes that invaded India in the fifth and sixth centuries.[3]

For the entire growth period—and, indeed, for the entire history of the society down to the coming of the British—there are only occasional allusions to education. From these occasional allusions it appears that, in general, the education that prevailed during the latter centuries of the Indic Civilization[4] still prevailed. The Rajputs of the growth period did patronize learning and did fill their courts with Brahmin scholars, dramatists, and poets.[3] Young merchants of rich families were sent for their education to a teacher, they lived with him in his house as disciples, they were expected to master all the highly technical training that the earlier vaisyas[5] had acquired.

It seems clear also that there were students in large numbers who sought out gurus as masters, for there was a strict enforcement of the old law requiring students to beg alms daily,[6] and it can only be supposed that the kind of training, curriculum, and the purposes of this tutorial education were the same that they had been in the earlier society. There was at least one great monastery[6] that was an advanced center of learning like the earlier Indic monasteries.[7]

There were also other organized educational institutions founded and maintained by private individuals and by kings as privately operated institutions: in the ninth century a king appointed a renowned scholar to teach grammar in, or in connection with, a temple; a tenth-century king founded a dormitory or hostelry for students who had come from a distance to attend a temple school; a tenth-century village chief gave lands and a dwelling house to a community of scholars; and a contemporary wealthy citizen endowed a college.[6] In the ninth and tenth centuries some educational centers appear to have given some form of literary examinations to their advanced students.

There is no evidence of any important difference between Hindu education, down to the foundation of the universal state, and the earlier Indic education.

In A.D. 1517 the Muhammadan Mughals established their empire as the universal state of the Hindu Civilization.

Rawlinson remarks[8] that the "high degree of culture" in India under the Mughals was "largely the result of the excellent system of education." The Mughal system of education appears to have been identical with that in other parts of the Islamic world[9] and therefore does not require a separate description. Many of the Mughal rulers and nobles encouraged education by endowing individual scholars as well as mosque schools and colleges.[10] Hindu Sanskritic and vernacular education was continued side by side with the Islamic education and, during the last years of Akbar's reign, some provision seems to have been made for the admission of a few Hindus to the Muslim colleges.[10]

The failure of the effective power of the Mughals at the beginning of the eighteenth century was followed by a hundred years of disorder and violence until the coming of the British at the end of the century. The establishment of the British Raj as the second alien universal state may be dated from about the second decade of the nineteenth century.

During the whole history of the Hindu Civilization, the education that had prevailed during the latter half of the Indic Civilization appears to have continued: education under gurus by the tutorial method, specialized training for vaisyas, advanced higher education both by gurus and in academic communities for the few.

11. The Islamic Civilization

The rise of Islam* is dated from Muhammad's move to Medina A.D. 622. Its enormous expansion in the seventh century was not, however, the result primarily of a religious movement, but of the fifth great Arab emigration out of the desert.[1] The effect of this emigration was to spread the religion and education of Islam from the shores of the Atlantic to the Hindu Kush and, later, beyond into India. The political organization of the Arab Caliphate served as the last universal state of the age-old Syriac Civilization.

The first collapse of the caliphate came in the ninth century and the final dissolution in the thirteenth, but the caliphs were without power after the beginning of the tenth century. The fall of the caliphate was followed by an interregnum with a series of small successor states, confusion, and barbarian intrusions. This interregnum ended with the rise, towards the end of the thirteenth century, of two daughter civilizations out of the chrysalis church which was Islam: the Iranic and Arabic societies. The home ground of the Iranic society was Iran, Anatolia, and the Oxus-Jaxartes Basin, and that of the Arabic, Arabia, Iraq, Syria, and North Africa. After the Ottoman conquests of Syria, Egypt, and Algeria, A.D. 1516–1517, these two societies fused to form the Islamic Civilization.

Toynbee[2] has drawn a comparison between this pair of Islamic societies affiliated to the Syriac Civilization and the pair of Christian societies—the Orthodox and the Western—that are affiliated to the

* "Islam" means "submission," that is, to the will of God; a "Muslim" is "one who submits."

Hellenic Civilization. And he has pointed out the difference in the histories of these two pairs of societies: the two Christian societies, once they had become differentiated and segregated, geographically and linguistically, from one another during the interregnum that followed the fall of the parent Hellenic Civilization, continued thereafter to develop separately. The two Islamic societies, on the other hand, within about two and a half centuries after their emergence from the interregnum that followed the fall of the caliphate, fused to form the Islamic Civilization. The Western Civilization had, indeed, made an unsuccessful attempt forcibly to incorporate the Orthodox Christian into itself in the course of the Crusades; the Iranic attempt, under the leadership of the Ottomans, forcibly to incorporate the Arabic into itself was successful.[3]

It is therefore historically appropriate to think and speak of the Iranic and Arabic societies as wings of the Islamic. It is even more appropriate to view them as wings or branches of one civilization in considering the education that prevailed in the two, for in neither was secular education separate from that of the church in the way that it was in both of the Christian societies. Education in both was thoroughly Islamic in the sense that it was based on the sacred book of that religion. Any account of education must therefore begin with the rise of Islam.

According to Hitti,[4] the three main divisions of Arabian history are the early Sabaeo-Himyarite, ending c. A.D. 500, the Jahiliyah (the "time of ignorance," that is, no revelation), ending with the rise of Islam, and the Islamic period. During the second period North Arabia was ringed about with cultural influences from Byzantium, Syria, Persia, and Abyssinia; Christianity and Judaism had both found a footing in the land, and there was some cultural and religious penetration. But the cultural influence were not vital enough to transform the native life, and the two religions did not make a deep impression on the North Arabian mind. At the same time, the native paganism no longer satisfied the spiritual needs of the people, and the national life that had early received a sort of political organization in South Arabia was, by the beginning of the seventh century, utterly disrupted. "Anarchy prevailed in the political realm as it did in the religious. The stage was set, the moment was psychological, for the rise of a great religious and national leader."[5] The fullness of time had come.

In or about A.D. 571 a child was born into the powerful Quraysh tribe at Mecca. This child was Muhammad. Little or nothing is known of his early life. When he was about twenty-five, he married a wealthy widow. Some time thereafter he began the practice of frequently secluding himself and meditating. In these meditations he sometimes heard voices. Finally a voice called to him: "Arise and warn!" He obeyed and so, about the year 609, announced his mission and began preaching. The first announcement and the first preaching were not taken seriously by his tribe; Muhammad then confined his preaching to a small circle that included only his wife and family and most intimate friends. The first convert was his wife, the second his cousin Ali, and the third his friend Abu-Bakr. After about three years of secret preaching his doctrine came to public notice and there were two noteworthy results. A number of families outside his own tribe were converted to his teaching, and the ruling oligarchy became vehemently and actively hostile to Muhammad and his doctrine.

The reason for the hostility of the oligarchy was Muhammad's denunciation of idolatry, a necessary corollary of the pure and spiritual monotheism that was the core of his teaching. The oligarchy probably feared that this denunciation might bring down on Mecca the wrath of these local divinities whose genuineness was being impugned, and they certainly feared that if the people accepted Muhammad's teaching it would disrupt or halt the lucrative pilgrimage traffic that was attracted to Mecca by the shrines of the local deities. The persecution forced some of the Meccan believers to migrate to Abyssinia and put themselves under the protection of the Christian Negus. Others, including Muhammad and his family, remained in Mecca but were shut up in their own quarter.

Thus for the first thirteen years of his mission, Muhammad was, from any worldly point of view, a complete failure: he had won only a handful of converts, most of these had been compelled to flee the country; he had brought on himself the implacable hostility of the ruling group in his native city. Yet he persisted in his mission. It seems clear that a prophet who did so persist could have been inspired only by a deep and unshakable conviction of the authenticity of his call and of the genuineness of his conviction.

Then Muhammad was invited by a deputation from Medina to come to that city. In A.D. 622 he accepted the invitation and there became the honored prophet, statesman, and political leader. The removal to Medina was the Hejirah, and from it dates the rise of Islam. From it dates also the end of the purely prophetic phase of Muhammad's career and the beginning of the second phase, which was political and military as well as religious. In Medina Muhammad was at once prince, general, statesman, teacher, and prophet. From this unity of functions in the person of the Prophet sprang the unity of the several sociological functions, so that in Islam there were no such distinctions as those that prevail in the West between church and state, ecclesiastical and civil, clerical and lay, canon law and civil law, religion and politics, even religious and secular.

In A.D. 624 a battle was fought between Muhammad's Medinan forces and his kinsmen of Mecca; Muhammad conquered; from then on the Islamic power was secure in North Arabia. In this battle Muhammad took captive some Meccans. Those who had money redeemed themselves by payment of a sum thereof. But there were certain captives who had no money, but were in possession of a literary capital: they were able to read and write. This capital was accepted by the Prophet as a ransom: that is, freedom was given to the captive who would teach ten Muslims to read and write.[6] This is the earliest record of teachers in Islam and it is an indication of the value set on teachers, and perhaps on literacy and education also, by Islam in the very beginning.

In A.D. 628 Muhammad concluded a treaty with the Meccans according to which Meccans and Muslims were to be treated equally; A.D. 630 he completed the conquest of Mecca and smashed the idols there. This year is called the "year of delegation" for during it, delegations came from all over Arabia to offer allegiance to the prince-prophet. Muhammad contented himself with requiring a verbal profession of faith and the payment of a small poor tax. Muhammad had proved himself to be the great national leader, and Islam had proved itself to be the religion, demanded by the time.

The political and social organization of the Arabian peoples had always been based on the vital bond of tribal kinship. With the acceptance of Islam, this bond was replaced by that of faith. The new community of the faithful did not have—and never was to have—a priesthood, or hierarchy, or central see. The foundation of the faith was, and is, the belief that there is no god but God and Muhammad is his Prophet, and that the Quran is the Word of God. The orthodox belief is that this book was dictated by the angel Gabriel to Muhammad from an archetype preserved in the seventh heaven. Not only is the meaning of the book the direct inspiration of God but so is every word, indeed every letter. The word Quran means "reading," "lecture," "discourse": the book is a strong and living voice intended for oral recitation. It is perhaps the most widely read book ever written, for in addition to its use in worship, it is the textbook from which nearly every Muslim learns to read and write.

In A.D. 651 the Caliph Uthman had a fixed text of the Quran made and, of this, three copies. All other texts and copies of texts were destroyed and from the fixed text all later copies have been made. The text of the Quran is therefore settled in a way that the text of no other sacred book ever was: there are no variorum readings, no differences in punctuation even, between one copy and another. Further, apart from the official translation into Turkish, there is no authorized translation of the book into any foreign language: Arabic is the language used in Heaven, Arabic is the language in which the book was dictated to Muhammad, Arabic is therefore to be learned by those who would know the Revelation.[7] The book is the source of all theology, all law, all social theory in orthodox Islam.

In addition to the Quran, Muslims accept also the "Hadith"— "Traditions." After the remarkable spread of Islam they realized that many social and legal problems could not be solved by reference to the Quran because the Revelation had not addressed itself to the problems. They found an answer to these latterly arisen problems in the Traditions. The Traditions were taken to be the utterances either of the Prophet himself or of his immediate companions who knew his thoughts, and were therefore authoritative. At first the Traditions were transmitted only orally but, in the third century after the Hejirah, they were set down in writing and became second in authority only to the Quran, and therefore unassailable. A single Tradition is believed, in many cases, to represent the actual words of God, as a verse of the Quran is the eternal word of God. The Traditions were therefore to be accepted without cavil or dispute.[8]

In the Muslim family, as in all others, the education of the child was by the apprenticeship method. But in the Muslim family it was the duty of the father to teach the child, as soon as he had learned to talk, "the word": "There is no god but Allah" and to begin to teach him the ritual prayers. The child was to know the prayers by the time he was six years old.

At the age of six or seven[9] the child entered the elementary school. The school was always, in all Muslim lands, either the mosque itself or an adjunct thereof; it appeared very soon after the death of the Prophet and increased with the spread of Islam, there being one in connection with most mosques as soon as they were built. The primer and the basic textbook was always in all Muslim lands the Quran. The major part of the efforts of the students was spent in learning to read the book and in memorizing it. Hitti says that "throughout the whole curriculum memory work was especially emphasized"; Totah that the child "had to accomplish in about three years the remarkable feat of learning [the Quran] by heart."[9] Whether all children perfectly learned the book may perhaps be doubted, but Totah's assertion is a clear statement of the ideal that was very frequently attained in practice. Further, since the slightest error in vowelling[10] or pronunciation of the eternal word of God was a sin, well-nigh absolute accuracy in the memorization and recitation of the book was expected and attained. In the twelfth century, in Damascus, a traveller noticed that the children, in doing their writing exercises, were not using verses from the Quran but from secular poetry. The reason was that in erasing and rewriting the sacred word, there was danger of discrediting it. Other schools seem not to have been so scrupulous, and the book was generally used as the primer for writing as well as reading.

In addition to reading, the elementary school taught grammar, penmanship, arithmetic, some poems, and stories about the prophets (Muslims believe in the genuineness of the Hebrew prophets; that Jesus was one of them; that Muhammad was the last and greatest of the line). Girls were taught in the lower schools, especially in order that they might receive religious instruction, but they were not encouraged to go further.

Teachers of all grades throughout the Islamic world were originally held in high respect, and the teachers of the higher grades continued to be so respected; but, in the course of time, the elementary school teachers sunk lower in social status, possibly because it was thought that any one who could read and write could do their job.

Parents who were financially able did not send their children to the elementary schools, but hired private tutors. The subjects that were taught by the tutor in the home were the same, and with the same emphasis on the primacy of the Quran, as in the public elementary school, but with more attention to secular literature and the art of versification.

There seems to have been no fixed number of years for attendance at the elementary school or for study under the private tutor: the child went ahead as he was able and "graduated" from the school or from the tutor when, in the opinion of the teacher, he had learned what was usually expected of students.

The schools, both elementary and higher, grew in number and spread geographically with the spread of Islam and the increase in number of converts. During the ninth and tenth centuries—the end of the caliphate and the beginning of the interregnum—there was a considerable growth, especially in the number of the higher schools.

The first higher schools that appeared in the Islamic world were, like the elementary schools, in, or in connection with, the mosques. They existed from the time of "those who had known the Companions of the Prophet" and seem to have been continuations of the elementary school, the student advancing to them when he had completed the work of the lower grades. At first the curriculum of these mosque schools included the Quran, the Traditions, the Arabic language and the "religious sciences" related to the Quran. Later there appeared private higher schools. In these a scholar gave instruction, in his own home, in subjects that were not available in the mosque schools—especially, after about the middle of the eighth century, the subjects of the Hellenic Quadrivium—or advanced work in subjects that were. In some of the private schools technical instruction was given as a supplement to the prevailing apprenticeship system for the trades and professions. These private schools were all small, but in the eighth and ninth centuries became very numerous.

Both the teachers in the mosque schools and in the private schools were recognized as being more competent and of a higher social status than the elementary school teachers.

The next stage in the development of Islamic education was marked by the appearance of the "Houses of Wisdom." With the persecution of pagan and heretical scholars in Constantinople in the sixth century under Justinian, many of them removed to Syria, Mesopotamia, and

Persia, and particularly to the schools at Edessa, Nisibis, and Junde-shapur. When Islam, in the seventh and eighth centuries, expanded into these lands it came into direct contact with a classical Hellenistic thought. This Greek thought was new and attractive to the Muslims, and the ninth century became the great age of the translation of Greek philosophy, medical literature, mathematics, and the other sciences into Arabic. The first important "House of Wisdom" was founded, with an endowment, by the Caliph al-Mamun at Baghdad towards the beginning of the ninth century.[11] It was primarily a translation bureau, with a large library of manuscripts and many competent specialists to translate them.

With the library, the scholars, and an endowed foundation, it was inevitable that the "House of Wisdom" should attract students, and so it became a new type of higher school: an academy of secondary and higher studies. It was the prototype of very many other ninth-century foundations. Connected with it was an observatory and, with the observatory, a school for teaching astronomy. Under the influence of the newly translated Greek medical literature Arabic medicine advanced apace, hospitals were founded, and most of them served also as centers for medical studies. Leclerc writes that "at the end of the eighth century their whole scientific possessions consisted of a translation of one medical treatise and some books on alchemy. Before the ninth century had run to its close, the Arabs were in possession of all the science of the Greeks; they had produced from their own ranks students of the first order, and had raised among their initiators men who, without them, would have been groping in the dark; and they showed from this time an aptitude for the exact sciences, which was lacking in their instructors, whom they henceforward surpassed."[12]

That there was an elite of very highly educated men under the caliphate is fully recognized, but there is little evidence about the cultural level of the masses. There was no such thing as systematic adult education, but the mosques in almost all towns and cities were educational centers. The mosque, being the civic as well as the ecclesiastical center for the people it served, was the scene not only of the reading of prayers and sermons but also of public messages, lectures, and discussions. In many mosques there were, regularly or irregularly, lectures on the Quran and the Traditions, and on literary and poetical and legal subjects as well. All Muslims had free access to these lectures and assemblies and the mosque "remained until the eleventh century the extension school of Islam."[13] The mosques became also repositories for books; through gifts and bequests, many mosque libraries became large and their holdings representative of the best knowledge of the time, though the holdings in religious literature were especially good.

There was another kind of educational group that was of some influence among the more highly educated. This was a sort of literary salon that was held in the homes of the members of the group. These developed so that several of the early caliphs attended, or held in their palaces, these discussion groups and listened to and participated in talks about religion and literature.

Still another educational agency flourished in the ninth century. This was the commercial bookshop. Hitti[13] quotes one writer to the effect that A.D. 891 there was a street in Baghdad that had in it over one hundred book dealers—and there were many other streets with other book dealers. Many of these shops were inconspicuously small and poorly stocked, but others were larger and served as a kind of meeting place for book lovers and students.[14]

The third stage in the development of Islamic education was marked by the appearance of still another kind of school that had still another purpose. In order that the purpose of this school may be understood, two prior developments must be taken into account.

The first of these was the division in Islam between the Sunni and the Shiah. Originally the Shiah was the faction of one of the rival Meccan houses[15] that claimed to be the true successors of the Prophet through the house of Ali, the second convert to Islam and one of the first Companions of the Prophet. Dispute had arisen about the succession because Muhammad himself had nominated no successor. When he died, the earliest and most faithful of the converts had elected Abu Bakr, the third convert, as his successor; upon his death two years later, Umar, another early convert was, it seems, elected; upon his death Ali was elected. The Sunni doctors always held that the caliphate was an elective office;[16] the early Shiah view was that the true Caliph was of the house of Ali. This original difference and rivalry about the succession developed into further differences in the interpretation of law and doctrine; the Shiah later became, in many parts of the Islamic world, partially identified with the national state in which it was dominant,[17] and so the differences became more formidable and finally irreconcilable. The Sunnis regarded themselves as the "orthodox" and the Shiahs as "heretical."

The second development that must be noticed is the entrance of the Turks into the Islamic world and their rise to power. In the sixth century A.D. the Turks had erupted out of the Central Asian deserts and one stream of them had flowed into the Oxus-Jaxartes Basin. There, at the close of the tenth century, the Seljuk Turks had been converted to Islam. As the Arab Caliphate broke down, the Turks flowed in to take possession of its derelict territories. In the course of the eleventh century they advanced from the River Oxus to the shores of the Mediterranean and the Black Sea Straits (and this was one of the events that provoked the First Crusade)—going clear across the territories of the now defunct caliphate into those of Orthodox Christendom in Anatolia; in the twelfth century, war-bands of Turkish mamluks in the service of Saladin went into Egypt and, in the next century, took control of Egypt and Syria for themselves.[18]

In the eleventh century the rulers in the Mesopotamian quarter of the Islamic world were Seljuk Turks who were Sunni Muslims. It was these rulers who established the first of the new and different kind of schools that mark the last stage in the development of the Muslim educational system.

This first school of the new type was founded in Baghdad A.D. 1065–1067 by Nizam ul-Mulk who was the Grand Vizier of the Seljuk sultans Alp Arslan and Malikshah. (Nizam was also the patron of Omar Khayyam.) The school was called the Nizamiyah. Hitti[19] regards this school as the "first real academy" in Islam in the sense that it was the first to make provision for the physical as well as the intellectual and spiritual needs of its students, and that it became the model for later foundations for higher learning.

The Nizamiyah had two sections or divisions, and these two divisions arose from the double purpose the school was to serve.[20] It was a seminary for the study of orthodox Sunnite law and theology and therefore a means of combating the Shiite heresy, and it was a college for the training of civil servants. It served the further purpose of demonstrating to the people that the sultan was a patron of the arts and of higher education. The Seljuks, and other non-Arab sultans, spent large sums on academic foundations and on promoting education in general. Hitti suggests [20] and Totah asserts[21] that their motive in so doing was to strengthen their position with the people.

The necessity for establishing agencies for combating the Shiite heresy arose partly from the fact that, in very many cases, the "Houses of Wisdom" had become centers of Shiite propaganda.[22] This was especially true in Egypt, where the great school in Cairo, with its library of over six thousand volumes, taught the entire Hellenistic Quadrivium, philosophy, and other sciences. Miller sees an "inherently close connection between Shiah mysticism and Greek metaphysics"[23] (especially Neo-Platonism) and so a certain inevitability in the assumption of Shiite tendencies by the translation bureaus and connected schools. He sees, therefore, the chief motive in the foundation of the Nizamiyah and other colleges in the desire of the orthodox Sunni sultans to combat heresy.

The necessity for training civil servants had arisen from the circumstance that as the Turks acquired more power and territory and subjects in Muslim lands, they found that their nomadic tribal army and organization were simply inadequate to the task of ruling the sedentary population within their territories. Further, their very successes had attracted more Turks into their empire. Prior to this time, the only training that civil and military office holders received was either by the apprenticeship method or on-the-job training in the practical experience of office holding or of war.[24] Hence the necessity for a system of training for the rulers which would produce more, and more competent, administrative officers.

The Nizamiyah was founded, accredited, and supported by the state and was the first, or one of the first, higher schools that was a government institution. It very soon became widely famous, and widely copied. The features that earned it its fame seem to have been its boarding department, the competence, even brilliance, of its faculty, and the continuing support of its founder. The backbone of the curriculum was the Quran, the Tradition and Arabic poetry; these were the "humanities" of Islam and occupied about the same place in Islamic higher education as did the "classics" in the later European universities.[19] In the study of the humanities memorization continued to be stressed: al-Ghazzali, perhaps the most famous of the Nizamiyah faculty, learned by heart three hundred thousand Traditions, and so earned his title of "The Authority of Islam"; another scholar is said to have learned one million.[19] These two were indeed exceptional in the amount of material that they memorized, but they seem not to have been exceptional at all, either among faculty or students, in regarding memorization as basic and in acting on the belief.

As the "science of Tradition" became more elaborate, it gradually became the basis of the curriculum—though of course the Quran was never displaced. And later, as will be seen, the curriculum became fixed into ten subjects.

The Nizamiyah was the model for many similar foundations: Totah mentions[25] some two hundred thirty-eight higher schools and records the fact that whenever a school was founded some kind of productive investment was made for it by way of endowment. In all, or almost all, cases, it was real estate that would yield a more or less regular income; Saladin, for example, endowed one of the schools in Cairo with thirty-two shops and one in Jerusalem with a whole street.

From the time of their foundation until at least the twelfth century the great schools in Iraq were the centers of learning in the Islamic world: they influenced the schools, both in curriculum and organization, of Egypt and of Spain and, later, of India. The original two divisions into liberal arts and government seem to have persisted.[26]

The Nizamiyah was renovated and reorganized at the beginning of the twelfth century; it was the most splendid of the thirty or more colleges in Baghdad at the end of that century; it survived the sack of the city A.D. 1258 by Hulagu and the second Mongol conquest under Timur Lane A.D. 1393; it had finally ceased to exist by about A.D. 1800.[27]

The finally developed curriculum of these higher schools included the Quran, Arabic literature, history, mathematics, and some music, law, and jurisprudence. A certificate or license from one of them conferred on the graduate the title of Doctor of Law and Tradition and opened to him a career as a judge, or professor, or mosque preacher, or mufti, that is the head of the local group of those who were "wise in the law," the chief jurist.

By the time of the dominance of the Ottoman Turks, the school system had become fixed into three grades: the primary schools, the colleges, and the higher colleges, of university grade. The primary schools were still attached to the mosques and many of them were supported by endowments, generally, although not always, given by the state. The basic curriculum of the primary schools continued to be the Quran and reading, writing, grammar, and arithmetic, with some Arabic literature other than the Quran. The curriculum of the colleges included the fixed ten subjects: grammar, syntax, logic, metaphysics, philology, tropics, stylistics, rhetoric, geometry, and astronomy (can one detect in this course the influence of Hellenistic rhetorical studies?); the higher colleges or universities taught the whole group of sciences connected with the Quran and the Tradition, that is, law and theology.[28]

There was no compulsory education, but it appears that educational opportunity was open to any Muslim child who lived in a town that was large enough to support a mosque and a mosque school. Primary education was free, being largely state supported, and in some cases some of the students were fed and lodged. The students in the colleges and universities were also partially supported. Upon completing the college the graduate received a sort of degree and was called *Danishmend* (this term appears in several of the early sources as *Talisman*);[28] they were now entitled to teach in primary schools or to assume certain ecclesiastical duties.

Students who sought careers as jurists had to take the law course offered in the higher schools. This course gave an intensive further training in the Quran, Quranic exegesis, the Tradition and its interpretation, together with a study of the law as it had gradually become fixed for Islam since the time of the Prophet. In the beginning it had been chiefly in Medina that speculation and theorizing had originated, and Medina, after the removal of the seat of the caliphate to Damascus and then to Baghdad, had not been at the center of public affairs. Hence at the outset much of the legal theory had been only theory, developed without reference to the actual circumstances of the application of the law. And this is why so much of Muslim law remained purely theoretic and included so many principles that were rarely, if ever, applied.[29] And it is why there was a need for the work of the muftis.

When the student had finished the higher law course he was examined personally by the mufti and, if he passed the examination, could become a professor in one of the colleges. Or he could, with some further study, aspire to become a mufti himself. The jurists were of two grades: those who were actual judges and tried cases, and those who were members of the body of "men learned in the law," that is, muftis. A mufti was assigned as an associate to the trial judge in every important city. Whenever a case required a learned knowledge of the law, the trial judge of a private citizen could submit the question in writing to the mufti. It was his duty to give an answer that applied the law to the case. Muftis, like professors, enjoyed a very high degree of esteem and prestige, as well as a high income.[28]

Under the Ottomans these schools—primary, college, and higher—did not supply any of the officers of the government or administration except those who applied and ruled on the Muslim law. All government officials were trained under that remarkable and unique educational institution, the Osmanli slave household, which will be treated separately below.

In Spain, Muslim primary education was the same as that in other Muslim lands except that it was mainly a private, not a state, matter. Yet it was so widespread that a large percentage of Spanish Muslims could read and write. And in Spain the elementary teacher enjoyed a higher place in the social scale than he did in other Muslim lands. Also, girls were far more frequently found in the elementary schools.

The basic curriculum of the colleges and higher schools was the same, or very nearly the same, as it was in other lands: it provided training both for private careers and for official appointment under the government. A number of the more important towns—Cordova, Malaga, Seville, Granada—had higher schools of university grade. At Cordova, according to Hitti,[30] the enrollment "must have reached into the thousands" and the certificate of graduation from it, and certificates from the other universities, led to the most important and lucrative positions both under the government and in private life.

Although the basic curriculum of the Spanish Muslim universities was the same as that in other Muslim lands, in some of them, especially Granada and Cordova, there were advanced courses or departments in botany, astronomy and mathematics, philosophy, medicine, and chemistry. It was in the first four of these subjects that Muslim Spain made the greatest advances—and its greatest contribution to Western learning. But by the beginning of the fifteenth century, the work of the Spanish universities, both in advancing knowledge and in contributing to the West, was done.

One feature of academic life in Spain that may be remarked was the occasional meeting or commemoration, open to students and to the public, in which members of the faculty and, rarely, some others, recited poems of their own composition, or delivered orations or lectures on some subject in which they were especially competent.

In the Muslim centers in India—at Ghazni, Agra, and Delhi—the same system of education was continued: primary, college, and higher schools, with the same basic curricula and, in the higher schools, the same combination of training in the "humanities" and for government posts.

We have seen that Muslim enthusiasm for education was, from the very beginning, great. It continued to be so under the Arab Caliphate, under the Seljuk Turks in Iran and Iraq, under the Ottoman Turks throughout their empire, under the Umayyads in Spain, under the Mamluks in Egypt and in the Muslim world in India. But we have seen also that, from first to last, the basis of all education, both cultural and legal, remained the same: the Quran and the Traditions. The Muslims did, it is true, adopt Greek philosophy and science with enthusiasm, produce a large number of first-rate philosophers and historians and scientists, contribute largely to advances in medicine and mathematics and other subjects, and create a culture of a very high order. But after the fixing of the curriculum of the colleges into the ten subjects and with the development of their teaching methods into final form under the Osmanlis, no change in either was permitted from century to century. Education was stereotyped under this universal state and the whole system, which now looked backwards rather than forwards, and which "had once carried its earnest pupils to the forefront of human knowledge was in time to hold them firmly at a stage which the rest of the world had long passed through and left far behind."[31]

In other Muslim lands the core of the curriculum was always the same and, since it was, education looked backwards to the Revelation and the Traditions. A concomitant was of course a reluctance to adopt innovations and a dependence upon theology. One illustration of the reluctance to adopt innovations may be seen in the Muslim refusal to print their books. They quickly adopted paper as soon as they became acquainted with it, and they produced books in very large numbers all over the Muslim world; so it might have been expected that they would have adopted printing as it was made available to them. Block printing was in use in Europe at the beginning of the fifteenth century (image prints and playing cards seem to have been the earliest items printed) and by the middle of the century, Gutenberg had, four hundred years after its invention in China, invented movable type. But Muslims refused printing. After, and in spite of, a great deal of opposition to the project, the first press was set up in Constantinople in 1729 and from it came a history of Egypt. The appearance of the book aroused such a storm of further opposition that the press was abandoned, all further attempts were given up, and no book was printed in Muslim lands until the year 1825, when a press was set up in Cairo.[32]

12. *The Early Period of the*
Western Civilization

We have seen[1] that towards the end of the Hellenic Civilization, three types of Christian schools appeared: the monastic, the episcopal, and the parish.

In Western monasticism from the beginning, the importance of a knowledge of reading and writing for all monks and nuns had been emphasized because the reading of the Scriptures and of the daily Office was deemed indispensable to the devout life, and because it was considered a part of the duty of monks to make copies of the manuscripts of the divine word and of other Christian writings.[2] Thus, in an early (A.D. 534) rule for nuns it was laid down that they were all to learn to read, were to spend two hours each day in reading, and were to copy manuscripts. Similar prescriptions appear in other sixth- and seventh-century rules for nuns. The several sixth-century rules for monks made similar prescriptions, but more emphatically; and the Benedictine Rule, which came to dominate monasticism in the West, set out in detail the requirements for the education of children and for the means and tools of writing and reading. Latin— Church Latin—was of course the language, but the texts that were read included none of the Latin classics—only Christian writings.

The second type of school was the episcopal school.[2] The bishops always had around them a group of young men and boys as assistants, the children acting as lectors. Through the attendance on and association with the bishops these youths learned, more or less by the apprenticeship method, what they came to know of Canon Law and dogma and liturgy. After the collapse of the Roman social and political system and of the classical schools, these attendants no longer had a grounding in elementary education or in secular culture, and it therefore became necessary for bishops sometimes to give elementary education as it was generally necessary for them to give the specialized theological and dogmatic training. This was the beginning, in the sixth and seventh centuries, of the episcopal school, which later, in some instances, developed into a university.

The third type of Christian school was the parish or presbyterial school. When the waves of barbarians broke over the Roman world and the tide of barbarism threatened to engulf the social and cultural and educational systems, and as the number of Christian converts had increased, the very continuity of the Christian life through the priesthood was threatened, for the supply of priests was endangered. The answer was to make an adaptation of the system already in use in the episcopal schools: the Second Council of Vaison, A.D. 529, enjoined "all parish priests to gather some boys around them as lectors, so that they may give them a Christian upbringing, teach them the Psalms and the lessons of Scripture and the whole Law of the Lord and so prepare worthy successors to themselves."[3] It appears that a similar action had already been taken in Italy, and was taken later in Gaul. Marrou remarks[3] that this action was a "memorable" one, for it marked the beginning of what was later to develop into the ordinary village school in which the two functions of teacher and village priest were "intimately associated"—an institution new with the West, unknown in any general or systematic form to the Hellenic society.

All three of these schools were limited in range and purpose: they were to produce monks and clerics. But as the secular schools disappeared they remained, throughout the interregnum between the dissolution of the Hellenic society and the appearance of the Western, the only carriers of culture. The level of culture was as low, during the interregnum, as it ever became: what was taught was only reading and writing, learning a part of the Bible, or at least the Psalms, by heart, and a minimum knowledge of dogma, Canon Law, and liturgics. There were a very few who had somehow retained some knowledge of the Latin classics, but the general attitude of schoolmasters in the West during the interregnum was to avoid all mention of the pagan, devil-inspired culture of the classical world. If even the bishop, in the episcopal school, took too much trouble over the teaching of grammar, he was apt to cause a scandal, for the pagan classical schoolmasters had emphasized grammar, and Christian teachers should dwell only on the Scripture. The cultural level was so low, and literacy limited to so few, that the school teacher had become a "shadowy figure who had mastered the mysterious secret of how to write."[4]

In Italy the classical schools persisted longer than they did in the rest of the Roman West: there were still teachers of grammar, rhetoric, law, and medicine in the city of Rome as late as the middle of the sixth century. But then, in the latter half of the century, came the Lombards, and, during the seventh century, education and culture in Italy reached as low a level as in Merovingian Gaul. The secular school collapsed, but the church monastic and episcopal schools continued. The collapse of the secular schools was not, however, altogether complete: there continued intermittently to be schools for laymen taught by laymen in many of the important towns. Instruction, though on a low level, was given in grammar and law, in the art of writing letters and drawing documents.[5] And the Irish monasteries were founded in Italy and Gaul and Germany in the early seventh century.[6]

From the last quarter of the seventh century may be dated the appearance of the Western as a civilization independent of its sister society, the Orthodox Christian, and of its parent, the Hellenic. During the first century of its growth the only education, other than that ubiquitous and omnipresent apprenticeship education, was given in the monastic and parish and episcopal schools and thus was established the intimate connection between the church and the school. This connection was stereotyped by the legislation of Charlemagne and the Palace School that he established.[7]

The relevant legislation was the enactment that "every Monastery and every Cathedral should have a school for the education of young clerks."[7] Further, now, for the first time, the monastic schools admitted students who were not to become monks, although the cathedral or episcopal schools continued to serve exclusively for future clerics. The foundation of the Palace School (c. A.D. 781) with the great Alcuin at its head, and with the most learned scholars of the day on its faculty, was intended primarily as a seminary for the training of future bishops and abbots of the Carolingian Empire. The maximum secular knowledge taught in any of the schools was the seven "liberal arts" of the Trivium and Quadrivium.[8] The Trivium included grammar, which used some literature by way of illustration, and rhetoric and dialectic. The Quadrivium included arithmetic, geometry, astronomy, and music. In Alcuin's time only Aristotle's *De Interpretatione* and the translations of Porphyry were known; of Plato, only three dialogues were known: the *Timaeus, Phaedo, and Meno*—all in the Latin of Boethius.

Although the knowledge of Plato was fragmentary and obscured by the translation, yet the obscure fragments gave a hint of the doctrine of Ideas,[9] and the influence of this doctrine was very great:[10] it gave focus to the question that was to become the absorbing intellectual interest of later scholastic thought, the question of the reality of universals. At this early stage, "the one stimulating and interesting morsel" of intellectual food that had been saved from the "wreckage of a by-gone civilization" and that could be set before the hungry intellect of the ninth-century student was the morsel of logic.[10] Aristotle's book supplied that morsel of logic and Plato's dialogues gave the hints about his doctrine of Ideas; Aristotle was the source of the dialectical method, and Plato had raised the question about the importance and status of the universals, the Ideas.

The question did not come into prominence until the issues of the conflict were brought out by Eriugena[11] about the middle of the ninth century, and the major controversies did not appear until the eleventh and twelfth centuries, but the ground for the prolonged discussion was laid already at the opening of the ninth century, for "at the very threshold of Logic the student was encountered by this question of the reality of Universals—on the face of it (as it is apt to appear to the modern mind) a dry, abstract, uninviting topic. . . . Yet no sooner does he approach it than the student finds himself led by imperceptible steps from Logic into Physics, and from Physics into Metaphysics, and from Metaphysics into Theology. Indeed, the solution of the most momentous questions to which the human intellect can address itself is inextricably bound up with the solution of a question which 'common-sense' will undertake to clear up in five minutes, or which it will indignantly pronounce too trifling to be asked or answered. Yet he who has given his answer to it, has implicitly constructed his theory of the Universe."[12]

With Roscellinus (c. A.D. 1100) and his "pure, unadulterated, extravagant nominalism" appears the "first wholly new idea" in philosophic thought since Eriugena.[13] From him the speculative impulse was transmitted to Abelard, and Abelard inaugurated the intellectual movement out of which the French universities sprang. Abelard was a professor at the cathedral school in Paris.

However, probably the earliest of the Medieval Western schools that could be called a university was the school at Salerno. Already in the tenth century the city was famous for the skill of its physicians. The famous physicians seem to have attracted students to themselves so that by the first half of the twelfth century some kind of organized teacher-student association was described as "existing from ancient times." Of the eleventh century revival of interest in legal, theological, dialectical, and medical studies, that in medicine appears to have been the earliest. This interest, together with the beginnings of medical instruction in Salerno, led to the establishment, in the twelfth century, of the "university"—which was primarily or purely a medical school.[14] Salerno was the one exception to the general rule that southern Italy took no part in the great intellectual movements of the twelfth, thirteenth, and fourteenth centuries.

In northern Italy, as we have seen, lay schools for lay students had continued a precarious and intermittent existence during and after the Lombard invasions. And the study of Roman law had continued and appears to have been amalgamated with the ordinary curriculum. The study of grammar and rhetoric was regarded rather as an aid to the preparation of legal documents than as a preliminary to the further study of the Scriptures and the Fathers. Already by about A.D. 1000 Bologna[15] was a center of studies and had begun to attract some scholars from outside the city; and later in the eleventh century, the study of law had begun to be a professional study separate from that legal study which was a part of general education. About A.D. 1142 the *Decretum* of Gratian, a codification of Canon Law, was published. It was almost immediately adopted as the recognized authority and textbook by teachers and by the ecclesiastical courts. During the latter part of the eleventh century and the whole of the twelfth century foreign students, both from Italian cities other than Bologna and from other lands, chiefly Germany, flocked to Bologna for the study of law.

A majority of the Italian students and all of the other students in Bologna were, as resident aliens, without civic rights in the city. Citizenship in an Italian town of the age was an hereditary possession of great importance, and in the absence of an express agreement or treaty between two towns, no citizen of one had rights in another. Hence the prolonged exile of studentship from one's own city was a serious penalty. Further, many of the students at Bologna were mature men of good family and high social position in their own cities. And finally, in the course of the eleventh and twelfth centuries throughout the cities of Europe there was a great movement towards the formation of associations of all kinds, notably into the guilds. As a consequence of the operation of these several factors, the alien students resident in Bologna organized themselves into associations that were particular kinds of guilds—*collegia*. As the numbers of students in the guilds increased they became more and more important to the commercial welfare of the city and were recognized by the city as duly constituted legal associations with rights of their own; and thus the student members secured for themselves a kind of artificial citizenship in the city of their temporary adoption and in place of the native citizenship they had temporarily renounced by leaving their own city.

The legal authority of the student guild (as of other guilds) over its members was based on the oath taken by each member. To break the oath was to commit perjury, and perjury was a mortal sin; the guild was therefore able to exercise considerable authority over its members. These associations or guilds of students at Bologna were the "universities." The term "university" did not, in the twelfth and thirteenth centuries, mean a place where all subjects were taught: it meant merely an aggregate of persons, or, in a somewhat more technical sense, a legal corporation. The phrase *universitas vestra* when addressed to a group of persons meant merely "the whole of you." Thus the universities at Bologna were guilds of foreign scholars; the purposes of the universities were the same as those of other guilds: a part of the statutes of the German Nation or German University in Bologna states the object as the cultivation of "fraternal charity, mutual association and amity, the consolation of the sick and support of the needy, the conduct of funerals and the extirpation of rancour and quarrels, the attendance and escort of our Doctorandi to and from the place of examinations, and the spiritual advantage of members." The first allusion to a student university in Bologna dates from A.D. 1174. By the end of the century the universities were extremely powerful: professors and townspeople alike could be controlled by a corporation which could destroy the income of the former and the trade of the latter by the simple expedient of migrating to another town. And the threat of migration was a real threat: a half-dozen late twelfth- and thirteenth-century schools were founded as offshoots of a parent school by student migrations. In course of time the universities acquired control over the professors and over the curriculum, as they already had control over certain aspects of the conduct of their members— for example, as regards entertaining and gambling.

Thus the school at Bologna arose out of the universities of students; these universities were the controlling authority over the life of the school and the professors and curriculum, and were influential in the affairs of the city. The twelfth-century student wandered from school to school, from subject to subject, and from master to master at his pleasure. In his wanderings he would have acquired the seven subjects of the Trivium and Quadrivium and would eventually have stood a kind of examination in which he publicly defended a thesis. If the examination were successfully passed, then he himself could, with further work, qualify as a teacher and could assume, after the completion of the advanced work, either or all of the three synonymous titles[16] of Master, Doctor, Professor.

Bologna was one of the two archetypal universities: Paris was the other. Rashdall holds that Paris and Bologna "might almost be said to be the only *original* Universities: Paris supplied the model for the Universities of Masters, Bologna for the Universities of students."[17]

In France, in the time of Charlemagne, the Palace School had not been located in Paris: the school was probably migratory, moving from place to place as the great Charles himself moved. After Charles, education was confined to the cathedral and monastery schools. By the opening of the eleventh century the most important school was the Cathedral School at Chartres. At Chartres during the first quarter of the century under Bishop Fulbert the Trivium and Quadrivium constituted the curriculum.[18]

The teaching of grammar included literature by way of illustration and used Donatus as the textbook for beginners, Priscianus for the more advanced. The teaching of dialectic used the logical works of Aristotle, Porphyry's *Introduction,* Cicero's *Topica* and Boethius's discussion of logical categories and the kinds of syllogisms as commentaries on the main texts. In arithmetic and geometry, Boethius was again the textbook; astronomy had for its practical object the computation of the church calendar; music seems to have been studied rather intensively. These seven liberal arts were the handmaids of theology, which was the queen of the sciences. Some of Canon Law, Roman Law, and Charlemagne's laws appear to have been included in the higher study of theology, which not only expounded the Scriptures but was also concerned with the philosophic-theological controversies of the age.

Towards the close of the eleventh century the reputation of the Cathedral School in Paris had begun to increase, and after Abelard's professorship there, Paris became a city of teachers. One of the great educational movements of the eleventh century was the gradual transfer of teaching activity from the monks to the secular clergy, chiefly because the old Benedictine and Cluniac monasteries had in so many cases sunk into "rich corporations of celibate landed proprietors, whose highest ambition was the aggrandizement of the house to which they belonged."[19] The secular clergy teaching in Paris in the twelfth century had organized themselves into a Guild of Masters of which the first mention occurs c. A.D. 1170. This date may be taken as marking the beginning of the university there. There were no written statutes for the university until about 1208, although the first "town versus gown" riots occurred in 1200. At some time during the first quarter of the thirteenth century the first "nation" organizations came into existence and, during the second quarter, a common rectorship was set up by the United Nations. The four student nations at Paris were the French (which included all Latins), Normans, Picards (which included the whole of the Low Countries), and English (which included the Germans). The rector gradually emerged as the head of the university.

It should perhaps be added that Paris was also the home of the "collegiate" system: about 1257 Robert de Sorbonne, chaplain to the king, founded the "college" or "house" of Sorbonne as a college for sixteen men, four from each nation, who had already taken the master's degree and wanted to go on with the advanced studies that led to the Theological Doctorate. By the sixteenth century "the Sorbonne" included the whole Theological Faculty of Paris.

A second French university was founded at Montpellier in the twelfth century on the model of the school at Paris—a university of Masters.

In England, Oxford seems to have originated in a migration of students and masters of the English Nation from Paris about A.D. 1167; in 1209 a migration from Oxford founded the university at Cambridge.

Thus by the end of the twelfth century there were six universities in the West: Salerno, Bologna, Reggio (founded by migration from Bologna), Paris, Montpellier, and Oxford. In the thirteenth century in Italy four original university foundation were established and four more by student migrations; in France three new universities were established, in England, Cambridge; in Spain and Portugal, four.

In the thirteenth century the term *Studium Generale* came into general use, and this is the term that perhaps most closely corresponds to the vague British and American idea of a "university." The *Studium Generale* at this time meant, not a place where all subjects were studied, but an institution with three characteristics: it had students from all parts, it had a plurality of Masters, and it had at least one of the higher Faculties, i.e., Theology or Law or Medicine. By the fourteenth century popes and emperors were founding universities by bull and charter, and Rashdall[20] excludes from the "category of universities all bodies" which came into existence after A.D. 1300 that were not founded by pope or emperor. In the fourteenth century there were five papal and two imperial foundations in Italy, three papal and one imperial in France, none in England, one papal foundation and two by royal charter in Spain, as well as papal foundations in Prague, Vienna, Erfurt, Heidelberg, Cologne, Cracow, and Buda, and Fünfkirchen in Hungary (the two latter foundations were extinct within a century). The fifteenth century witnessed the foundation of two more universities in Italy, nine in France, three in Scotland, seven in Spain, eleven in Germany and Switzerland, as well as one at Pressburg (Poszony) in Hungary and one each at Upsala and Copenhagen. Thus the total number of twelfth-century universities was six; thirteenth century, sixteen; fourteenth century, twenty-two; and fifteenth century, thirty-five; giving a grand total of seventy-six for the four centuries.

In the twelfth and thirteenth centuries the larger universities probably had between two and five thousand students each and the number at the largest—Paris and Bologna—in later centuries probably never exceeded six or possibly seven thousands.

During the first three "university centuries" there was no student discipline as it is known in academic institutions today; students entered the university—after the beginnings at Bologna—at an average age of between fourteen and seventeen years; they all, in all universities, spoke Latin, and they all, or nearly all, wandered from university to university and from teacher to teacher. As a result, intercourse between the different universities in different parts of Europe was perhaps easier then than at any later date, and the spread of ideas from one center to another occurred perhaps more readily. Further, on the whole, students seem to have been rather more eager to learn than masters were to teach, so that in the student universities instruction was probably better and the various chairs more competently filled than in the universities of Masters.

We have seen that the chief purpose of the Carolingian schools had been the production of clerics, that the rudiments of the seven liberal arts represented the maximum knowledge of the time, that they were regarded as preliminary to the study of the Scriptures, and that, of the whole curriculum of studies, logic was the item that was most interesting and exciting to the student. We have seen also that only fragments of the writings of Plato and Aristotle were available to the scholars of the time. During the ninth and tenth centuries logic continued to be the "one stimulating and interesting morsel" that could be offered to the student, no more of Plato or Aristotle came to the attention of the West, and the intellectual fare continued to be chiefly the Scriptures and the writings of the Western Church Fathers.

The primary intellectual interest of the Fathers had of course been the Christian faith and the dominant attitude was that the Scriptures, rightly interpreted, contained all knowledge necessary for salvation and, indeed, all knowledge that men required or should seek to acquire. This attitude and this interest did not of course stifle all inquiry about history and nature, but it did relegate all knowledge other than that clearly related to the Scriptures and their interpretation to a secondary and subservient place. This attitude and this interest, on the whole, were taken up and continued during the centuries immediately following the emergence of the West as a separate civilization. As a consequence, there was little interest in the observation or investigation of the natural world, in the discovery of facts.

That "wonderful deepening and broadening of the stream of human culture"[21] in the late eleventh and twelfth centuries found its characteristic expression in Italy in the greatly increased interest in the study of law and resulted in the rise of the University of Bologna and its offshoots in other cities. In France the twelfth-century renaissance found its characteristic expression in the "great outburst of dialectical and theological speculation" that did not originate in Paris but found its ultimate home there, and resulted in the rise of the University of Paris and its offshoots elsewhere. In both France and Italy the intellectual movement was primarily, although not wholly, secular. The late eleventh- and early twelfth-century speculations in France were original with the West and were creative to a remarkable degree. But by the beginning of the thirteenth century and largely in consequence of the opening up of communications with the Orthodox Christian and Islamic worlds during the Crusades and after, the whole of the works of Aristotle were making their way into the West.

The creative originality of the twelfth century was stifled under the weight of the works and thought of "The Philosopher," whose pronouncements were accepted as authoritative.[22] In the thirteenth century, as soon as the student had the rules of grammar and enough Latin for ordinary use, he set to work mastering the semi-technical but unliterary language of logical disputation so that he could enter into the dialectical fray of the schools. The acquisition of the works of Aristotle enormously widened the range of dialectical and logical studies, but intensified the method. The method of mastering a subject, after the rudiments of the seven arts had been learned, was the method of disputation. Robert of Sorbonne said that "nothing is known perfectly which has not been masticated by the teeth of disputation" and his assertion was but a reflection of the consensus of the time. The student was always ready to dispute the thesis of any opponent and to defend any prescribed thesis. The study of grammar sank to a subsidiary place, that of rhetoric sank almost as low, the classics were not taken up at all: all attention was devoted to logic and to Aristotle, and "henceforth the poets, the historians, the orators of ancient Rome were considered unworthy the attention of ripe students of 14 or 16 in the University Schools."[23]

The education given at the universities in the seven arts in the thirteenth and later centuries was secular: "A student in the Arts would have been as little likely to read the Bible as he would be to dip into Justinian or Hippocrates."[24] The church provided little professional education for the future priest and less for the ordinary layman; even the bishops seem, in so far as they required any real standard of learning from candidates for holy orders, to have insisted mainly on secular learning."[24] Seminaries for priests, catechisms, instruction and preparation for the first communion, and so on, are the product of Counter-Reformation, not of the education, clerical or other, of these centuries.

This, in very brief, was the educational situation in the West until the rise of modern Western science, the elevation of the vernaculars to the dignity of literary languages, and the emergence of individualism with that literary and artistic revival called "*the* Renaissance."

The legacy of these early medieval Western universities to the educational ideals and standards of the modern West is enormous. Rashdall[25] is emphatic in showing that if the term "university" is appropriate for a modern Harvard or Oxford or Heidelberg or a medieval Paris or Bologna or Cambridge, it cannot be applied in the same sense to any school of antiquity. The ideas that teachers should be united into a corporate body, that teachers of different subjects should teach in the same place and be joined by a single institution, that an attempt should be made to have the body of teachers represent all human knowledge, that studies should be grouped into different faculties, that students should, after their preliminary training, confine themselves, at least partially, to one faculty or department—all this derives from the great twelfth- and thirteen-century academic foundations.

It should be added that the kings and princes of the Middle Ages got their statesmen and civil servants from the universities. Thus again, it was a literary and philosophical training that seemed to qualify a man for the affairs of the world.

III. In One Abortive and Two Arrested Civilizations

13. The Abortive Far Western Christian Civilization

When the Romans of the empire occupied the British Isles they did not succeed in imposing effective rule on the Celts of "the Celtic Fringe" in Ireland, in what is now Wales, and the rural districts of what is now England. Patrick had introduced Christianity to the Celts in Ireland in the first half of the fifth century; then the English (Angles and Saxons and Jutes) invasions had the effect of segregating—though not of wholly insulating—Ireland from the continent. The Celts of Ireland, in response to the double social challenge of the disintegrating Hellenic Civilization and the nascent Western Civilization, originated a civilization of their own, and their originality is manifest in their church organization, literature and art, and their ritual and hagiography.[1]

The Irish Church—and Irish monasticism, for they were one and the same thing[2]—was organized on a tribal, autonomous, and cellular basis in accordance with the local social system. A monastic cell was established in many, or most, of the districts of Ireland; around the nucleus or mother-foundation arose daughter-foundations that were federated with it; the initiative in founding the monasteries was often taken by the local chieftain; the abbot, as head of the mother-foundation, was the chieftain of an ecclesiastical clan, most of whose members were descended from the same common ancestor as himself. The Latin name that the Irish gave to these monastery-clusters was *civitates*—the name for the Hellenic city-states that, after they were Christianized, had become the sees of bishops—though the Irish *civitates* differed from their continental namesakes in that they were monasteries, not towns. Further, in the Irish monastery or monastery-cluster, the office of bishop was sometimes held by the hereditary abbot and sometimes by a "tame" bishop who lived in the monastery and was subject to the abbot's control. The abbot was the administrative head of the Irish *civitas* and this executive function was so characteristic that the term "abbot" came to mean executive authority of any kind.[3]

The abbot's functions were thus those of the chieftain of a clan; and, as clan chieftains were not always the eldest sons of chieftains but were chosen from the chieftain's family on the basis of personal fitness, so also were abbots chosen. Thus in the Irish Church there were no strict lines of hierarchic authority, as in the Roman Church, nor were there territories of episcopal jurisdiction; there were even bishops without dioceses.

The Irish adopted a peculiar non-Roman form of tonsure, possibly from the Druids;[4] and they developed their own hagiography in which Irish saints were given a place of equal eminence with the most exalted figures in the Bible: Patrick ranked as high as Moses, and Bridget as high as the Virgin Mary.[5]

About the middle of the fifth century there was established at Armagh in Ireland, probably by Patrick, a school to train young men for the priesthood. During the next three-quarters of a century some sixteen schools were established; like the first school, these were probably originally ecclesiastical seminaries that were later converted into monastic schools.

The heart of the Irish monastery, and of the monasteries that the Irish established on the continent, was the monastic school with its accompanying scriptorium and library. These schools in Ireland became centers of instruction that drew students from all over the land and even from abroad. From the seventh century the Irish monastic schools were the chief centers of learning, both in their native land and on the continent. The primary knowledge sought was that of the "science of the Scriptures." The libraries seem to have had large holdings in manuscripts, especially of Biblical texts, the scholars were well grounded in their subjects, and, in some of the schools at least, it appears that students were given not only books but also board and lodging.[6]

Religious and literary education were carried on concurrently and simultaneously: the "liberal arts" studies of the Latin (and, a little later, Greek) languages and secular literature had in theory the purpose of rendering the mind fit for "the study of the divine thought" of the Scriptures and of the Christian tradition. There seems to have been no suspicion attached to the Hellenic classics and no idea that they might conflict in teaching the Bible. This, of course, stood in contrast to the attitude of the contemporary Roman Catholic monasteries on the continent.[6] On the continent, pagan secular literature was associated with the pre-Christian attitudes and beliefs and with the state of society that Christianity had tried to reform and transfigure. The Irish, having not previously known the pre-Christian Hellenic society and culture, had formed no such associations and regarded Latin as only the language of the church.[7]

According to Graham,[8] the characteristics of the Irish monastic school were derived from the three different and distinct elements from which their tradition and training were derived: the native Irish culture, Christianity, and Hellenic culture.

Before the introduction of Christianity, the Celts of Ireland had developed a code of laws that proved, in the event, to be adaptable to the requirements of the society after it had become Christianized. Already native learning had been actively cultivated and a learned class had arisen. This class was that of the Druids (priests, poets, historians, judges, bards) whose functions had, by Patrick's time, become specialized. The Druids had a knowledge of letters, they wrote down their learning in books, and they cut inscriptions in wood and on stone.[8]

A late third-century king of Ireland is said to have founded three schools, one of military science, one of law, and the third of general literature. The third seems to have been the native predecessor and precursor of the lay school that arose after the introduction of Christianity. The first two were apparently exclusively professional, and the third seems to have developed also into the "Bardic School" in which poetry, history, and vernacular literature were taught. It was attended by two different groups of students: those who were seeking admission to the Bardic Order, and those who were seeking a general liberal education.

The members of the Bardic Order had, by the third quarter of the sixth century, become so numerous and their various demands so exacting that the abolition of the order was contemplated. It was, however, not abolished but, instead, the system of public secular education was reformed and reorganized. The order was saved by a Christian saint, Columba, who had received a part of his education in a Bardic school, and the reorganization plan was devised by a secular priest. The plan provided for a college in each of five provinces. Under each college were district schools; all schools were endowed with lands and each was headed by a distinguished lay scholar. Tuition was free. The several subjects in these schools—law, poetry, history—were commonly taught by members of the same family through successive generations.[8]

It seems that between these lay schools and the Christian monastic schools there was no antagonism. The monastic schools gave instruction in both Latin and the vernacular, in both literatures, and in both as leading to the divine knowledge. The student bodies in the monastic schools included not only those who had the intention of becoming monks but also those who intended to remain laymen but desired a wider general education.

Some children were entered in the monastery schools at a very early age, others at adolescence. There were, consequently two divisions: the one for the very young, the other for adolescents and older children. Nuns often took care of the young, who began their schooling proper at about the age of six or seven. The boys lived in the monastery and were taught only by the monks. They were tonsured and given ecclesiastical dress, unless their parents objected. They followed all the ascetic practices except fasting, took part in religious services, and did manual work within their capacity. The essential aim of their education was to teach them the Christian virtues and the ecclesiastical discipline, but a certain amount of literary instruction was always connected with this religious training.[9]

Upon entrance into the monastery the child was taken over by a monk who became his master; student and master lived beside each other, the student learned from the master both by the apprenticeship method and by systematic instruction. Some masters had two pupils, but the usual arrangement seems to have been the tutorial, with one master for each student. There appear to have been "classes" for instruction only in the cases of a very few outstanding teachers who attracted students—or disciples—in such numbers that it was impossible to give individual instruction to them all. But even where there were classes the personal relationship between master and student was emphasized. Sometimes a more advanced student might become the teacher of one less advanced, but in such cases, the elder student appears to have taught only reading. The monastic schools seem always to have retained the tutorial tradition of close personal association between the teacher and the student.[9]

This tutorial tradition had a firm basis in the ancient Irish custom of fosterage: a child would be entrusted as a foster son to a tutor who formally took over the care and responsibility for his charge as if the latter were his own son. The foster parent prepared and tutored his foster son for his future profession, and the relationship between the two was always close and personal. In return for the fatherly care and instruction that he received certain duties were incumbent upon the foster son: he was to assist his tutor in the latter's old age, and to give him certain material gains earned during the apprenticeship.[10]

In the monastic schools the child's literary training began with the alphabet, followed by a syllabary, and then by selections for reading. The first text was the Psalms. The teacher wrote on the pupil's wax-coated wooden tablet a psalm; the pupil then read it, copied it, and finally memorized it. Only when the student had mastered all of the Psalter did he pass on to the rest of the Scriptures. The teacher took occasion in the lessons to comment on the texts. The more advanced students seem to have been given some slight instruction in arithmetic and astronomy and possibly in some other subjects.[9]

Elementary studies seem to have ended at this point and it appears that the majority of students did not go further. But for the gifted and scholarly, the Irish monasteries of the time offered opportunities for learning unrivalled elsewhere. There is no accurate information about the number of volumes or manuscripts in the libraries of the Irish monastic schools, but the holdings of the libraries of the continental monasteries that had been founded by Irish monks suggest that they were large: St. Gall in the ninth century had over five hundred volumes, and Bobbio in the tenth about seven hundred. In these collections Greek and Latin classics were well represented.[10]

The Irish copyists had developed a characteristic script that was based on the Roman half-uncial. This script was carried abroad with Irish learning, and manuscripts in England, Switzerland, and Italy testify to its wide currency.

Another unique characteristic of Irish monasticism was its missionary fervor. Within a very short time after the foundation of the first monastery in the fifth century, there were monasteries in nearly every district in Ireland. In the sixth century Irish missionary-monks had founded monasteries in Scotland at Iona and in Britain at Lindisfarne, and in the early seventh century, on the continent at St. Gall in German territory, in Bobbio in Italy, and at Annegray, Luxeuil, and Fontaines.

And this original missionary fervor and the fervor for learning was not exhausted in the sixth and seventh centuries: Irish learning kept its vivifying power and gave again in the ninth century the stimulus it had afforded the continent in the seventh. On the continent the so-called "Carolingian Renaissance" of the late eighth and early ninth century borrowed heavily from the Irish. Among the foreign scholars summoned by Charlemagne to his court and school were several notable Irish scholars. Outstanding among them all in the ninth century was the very great John Scotus Eriugena—perhaps the first Western scholar with a mastery of Greek. Another nine-century Irish scholar, one Sedulius Scotus, was also a Greek scholar, an outstanding poet, and a man of encyclopedic knowledge as well. It seems certain that these two Irishmen had learned their Greek in Ireland and that Greek was taught in the Irish schools in the ninth century, although the channel through which the Irish acquired their knowledge of Greek remains a mystery.[6]

Alcuin, the architect of Charlemagne's educational plans, had high praise for the Irish monks for their services to the church in Britain and Gaul and Italy; most of the influential churchmen of the continent welcomed and encouraged the Irish scholar-monks. Gougaud[11] summarizes the work of the Irish on the continent in the ninth century: "During the reigns of the great emperor (Charlemagne) and his successors, the Irish taught the Franks orthography and grammar; they commented on the Scriptures; they brought from their island biblical and liturgical manuscripts, collections of canons and penitentials; above all, they copied many books on the continent. The libraries of continental Europe preserve to the present day a large number of such books which they scattered along their route— and whither did they not make their way? Especially great was the wealth of codices of Irish origin possessed by the libraries of Bobbio, St. Gall and Reichenau."

Thus the Irish Church grew and pospered in almost complete independence of Rome. This was of course made possible by its geographical remoteness and the fact that the Anglo-Saxon invasions of Britain in the fifth century interposed an insular barrier between Ireland and the Holy See. The whole monastic organization of the Irish Church was a standing offense to the carefully regulated authority of Rome and the two met in inevitable conflict when the adherents of the Roman Church, which had been introduced into Britain by St. Augustine, clashed with the leaders of the monasteries of Iona and Lindisfarne, which had been founded in Britain by Irish monks. The climax of the struggle came with the victory of the Church of Rome at the Synod of Whitby, A.D. 664. The nominal points at issue at the synod were the method of calculating the date of Easter and tonsure, but the real issue was whether the Church of Rome could or would tolerate the existence of a semi-autonomous rival which did not follow the Roman discipline and authority. Rome won. The vitality and influence of the Irish Church did not, however, immediately dwindle and die, but lingered on in England for another century. The last recorded mention of the affairs of the Columban Church occurs A.D. 1221.

Thus the challenge of the great and powerful Church of Rome was too severe for the resources of the younger Irish Church and Far Western Christian Civilization; the succeeding challenges of the Viking invasions in the ninth and tenth centuries and the rising political authority of England in the twelfth century rendered abortive the civilization that had begun to grow in the fifth: the challenges were excessive in their severity.

14. The Arrested Spartan Civilization

Two Peculiar Communities

Civilizations come into existence as responses to challenges from the physical environment or from the human environment or from both; challenges from both have ranged from severe to easy; the optimum challenge is a mean between the two extremes; a challenge that verges on the unduly severe is likely to produce a response that immobilizes the responding society, and such a society is said to be "arrested."[1] The Polynesians, Eskimos, and Nomads are all examples of societies that have come into existence as responses to very severe physical challenges, that have attempted and achieved a *tour de force,* and so have been arrested in an early stage of development.[2] Education in these three societies was always by the apprenticeship method.

The two other arrested societies were responses to very severe challenges from the human environment that were produced by extraordinary local conditions—and both produced extraordinary educational systems. These two peculiar communities were the Spartans and the Osmanlis. Because of the similarity between the two challenging human environments, the two responses were, in significant ways, similar.

In both communities the problem was for a very few masters to establish and keep control over a very large number of subjects: Toynbee estimates[3] the ratio of the actual Osmanli ruling institution to the total population at about one to one hundred fifty and that of the

228

whole ruling class to it at about one to fifty; Xenophon estimated[4] the ratio of the ruling class in Sparta to the total population at about one to one hundred. Both ruling classes solved the problem by creating ruling institutions the requirements for admission to which were rigid, in which the education for the rulers was severe, austere, and relentless, and which ruled in a fashion that earned for the masters the bitter hatred of the subjects. Xenophon says that there was not a man among the Spartan subjects but "would be delighted to eat [the masters] alive,"[4] and the hatred of the Greek subject population for their Osmanli masters was shown—among many another instance—by the slaughter of every Osmanli man and woman and child in the Peloponnese by the Greeks there at their first opportunity.[5]

Another characteristic of the two communities was the veil of secrecy that was deliberately drawn before the institutions of the ruling class, and especially the organization and the education. Among the Osmanlis, the students at the schools were immured during the whole period of training and were vowed to secrecy about all the affairs of the schools when they were released, and no outsiders were admitted to the schools at all. In Sparta, a profound obscurity envelops all institutions before the end of the fifth century B.C.[6] and this obscurity was—and is—the result of a deliberate Spartan policy to allow only misleading information to filter through to the outside world. From about the last quarter of the seventh century to about the last quarter of the fifth, none of the many Greeks who referred to or commented upon Sparta was a Spartan, and the philosophers and historians of the fourth century had "even less direct material to work upon than is accessible to modern scholars."[5]

For these reasons, the amount of available information about education in both of these peculiar communities is deplorably scanty, but the intrinsic interest of the two systems, as well as the light they throw on the possibilities of adaptation and training of human beings in extaordinary circumstances, makes it desirable to give brief accounts of what is known about them. Each community succeeded in solving the immediate problem with which it was confronted; the solution was, in each case, an heroic achievement; each was a miracle of determination and ingenuity; but each bore within itself the seeds of its own dissolution, for each "grandly disregarded" the fundamental customs which make up what is called "human nature" and, in the end in each case, human nature reasserted itself and destroyed the system.

We have seen that the Hellenic Civilization as a whole came into being towards the end of the twelfth century B.C. as a response chiefly to the physical challenge of the barren lands of the Aegean islands and coastlands.[7] The Greeks successfully responded to this challenge by establishing themselves in the arable lowlands and developing agriculture sufficiently to feed themselves. But this gave rise to an increase in population such that the available arable lands could no longer sustain it. The solution to this problem that was followed by many of the Greek states was that of getting rid of the surplus population by establishing overseas colonies. During the eighth to the sixth centuries Greeks founded colonies in the toe of Italy, on Sicily, in the Cyrenaica, on the north coast of the Aegean, and as far west as Marseilles.

The solution of overseas colonization, however, was not adopted by the Spartans.[8] They, being a land-locked people, did not take to the sea, but, instead, to the land of their neighbors, the Messenians. The first Messeno-Spartan War—which was contemporary (c. 736–720 B.C.) with the first Greek settlements in Sicily and Thrace—ended with a Spartan victory but not with a completely subdued Messenian people. The Messenians nursed their anger and pride and hatred of the Spartans and rose again seventy years later. After thirty long years of war, the Spartans were again victorious. But they now found themselves under the necessity of maintaining their state in perpetual readiness for war, of training themselves as soldiers and nothing but soldiers, of remaking their state into one permanently organized war. They did this—as did the Osmanlis much later—by taking existing institutions and modifying them so as to fit the needs of the conqueror state.[9] Nilsson regards[9] this adaptation as the work of "one man, or of several men working in the same direction" because everything was made to lead in a purposeful way towards one goal; Chrimes, on the other hand, sees[10] the institutions not as the work of any one man or group of men, but as "a spontaneous growth from conditions of society in a very remote period." Toynbee takes a middle course between these two views and supposes that the Spartan institutions were the result of the work of a series of Spartan statesmen during the century after the outbreak of the Second Messeno-Spartan War, c. 650 B.C.

Under the Osmanlis, as will be seen below, free-born Muslims were excluded from the rule entirely, while under the Spartan institutions, free-born Spartiates bore all the burden of rule. After the second war with the Messenians, the victorious Spartans divided the Messenian land and the Messenian people among themselves. Each Spartiate "peer" received an allotment of land that was calculated to support him and his family and, with the land, a number of Messenian families to work it. These families were bound to the soil as serfs (helots). Thus the Spartiates were freed from the necessity of having to make a living by the sweat of their brows in order to be bound to the necessity of permanent and perpetual military training and service.

Among the Spartiate peers, although there was equality of holdings of Messenian land and serfs, there was not equality of wealth, for some had originally held, and continued to hold, more Spartan land than others. This inequality of wealth, however, could not, under the Spartan institutions, be reflected in differences in the way of life, for all peers, as soldiers, lived the same common life.

The social classes were rigid: at the bottom were the serfs, attached to the hereditary estates of individual peers, with no freedom whatever.[12] Then there were the free-born Spartiates who had not satisfied the requirements for entrance into the select ruling class of peers. These were the "unprivileged" or "inferiors." The elite, the rulers, were the Spartiate peers, the privileged class. There were also two hereditary kings, but now the only substantial power remaining to them was the military command when the army was on active service. At other times the kings and other members of the two royal families led the same life and submitted to the same discipline as did the other peers.

One of the ways in which the Spartan system set at nought the ordinary demands of human nature was in the several devices used to breed soldiers. It sought quantity by penalizing, both legally and socially, the deliberate bachelor and by encouraging the getting of sons: the father of three sons was exempt from mobilization, the father of four or more was exempt from all obligations towards the state.[13] It sought quality of the human stock in a way reminiscent of the breeding of the Osmanli future sultans[14]—and of non-human stock: if a husband could find for his wife a better sire than himself for her children, and did so, his conduct was socially approved rather than condemned, and if he neglected to do this when he himself was "below par," his wife might, it seems, undertake such an arrangement with impunity.[15]

Once the child was born it was inspected—not by the parents, but by the state—for weakness or defects. If it was found to be defective, it was left out (usually on the dung-heap) to die; if healthy and strong, its life was preserved and it was reared by the mother to the age of seven. At this age the child and his education were taken over by the state.

The child was assigned to a "pack," an age-class, that included other children of his age and sex—for girls were also so assigned. Within this system of packs or age-classes there was a cross-division in which children of all ages were brought together in a "herd." The purpose of these herds seems to have been that of putting the older children to work in training the younger. The leaders of the herds were, as a rule, about twenty years old or twenty-one, were members of distinguished families, and had individually distinguished themselves during their twelve- or thirteen-year long education in the packs and herds.[16] The authority of these leaders over their herds seems to have been very great. It was also the unofficial business of every peer to supervise, in some way, the education of the children in these herds, as it was the official business of a government agent appointed for the purpose.[17]

After the twelve or thirteen years in a herd, and at the end of the boy's twentieth year, he was eligible for election to one of the adult "messes." He had to be elected to membership and it appears that a single negative vote from a member was sufficient to bar him from membership.[18] And only members of messes could "graduate" into the select company of peers.

When we ask what was the education received by the Spartan children we find the veil of obscurity before the Spartan institutions almost impenetrable. It appears that they were all taught to read and write, but were given little in the way of literary training. The bulk of the training was devoted to the development of the "Spartan" character and of the body and the arts of the soldier. The child learned to be a soldier—this sums it up. There is some evidence that the Spartans did not completely ignore the arts in education and that the dance, music, and recitations were highly regarded.[19] It is clear, however, that there was no emphasis at all on—indeed no place for—the literary and philosophical education that was, in the fifth and fourth centuries, becoming characteristic of the rest of Greece. "Thenceforward," as Toynbee says, "Sparta was in Hellas but not of it," and Marrou writes of "The Great Refusal" by which Sparta renounced the arts and even athletic sports as sports—because they were too disinterested and tended to develop strong personalities—in favor of the completely totalitarian military state.[17]

The only sort of "examination" to which the scanty evidence gives any clue was by competition. There appear to have been competitions in all the physical sports (although the Spartans did not send teams to the Pan-Hellenic games) and there certainly were pitched battles and whipping competitions. The pitched battles were between opposing packs or herds and were fought with the ferocity that was one of the traits the education system was designed to nurture. The annual whipping competitions seem to have been sheer tests of the amount of pain the boys could endure without whimpering: there were instances of boys being whipped to death without making an outcry. The theory underlying the whole Spartan education system was, according to Chrimes,[19] "that boys were just so many wild or half-wild animals, to be treated as such until they were tamed, and not allowed to lose their wild characteristics altogether." The system did not provide education for all the inhabitants of lands ruled by Sparta, nor even for those who were in some sense citizens of Sparta, but only for the free-born sons and daughters of free-born Spartiates, for only these might become eligible for one of the "messes."

The effectiveness of the physical and military training is shown by the fact that the Spartan army was invincible for two centuries and more. The kind of character that was developed can perhaps be illustrated by repeating two or three of the stories that have made the name of Sparta famous—or notorious—throughout the world. One aspect of the education of boys in the herds was that they were ordered to steal and were punished if they were caught. Plutarch writes[20] that "to show what earnestness the boys put into their stealing I will cite the story of the boy, once upon a time, who had stolen a fox and was hiding it under his shirt; and although the creature was tearing the boy's belly with its teeth and claws the boy bore the torture, rather than be found out, until he fell down dead."

The story of Leonidas and the Three Hundred at the Battle of Thermopylae is perhaps too well known to need repeating; it also is illustrative.

Toynbee adds[21] to these two stories the item that the last two years of the youth's training before he came of age and was eligible for election to one of the messes were probably spent in the "Secret Service." This was nothing more nor less than an official "murder gang" whose function it was to discover serfs who had shown themselves to be either restive or outstanding in character or ability and to destroy them; service in the gang served the educational purpose of toughening the youths to the harsh life of ambush and war.

The most notorious single deed of the Spartans was that reported by Thucydides:[22]

The whole policy of the Spartans towards the Helots [serfs] is governed by considerations of security; and one of the acts into which they were led by their fear of the rising generation's spirit and numbers was the following. They proclaimed that all Helots who could show a distinguished war record should present themselves for selection to receive their freedom. This was simply a trap—the calculation being that those Helots who considered that they had the best claim to liberation would be just the Helots who would have the spirit to take the initiative in falling upon their masters. So they selected two thousand of them; and these two thousand gave thanksgiving for their manumission by crowning themselves with garlands and visiting the shrines of the Gods in procession. But the Spartans were not long in making away with them—and this with such secrecy that nobody ever knew how each of the victims had met his end.

On "graduating" from the herd and pack, the young man became eligible for election to one of the adult messes. If he were not elected, he was not and never could become one of the privileged peers, but remained a member of the class of "inferiors," or unprivileged. If he were elected, he remained a member of his mess from then on until he was sixty years old. There seem to have been only two reasons sufficient to bring about his expulsion from his mess, and from the class of peers: the first and most important was his having shown cowardice in battle, the second was his having failed to make his contribution to the common table.

The main features of youth education—supervision, selection, specialization and competition—were also features in the life of the mess. The peer married and established a family, but he could neither eat nor sleep at home—a bridegroom had to spend even his wedding night in barracks. As he became older he was allowed, from time to time, to sleep at home, but never under any circumstances to dine there—even one of the kings, when, after his return from a long absence and victorious war, he sent to his mess for his portion of food that he might eat it at home, was refused and fined for having made the request.[23]

The sanction in Sparta for enforcing these disciplinary rules and for making death preferable to cowardice was that of public opinion as well as the law. Xenophon's comments[24] are to the point: one of the remarkable achievements of the Spartan institutions, he says, is that they

. . . have made it preferable to die a noble death rather than remain alive in disgrace. As a matter of fact, investigation reveals that there are actually fewer deaths in battle among the Spartans than in armies which give way to their fear and prefer to leave the field; so that in reality courage turns out to be a more effective survival-factor than cowardice. The path of courage is easier and more agreeable and smoother and more secure. . . . And I ought not to omit to explain how Lycurgus made sure that his path would be followed by his Spartans. He made sure of that by ensuring inevitable happiness for the brave and inevitable unhappiness for the cowardly. In other communities, a coward's only penalty is to be branded with the epithet. For the rest, he is free to work and play cheek by jowl with men of valour if he chooses. In Sparta, on the other hand, everybody would be ashamed to take a coward for his messmate or to take him for his partner in athletics. And it will often happen that when they are picking up ball teams the coward finds himself left out, and that in choirs he is pushed out into the least honorable positions, and that he has to yield precedence to everybody in the street and at table and to make way for his juniors and to keep his womenfolk indoors and to bear their reproaches for his lack of manhood and to resign himself to having no housewife in his house and to pay a fine on that account into the bargain, and never to show himself out of doors with his skin oiled, and in fact to do nothing whatsoever that is done by Spartans who have no stain on their reputations—under pain of receiving bodily chastisement from his betters. For my part, I am not at all surprised that, in a community in which cowardice is visited with this terrific penalization, death is preferable to a life of such reproach and such dishonour.

The order given by the law to all Spartiates was, as Herodotus writes,[25] always the same: "In action it is forbidden to retire in the face of enemy forces of whatever strength. Troops are to keep their formation and to conquer or die."

Marrou shows[26] that during the period of the dominance of the typically Spartan institutions, severity in training was slowly but steadily on the increase. For example, in the beginning, the gymnastic exercises of the children were in part ritualistic and were performed to musical accompaniments. Later, the Spartan nudity of the children—boys and girls alike—lost its ritual value and led to competitions between the individual children and the packs to see who could "best resist the terrible summer sun" and who could last longer while exercising in its heat. In the beginning, the battles between the packs and herds had been a harmless scramble by the children for the prizes of cheese. Later, in Roman times, the battles were fought with a savage ferocity and they and the whipping competitions were conducted before crowds who flocked to see them.

Sparta was thus completely and utterly totalitarian to an extent not yet achieved by any modern state. The education of the youths —that is, of that one per cent of the population that ruled (the other ninety-nine per cent were not recognized in the educational scheme at all and presumably all their education was by the apprenticeship method)—was directed to one end and one only: the youths learned to be soldiers. To this end the arts, literature, even athletics as sports, were all sacrificed.

The decline of Sparta may be dated from her victories in the war against Athens 431–404 B.C.[27] Toynbee writes:[28]

A people trained consummately but exclusively for warlike contact with its neighbours found itself suddenly compelled, by the outcome of one particular war, to enter into non-military relations for which they were not only unprepared but were positively unfitted by their own peculiar institutions and habits and ethos. These peculiarities which the Spartans

. . . had developed in order to grapple with a previous problem, and which had given them superhuman strength within the limits of the narrow environment within which their lines had previously been cast, now took their revenge upon this peculiar people by making them inhumanly or infra-humanly incompetent to live in the wider world into which the fortunes of war had eventually carried them. The very exactness of their adaptation to their previous environment made any readaptation to a new environment so difficult for them as to be virtually impossible; and the very qualities which had been the secret of their success in the one situation became their worst enemies when they found themselves in the other. . . . The contrast between the Spartan at home and the Spartan abroad was a by-word in Hellas; for whereas, on his own ground, the Spartan admittedly rose above the ordinary Hellenic standards of personal discipline and disinterestedness, he fell below those same standards in at least equal measure as soon as he found himself out of his own element.

And so the power of Sparta declined. Messenia was liberated from Sparta in 370–369 B.C.; in the latter half of the third century, according to Plutarch,[29] "not more than seven hundred Spartiates survived, and of these perhaps one hundred may have owned land and an allotment, while the remainder were a destitute and disfranchised mob." Nabis, the last king of Sparta, was assassinated in 192 B.C. and Rome invaded Sparta in 195 B.C. In the Roman period Sparta was entirely archaistic and presented "the rather pathetic spectacle of a museum city, clinging tenaciously to all its ancient institutions for the sake of attracting tourists."[30]

15. The Arrested Osmanli Civilization

We have seen[1] that the nomadic Turks had erupted out of the Central Asian deserts in the sixth century A.D., were converted to Islam at the end of the ninth, and had flowed westward into the derelict realm of the defunct Arab Caliphate in the eleventh century. When early in the thirteenth century, the Mongols under Genghis Khan erupted out of the same deserts, they drove before them an unknown number of Persian and Turkish refugees, some of whom found a temporary halting place deep in the Anatolian territories of the now disintegrating Orthodox Christian Civilization. One nameless band of these refugee Turks was led by a chief named Suleiman. Suleiman's son Ertoghrul had finally established the band on a small strip of territory on the northwestern edge of the Anatolian plateau. Ertoghrul's son Osman (Othman, Ottoman) gave his name to the band and set himself the task of enlarging his territories at the expense of the East Roman Empire. By A.D. 1326, the Osmanlis had captured Brusa; by 1355, crossed the Dardanelles; by 1360, captured Adrianople; by 1371–1372 completed the conquest of Macedonia and, therewith, the effective establishment of their rule as the universal state of the Orthodox Christian Civilization, although the city of Constantinople itself was not captured until 1453.

The originally nomadic Osmanlis were now confronted with the problem of governing a sedentary population, spread over extensive territories, in which their Christian subjects outnumbered those of their own faith. The response to this challenge was the establishment, development, and continuation of an institution—essentially an educational institution—that was unique and perhaps the most remark-able educational institution ever devised. This was the Ottoman slave-household. It was the ruling institution of the empire. It was established as a fully developed institution by Muhammad the Conqueror shortly after the capture of Constantinople, although slaves had been used by the earlier Osmanlis.

The use of slaves in positions of authority was not an Ottoman invention but a practice that had been current in other nomad empires over sedentary peoples: in the Parthian Empire in the last century B.C., in the Arab Caliphate in the ninth and tenth cen-turies A.D., in the Umayyad Caliphate in Spain,[2] in the Samanid prin-cipality in Balkh and Bokhara of the same time, in the Mamluks in Egypt.[3] But only the Osmanlis elaborated and refined the practice to the highest pitch: every single member of the ruling institution of the empire, "from gardener to grand vizier, save only the mem-bers of the royal family" were slaves, the personal property of the sultan, over whom he had absolute power.[4] Originally the slaves had been acquired by capture, or purchase, or gift or tribute, but these four methods were soon, for the most part, reduced to two: capture and tribute.[4] There were two sets of professional slave-raiders who kept the Ottoman slave market supplied, and one set of these, in the middle of the seventeenth century, supplied about twenty thousand head annually to Constantinople.[5] Not all of these slaves who were supplied to the capital came into the possession of the sultan, for every great member of the sultan's household built up his own slave-household after the model of that of the sultan.[6] A further peculiarity of the system was that the slave must have been born a Christian and must have become a Muslim.

Perhaps even the members of the royal family might be said to be included in the slave-household. Lybyer notes that the sultan him-self was the son of a slave, the mothers of his children were slaves, his daughters were married to slaves and his sons were the consorts of none but slaves.[6] To this Toynbee adds[7] the note that the sultans bred their children from selected female slaves "as their nomad fore-bears . . . had bred pedigree cattle from selected stock" and that their attitude toward their progeny was much like that towards the progeny of flocks and herds. Muhammad the Conqueror sought and obtained from "those learned in the law" a judgment that—"in order

to secure the peace of the World"—it was allowable for his successors to have all their brothers put to death, for all those that did
not succeed to the throne endangered it. Muhammad then issued
an edict that made the wholesale assassinations an order rather than
merely allowable, and his successors duly obeyed the order.[7]

This attitude towards superfluous offspring seems to have been
about the same as that of a modern householder towards the pet
cat's superfluous kittens. It is an evidence of the "grand disregard
of human nature" which was the basis of the selection and training
of the slave-household. Lybyer writes:[8]

Perhaps no more daring experiment has been tried on a large scale upon
the face of the Earth than that embodied in the Ottoman Ruling Institution. Its nearest ideal analogue is found in the Republic of Plato, its
nearest actual parallel in the Mamluk system of Egypt; but it was not
restrained within the aristocratic Hellenic limitations of the first, and it
subdued and outlived the second. In the United States of America men
have risen from the rude work of the backwoods to the Presidential
chair, but they have done so by their own effort and not through the
gradations of a system carefully organized to push them forward. The
Roman Catholic Church can still train a peasant to become a pope, but
it has never begun by choosing its candidates almost exclusively from
families which profess a hostile religion. The Ottoman system deliberately
took slaves and made them ministers of state. It took boys from the sheep-
run and the plough-tail and made them courtiers and the husbands of
princesses; it took young men whose ancestors had borne the Christian
name for centuries, and made them rulers in the greatest of Muhammadan
states, and soldiers and generals in invincible armies whose chief joy was
to beat down the Cross and elevate the Crescent. It never asked its novices
"Who was your father?" or "What do you know?" or even "Can you
speak our tongue?"; but it studied their faces and their frames and said:
"You shall be a soldier and, if you show yourself worthy, a general," or
"You shall be a scholar and a gentleman and, if the ability lies in you, a
governor and a prime minister." Grandly disregarding that fabric of fundamental customs which is called "human nature," and those religious and
social prejudices which are thought to be almost as deep as life itself, the
Ottoman system took children forever from parents, discouraged family
cares among its members through their most active years, allowed them
no certain hold on property, gave them no definite promise that their sons
and daughters would profit by their success and sacrifice, raised and
lowered them with no regard for ancestry or previous distinction, taught

them a strange law, ethics, and religion, and ever kept them conscious of a sword raised above their heads which might put an end at any moment to a brilliant career along a matchless path of human glory.

Toynbee adds[9] to this the comment that the essence of the system was the selecting and training of "human watch-dogs" to keep the sultan's "human cattle" in order and his human neighboring enemies at bay; from this band of "human watch-dogs" the conquering Osmanlis were themselves excluded; and this was necessary because the system of training made such excessive demands upon ordinary human nature that only one had been wrested from his own family and social environment and forcibly introduced into an alien environment "as an isolated human atom" could submit to or profit by it. The free Muslim Osmanlis, with their pride of family and clan and religion, could not be expected to submit to such a training, and if they had been admitted to the slave-household, they would have disrupted both it and its educational system by introducing an aristocracy of blood, not of intellect, into it. Indeed, when finally they were admitted, the system did break down.

It should be emphasized that slavery in Muslim lands had none of the stigma it has borne in the West. Slave status was regarded as accidental and temporary, not as permanent or as arising from inferior capacities or native endowments—there seems to have been no trace of the Aristotelian idea that men are "by nature" either slave or free. Further, slavery had, in many times and places, been the broadest and most direct avenue to power and fortune and positions of prestige and honor. And finally, there was the teaching of the Prophet himself that slaves were to be treated with kindness and generosity, and were to be fed and clothed as were the free members of the family.

The results of the training received by members of the slave-household impressed those Western observers who saw fractions of it in action. Rycaut writes:[11] "In the Turkish camp no brawls, quarrels, nor clamours are heard; no abuses are committed on the people by the march of their Army, all is bought and paid with money, as by travellers that are guests at an inn; there are no complaints by mothers of the rape of their virgin-daughters, no violence or robberies offered on the inhabitants." Rycaut adds, perhaps with exaggeration although in all seriousness, that "this regulation . . . proceeds from nothing more than the strict prohibition of wine upon pain of death." (There were perhaps other contributing factors, e.g., the training that the army had received.) This remarkable discipline continued as a tradition in the Turkish army long after the slave-household had ceased to function. Toynbee reports,[11] from his own observation, on the extraordinary restraint shown by a Turkish army in taking over a town in Anatolia in 1921, at which date the use of alcohol by a soldier on active duty was still punishable by death.

Another Western observer of the sixteenth century[12] further reports on the discipline of the soldiers in peace time:

What struck me as particularly praiseworthy in that great multitude was the silence and good discipline. There were none of the cries and murmurs which usually proceed from a motley concourse, and there was no crowding. Each man kept his appointed place in the quietest manner possible. The officers were seated; the common soldiers stood up. The most remarkable body of men were several thousand Janissaries, who stood in a long line apart from the rest and so motionless that, as they were at some distance from me, I was for a while doubtful whether they were living men or statues, until, being advised to follow the usual custom of saluting them, I saw them all bow their heads in answer to my salutation.

And he offers an explanation:

It is always the way of the Turks, whenever they come into possession of a man of uncommonly good parts, to rejoice and be exceeding glad, as though they had found a pearl of great price. And, in bringing out all that there is in him, they leave nothing undone that labour and thought can do—especially when they recognize military aptitude. Our Western way is different indeed! In the West, if we come into possession of a good dog or hawk or horse, we are delighted, and we spare nothing in our efforts to bring the creature to the highest perfection of which its kind is capable. In the case of man, however . . . !

We may now examine the institution that produced these results. As has been seen, it was founded by Muhammad the Conqueror soon after A.D. 1453. Muhammad had some precedents for the institution in the habit of the Turks of recruiting their official administrators and soldier-statesmen from alien sources; and for the human material of the student body he had the children secured by levy, chiefly upon the Christian subject races of the Balkans. A Law of Draft of Murad I (1360-1368) had secured a steady supply of this human material.

Muhammad was himself a man of vast attainments and of multiplicity of interests. Those interests which absorbed much of his attention and in which he excelled included literature and linguistics, sports of all kinds but especially horsemanship and archery, gardening—and education. It was he who, with the aid of his Croatian Grand Vizier, fixed the hierarchical order of "those learned in the law" and organized the curriculum of the Islamic colleges in his empire into the ten fixed subjects. Under him, learning and literature became the fashion for all the nobility and upper classes. Miller comments that, in his passion for learning, he "even organized a system of education for the women of his harem."[13] Most of the subjects in which he was interested came to be included in the curriculum of the palace school.

It is possible, though by no means certain, that the University of Constantinople after its reorganization A.D. 1045 suggested some ideas for his school to Muhammad; it is certain that the Muslim Nizamiyah and the similar higher schools were suggestive to him, especially in their capacity as training grounds for civil servants. The immediate occasion for the founding of the school was the urgent need for a sufficiency of adequately trained civil servants and soldiers to man the administration and army of the now vast empire.[13]

When the slave children, aged about twelve to fourteen, were brought to Constantinople[14] they were sent at once before a board of expert examiners and given severe physical tests and a kind of "intelligence test." Only those who were physically perfect and in the "upper quartiles" of their group were admitted as students (pages) into the palace school. Upon admission, the pages were cut entirely off from their families so that most of them lost all track of their original home ties and often even of their own original identity. They were kept immured in the palace school and, at the outset, were isolated even from each other. They were of course celibate —before the middle of the sixteenth century no woman was allowed within the whole vast palace where the sultan spent most of his time. They wore uniforms; their day was rigidly scheduled, with an appointed task for each hour. In all these respects, the school of the pages closely resembled the more strictly run monasteries of the medieval West. It differed from those monasteries in its education, which was wholly secular, and in its purpose, which was to produce administrators and soldiers.

When the system was at its height under Suleiman in the middle of the sixteenth century, there were nine schools within the Grand Seraglio. Of these, five were preparatory schools and four were advanced vocational schools. Each school was a separate and independent unit, but all nine were closely correlated with each other so that the system as a whole was also a unit. The curriculum was organized with a view to promoting from one school to another in order and to appointment to official posts—both military and civil—of the corresponding grade.

The preparatory school course averaged six to eight years and the advanced course eight to six years, depending upon the ability and industry of the student. There seems to have been no such thing as a required period of time for the completion of a required part of a subject. Instead, when the student showed himself competent in a part of the subject at one of the periodic examinations, he was immediately promoted, so that the only limitations upon the student's rate of progress were his own ability and industry. This system was in fact successful as long as it was adhered to: the best, and only the best, rose to the top—and they rose fast. Only between about twelve to twenty-five per cent of the pages who entered the school completed the course; the others were weeded out by frequent screening tests and examinations. Those who were so weeded out filled minor offices in the state, or remained to perform duties within the Grand Seraglio.

The faculty of the palace schools were composed of members of the Muslim body of "those learned in the law" and, though in smaller number, the more famous scholars, poets, musicians, and mathematicians of the time. Instruction in classes was given daily and there were periodic lectures for the entire student body.

The aim of the school was to produce men of character and ability who could serve as statesmen and warriors and loyal Muslims and who would at the same time be polished courtiers excelling in politeness and the forms of etiquette (this, with the strictness of the training, is strongly reminiscent of the education of the Japanese samurai). To this end, all pages were drilled in the ceremonies of Islam and Turkish etiquette, and they were taught the following course of studies: the liberal arts, physical exercises and the arts of war, and vocational training, with almost equal time allotted to each division.

The liberal arts curriculum included the Turkish, Arabic, and Persian languages, Turkish and Persian literature, the Quran and commentaries on and exegeses of it, theology, jurisprudence and law, Turkish history, mathematics, and music. The language instruction was begun in the first year of the preparatory course, the other and more difficult subjects were added as the student was ready for them; the liberal arts curriculum was taught throughout the entire course. Physical or manual exercises were a part of the daily routine also from beginning to end. The more advanced physical exercises included weight-lifting and wrestling, archery, swordsmanship, horsemanship, and a game played with a wooden ball on a cord.

As a student was periodically examined and showed more aptitude for one kind of training rather than another, or as he declared his own preference or inclination for one rather than another, he was placed in the course that he preferred or that was suited to his natural bent. Those whose inclinations and abilities showed them fitted for the army were enrolled in the corps of the Janissaries ("Yenicheri," "new troops"). In the sixteenth century they were about one-fourth of the slave family.

When we ask how it was that human beings could be induced to undergo and then to profit from so arduous, austere, and relentless an educational program the answer must be sought in the incentives that were offered. The pages were apparently paid—and fed, clothed, and housed—from the first day of their enrollment. They were of course punished—and severely punished—for any infraction of the rules or breach of discipline. But the system relied far more on its rewards than on punishments. There was a carefully graduated scale of rewards, both monetary and in privileges, the student could advance as rapidly as he was able, and he was encouraged by being allowed to select the course and the subjects of study, within limits, for which he was best suited and in which he might excell

And he knew of the rewards that awaited him when he had successfully completed the course.

The system proved itself sound, for the students did work unremittingly, for the most part using their recreation time for study or for physical or manual exercises.

At the end of the course there were elaborate ceremonies of graduation or departure and after the ceremonies "the page who thus rode forth into the outside world had been ennobled for life by the service which he had performed for the sultan and by the training he had received."[15] He was henceforth certain of a permanent job at high wages, he was exempt from all taxes, he could advance as fast as he was able and as far as the highest offices in the land save only the sultanate itself, he enjoyed a set of privileges "which in Western minds were associated only with nobility."[16] By the sixteenth century he was no longer subject to the civil courts, but only to courts composed of his own higher officers. He could establish a family of his own, accumulate property, form his own slave-household and model it after that of the sultan. And he was the sultan's slave: the sultan could take his property, withdraw his honors, or demand his head.

Lybyer writes:[17]

There is reason to believe that human history has never known a political institution which during so long a period was so completely dominated by sheer intellect, and thereby so unerringly held to its original plan and purpose, as was the Ottoman Ruling Institution. The democracy of Athens attained an unexampled level of average intelligence, but under its sway, the exceptional mind received discouragement rather than exceptional training. The free democracies of the present age allow the gifted individual opportunities to fight his way upward, but against obstacles which sometimes become insuperable. These systems are unquestionably superior on the whole to the Ottoman scheme, because of their inclusiveness and individual freedom, but as regards sheer efficiency, unobstructed opportunity, and certainly of reward, their operation is wasteful, clumsy and blind by comparison.

It was remarked above that the closest ideal analogue to the Ottoman institution is perhaps the Republic of Plato, and Plato certainly would have approved a number of the main features. He would have approved the careful training of both the bodies and the minds of the students, the division into soldiers and rulers, the freedom from family ties on the part of the rulers, the long course of education and, above all, government by the wise. He would certainly not have approved the lack of regard for birth and, still less, the education that was not based on and directed towards an understanding and grasp of the Good.[18] It would have been possible for Muhammad the Conqueror to have known of Plato's proposals for the education of rulers; whether in fact he did know of them, or not, is not known.

So much of the inner workings of the palace school is also unknown: the textbooks used in the courses, the length of the class periods, the methods of teaching and of studying. A large part of this ignorance derives from the fact that there was, from the beginning to the end, a veil of secrecy before everything beyond the third gate of the Grand Seraglio, and that the pages were vowed to secrecy about the curriculum and all else within the school. Very little knowledge about the Grand Seraglio sifted out beyond the members of the slave-household: the outer world could only be astonished by the results that were produced, without knowing exactly how they were produced. It would seem certain that the teaching methods in the palace school were about the same as those in the Muslim colleges and higher schools, for so many of its faculty were members of the body of "those learned in the law" and had themselves graduated from one of the higher schools. It would follow that a great deal of emphasis was placed on memorization of the Quran and the Traditions and, possibly, of texts of Persian and Turkish literature.

But the system, with its "grand disregard" for the "fundamental customs" of human nature, was unable, in spite of its rigor, austerity, and inflexibility, permanently to set at nought the demands of that human nature. The first of the "fundamental customs" that demanded satisfaction was the pretension of birth and heredity, the desire of fathers to secure for their sons the advantages that they themselves had enjoyed as members of the sultan's slave household. At the very end of his reign Suleiman had permitted a few of the sons of Janissaries to be enrolled in the corps. In A.D. 1568 the Sultan Selim II formally recognized this privilege of the Janissaries. Within a generation after this formal extension of the privilege a majority of the Janissary corps was reckoned to consist of the sons of Janissaries. Now the Janissaries were of course Muslims, and their sons were born Muslims, and with this admission of certain Muslims into the privileged ranks it became "a psychological impossibility" to keep out free-born Muslims. By the end of the sixteenth century free-born Muslims were admitted to the Janissary corps and, soon after, to other schools in the palace. And so within about three generations, by the end of the seventeenth century, the slave system of government had, in Miller's phrase, "virtually broken down" although the palace school was still functioning and many slaves were still employed in government offices.[19]

Thus the rigorous selectivity and promotional standards of the system were undermined, for if a child was admitted to the school and kept in it and finally graduated from it to a position of honor and responsibility, not because he had proved himself abler and more industrious and more intelligent than his competitors, but because he was the son of a father who had enough power to ensure his admission and graduation, the teachers and examiners could not be expected to enforce their standards as rigorously on the other students, nor could the other students so confidently expect rewards for sheer merit. Neither the schools nor the slave-household institution crumbled all at once; the momentum gathered at the beginning and during the period of peak efficiency was too great to be dissipated suddenly: the sultan "solemnly and forever" renounced the privilege of "exacting tribute of children from the said Provinces of Georgia and Mingrelia" only in 1774,[20] the Janissaries were not finally extirpated until 1826 by Mahmud II, and the palace school was not finally abolished until about the same time and by the same ruler.

After the humiliation of the Peace Treaty of 1774,[20] the Sultan Selim III had begun a process of "Westernization" of his empire. In A.D 1793 he had sent diplomatic missions to the Western European capitals with Turks as ambassadors. But the Turks, with their complete ignorance of geography, Western ways, and Western languages, proved to be wholly incompetent and had to be replaced by Greeks. The Greeks had none of the "classical" Islamic education that had so distinguished earlier generations of Turkish Muslims; but they had had the opportunity, in following commercial careers, to come into contact wtih the West and to learn Western ways and languages. The Muslim education of the Osmanlis had, in the end, proved itself as inadequate to the needs of a later day and changed circumstances as had Islamic education as a whole.[21]

Yet the Osmanli achievement was great. Toynbee's summary is as follows:[22]

The makers of the Ottoman slave-household forged an instrument which enabled a tiny band of Nomads, who had been ejected from their native steepe and cast away in an alien environment, not merely to survive and hold their own in this strange world, but to impose peace and order upon a great Christian society which had gone into disintegration, and to threaten the life of a yet greater Christian society which has since cast its shadow over the whole of the rest of Mankind. Our latter-day Turkish statesmen have simply filled part of the vacuum which has been left in the Near East through the disappearance of the incomparable structure of the old Ottoman Empire by erecting on the desolate site a ready-made "go-down" of a standard Western pattern in the shape of a Turkish national state.

PART THREE

Comparisons and Conclusions

16. Comparisons Among Nineteen Civilizations

The foregoing chapters have given accounts of education in one abortive, three secondary, seven tertiary, and two arrested civilizations.* Education in each of these had its own peculiar and distinctive characteristics, and these peculiarities arose out of the different circumstances and the differentiating ethos of the several societies. At the same time, certain similarities among the several educational "systems" have emerged. It would be expected antecedently that there would be more points of likeness among the secondary civilizations than between any one of these and the tertiary civilizations, and this for two chief reasons: the secondary civilizations all arose out of primary civilizations without the instrumentation of a chrysalis church, and in them all writing was not, at the outset, in general use; the converse was true of the tertiary civilizations. The antecedent expectation was seen, in the several accounts, to be justified, and especially so in those of the growth phases. There were greater divergencies and differences among the civilizations in their time of trouble and universal state phases, but even in these divergencies and differences there were certain general tendencies that were common to those phases and were significant.

Six of the nine secondary civilizations have not left sufficient evidence about their education to justify inclusion in the above account: only the Sinic, Indic, and Hellenic societies have done so. However, education in some of the other societies that are noticed in the

* What is known of education in six other civilizations is recorded in Appendices I and II, pp. 293 and 314.

Appendices below shows certain similarities to that in these three societies. It now remains to bring out and to state the major points of similarity—or even identity—among the different societies in respect to their fundamental beliefs and their educational practices.

In the earliest thought of China, India, Mesopotamia, and Egypt there was no sharp distinction drawn between the self and other; this distinction was drawn in early Greek philosophy and in its successors in the West—with enormous and far-reaching consequences. It is this fundamental difference that lies at the root of some or many of the other differences between Greek culture on the one hand, and Sinic and Indic on the other.

In the Sinic, Indic, and Hellenic societies alike, however, there was, at the beginning of the times of troubles, very great attention paid to the theory and processes of learning, probably as a part of the general increase of speculative interest in all questions. In China the doctrine that came to be widely influential was that of Mencius, who taught that all men are nearly alike. The nature or native endowment of each man is similar, especially in the fundamental characteristics, to that of every other man, although there are hereditary variations. As a man grows and matures, his essential nature is to be educed and developed. That which educes his nature and leads him to realize his full being is the "Way." Both man's nature and the Way are linked with and derived from the cosmic order, the very structure of the universe itself. But the Way cannot be followed by a man alone and unaided; there must be a cultivation, a building, of the Way in human experience. That which cultivates the Way is called *chiao*—education, culture, cultivation. *Chiao* means not only teaching but also civilization, government, religion, and some kinds of associations. Thus there is a strong suggestion of similarity between this conception and the general idea of the Greek *paideia* as education by the whole community in all its aspects. The purpose of education into the Way is to produce the "superior man" who shows certain definite characteristics and who has realized that nature of his which is linked with the cosmic order.

In India, the fundamental purpose of education was closely related to the fundamental purpose and highest goal of human life. This goal was the full, self-conscious awareness and realization of the intimate link between the individual self and the universal spiritual reality, and of the dependence of the former upon the latter. The similarity between this Indic conception of self-realization and the Sinic conception of the realization by man of his essential nature is clear.

In Greece, in the philosophy of Plato, the conception is quite differently stated and is perhaps fundamentally different. There are, however, similarities that may be noted. Plato held that the Ideas are universal principles, fixed in the nature of the universe itself; Mencius held that the Way and man's essential nature are universal and fixed in the structure of the universe itself. Plato held that the Idea of Good is the prime reality and the source of all reality; the Upanishadic doctrine was that the Brahman is the prime reality and the source of all reality. Plato held that the goal of life and of education was the direct apprehension and awareness of the Good; the Upanishads taught that the goal of life was the realization of Brahman; Mencius held that the highest aim and the final achievement of individual self-cultivation was that state of awareness in which the individual becomes one with the ground of his being. These are striking similarities amidst the differences. On the other hand, Plato did not teach that there is an identity between the self and the Good, nor so close a kinship between the self and all living things as the Upanishads taught, nor that the Way is derived from the cosmic order; yet, the final apprehension of the Good by the philosopher, after his long and arduous training, seems to be remarkably like the Indic realization of the self and the mysticism of Mencius.

The philosophy of Plato was not the universally or even generally accepted philosophy of Greece of the time of troubles, although it was representative of one characteristic strain of Greek thought. It is remarkable that in Greece at least one philosopher of the time held ideas that were similar to the philosophy that was dominant in India and to the philosophy that was to become so influential in China.

In all three civilizations alike, the primary aim of the aristocratic education of the periods of growth was the development of the character of the student; the training was fundamentally moral training. However, the very statements that the primary aim was the development of character rather than of mind, that the training was fundamentally moral rather than intellectual, and general rather than technical or professional—these statements all assume distinctions between mind and character, morals and intellect, a man's inner being and his outward behavior. These distinctions derive from a later time and a different way of thinking: they would have seemed unreal, forced, artificial to the guru, to the Chinese *chun tzu,* and to the Greek tutor; these teachers would have thought that the morally cultivated man, the ideal man, was cultivated in his behavior as well as in his inner nature—that his behavior was somehow an expression of his inner nature and not separable from it.

Coupled with this attitude was the belief that the *culture* of the inner man and the knowledge about how to speak and how to behave and how properly to perform sacrifices were priceless possessions of which only a few were worthy. This belief was, in large part, the basis of the further belief in all three societies that not everyone should receive or could profit from education, but only those who had proved themselves morally worthy of being chosen by a tutor and retained as a pupil. It was perhaps also the basis of the belief that the imparting of knowledge, of the training that developed character, was not something for which a teacher ought to take pay. And this belief was confirmed by the relation that existed between tutor and pupil: it was one of friendship and love, close and intimate and personal as the relations between members of a family—as, in India, and also in Egypt, tutor and pupil were members of the same family. The establishment of such a relationship and the development of the values that arose from it were not things for which pay could be given or received, although, as between friends today, one could give and the other could receive presents as expressions of esteem and affection. Such tutor-disciple education was of course wholly private; there was no trace of official state control over, or even concern with, education in either society in the growth period.

In all three civlizations education involved an ideal, and the ideal was believed to be somehow grounded in the nature of the universe. In Greece, the striving of the Homeric hero, who was the pattern held up by the tutor for emulation by the pupil, was always towards an Absolute Beauty and a Perfect Valor that far transcended any actual heroic deed or heroic life. A little later, the Greek conception of ideal man dominated their education; this ideal was believed to be real, to be independent of any human conception of it, to be the guide and criterion according to which human character was to be shaped. In India, the ideal was self-realization, but the self that was to be realized was not the narrow social self nor the physical self nor anything but that larger spiritual self that was conceived, in the early period, as somehow related to a universal spiritual self—although the clarification and formulation of the belief did not come until later. And it appears that in China, in the early period, an ideal controlled the aristocratic education although the evidence about it is less clear than for Greece and India.

Greece was unique among the three secondary civilizations in developing the conception of the *polis,* in the degree of emphasis she placed on the ideal of man as necessarily and essentially a member of the political community. It is this characteristic and unique Greek conception and emphasis that supports the view that the Greek *paideia* as culture is the source of all later, Western notions of "culture." As a result of this and other developments Greek education was, by the end of the growth period, slowly beginning to be democratized. This does not appear to have been the case in either China or India.

In all of these societies there was, at the very beginning, an aristocracy that had emerged as the leaders in responding to the successive challenges. All that is known of education in the earlier societies is of the education of the aristocracy.

This aristocratic education in the three societies used as teachers the members of the aristocracy themselves. We may suppose that among the minority, before their appearance on the stage of history, education had been by the apprenticeship method. As the society developed and as more began to be expected of the nobility, it gradually became necessary for the young aristocrat to have some education beyond what he acquired in his own family or by observation. He was then entrusted to an older man who acted as his companion and tutor. This was the case not only in these three societies but also, and notably, in pre-Greek Rome, in Ireland, and in Egypt.

The tutor was himself an aristocrat and a member of the leading minority. He was under no obligation to take a pupil, but it was expected of him that he should do so as partial fulfillment of his obligation to the group, and he himself recognized it as a duty. The tutor was not, however, expected to accept a particular pupil, and the right to reject any applicant as unworthy was reserved to him. This was true especially of the Indic guru. In India and China, as in Egypt, the pupil became a member of the household of his tutor and served him even as he learned from him; tutor and pupil were similarly related in the Irish communities, though apparently not so in the Hellenic society nor in Rome. The personal relationship between tutor and pupil was close and intimate; in China and Egypt so close and so intimate that the tutor was regarded as a second father; in India and in Ireland the relationship was almost equally close.

The tutors were those, in all three societies, who had proved themselves to be among the ablest and wisest not only of the people as a whole but even of their own much smaller social group. They emerged as tutors on the basis of their own proved merit. The tutor enjoyed, in his own right, a high social position and his prestige seems to have been enhanced when he became a teacher. He received no pay for his teaching. In none of the three societies did a teacher take pay until the very end of the growth period, and then only in Greece.

The method of education was tutorial-apprenticeship: the pupil associated constantly with his tutor and observed his speech, his manners, his social and moral attitudes, and so, little by little, learned all these things from his tutor and his tutor's associates. In addition, he was given lessons in what he was expected to know: in etiquette and ceremonial and manners, in music and poetry and (in Greece) oratory, in (in China) arithmetic, in sports and games. There were no examinations—or perhaps it might be said that the whole process of education was one long informal examination: the tutor, being so intimately acquainted with his pupil, of course knew from day to day how much his pupil had learned and so advanced him according to his achievements and as he was able to proceed.

The entire education in all three societies was general rather than technical or professional. The content was determined by the consensus of the group, not by a few professionals, and was already traditional by the time of the emergence of the society. The content changed during the course of the growth period; for the stages of the change the evidence is clearer from the Hellenic Civilization than from the other two.

In all three civilizations all teaching was oral throughout the growth periods despite the knowledge and use, in China, of writing from the outset and, in Greece, from a somewhat later though still relatively early date. In all three, great stress was laid on memorization, and all three early literatures were transmitted during the earliest periods by oral tradition alone. This transmission of literature by oral tradition was characteristic not only of these civilizations in the growth periods but also of the Andean society, which was always without writing, of the Sumeric, the Babylonic and its Hebrew wing during the early period, the Arabic, Iranic, Islamic, and Hindu; and education in all these civilizations laid great emphasis on memorization.

In all three civilizations the social position of women seems to have been higher and women's education more general and complete in the early periods than at any later stage.

These are the chief points of likeness and difference among the three secondary civilizations during their growth periods.

In the Hellenic Civilization the educational revolution of the sophists occurred during a period that just overlapped the end of the growth period and the beginning of the time of troubles, so that the account of that revolution can as conveniently and appropriately be included with the one historical period as with the other. Well before the end of the growth period in Greece, the earliest philosophers had begun to do their speculative work, and by the beginning of the time of troubles, the differences of opinion and belief that were to produce the later philosophical "schools" had begun to appear. The sophists undertook to teach a particular skill, rhetoric, with a particular purpose, that of winning cases in the courts; and some of them appeared not to be concerned with the development of character as a primary object or even as an adjunct of the higher education they undertook to give. This was perhaps the first rift that resulted later in the great divorce between education as intellectual training and education as the development of character.

In the Sinic and Indic civilizations there were parallel increases in philosophical speculations and appearances of wandering scholars; in China the increased speculation gave rise to the many different "schools" of philosophy; in India, to the proliferations of the

Upanishadic philosophy. This outburst of speculation arose as the challenges facing the society increased in severity and as the accepted order felt itself increasingly unable to meet them, with the result that the received institutions and ways and beliefs were felt by more and more men to be in need of critical examination. With the increase in speculation there was an increase also of scholars and teachers, and the creativity which found no outlet in devising satisfactory responses to the intensifying social challenges now manifested itself, instead and in part, in devising philosophies. The philosophers were also teachers, and this period in all three societies witnessed the appearance of more teachers and of the wandering teachers. All three societies also manifested an increasing interest in primary education and all three established primary schools. Only in Greece, however, did many of these receive state support. There was an extension also of higher education, with the establishment of higher schools, and an extension and elaboration of the curricula, with some development of specialized or professional education in addition to the general education. In all three societies there was a great increase in the use of writing and in the publication of books, and in two of them, China and Greece, this was reflected in the greatly increased bookishness of the education. In all three there was a strong tendency, after the creativity manifested at the beginning of the period had spent itself, towards formalism, institutionalization, the fixing of curricula and texts, of methods and procedures. And, in Greece, there was an increasing state interest in and control over education.

In all three civilizations under their universal states the tendency towards formalism, curriculum-fixing, rigidity, and stereotypes that had manifested itself in the preceding period now came to completion; the educational system, content, and methods were petrified. This was far less true in the Indic than in the other two civilizations and for a reason that seems clear. In the Indic society, education remained oral and tutorial to a greater degree than in the other two; the very use of the method of personal conversation in teaching, instead of the written word, had—as it still has—the effect of eliciting responses from both student and teacher that are less likely to arise from the use of fixed methods and established exegeses. The responses elicited by the common study of a literary classic or a philosophical problem are not to be labelled "right" or "wrong" as answers can be in mathematics and some of the physical sciences. And when the study of a literary classic has been reduced to a "received standard version" of topical analyses, lists of places and persons, fixed, official interpretations and exegeses, the student's responses to that classic are likely to be pedantically labelled "right" or "wrong" as in a different kind of subject altogether where such labels are appropriate. This pedantic exegesis of received texts became the characteristic of higher education in the Sinic and Hellenic societies to a far greater degree than it did in India.

In China at the very beginning of the universal state the language was standardized, soon thereafter the dominant philosophy was standardized and made official, and the learning of the script, of the received classics, and of the official philosophy became the mark of the "superior man" as it became also the chief avenue to appointment and promotion in the civil service. Within a century of the foundation of the universal state, the edict was issued that laid the basis for the system of state schools and state examinations. The language and the classics in which the scholar and the civil servant were trained had long since ceased to be intelligible to the people, and so the gap in education between the two classes was rendered unbridgeable—and remained so in China until the twentieth century.

In the Sinic and Hellenic societies the central imperial government took an increasing interest in and assumed an increasing control over education, especially advanced education. In the Sinic society this interest and control appeared very early under the universal state and was more complete than in the Hellenic; in both the reason was the need for competent civil servants in increasing numbers as the empire became increasingly bureaucratized. It is interesting and significant that in both societies the education that led to appointment to and advancement in the civil services was basically "classical" and literary—not professional or technical, except in so far as the Roman legal training was professional. But even in Rome, the professional legal training was no better guarantee of advancement than was the literary and rhetorical training. These civil servants, with their literary and philosophical education, received, of course, professional training "on the job" after they were appointed. Their success and efficiency in administering the affairs of the two empires was very great. In India also, it was the man with the literary and philosophical education who, for the most part, administered the affairs of the state, although neither the Mauryan nor the Guptan empires had a system of state controlled schools, as did the Han, nor even as much official interest in education as did the Romans.

In India under the universal state several great centers of higher learning, both Buddhist and Brahman, were founded, and to these students of all classes were admitted. This democratized education to a considerable extent, although it in no way intruded on the fixed caste system. In Rome there was a far greater democratization of education; in China, far less; but in all three societies the process of democratization was greater under the universal states than during the preceding period, and nonexistent (except in Greece at the end) in the growth periods. And the Sinic and Hellenic universal states established great centers of higher learning.

Another significant change in the educational attitude in the universal state phase in the Sinic and Hellenic societies was the increasing tendency to view education as a product rather than a process. When it is regarded as a product it is conceived as something that can be "got," complete and finished, or relatively so; for example, it is not uncommon now to hear one person ask of another, "Where did you get your education?", expecting the answer, "At such-and-such college." The implication is that the graduate has learned all he need to know of the techniques and skills of language and mathematics and of all the accumulated knowledge about man's relations to other men, his indebtedness to the past, the natural order and his relation to it, and about the realm of aspirations and values—all he need to know, that is, except what is required for his particular job. It is even possible to hear an undergraduate say that he does not need to read a book on history—or literature or philosophy—because he has "had" history—or literature or philosophy. That this implication is real and not fancied is borne out by the remarkable abstention on the part of (American) college and university graduates from any further reading or investigation in any field in which they "had" (or even did not have) an undergraduate course.

When, on the other hand, education is regarded as a process, it is perhaps inevitable that it be regarded also as unending so long as the man is alive. There is in the human being a hunger and thirst for knowledge that appears to be as innate as his appetites for food and drink. And if the appetite for knowledge is stifled—as some kinds of social conditions can stifle it, or murdered—as some kinds of pedagogical systems can murder it, or withered—as, it would seem, the blight of laziness can do, then the man does not so obviously die as when his appetites for food and drink are left unsatisfied, but a part of him dies, and as Plato somewhere remarks, he walks lame and impotent to his grave. But if the appetite for knowledge is fed, then the man continues to live and to grow and there is no end to the process of learning, that is, of education, until death or senility.

In the Sinic society under the universal state the great changes were the greatly increased bookishness, the fixing of the script, the standardization of Confucianism as the official philosophy, the petrifaction of the curriculum and the texts of the classics, the establishment of a state school or schools of higher studies, the beginnings of the state examination system, the requirement of a literary, classical education for most civil servants, the vast increase in state control, and the increase of the tendency to view education as a product rather than as a process.

In the Hellenic society the great changes were the greatly increased bookishness, the petrifaction of the curriculum and the texts of the classics, the establishment of a state school of higher studies, the requirement of a literary and classical or legal education for most civil servants, the increase in state control, the vast increase in democratization, and the increase of the tendency to view education as a product rather than as a process.

In the Indic society the great changes were the establishment of great centers of higher learning, the increase in democratization, the tendency towards formalism, and the fixing of stereotypes.

In the Hellenic and Sinic societies the great changes from beginning to end were from entirely oral to bookish, from wholly private to largely state, from tutorial to class and lecture (although more so in Greece than in China), from an ideal regarded as transcendental and grounded in the cosmic order to the near-evaporation of the ideal, or to an ideal that was this-worldly and involved only a part of the human individual, not the whole man.

Turning now to the tertiary civilizations, it may be remarked again that they were all derived from a preceding secondary civilization through a chrysalis church, that they began their careers either already in possession of an alphabet and writing or (as in Japan and Russia) very soon had both provided for them by the church, and that they all had a literature of a sort from the outset. They all started with ethics, goals, ideals and a set of beliefs, including the beliefs that the way of salvation is open to Everyman, and that there is a brotherhood of all men, or, at the least, of all believers. In none of the tertiary civilizations was education aristocratic in the way that it was in the early periods of the Sinic and Hellenic societies, nor was it either oral or tutorial to the same extent, or private.

The basic controlling belief of the earliest civilizations in their growth periods was the belief that the goal and purpose of education was that of bringing man into harmony with the cosmic spiritual order, of bringing him to a realization and awareness that his own individual self is akin to the ultimate reality, or may recognize and somehow become like that reality. Education, under this controlling belief, was fundamentally moral training—character training: no distinction was drawn between moral training and the training of the mind. And this education was reserved for those who had shown themselves worthy to receive it, as it was imparted by those who had, in their lives, shown themselves to be superior. In the three secondary civilizations this original controlling idea—during the long histories of each, but especially during their times of troubles and the last, or universal state, phase—gradually became dissipated or formalized. One result was that men felt themselves in need of something new and better and quickening. And the higher religions appeared: Christianity in the Hellenic society, Buddhism in India and later in China, and post-Buddhaic Hinduism in India.

As Toynbee has observed in the final chapter of his *Historian's Approach to Religion,* not only these three religions, but also the other higher religions as well—Judaism and Islam and Zoroastrianism—agree in asserting that man's goal is to seek communion with the ultimate spiritual reality and to bring his individual self into harmony with it. No doubt the teachings and counsels of the higher religions are on a higher level of awareness and significance than are the controlling beliefs of the early stages of the secondary civilizations, but it is evident that, on this fundamental point, the essential doctrine is the same. One of the distinguishing marks of the higher religions, however, is that they all have missions to all Mankind, not merely to an elite or to the local tribe or group or nation. And so, in none of the tertiary civilizations which arose through chrysalis churches was education aristocratic in the way that it had been in the early periods of the secondary civilizations.

During the interregnum following the disintegration of the Sinic society some few Confucian schools were maintained in different parts of the land and, in these few, the teaching of the classics and the system of examinations were continued, but learning was kept alive mainly in the many Buddhist monasteries. During the interregnum following the disintegration of the Hellenic society there was a continuation of the classical schools and of the secular primary schools in the Byzantine Empire, and, with these, the monastic and patriarchal schools; in the West, the classical schools all but ceased to exist so that learning was kept alive only in the monastic, episcopal, and parish schools, and the stream of classical learning dwindled to the merest trickle. During the interregnum following the breakdown of the Indic society there appears to have been little or no break in the continuity of education, although there probably was diminution in the numbers of masters and pupils. In both of the offshoot societies, the systems of writing, the texts that were first used, and the methods of education were taken over from the main society, and these elements from the main society remained dominant even as they were being gradually domesticated in the offshoot throughout the period of growth of the latter. In the Islamic society the pre-Islamic oral literature persisted, but was as nothing in significance and importance in comparison with the dominance of the sacred book of the religion and the traditions that were believed to have emanated from the prince-prophet.

Thus the seven tertiary civilizations that have been studied can be thought of as falling on a kind of scale of relative continuity with the education of the earlier, apparented society. On such a scale, the Islamic society lies at one extreme of lack of continuity with the education of the earlier society, and the Hindu at the opposite extreme of apparently complete continuity. Next to the Hindu in relative completeness of continuity falls the Orthodox Christian

Civilization, with its classical, secular schools. In this society, however, the monastic and patriarchal schools existed alongside the classical schools, and the former gave a peculiarly Christian education that had not been present in the schools of the apparented society. In the Russian Offshoot of the Orthodox Christian Civilization, the education that was introduced under the aegis of the church was not, in the main, that of the Byzantine classical, secular schools, but that of the monastic schools, so that the Russian society began its career with less of the classical heritage.

Next to the Islamic in relative discontinuity falls the Western Civilization with its heritage of the "seven liberal arts" from the classical tradition and its canon law as a development out of Roman law, but with its bias against the old pagan, classical education and the limitation of the range and purpose of its three types of schools to the production of monks and clerics.

Education in the Far Eastern Civilization falls about midway in the hypothetical scale between the relatively extreme discontinuity of the Islamic society and the almost complete continuity of the Hindu. In the few Confucian schools that persisted in the land during the interregnum, the education given was the same as that of the latter days of the apparented civilization; but in the Buddhist monasteries most intellectual energy was spent on learning, translating, and adapting Buddhist texts. In the Japanese Offshoot of the Far Eastern society the education that was borrowed from China was, initially, that of both the Confucians and the Buddhists, but, in Japan as in the main society, the Confucian classics continued as the state education while the Buddhist influence was confined to private learning. In both the main society and its offshoot, the influence of Buddhism among the people was very great even as it was apparently wholly without influence upon the education required to pass the state examinations.

Each of the three societies that lie in the intermediate ranges of the hypothetical scale suffered a "renaissance" of the classical literature and thought and education of its apparented earlier civilization. The renaissance was, in each case, essentially the evocation of a dead culture—or of aspects of that culture—by a civilization that was a living, "going concern," as Toynbee has shown. The dead culture that was evoked was that of the society that was apparented to the living civilization; there have been many such evocations. Thus, so far from its being true that there was one "Renaissance" which was the revival of the classical, Hellenic influence in Western letters and arts in the fourteenth, fifteenth, and sixteenth centuries, there have been, instead, many "renaissances" before the "Renaissance": the eleventh-century political renaissance when the Lombard city-states of Northern Italy turned to the organization of the Hellenic city-states for the model of their own system of government by responsible magistrates instead of by their bishops; and the twelfth-century renaissance in philosophy when the influence of Aristotle began to stifle the indigenous Western creative originality.

In the Orthodox Christian Civilization, the ninth-century literary renaissance was clearly a return to and a revival of the texts that had been produced by the earlier Hellenic Civilization and this return was marked by the compilation of encyclopedias and anthologies of the earlier literature. Similar compilations marked the revival, in the Far Eastern Civilization, of the earlier Sinic literature, which was characterized by an increasing emphasis on form and a decreasing emphasis on content. The later Far Eastern philosophical renaissance, which was known as Neo-Confucianism, was essentially a reinterpretation of Confucianism in the light of Buddhism and was on the whole archaistic and conservative. All of these renaissances occurred towards the ends of the growth periods of the several societies or early in the time of troubles.

In the universal state phases of the tertiary civilizations there was, in each case, a gradual stereotyping and petrifaction of the intellectual life.

In the Far Eastern Civilization, for example, after Neo-Confucianism had won the day, there was an increase in pedanticism and dogmatism and a general stereotyping and petrifaction of the intellectual life. Then, after the expulsion of the Mongols and the establishment of the Ming, there was an even more exacting pedanticism and formalism which continued to be extended and intensified in the training of the scholarly civil servants. Underneath this scholarly surface the vernacular literature arose, propagated itself, and became the literature and education of the masses of the people. In the Orthodox Christian Society the successive refoundings of the university—each time with essentially the same classical curriculum, the same state support, and the same purpose of producing civil servants—indicate a similar progressive stereotyping and growth of formalism. By contrast with the Far Eastern society, Byzantium produced no flourishing vernacular literature under the incubus of classical literature and scholarship.

In Russia there was very little education—other than that given by the universal apprenticeship method—during the time of troubles or the early stages of the universal state. The real beginnings of Russian education, after the Kievan period and after the prolonged and devastating time of troubles, came with Peter's attempt to Westernize the society. In the other offshoot civilization, Japan, the original subject matter of education had been taken over from China. The purpose of the schools was to produce civil servants. The character-education of Bushido was characteristically Japanese, but two of the major influences on it were Chinese. Under the universal state of the Tokugawa Shogunate the schools were dominated by Neo-Confucianism, and their purpose continued mainly to be that of producing civil servants. The schools became increasingly stereotyped and formalized and petrified until the Meiji Revolution and the beginnings of Westernization of the school system.

In the Islamic world in its later stages the schools became increasingly stereotyped; no changes were allowed in curricula or methods; and the purpose of the state schools was to produce civil servants.

17. Conclusions

by
Arnold J. Toynbee

Education is a specifically human activity. Unlike other animals, man inherits something over and above what is transmitted to him automatically by physical and psychic heredity. He also inherits a culture which the members of the rising generation acquire, not as an automatic birthright, but through being inducted into it by their elders. Human culture is not built into human minds; it is a mental tool that is transmitted, held, and operated by them, and it is detachable and variable. Our minds are like handles to which alternative systems of culture can be fitted. Our culture does resemble our physical and psychic constitution in changing in the course of transmission; but its rate of change is incomparably faster than nature's. Even when the intentions of all concerned are conservative, the transmitting generation never succeeds in handing on its cultural heritage in quite the form in which it received it from its predecessors; and the time span of one generation is infinitesimally short compared to the age of the human race up to date.

In most human societies in most times and places so far, education, in the broad sense of the transmission of a cultural heritage, has been an unself-conscious and unorganized activity. People have mostly acquired their ancestral culture in the way in which they learn their mother tongue. They associate with their elders and learn from them unconsciously, while the elders, on their side, are hardly more conscious of being teachers. Both the importance and the persistence of this kind of education have been brought out very clearly by Professor Myers in this book.

This unsophisticated kind of education continues to play an important part even in societies in process of civilization in which organized and formal systems of education have come to be established. Even in educational institutions in which the official staple is book learning, the forming of habits and the training of character are still largely left to be taken care of by the spontaneous effects of the social relations between the rising generation and its elders; and what the child brings with him from his home may count for as much as what is deliberately impressed upon him at school. The importance of the home's contribution comes to light when an educational institution that has been the preserve of some privileged minority is thrown open to a wider public. One of the most effective privileges hitherto has been the privilege of being heir to a richer cultural heritage than is accessible to the unprivileged majority, and this richer heritage is transmitted through the family as well as through schools and colleges. This becomes apparent when children with a poorer cultural heritage are admitted to the minority's schools. They find it difficult to obtain as much benefit as their privileged schoolfellows obtain from the same course of formal education, because they bring less with them. To him that hath shall be given. This is not just, but it is one of the facts of life. It takes more than one generation for a family that has made its way out of a less privileged into a more privileged social class to acquire the full cultural heritage of the class to which it has won admission.

A society enters on the process of civilization as soon as it can afford to maintain a minority, however small, whose time and energy is not wholly taken up in producing food and the other primary necessities of life. This leisured minority is the social milieu in which an unorganized and unself-conscious apprenticeship in the older generation's way of life comes to be supplemented, more and more, by the organized and self-conscious kind of instruction which is what we commonly mean today in our society when we use the word "education." This development, which is one of the accompaniments of civilization, is what makes possible the enrichment of the cultural heritage that the word "civilization" implies. But every good thing has its price, and the introduction of formal education has several awkward consequences.

One consequence is to make education become a burden on the

mind. In the act of making it formal we make it cumulative. The successive cultural achievements of successive generations are recorded and handed on, while the capacity of a single human mind in a single lifetime remains within constant natural limits. How is a limited human mind to cope with a cultural heritage that is perpetually increasing in bulk? This problem is aggravated when people begin deliberately to extend the range of human knowledge by systematic research. There will be a temptation to try to facilitate the acquisition of the growing heritage by simplifying its content at the cost of impoverishing it. For educational purposes the culture may be reduced to a conventional form in which it will tend to become impersonal, secular, and abstract; and in this process the living essence of the culture may slip out of the meshes of the educational net. The apprenticeship for life may be ousted by a course of instruction set by syllabus. Ordeals that are initiations into successive stages of life may shrivel into examinations in arbitrarily selected bodies of cut-and-dried knowledge.

Another consequence of formalizing education is to make it esoteric. When poetry, sacred or secular, is preserved over a series of generations by being committed to memory or to writing, the work of art "freezes" the language in which it is conveyed. Of all man's cultural tools, his living language is perhaps the one that changes most rapidly. It quickly parts company with the language of a work that has become a classic, and the classical language soon becomes archaic and finally ceases to be intelligible to anyone who has not had the leisure to devote himself to the study of it. Mastery of a language that still enjoys high cultural prestige but is at the same time a "dead" language for all but a learned minority gives this minority a monopoly that carries power with it and that may therefore come to be prized and clung to for its own sake.

This may happen even when the transmission of a classical literature is still oral. History shows that in societies in which the human mind's natural powers of memory have not been weakened by dependence on written records, large bodies of literature can be handed down, word perfect, for centuries by memorization, unaided by writing. And indeed, many societies, long after they have acquired the art of writing, have cherished a strong and persistent prejudice against committing to writing anything that is felt to be of social and cultural value—for instance, laws, and still more, liturgies. Writing seems usually to have come into use first of all for prosaic practical purposes such as the recording of inventories, contracts, and correspondence. It has to become well established and familiar before people can bring themselves to use it for higher cultural ends.

The earliest scripts have been the clumsiest and the most complicated and therefore the most difficult to learn to read and write. So, when the scribe's monopoly of understanding a classical language is reinforced by a monopoly of manipulating an archaic script, he becomes doubly entrenched in his position of privilege, and acquires a vested interest in opposing the literary use of the vulgar tongue of his own day conveyed in an easily mastered system of writing. The Egyptian hieroglyphic script, the Sumerian cuneiform, and, above all, the vast array of Chinese characters are examples of scripts that have been misused to defeat the purpose of the art of writing by making it a barrier to communication instead of a channel for it. For this reason the invention of the alphabet has been a turning point in the history of education, if we think of this history as being the story of the effort to make formal, as well as spontaneous, education one of the fundamental rights of all men instead of leaving it to remain the privilege of a minority. Yet, during the first three thousand years since the discovery of the principle of analyzing the sounds of human speech into their elements by the unknown genius to whom the invention of the alphabet is due, this principle has never been applied with complete rationality. Every known version of the alphabet retains letters that are superfluous because they are duplicates or compounds, and lacks letters required for conveying some of the sounds that occur in the language to which this version of the alphabet has been geared.

Successive breaches in the scribe's monopoly have been made from various motives. For instance, the government of a widespread empire, embracing all, and perhaps more than all, the domain of an entire civilization, may find the traditional privileged minority inadequate or unsuitable for supplying the imperial government with the administrators that it needs; and then this government may deliberately call into existence a new class of educated people to fill or supplement the ranks of its administrative hierarchy. In China at the turn of the second and the last century B.C., the imperial government entered into an alliance with the Confucian school of philosophers whose literary stock-in-trade was the classics that Confucius had canonized. The result was a considerable extension of the educated class in China and a concomitant broadening of this class' social basis. A wholly new "intelligentsia" may be called into existence by an imperial government that has become converted to an alien culture or has brought an alien culture in with it. This was one of the effects of the "reception" of Western culture in Russia in and after the reign of Peter the Great, and of the introduction of Western culture into India by the British raj.

Missionary religions, again, have called into existence new corporations of educated clerics in their zeal to propagate themselves to the ends of the earth; and their leaders, looking upon the whole human race as prospective converts, have been, perhaps, the first people in the world to conceive of universal education. In China, in particular, the inventions of printing and paper appear to have been stimulated by the eagerness of Buddhist missionaries to bring spiritual enlightenment within the reach of the masses.

This vision of universal education was caught by the higher religions before the economic means had been provided for translating it from an ideal into a reality. During these first five thousand years of the history of civilization, one of the most characteristic, and most ugly, features of this new way of life has been the monopoly of its amenities, spiritual as well as material, by a small minority of the members of societies in process of civilization. This blot on the scutcheon of civilization during its first phase has not been due solely to the selfishness of the ruling minority. Even if all the members of this group had succeeded in rising above their natural human egotism and had tried with all their might to share their cultural heritage with the unprivileged majority of their fellow human beings, they would have been defeated, till the other day, by the smallness of the economic surplus, remaining in hand after the satisfaction of elementary economic needs, that human society was able to produce before the modern industrial revolution. This revolution started in the Western World about two hundred years ago and, since then, has been increasing in momentum and been communicating itself from the Western peoples to the rest of mankind. But in a pre-industrial agricultural economy, in which human and animal muscle power has not been reinforced by mechanical power, all but a small minority of the members of society are condemned to live as a peasantry whose puny production cannot provide amenities, in addition to such common necessities as food, clothing, and shelter, for more than a small minority. This injustice was made intolerable by the appearance in the world of higher religions which divined and proclaimed the infinite spiritual values of every human soul, irrespective of the social class in which it has been placed by the accident of birth. An injustice that has long since been intolerable has now been made unnecessary by the industrial revolution, which has brought it within our economic power at last to provide the amenities of civilization for mankind in the mass —always supposing that we do not use the new power, generated by the progress of technology, for the mass self-destruction of the human race.

Our present industrial revolution is, of course, only one in a long series of technological advances; but it is perhaps the first, since the invention of agriculture, that has been potent enough to provide appreciable social and cultural benefits for *all* members of a society that has made it. At the dawn of civilization the quantitative yield of agriculture was increased in the river valleys of Southwest Asia and Egypt by the invention of water control. In the seventh and sixth centuries B.C. the qualitative value of the yield was increased in Greece by the invention of specialization in luxury crops to be traded in exchange for staple foodstuffs and raw materials. These too were brilliant economic revolutions, but they were comparatively minor ones in their material effect. Our present day industrial revolution is the first that has opened up the prospect of providing the material means for raising the standard of living of the world's vast peasantry above the neolithic level that was attained round the rim of "the Fertile Crescent" during the age preceding the dawn of civilization there. This present possibility of bringing the benefits of civilization to the whole of the great unprivileged majority of the human race carries with it a moral command to execute the act of justice that is now at last within our power. This is the new requirement with which mankind, and consequently the ancient human institution of education, is confronted today. The educational problems involved are of the same order of magnitude as the requirement itself.

One problem is presented by the unalterable and inescapable fact that a human being has a strictly limited capacity. The maximum natural endowment of ability and energy that can be in action over the maximum effective life span is something that is fixed within very narrow limits of marginal variability. On the other hand, human knowledge is cumulative in the field of science and technology; and in the field of the humanities, as well, knowledge tends to accumulate within the time spans of particular civilizations and higher religions, and sometimes outlives the disintegration and disappearance of these social matrices of humane culture. This accumulation of culture confronts the givers and receivers of formal education with a Psyche's task of ever-increasing difficulty; and this difficulty confronts all individuals alike, in every civilization and in every social class.

In modern times the Western Civilization has been sensationally successful in deliberately and systematically extending the bounds of knowledge and in applying the knowledge of non-human nature, that has been gained in this way, to the practical purpose of increasing human power over man's non-human environment. One of the devices by which these successes have been achieved has been specialization. And there is a temptation to carry specialization to still farther lengths as a possible means of coping with the overwhelming mass of new knowledge that specialization has won for us. At the present time this temptation is reinforced by the new demand of governments and non-governmental corporations and foundations for specialists in natural science and technology, now that technological and scientific knowledge is expected to count for more than military prowess and administrative skill in the arena of international power politics.

Any state or people that succumbs to this temptation seems likely to defeat its own purpose. The modern marriage of technology with science has proved fruitful because science has been pursued primarily for its own sake, without any immediate view to a practical application of its discoveries. And even the disinterested pursuit of science becomes sterile if it runs in narrow ruts. Specialization in particular branches of natural science soon runs dry if it is cut off from its source in comprehensive and philosophical scientific thinking. Moreover, even a scientist who takes the whole of non-human nature into his purview cannot afford to leave human nature out of it. "The proper study of mankind is man," because man's dealings with himself and with his human neighbors are the part of man's business in which he has been conspicuously unsuccessful up to date; and the penalty of failure here becomes heavier, the greater the power over non-human nature that the advance of natural science places in man's hands for him to wield, in his perversity, against himself. The need for balancing an education in natural science and technology with an education in the humanities has been recognized and acted upon by, for instance, the Massachusetts Institute of Technology, which is one of the most distinguished educational institutions of the present day; and the wisdom of this broadminded policy has been recognized in the educational world. This should be noted and taken to heart by the advocates of extreme specialization in the various branches of technology and natural science as a supposed key to dominance in a competition for power between states.

Meanwhile, the ocean of knowledge has grown to an immeasurable size, not only in the field of natural science but in the field of the humanities as well. In the past, when the different civilizations were living side by side more or less in isolation from one another, a humane education demanded no more than the mastery of the "classical" language, literature, and philosophy of some single civilization—for example, the Chinese classics for the peoples of Eastern Asia and the Greek and Latin classics for the peoples of the West. But, since the modern Western Civilization has made its recent impact on the rest of the world, the children of other civilizations have been finding that a mastery of their own ancestral culture is no longer enough to enable them to hold their own. If they are to survive "under the strenuous conditions of modern life" (to quote a phrase from the mandates chapter of the Covenant of the League of Nations), they must now learn something about modern science and technology and must also learn something about its Western inventors, to whom this new knowledge has given a temporary dominance over other peoples. Under Western pressure, the non-Western peoples have been stealing a march on the Westerners in broadening the traditional range of their education in the humanities. And the West, in its turn, in going to have to follow its unintended pupils' example. For, in our lifetime, we are seeing the West rapidly losing its recently won supremacy, as one non-Western people after another acquires the Western technological and scientific "know-how" and thereby begins to recapture its normal position in the world which it had temporarily lost when the modern West took the world by storm through taking it by surprise.

The non-Western peoples' self-education in Western knowledge may be proving effective, for the moment, as a key to the recovery of power, but it is a shallow knowledge, compared to their traditional education in their ancestral humanities, and this new knowledge will prove a poor exchange for the old unless it is deepened. The typical Westernized—or, as he might prefer to say, modernized—non-Westerner of today has qualified himself for the exercise of some modern Western profession—say, medicine or engineering—and he has learnt his profession in some Western language, but he is likely to be ignorant of the Greek and Latin classics, which are the source of the modern West's secular culture, and ignorant of Christianity, which is the source of an agnostic or an atheist Westerner's spiritual outlook, as well as of his ethical principles. So the non-Western convert to Western Civilization will have abandoned his own ancestral cultural heritage without having succeeded in acquiring its Western equivalent. But the peoples of the world cannot learn to understand each other if they confine their attention to the present surface of life and ignore the historical depths. We cannot truly know a person, a people, a civilization, or a religion without knowing something about its history; and here, by yet another route, we are again brought face to face with the problem created by the inordinate increase in the quantity of our knowledge.

Today our knowledge of the past is increasing at an unprecedented rate, and this at both ends of its ever lengthening vista. The archeologists are making history by exhuming buried and forgotten civilizations as fast as the politicians are making it by taking new action for contemporary historians to study. The public records produced in the United Kingdom during the Second World War, which lasted less than six years, are said to equal in quantity the whole amount of the surviving previous records of the United Kingdom and its component states the Kingdoms of England and Scotland. The wartime records of one single government department in London would extend, it is said, for seventeen miles if the files were stacked on edge, as tight as they could be packed, in a row. The records of archeological excavations are also formidably extensive; and, in between, our knowledge of comparatively well known periods in the histories of the civilizations and the religions has been increased and, in the process, transformed by the study of previously unknown or neglected documents and by the reinterpretation of previously familiar ones.

In the meantime, economics has opened up the study of an aspect of human activity that was previously ignored; anthropology and sociology have opened up the study of the structure of human society and the nature of human culture at all levels, from the most primitive to the least uncivilized. And psychology has added a new dimension to the study of human nature. The Greek sciences of epistemology, logic, and ethics had explored the rational and purposeful surface of the human psyche; psychology is probing the irrational and emotional depths; and here, once more, the questing human mind finds itself confronted by infinity. To quote the Gospel according to St. John, "the World itself could not contain the books that should be written" by a competent psychologist if he were to set himself to make an exhaustive record of all the psychic events that occur in a single psyche within the shortest period of time that the subtlest recording instruments can measure.

This immense and growing mass of knowledge about man and his non-human environment daunts the minds that are exposed to it and throws them on the defensive. In self-defense we are tempted to ask ourselves again whether our institutions for formal education cannot simply reject the greater part of this formidable load, or, short of that, divide it up into packages that can be distributed between different pairs of shoulders without a risk of breaking any backs. The reply to this cry of distress has to be in the negative. "Homo sum, humani nihil a me alienum puto." "I am a human being, so I cannot be indifferent to anything that has to do with human life and human nature." Every man, woman, and child that is alive today is living in a world in which mankind is now faced with the extreme choice between learning to live together as one family and committing genocide on a planetary scale. Neither the human race nor any living member of it can afford to ignore the present human situation. We must cope with it if we are not to destroy ourselves; in order to cope with it we must understand it; and trying to understand it commits each and all of us to making some acquaintance with at least three vast realms of knowledge: a knowledge of non-human nature; a knowledge of human nature; and a knowledge of the characters and histories of the local and temporary cultures—some relatively primitive, others relatively advanced—that man has created and transmitted and modified and discarded in the course of the ages that have passed since his pre-human ancestors became human. Formal education's minimum task has thus become a big undertaking in our day; and every child will have a strenuous course of formal as well as informal education to run in order to grow up into being an effective citizen of our new world.

How, then, are our educational institutions to convey this overwhelmingly massive heritage of knowledge to a puny and ephemeral human mind? The task would be an intimidating one even it we could confine it to the education of the privileged heirs of the Western cultural tradition. These, if anyone, should be receptive to an education of this comprehensive kind; for it is they who have called into existence the world-wide social framework within which the whole human race is now living. This has started as a Western framework (though, no doubt, it will turn into a very different one); and the privileged minority in the Western society have played the chief part in giving it its present shape. So they, if anyone, ought to feel at home in it. Yet how hard it is, today, to educate even this favored minority to cope with what is its own heritage. And before we have seen our way to solving even this limited educational problem, we have to plunge on into the still more difficult problems of educating the unprivileged majority of Westerners and the huge non-Western majority of the human race, for whom the present Western framework of their life is something alien and uncongenial. Evidently this educational task is a tremendous one. Yet we cannot afford to shy away from it or to exclude any part of the human race from its scope. We have to help mankind to educate itself against the danger of its destroying itself; and this is a duty that we dare not repudiate.

This is not the first time that an educational task of this nature, and even of something like this magnitude, has confronted human beings who have found themselves responsible for the destinies of large portions of the human race. It may be true that the whole human race, in all the habitable regions on the surface of the globe, has never been drawn together into a single literally world-wide society before this was achieved, in the course of the last few centuries, by Western initiative. All the same, in the past, there have been unifications on a scale that, short of being truly ecumenical, has been great enough to seem ecumenical to the people involved. Nineteen hundred years ago, the Chinese Empire seemed to the inhabitants of the Chinese Empire, and the Roman Empire to the inhabitants of the Roman Empire, to embrace virtually the whole of the civilized world. Both societies were mistaken in their picture of themselves—as is demonstrated by the mere fact that these two "ecumenical" empires were co-existing, almost unknown to each other, at opposite ends of the same continent. Nevertheless, the educational problems that these predecessors of ours encountered as a result of unification on a sub-continental scale are sufficiently like our own truly ecumenical problem of the present day to be worth our notice. A glance at these partial precedents may perhaps at least give us warning of some of the pitfalls that we have to avoid, even if it does not throw as much light on the positive educational policies that we ought to pursue.

In the Chinese Empire in its first bout, under the Ts'in and Han dynasties, as well as in the Roman Empire, there was an attempt to extend the range of formal education from the privileged minority that had previously monopolized it to a wider circle. In both cases this attempt miscarried, in the sense that it failed to teach the whole population of an "ecumenical" empire how to live together permanently as a single family. Both empires went to pieces (though both were put together again temporarily after an interregnum). In both cases, the same two reasons for the miscarriage can be discerned within the field of education—though of course these are only part of the explanation of what happened.

One reason was that the former privileged minority's traditional system of education was impoverished in the process of being disseminated. It degenerated into a formal education in book learning, divorced from a spontaneous apprenticeship for life. The test of having been initiated into the traditional culture came to be the mastery of an arbitrarily selected and canonized corpus of classical literature, and the test of this mastery came to be an ability to imitate the original. In fact, the art of playing with words was substituted for the art of living.

A second reason for the miscarriage was that the range of formal education was limited, in both cases, to the humanities. Though both the Greeks and the Chinese of the "classical" age had made additions to mankind's technological equipment, and the Greeks had also been pioneers in the discovery of pure mathematics and physical science, an aristocratic prejudice against "the useful arts" outlived the aristocratic regime in both societies. Accordingly nothing was done in either society to try to raise the economy above the purely agricultural level at which it had always remained in Eastern Asia and to which it had been reduced again in the Graeco-Roman World when the effects of the agricultural revolutions in Greece in the sixth century B.C. and in Italy in the second century B.C. had been offset by the incorporation into the Graeco-Roman world of large economically backward areas in Northwest Africa and in the European hinterlands of the Mediterranean. The same aristocratic prejudice inhibited the Greeks from making that marriage between science and technology which was consummated in the modern Western World in and after the seventeenth century with such fruitful results. The consequence, in both the Graeco-Roman world and Eastern Asia, was that a swollen educated class remained parasitic on a peasantry whose productivity had not been stepped up to carry the additional load; and this increase in the peasantry's social burden was not compensated for by any cultural benefits that the peasantry could appreciate. The cut-and-dried book learning in the classics, to which the privileged minority's culture had been reduced, was not made accessible to the peasants, and if it had been, it would probably not have proved attractive to them. In these circumstances it is not surprising that in both cases the peasantry revolted and that the "ecumenical" empire, and the civilization embodied in it, collapsed. In this story from the past there are lessons for us today.

One lesson is that we must try to keep the several essential subjects of education in balance with each other. Undoubtedly the most important subject of all is man. The human race could not survive if, in each generation, we did not learn from our predecessors at least a modicum of the art of managing our relations with our fellow human beings and with ourselves. This is the essence of a humane education, but it cannot be learned just from a study of "the humanities" in book form. In the present day world, it is true, a considerable amount of book learning has come to be a necessary part of everyone's education. At the same time, the essence of a humane education has still to be acquired mainly through the informal apprenticeship that is the heart of education in all societies and all social classes at all levels. This is what makes and keeps us human. Book learning in "the humanities" can be a valuable supplement to it, but can never be a substitute for it. And it must be remembered that while an apprenticeship in the art of living with one's fellows is an indispensable part of the education of every human being born into the world, the bookish supplement to it originally came into existence as a vocational education for administrative officials in government service and for ministers of the higher religions. These are two highly specialized occupations; and, though the range of "the liberal professions" has considerably increased *pari passu* with the increasing complexity of civilization in the modern age, these walks of life seem unlikely ever to provide employment for more than a small fraction of the human race or to find more than a small fraction willing and able to seek its vocation in them.

If we were to try to force mankind in the mass to undergo a formal literary education, not merely up to the elementary or the secondary stage, but up to the standard required in order to qualify for one of the liberal professions, we should ruin the higher levels of this branch of education in trying to bring them down to within the capacity of people with no special aptitude for rising to them, and at the same time we should be running the risk of disgusting the mass of mankind with formal education of any kind. We must recognize that there is a diversity in human gifts, and that this diversity is valuable to society. Natural-born "intellectuals" are divided between those who are attracted to the humanities and those who are attracted to natural science. But "intellectuals" of both types are a rather small minority in every class, society, and race. What line of higher education an individual should follow ought to be a matter, not of privilege, but of personal aptitude. Most human beings in all races, societies, and classes are born with a practical bent, and these, when they reach the stage of more advanced education, will feel most at home if they turn from book learning towards an apprenticeship in technology, irrespective of what their family's social position may happen to be.

This does not, of course, mean that formal education should be depreciated or neglected; for, in a world in which peoples inheriting widely different ways of life have suddenly to learn how to live as one family, there are obvious tasks for formal education in the spheres of technology, science, and the humanities. Our first need is to communicate effectively with each other; and, in a world that is still a babel of mutually unintelligible languages, every child should be expected, whatever its vocation may be going to be, to learn at least one other language besides its mother tongue. This is not an excessive demand, as is shown by the fact that in Switzerland every child does already learn two other languages, and in Holland three, as a matter of course. The incentive is greatest for those, like the Dutch, whose mother tongue happens not to be a world language, so that they will be strangers in the wide world if they do not make the effort to become polyglots. The English-speaking peoples tend to be spoilt by the handicap of happening to speak a world language as their mother tongue.

Americans also tend to think of the rest of the human race as being potential immigrants whose business it is to learn how to live the American way of life, and the first step towards this, as Americans see it, is to learn the English language. Today, however, it is the Americans' turn to come on to other people's ground if America is to hold her own in her world-wide competition with Russia. Since the Second World War, an important new profession has made its appearance in American life. There are now hundreds of thousands of Americans working abroad in the service, not only of the United States Government, but of the great American commercial corporations and cultural foundations. These American citizens on service in non-English-speaking countries have been caught at a disadvantage by the traditional American aversion to the learning of foreign languages. On the other hand, Russia enjoys the advantage of a traditional mastery of foreign languages up to almost Swiss and Dutch standards, and this tradition seems now to have revived in Russia after a lapse during the early years after the revolution of 1917. It looks as if the Russians are likely to be the unintentional promoters of a new movement in the United States to make the learning of foreign languages one of the staples of American education. But it is not only the English-speaking peoples who need a stimulus in this direction. In a world that has to be "one world" now if it is to continue to exist, there is room for improvement even in those countries in which the standard of proficiency in learning foreign languages stands at its highest today in all classes.

But the world cannot become "one world" in spirit merely by improving its means of intercommunication. Closer acquaintance may produce hostility instead of friendship so long as different peoples, and different classes within the same community, have such unequal shares in the amenities of civilization as they still have. This inequality has been the consequence of poverty; poverty has been the consequence of technological backwardness; and this backwardness has been overcome by the modern marriage of technology with science. The world needs to educate its scientific-minded "intellectuals" and the technological-minded majority of its people to work together with a view to raising the minimum standard of material life for all mankind to a hitherto undreamed-of level. Now that we have discovered how to tap atomic energy, there is no reason why every Indian peasant should not soon be as well off as a present day Illinois farmer. A rise in material well-being of this magnitude might perhaps not be altogether good for the peasant's soul; but without a considerable rise above his present depressingly low level of material existence he will be unable to achieve the spiritual welfare that is the true end of man.

The greatest blessing that technological progress has in store for mankind is not, of course, an accumulation of material possessions. The amount of these that can be enjoyed effectively by one individual in one lifetime is not great. But there is not the same narrow limit to the possibilities of the enjoyment of leisure. The gift of leisure may be abused by people who have had no experience of making use of it. Yet the creative use of leisure by a minority of the leisured minority in societies in process of civilization up to date has been the mainspring of all human progress beyond the primitive level. In our present day, still archaic, industrial society, leisure is still thought of, by all but a privileged minority, in its negative aspect of "unemployment" in gainful labor; and for the industrial worker, the prospect of unemployment is at present a nightmare, because at present unemployment carries with it a loss of income and, worse still, a loss of self-respect. In our world today an unemployed worker feels as if he were an unwanted outcast from the working community. The

Greeks had a truer vision in seeing in leisure the greatest of all human goods; and they did indeed use the leisure that a minority of them enjoyed for worthy ends—as is witnessed by the etymological fact that the Greek word for leisure has provided most of the modern Western languages with their word for "school." In our world, the dawning age of automation is soon going to provide ample leisure for all industrial workers without loss of income or of self-respect or of social esteem.

No doubt, if this unheard-of leisure is thrust into their hands suddenly, they will partly misuse it to begin with. But, sooner or later, we shall surely be able to salvage some of it for employment on adult education of a formal kind. Our informal apprenticeship in life is, of course, lifelong; our experience of life educates us, whether we will this or not. But, in the poverty-stricken civilizations of these first few thousand years, formal education, even for a privileged minority, has usually come to an end at the close of adolescence, if not earlier; and this has had an unfortunate consequence. The student has been surfeited with book learning at a stage of life at which he has not yet acquired the experience to take advantage of this, and he has then been starved of book learning at a later stage in which, if he had been given the opportunity, he could have made much more of it in the light of his growing experience. In the rich society of the future, we shall be able to afford to offer part-time adult education to every man and woman at every stage of grown-up life. Already, in Denmark, a highly civilized people that has had the intelligence to carry out an agricultural revolution has used some of its modest profits, Greek fashion, for providing voluntary adult higher education for itself in the admirable Danish high schools (which are schools for grown-up persons, not for children). A Danish farmer will save money for years to enable himself to take a six-months' or a twelve-months' course, and he will make it a point of honor to choose his subject with an eye to raising the level of his culture and not with an eye to improving his economic position. In this present day Danish institution we have a foretaste of an educational advance that will be open to the whole of mankind in the coming age of "atoms for peace," automation, and the leisure that will be generated by an abundance of scientifically directed mechanical power.

But the quality of education of all kinds depends on the quality of the people who give it, and there has been a paradoxical tendency for this to deteriorate as the formal element in education has increased in importance. The spontaneous apprenticeship in life, which was the only form of education known to early man, was given by the leaders of the community. The child received it from his parents, and the young man from the community's priests and captains. The educational functions of these leaders were inseparable and indistinguishable from the rest of their activities, and therefore shared in their general prestige. But when a separate formal kind of education makes its appearance, it brings into existence a new class of professional teachers who work, like other professional men and women, for pay; and, in most societies in process of civilization up to date, both the pay and the status of the professional teacher have been lower than has been warranted by the lip service that society has paid to the value of formal education. This has sometimes set up a vicious circle, in which the depression and discontent of the teaching profession has deterred able people from entering it, and has thereby led to a further lowering of its standards and status, leading in turn to deeper depression and discontent. The lowness of the status of the teaching profession in the present day Western World has been satirized in George Bernard Shaw's trenchant and telling epigram: "If you can, do; if you can't, teach."

It is true that, in the modern Western World, the status of the teaching profession varies appreciably from country to country. In Austria a professor's wife used to rank with a colonel's, while in Prussia she ranked with a major's. If anyone had thought of grading her in England, she probably would have ranked no higher than a captain's wife there, whereas in Scotland she certainly would have ranked as high as a major-general's. Before the salaries of professors in the United Kingdom were evened out by subventions from the public purse to counteract the effects of inflation, poor Scotland used to pay her professors higher salaries than rich England cared to dole out in remuneration for the same work. Today, an English professor no longer gains an increase in monetary income if he is posted to a Scottish university; but his wife is still astonished at the deference—out of all proportion to her slender purchasing power—with which she is treated in the stores that she honors with her distinguished custom.

Perhaps one reason why, in Scotland, the status of professors remains high is that they still trail some clouds of glory from an ecclesiastical past. Till recently the ambition of every Scottish peasant family was to send a son into the Presbyterian ministry. The enterprise called for immense effort and self-sacrifice; and the professor was the good genius who won the whole family's gratitude by helping the aspiring student on his arduous road. This cannot, however, be the whole explanation, for the status of professors has also been comparatively high in France and Germany, where the professor has been, not a semi-ecclesiastical hierophant, but the civil servant of a secular state. And anyway, in the modern Western World, these instances of a relatively high status for teachers are exceptional. The relatively low status to which they have been depressed in most English-speaking countries, outside Scotland, is more typical of their status in the Western World as a whole.

What, then, can be done today to raise the Western teaching profession's status and standards? Here Russia may be doing the West another unintentional service by giving Western observers the impression that she treats her professors as grandees. Perhaps this impression, whether or not it is correct, may spur America into raising the status of the American teaching profession as an inescapable move in her competition with Russia for world power. This is not the best conceivable motive for an educational reform; but it is to be welcomed if it does move the American people to give American teachers large increases of salary and of leisure. America can afford already to be generous to her teachers, without needing to wait for the superabundance that is to be expected from "atoms for peace."

But a substantial improvement in the teaching profession's material conditions of life would not be enough in itself. It would merely be an enabling condition to open the way for a rise in the degree of esteem in which teachers are held in their own estimation as well as in the public's. This esteem cannot be high unless both the public and the profession become convinced of two things: first, that the teaching profession is performing a valuable public service, and, second, that it is maintaining a high professional standard in its work. The first of these two conditions will be fulfilled if it is realized that, in the present critical chapter of history, the teaching profession does have an indispensable part to play in helping the human race to save itself from self-destruction by helping it to grow into one family in which the odious traditional division between the privileged and the unprivileged will have been abolished. Here is a field in which the teacher of languages and the teacher of technology can both prove their worth. As for the professional standard to which the teacher can rise, this will depend on the amount of the leisure that is granted to him and on the use to which he puts it.

Since man in process of civilization first deliberately set himself to extend the bounds of human knowledge by purposeful and systematic research, it has been recognized that a university teacher must be given the opportunity to be a part-time researcher too if he is to retain his intellectual vitality and to communicate this to his pupils. We now have sufficient material resources to be able to offer the same opportunity to teachers not only at the university level but at all levels below it. Nothing could do more than this could to increase the teaching profession's efficiency, prestige, and self-respect. When we think of research, we should, of course, think of it in the widest terms. In the field of research into physical nature, no one would dispute that the telescope is as valuable and as honorable an instrument as the microscope. In the field of the humanities, there has recently been a tendency for the microscopists to claim a monopoly of the label "research" for their own kind of work and to refuse the title to their brethren the telescopists. Yet it is surely obvious that the Newtons and Einsteins have done no less to increase our knowledge and understanding of the Universe than their fellow scientists who have discovered previously undetected planets or galaxies. It is also obvious that this truism holds good for the humanities as well as for physical science.

Research, of whatever kind, is good for teaching, because it sets a standard of precision and thoroughness which the researcher-teacher will exact from himself and demand from his pupils. But here, as so often before, we are brought back to the problem set by the limits of the capacity of human minds. Even if formal education is to become lifelong, how can a single mind in a single lifetime acquire an education that will be exact and at the same time comprehensive? We cannot do without either of these conditions in a world that has become "one world" and that has also become scientific in its intellectual standards. Perhaps the solution will be for everybody—pupil and teacher, researcher and "practical" man or woman alike—to operate intellectually in two dimensions simultaneously. Everybody needs to have a glimpse of the bird's-eye view, with a radius of hundreds of miles, that one catches from a jet plane flying in the stratosphere. Everybody also needs to have a glimpse of the worm's-eye view, with the depth of thousands of feet, that one catches by sifting the successive strata that are brought to the surface by an oil prospector's drill as it burrows into the bowels of the earth. The capacity of a single human mind is narrowly circumscribed; it can never succeed either in surveying the whole surface of the globe or in probing the globe's interior to the center. Yet at least it need not confine itself to either of these intellectual quests exclusively. It can sample both, and such intellectual catholicity will be a liberal education. Let our students survey the history of all mankind all over the face of the planet since the age when man's pre-human ancestors first became human; but at the same time let them scrutinize the history of some local short-lived tribe or parish. Let them learn to communicate with their neighbors in languages that are not their own mother tongues; but at the same time let them master in detail the structure of some particular language and the art of some particular poet. This dual approach to the problem of education seems the most promising that we can make in the huge and complex new world into which we are being carried today by the rushing current of history.

Here are some of the reflections that are suggested by Professor Myers' exciting panorama of education in the societies that have embarked on the enterprise of civilization during these first five thousand years. Many other thoughts and questions will have presented themselves in the reader's mind while he has been following Professor Myers' work. This work opens up the horizon of the future by re-evoking the horizons of the past.

Appendices

Appendix I Education in Five Primary Civilizations

1. The Andean Civilization

The Andean Civilization arose as a mutation out of some primitive societies in response to the twofold physical challenge of the coastal desert and of the bleak climate of the almost soilless highland plateau of northwestern South America. The civilization was wholly unrelated to any earlier or later civilization and is therefore known solely through archaeological and literary records.

The civilization originated first in the coastal lowlands towards the beginning of the Christian era, and appears to have grown rapidly during the first five Christian centuries. Somewhat later, and apparently independently, a civilization appeared on the highland plateau.[1]

The breakdown of neither part of the society can be dated, but the time of troubles was well advanced—in the highlands at any rate —by the end of the twelfth century, and so would appear that the breakdown occurred at some time between the years A.D. 900 and 1100—perhaps about A.D. 1000.

The time of troubles came to an end about A.D. 1430, when the Inca Pachacutec succeeded in imposing a universal state on the highlands and lowlands alike.

Of education during the period of growth and the time of troubles nothing is known.

The Incas seem originally to have been a small tribe of mountaineers not different in any way from scores of other tribes. Their history unfolded in the space of about four centuries from 1100 to the final foundation of the universal state. During the time of troubles they rose gradually to the position of chiefs of tribal confederacies in competition with other confederacies. The first historical Inca consolidated his power in the neighborhood of Cuzco, in the highlands. He and his successors, by a skillful combination of martial prowess, tact, and diplomacy, extended the Inca sway from this center, first to the entire plateau, and finally, to the coastal region as well.

The Inca Empire was a marvel of rational planning and state socialism. At the summit was the Inca, the hereditary emperor, who held supreme temporal and religious authority. A small group of the elite helped him to rule. This elite was recruited primarily from young men of royal blood (the sovereign often had several hundred wives) and those few whom the emperor himself designated as fit members of this class. Beneath the elite came the minor functionaries, who supervised the lowest class, the peasants. The peasants cultivated the corn and legumes and tended the llamas and alpacas. A rigid hierarchy of caste was maintained, so that there was strict separation between social ranks.

The entire country was divided into districts based on the decimal system. Heads of families were divided into groups of ten. One man, the decurion, had power over the other nine. A centurian supervised a hundred families and so on up to a governor who administered the affairs of a group of forty thousand families. These officials had wide functions: they gathered statistics, made requests for seed, food, and wool, distributed the products obtained, oversaw inferior officials, and forwarded periodic reports to their supervisors.[2]

Land was parceled out to communities on the basis of population. The Sun God owned one part, the Inca one part, and the community one part. Land was cultivated in common for all three owners.

All except the elite, the widows, and the sick were required to work the lands of the Sun God and emperor. Tribute in goods was levied according to the needs of the provinces; and equality and justice were the ideals of the administration.

Since all administration was based on stable numbers, no fluctuation or movement of population was permitted. The emperor might, however, when necessary, move groups of families as colonists. Demand was limited to ensure stability of the economy. Each family was supposed to be self-sufficient.

The state maintained granaries and stockpiles of other types of food, clothing, and arms as war resources, as sources of gifts for the reward of merit, and to distribute in times of famine.

The marvellous roads of the Incas served as an instrument of unification of the empire. Inspectors, couriers, secret agents, and even the Inca himself made frequent tours of inspection, during which they heard complaints, observed conditions, and corrected abuses.

The Inca emperors in their conquests showed great moderation in victory. A conquered tribal chief was given presents and allowed to remain in authority. The modes of existence of the conquered tribes were changed as little as possible, though they were made subject to the rules and laws of the empire.

The members of the elite were the physical, moral, and intellectual guardians of the throne. Education was reserved for this class alone. The Inca Roca, who in the thirteenth century organized the schools in Cuzco, stated that the little people must not be instructed in what should be known only by the important personages.[3] The Incas admitted to their schools only the young people of a class superior to the others by the intellectual and moral qualities of its members. They saw little point in instructing those who were only to obey, just as they realized that none could command without having first been instructed.

The schools were erected at Cuzco on the main square near the imperial palaces. The teachers were the "amanta," a class of professional sages and jealous guardians of learning. They taught both religious and secular subjects, including mathematics, astronomy, statistics, theology, history, politics, poetry, music, and medicine. They composed tragedies and comedies and they themselves performed. They were entrusted with interpreting the law. Perhaps they also acted as engineers, directing the construction of canals, roads, fortresses, and cities.[4]

All instruction was of necessity oral, since the Incas were ignorant of writing. Knowledge of history, the law, religion, and science was transmitted from generation to generation by oral tradition. As a computer and statistical aide-memoir, the Incas used the quipu, an ingenious device consisting of leather thongs which could be knotted at intervals with small varicolored leather strips. By means of the quipu all records and reports and historical events were recorded. Instruction in its use was an important part of the education of the elite.

According to an early Spanish historian of the Incas, the first year of schooling was devoted to the study of language, the second to religion and the rites, the third to the use of the quipu, and the fourth to the study of history.[4]

The instruction ended in an examination of military character which took place annually or biennially at Cuzco. This examination permitted the Inca to assure himself that the future leaders of the elite were capable of being leaders of the army. The candidates were put on a diet of water and raw maize without salt for six days. After the candidates had been suitably refreshed, they then took part in a race at the city gates before the eyes of their friends and families, who cheered encouragement, praising the victors and jeering the losers. Next the candidates were divided into two camps for combat. Often they fought so hard that some were wounded or even killed. The physical exercises were concluded with wrestling and archery.

After the physical came the moral tests. The candidate had to remain for ten consecutive nights as a sentinel, take blows without complaint, and remain immobile when a chief threatened to crush his skull with a club or to stab his face with a lance. Finally, the candidate had to show his technical skill by making a bow and a pair of sandals.

A candidate who showed fear or fatigue was shamefully eliminated. The successful ones were received by the emperor who pierced the candidates' ears in the course of a magnificent ceremony. This ear piercing was a symbol that the young man now belonged to the elite. He now had the right to wear large ear pendants the size of which was proportionate to his social rank.

Baudin writes:[5] "The character that this teaching conferred was common to the entire elite and to the Inca himself. It is that revealed in the only pre-Columbian drama which we have: pride of caste, chivalric spirit, filial love, generosity towards the conquered, and royal magnanimity. Thus, this social class merits the name elite rather than that of 'nobility,' for no one could belong to it, unless he had surpassed the people and his peers in intelligence, knowledge, and virtue."

Very little is known about the origins and development of this Inca education. The Inca Roca in the last half of the thirteenth century seems to have established it. The great Emperor Pachacutec Yupanqui (fl. c.1425) reorganized the school of Roca. He erected new buildings and enlarged the teaching staff of "amantas," and, in accordance with the Inca policy of generosity towards conquered tribes, admitted the sons of defeated lords and chieftains to the capital school.[6]

Outside the capital there was no higher education. All Indians were required to learn Quechuan, the language of the Incas, and teachers were sent to the provinces for that purpose. In addition, there was universal military training. Special instructors taught the use of arms in every village to boys over ten years of age. Except for this instruction in Quechuan and in the use of arms, there seems to have been no formal schooling in the provinces.

Thus education among the Incas was wholly oral, reserved for the elite, humanistic, or classical rather than vocational or specialized, included military and physical training, and was inspired by an ideal of excellence. Education for the masses must have been by the apprenticeship method. Of education in pre-Incaic times nothing is known.

2. The Egyptiac Civilization

The Egyptiac Civilization arose out of a mutation of some primitive tribe or tribes in response to the physical challenge of the dessication of the homeland.[1] Wilson[2] writes that "the three concepts of challenge and response, the urban revolution (Childe), and the folk society (Redfield) are useful and instructive about that important transition between prehistoric 'barbarism' and historic 'civilization' but none of them provides a full and satisfying explanation of the phenomenon of such a transition within a comparatively brief time. No one can give that satisfying explanation, first, because our information is too slight on the times and, second, because there were certain spiritual imponderables at which we can only guess." But it is just the point of the notion of challenge-and-response that the "certain spiritual imponderables" are decisive, as well as free and not scientifically predictable.[3]

According to Wilson[4] the early development of the Egyptiac Civilization was a slow, internal, entirely native process from the beginnings to about 3250 B.C. (plus or minus 150 years). During this time the continuing success in irrigating the land and in farming the irrigated land had produced enormous changes. Perhaps the first of these changes was an increase in population. This required further responses, because the old customs that had been useful and effective, or even workable, with larger numbers, and these responses produced, or were, in turn, further challenges. The larger population brought about also further divisions and specialization of labor and this, in turn, produced some surplus of wealth and leisure as well as skilled professions. And a ruling class was produced.

At some time between 3400 and 3100 B.C. Egypt was in contact with the Sumeric society and borrowed from it certain elements. These were the idea of writing and other elements of which visible traces remain: the cylinder seal, bricks used in decorative designs, and monumental architecture. There seems, however, to have been no borrowing from Egypt by Sumeria.

At some time between 3200 and 3000 B.C. one of the ruling families of Upper Egypt went north, conquered the delta, established a united kingdom with a capital at Memphis, and thus founded the First Dynasty.

Toynbee dates the beginnings of the civilization at about the middle of the fourth millenium; the dates given above are adopted from Wilson.[5] The first and second dynasties continued to c. 2700 B.C.; the third through the sixth dynasties which, taken together, constituted the "Old Kingdom," continued to c. 2200 B.C. In the first six volumes of the *Study* Toynbee dated the breakdown at c. 2524, but with the revised chronology adopted in the last four volumes,[6] left the date open. Wilson dates the "First Intermediate Period" 2200–2050 B.C. and entitles the chapter dealing with it "The First Illness." The characterization of the Old Kingdom as "Egypt's rich and abundant youth" as contrasted with the despair and dismay and hopelessness of the first intermediate period strongly suggests that the Old Kingdom was indeed the growth period of the society and that the breakdown came at the end thereof, at c. 2200 B.C., despite Wilson's rejection[7] of the Toynbee pattern. We may therefore be not far out if we adopt the twenty-third century as the time of breakdown and beginning of the time of troubles of the Egyptiac Civilization.

Wilson[8] and Frankfort[9] hold that there were certain characteristics of mind common to the Egyptian and the Sumerian that transcended the differences between their cultures and that sharply differentiates their thought from that of modern Western man.

The first and most important characteristic common to the thought of both societies in contrast to that of the West seems to have been that there was no clear distinction drawn between man, on the one hand, and society and nature, on the other. The two did not have to be apprehended by different ways of thought or—in technical terms —by different modes of cognition. The nature of the individual human being was, for them, grounded in human society and human society was grounded in cosmic forces. Or, to reverse the order of statement, natural phenomena were apprehended and understood in terms of human experience. As Frankfort puts it,[10] "for modern, scientific man the phenomenal world is primarily an 'It'; for ancient—and also for primitive—man it is a 'Thou.' "

Phenomena were therefore not understood as effects of mechanical causes or as the results of a series of antecedents, but rather as appearances of a "timeless and boundless universe." This universe was the realm of the gods and was subject to their control or intervention. But neither phenomena nor the control or intervention of the gods was capricious or arbitrary. There was a cosmic force of harmony or order.

This conception is found in the Egyptian *ma'at* (truth, justice, righteousness, order, harmony). *Ma'at* is the universal principle of harmony and stability. It appears in and is derived from the first creation and is the continuing principle of harmony, of organization, of *cosmos* in all phenomena. According to the so-called Memphite theology of the earliest dynasties, there was intelligence behind the creation. Wilson[11] sees in "this idea of a rational principle behind creation the Egyptians' closest approach to a Logos doctrine." One may perhaps see similarities also to the Sinic conception of *Tao* and to the early Hellenic conception of the ideal as grounded in the natural order.

Thus the nature of man is grounded in the nature of the universe itself; it is not separate and distinct therefrom. The rules according to which he was to live his life were general and well understood, and they were not incompatible with a degree of liberty to develop his own personality in the exercise of freedom.

Wilson characterizes the attitude of the Egyptian of the growth period as optimistic, gay, self-assured, exuberant, and as exhibiting a lust for life and a determination to continue life and the pursuit of a more abundant life after death. This optimistic confidence was possible because of the high degree of geographic security of the land.

Egypt was, essentially, the delta of the Nile and the upper valley southwards to the First Cataract. The delta was protected by the surrounding desert and sea, and Upper Egypt by both the surrounding desert and the rock walls of so much of the valley. The cataracts were an effective barrier against any intruders who might have tried to use the waterway. Further, the life-giving floods of the river were regular and dependable, so that the whole of the Egyptian's experience was proof of the annual renewal of the necessary means of life.

In addition to these combined factors that made for geographical security against enemies and economic security of the means of livelihood, the Egyptian lived under the direct rule of a god. The pharaoh was a god who lived on earth among mortals, and in him resided the essential forces of the Two Lands. It was possible for the Two Lands—the Delta and Upper Egypt—to be a unity because the pharaoh was neither an Upper Egyptian nor a Lower Egyptian, but a god. And since it was under the protection and rule of a god that the Egyptians lived, he was guaranteed a measure of security that could not otherwise have been possible.

It is likely that there was also another factor that contributed to the Egyptians' confidence and optimism. He had, from the beginnings of his civilization, always succeeded in meeting challenges as they arose, in successfully responding to the difficult situations and problems as they appeared. Why, therefore, should he not be able to in the future? Why should he not be confident about the present life and the future life? The whole picture of Egypt of the Old Kingdom is one of a continuing increase in self-determination—the ultimate criterion of growth.

Wilson writes:[12] "Under the Old Kingdom, Egypt realized her high-

est material and intellectual powers . . . The Old Kingdom had
vigor, *savoir faire,* and confidence. In terms of what the ancients
seemed to be trying to establish as a way of life, the Old Kingdom
appeals as the most Egyptian of periods." Yet, he adds, the Old
Kingdom values "were chiefly earthly success and wealth."

For this period a book of etiquette for an official, the *Teachings
of Ptahhotep,* gives an excellent picture of the supreme values. It
has been summarized as follows: "The ideal picture is that of a correct
man, who wisely avoids impulse and fits himself by word and deed
into the administrative and social systems. An assured career as an
official awaits him. No moral concepts like good and bad come into
discussion here; rather the standard lies in the characteristics of the
knowing man and the ignorant man, perhaps best given in the words
'smart' and 'stupid.' Smartness can be learned. . . . So rules are
provided for a man's career. If he pays attention, he will be smart;
he will find the right way in all life's situations through his smartness; and through his correct attitude he will bring his career to
success."[13] It should be added that the entire text is not altogether
opportunistic and materialistic. In one passage honesty is urged as
the best policy, but this arises from experience rather than from
principle.

At about 2200 B.C. the sixth and last Old Kingdom dynasty came
to an end and there began the period of anarchy and violence, of
internecine warfare among a multiplicity of small states and local
dynasties, of loss of self-determination. Though the evidence is
defective, it is reasonable to suppose that the seeds of discord must
have sprung up before 2200 in order to have been able to flower
so completely and so suddenly.

"For the first three Dynasties" [that is, for the beginning of the
growth period] "we know little about the kings, less about the nobility,
and practically nothing about the people."[14] And, we may add, we
know little about education.

Writing, however, had been a possession of the Egyptians even
during the First Dynasty, and there was instruction in so difficult
and complicated an art as the making of hieroglyphics. By the end
of the growth period, the art of writing did form the basis as well as
the main content of all formal or quasi-formal education. It created
a great and unbridgeable gap between the learned and the masses.

It seems that only candidates for the priesthood and young officials in the civil service were taught to read and write, and that this knowledge was the prerequisite for both official and ecclesiastical office.

The process of learning to read and write was long and arduous. For the masses there was neither the leisure nor the energy nor the opportunity to learn, and so there arose an aristocracy of the learned, the scribes, in whose hands rested the control of all civil and ecclesiastical affairs. To be a "Royal Scribe" was an honor that was not disdained by the highest official. The class of scribes, in course of time, became exclusive and somewhat contemptuous of all who did not belong to it. And the power of the scribes became more firmly rooted than that of any other class, for it rested on an intellectual possession that was indispensable.

Little is known about the details of transmission of this intellectual possession, but it is clear that there were no schools as such.[15] A wise official or scribe, when he became old, would take a "son" or "sons" into his household as an apprentice or apprentices. The apprentice performed household tasks and took part in the daily work of his master; in return, the master instructed him in writing and reading, shared experiences with him, and perhaps even took him to court as business required. Some apprentices served as pages at court and participated in the ceremonies. Students from the provinces were sent to the capital for instruction in the court ceremonies and in etiquette. Only the sons of the nobles were accepted as apprentice-pupils. There was no "plan" or "curriculum" for the education that was given: all depended upon the master, who was not a professional teacher, that is, the master earned his living or maintained his place in society by some profession other than teaching.[15]

The close similarity between this Egyptian education of the Old Kingdom and those of early China, India, Greece, and Rome is clear.

The time of troubles of the Egyptiac Civilization lasted from the Seventh Dynasty, in the twenty-third century, to the foundation of the Twelfth Dynasty (the "Middle Kingdom") as universal state about 2050 B.C.

The outbreak of internal discord, the breakup into a multiplicity of petty states and the warfare between them, the increasing contempt for law and order and the rights of property, were all, according to both Toynbee and Wilson, not the result of any blow dealt to the society from outside, but were systemic and internal. There was an obvious failure of self-determination accompanied by or resulting in a loss of confidence and creativity. From this period we have a not inconsiderable body of literature recording the shock and dismay and despair with which the thoughtful Egyptian faced the crumbling of his once stable and secure world.

The reactions of the Egyptians to this calamity were like those of the members of other civilizations in similar periods. The successful official of the Old Kingdom was now poor and hungry. He had no administrative position, no provisioned tomb, no property to impress the world. What values were to be found now? Since the wisdom that had been so highly esteemed now produced no tangible evidence of success, and there was no certainty of future happiness, one answer was to pursue the sensual pleasures of the day: "Make holiday and weary not therein! Behold, it is not given to a man to take property with him. Behold, no one who goes [over there] can come back again!"[16]

Another answer was to seek death as a release from the intolerable conditions of life.

But still others, having lived through the shattering of the naturalistic and materialistic Old Kingdom values of earthly success and wealth, sought to discover other and higher and more enduring moral and spiritual values. This, again, is faintly similar to the creation of higher religions and philosophies by other societies in times of troubles. The similarity, however, is faint rather than clear, for the effort to discover and possess the eternal values was, in Egypt, abortive.

Wilson writes: "Gropingly and inadequately, they discovered that the things which are unseen may be eternal; and eternity was always their goal. If they had been able to make their discovery increasingly effective . . . Egypt might have been the first country to recognize the values in the common man and to continue attempts to work out a good life for the many. Unfortunately, the discovery of the essential importance of man in general turned out to be short-lived in Egypt, applying only to the time of troubles and its immediate aftermath, and Egypt soon returned to its materialism and absolutism."[17]

It is not possible, from the evidence, to draw distinctions between education during the time of troubles and that of the universal state.

The founders of the Twelfth Dynasty reunited the Two Lands by force of arms and established their capital at Thebes. The pharaohs were, on the whole, good rulers, so that Egypt again enjoyed peace and prosperity. The success of the state was sufficient proof of the capacity of the pharaohs to be gods, and so they *were* gods and, as such, the dispensers of *ma'at*.

Wilson suggests that Egypt, at the end of the time of troubles, had been on the verge of a great discovery and that she recovered peace and prosperity only at the price of losing a great potential. The discovery was of the value and sanctity and rights of the individual human being, of Everyman.[18]

Several Middle Kingdom texts suggest the new and different ideal towards which some thinkers of the time were groping. But the ideal did not succeed in establishing itself as that of the whole society. For, since the pharaohs, as gods, were the dispensers of *ma'at, ma'at* was still very far removed from Everyman. And it appears that, as the state waxed fat and the people became again well fed and contented with their lots, their thoughts no longer turned to questions about ultimate human rights. They re-turned, instead, to the conceptions that had dominated the society in the heyday of its youth: the Egyptians were the Chosen People; their special election was laid down in the original creation; all that was required, therefore, was to restore the order, the harmony, the *ma'at* of the early period and all would be well. This is perhaps the reason that the only really creative period in Egyptian history was at the beginning.

The earliest mention of classes and schools as such occurs in the literature of the period of confusion following the collapse of the Old Kingdom. Exactly when the schools appeared and teachers became professional teachers is unknown, but both existed in the Twelfth Dynasty and are mentioned frequently from thence onwards. At the beginning of the universal state period it seems to have been customary for children who were to be trained as scribes to leave their homes and go to the school at the capital.

The schools arose from the need of the state for trained officials after the disorder and anarchy following the collapse of the Old Kingdom; the need was for a technically and ethically trained bureaucracy. The training given in the schools was only elementary; the higher training continued to be given by nonprofessional masters to selected pupils. The pupils continued to be selected chiefly from the nobility, but probably also from families lower in the social scale.[19]

The subtitle of a popular work *The Teaching of Duauf* (probably Twelfth Dynasty) was: "Teachings that a man named Duauf composed for his son when he went up to the capital to put him into the School of the Books among the children of the great." The curriculum consisted almost entirely of reading and writing. For beginners three or four lines a day seems to have been the required amount. The texts used for study were drawn for the most part from the wisdom literature: *The Teachings of Ptahhotep* (Old Kingdom), *The Teachings of Kagemmi* (Old Kingdom), *The Teachings of Duauf*, *The Teachings of Amenemhet*, *The Admonitions of an Egyptian Sage to a King* (Twelfth Dynasty).[20] These texts were endlessly copied and recopied, and undoubtedly their maxims of practical wisdom and the successful conduct of life were committed to memory.

Although the training was almost all in reading and writing, it was not quite wholly so. There seems to have been also training in gymnastics and many types of sport, in jumping, dancing, swimming, riding, archery.[20]

However, even when the young man finished his schooling and became an official, he continued to practice his skill in writing. Many papyri from the thirteenth century contain model letters and copies of texts done, not in the ordinary abbreviated business script, but in the fuller and more difficult book script. These exercises were written by young officials who served their masters as assistants. The master had the young scribes do these exercises, which he then corrected with an eye to the beauty of the signs. The purpose of the exercises was to show that the pupil had become a master scribe, when his master or guild should decide that he had now the right to call himself a scribe.[21]

The reason that so many such papyri have come down to us is that they were put in tombs as testimony of the deceased's rank of scribe for this, even in death, was nothing inconsequential. In the underworld there awaited him, as the judge of the dead, Thoth, the divine colleague and patron of earthly scribes.[21]

The Middle Kingdom as universal state had been in process of disintegration over a period of time—perhaps half a century—before the Hyksos invasion. Wilson wonders[22] how it happened that so admirable and flexible a system collapsed so suddenly and guesses that possibly or probably it had an "inner structural weakness" inherited from its origin in a feudal state, or that there were serious problems of loyalty within the royal family. Toynbee would guess that Egyptian society followed the pattern of those other societies about which we have more information: that the loss of self-determination and creativity manifested in the breakdown had resulted in the time of troubles; during the internecine wars of the time of troubles, the society had become materially exhausted and spiritually enfeebled and war weary so that the peace enforced by the universal state was only a last—or next-to-last—rally before the final petrifaction of the society in its ultimate phase.

In any case, it seems clear that the Twelfth Dynasty had collapsed as an effective ruling power before the Hyksos invaders established themselves in the delta 1730 B.C.

The movement of the Hyksos into Egypt was a part of a larger and more general movement of peoples within and out of Southwestern Asia in the second millenium. The same movement sent the Kassites into Mesopotamia and the Aryans into northwest India. The Hyksos, *vis-a-vis* the Egyptians, were barbarians. They did not absorb the Egyptian culture, nor were they assimilated into it. For the most part they lived apart in fortified camps; they ruled—as they had conquered —by force; they exacted trubute; they allowed "shadow pharaohs" to continue at Thebes while they established their own headquarters at Avaris-Tanis. They paid no attention to the Egyptian gods, but introduced a god of their own.

The Egyptians paid the tribute demanded of them, bided their time, learned to use the new weapons of their masters—the horse, the chariot, the composite bow, new types of daggers—and, at long last, c. 1570, expelled the Hyksos and established the empire (Eighteenth Dynasty) as a continuation of the universal state.

Under the second universal state there seem to have been no manifestations of creativity at all: in art and architecture the forms and themes of earlier periods were repeated over and over again; the school curriculum remained fixed although the written language was obsolete by the end of the sixteenth century and was a dead language by the fourteenth; the individual peasant was only an element in a mass that was now organized to meet the demands of a geographically expanding empire. For the empire had expanded, during the fifteenth century, into Palestine and Syria. But this empire, and the successive forms that the Egyptian society later assumed were, in Toynbee's words "not a new tree with a life of its own, but the old tree's dead trunk artificially re-erected, and many times re-erected again, during the ages that elapsed while its massive bulk was weathering away and its hard grain rotting into dust."[23]

But the Egyptiac Civilization did endure more than two millenia.

3. The Indus Culture

During the whole early period in the life of Mankind down to the final recession of the last ice sheet from Europe and Western Asia at some time shortly after about 10,000 B.C., human economy was stagnant and the challenge offered by the environment severe enough to require man to use all his energies in simply staying alive. The surviving primitive peoples were also, as Toynbee has conjectured, recuperating from the strain of having achieved the mutation of Sub-Man into Man.

The economy of primitive man throughout that period was based on the gathering of some fruits and nuts and other edible wild vegetables, but chiefly on the hunting of wild animals. As the ice sheet receded and the climate of the land changed, so the herds of animals on which he had depended for his livelihood migrated or died. This complex of events presented to Primitive Man a physical challenge of the first magnitude: he had to adapt himself to the changing conditions or die. He did adapt himself, and his responses to the challenge were several and varied. We have already seen the nature of the response evoked by the peculiar conditions in the Nile Valley.

In Europe and Western Asia, the axe seems to have been invented as a weapon against the trees and shrubs; the dog was domesticated at first as a helper of the human hunter; a beginning was made in the cultivation of grain of the wheat and barley types. These responses —and probably also others of which we are ignorant—enabled Primitive Man of this early period to survive the changing climatic conditions and to maintain a precarious balance between the very small population of his tribes and the inhospitable environment. He still lacked any means of food production over which he himself could evercise much control and was therefore denied the possibility of increasing his numbers or of having leisure or of developing a civilization. It was with the invention of the techniques of Egypt and Sumeria that he at last gained a large measure of control over his food supply and entered upon a course of dynamic growth.

At some time after the rise of the two civilizations on the Nile and in the lower valley of the Tigris and Euphrates another civilization, the Indus culture, appeared in northwest India. Primitive Man had been in India for a long while: the earliest tools used by human beings in India can be dated to a time of the order of about three to four hundred thousand years ago. But, so far as is known at present, the earliest civilization began about 3000 B.C. The Indus culture is known only through archaeological findings and, even through these findings, only in its mature form. Nothing is known of its beginnings, of a period of growth, of a time of troubles. What is known of it in its later phase strongly suggests a universal state form of political organization and we can only conjecture that it either followed the pattern of other civilizations, or went through some unique process of development. Of these two alternatives, the former seems the more reasonable. Piggott says that an origin of the culture outside India is inherently improbable, although there certainly were trading contacts with Sumeria and there could have been influences.

The homeland of this culture is a great irregular triangle around the Indus River from the Makran coast to Kathiawar to the foothills of the Himalayas. The chief evidences for the culture derive from the ruins of the two great cities, Mohenjo-daro in the southwest, and Harappa in the north, lying some 350 miles apart, and from more than a score of small villages in the triangular area.

In the phase in which the culture is known there prevailed, for perhaps seven centuries, a state of almost complete and monotonous uniformity. It appears that this uniformity and regularity may be attributed to some type of strong centralized government that controlled production and distribution of goods, perhaps enforced tolls, did enforce a uniform system of weights and measures, planned similar layouts in the two great cities, maintained granaries, and regulated agricultural production. In addition, there was probably also a fairly rigid commercial code, standardized techniques of production, and rigidly controlled trade.

The political administration was probably of a priest-king type in this urban and literate society. The society did have writing. The writing has, so far, not been read or even transliterated. It is pictographic but is not apparently related to Egyptian hieroglyphics nor to Sumerian cuneiform and it has no descendants. The language of the people is unknown but, almost certainly, was not Indo-European.

In town planning, engineering, sanitation, sculpture, agriculture, and other arts and skills the culture had reached a high point by the time of the foundation of the two great cities, but seemingly made no progress during the period that is known.

At some time probably before c. 1500 B.C., but not very long before, the cities and villages of the Indus culture were invaded by a people from the west. It seems likely that the intruders were either the Aryan invaders of northern India, or closely related to them.

Of educational practices among the Indus peoples nothing is known.

4. The Sumeric Civilization

The Sumeric Civilization arose out of a mutation of some primitive society in response to the double physical challenge of dessication and the intractability of the two rivers of its homeland, the lower Tigris-Euphrates Valley. The environment of the society, although fluvial like that of Egypt, is radically unlike the Nile environment. The two rivers may rise unpredictably, there are heavy—and also unpredictable —rains which convert the land into a sea of mud, there are scorching winds and there are severe thunderstorms.

There had been primitive peoples in the land for thousands of years before the Sumeric Civilization emerged; finally, a group of those people worked out the physical response of planned irrigation by means of dams and canals to the physical challenge of the rampant flooding waters of the rivers. They did this by means of cooperative action. This cooperative action in the physical sphere had its counterpart politically in the primitive democracy of the villages and towns —as men cooperated in controlling the waters and using them for irrigation, so they cooperated in governing themselves: political power rested in an assembly of adult freemen. But this power normally was vested in a council of elders, and we may suppose that those who were elected or appointed elders were those who had shown the creative leadership necessary first to set the civilization on the road to growth, and then to devise adequate responses to the successive challenges as they presented themselves.

The Sumeric Civilization came into being about the middle of the fourth millenium B.C. and seems not to have broken down until about a thousand years later. During this period of growth the Sumerians invented writing, using cuneiform script of syllabic character, at first to keep the increasingly complicated accounts of the towns and cities and temples. In time, however, and in a relatively short time, this script and language became the vehicle of a significant literature that was primarily religious and cultic.

The time of troubles of the civilization lasted from the breakdown at about the middle of the third millenium to about 2079 B.C., when the universal state—the Empire of Sumer and Akkad—was founded. The empire endured until 1686 B.C.

During the time of troubles the Sumerian language had begun to give ground to Akkadian, a Semitic language of radically different structure and vocabulary. By the time of the foundation of the universal state Akkadian had completely supplanted the earlier language as the spoken tongue, although Sumerian continued as the written language of all religious and cultic texts to the end of the civilization and, even later, into the Babylonic Civilization.

Throughout the third millenium, that is, through the growth period and the time of troubles, the civilization was politically organized into a number of city-states. Central to the city-state was the temple of the city god. The temple was usually the largest land owner, and its lands were cultivated, its irrigation works operated by, serfs and sharecroppers. During the time of troubles, when the city-states engaged in increasingly violent wars with one another, one or another of them would succeed in gaining dominion over weaker neighbors. This was translated into the conception that one god had gained a victory over those of the weaker states for, as Toynbee observes, "the relations between the Gods were simply a transposition of political facts into theological terms."[1] But that the political facts *were* so translated and transposed accounts, at least in large part, for the continuing importance of Sumerian as a cultic language.

The materials for a systematic account of education in this civilization do not exist. The available evidence throws only feeble and fitful rays of light on an otherwise almost wholly obscure picture.

Meissner[2] conjectures that there must have been schools to continue the tradition of the occult and real sciences even during the earliest period of the civilization. He conjectures further that since Hammurabi (about 2000 B.C.) makes no mention of the schools of his time, they were not state operated, but were private institutions of the temples and of individual teachers. There is evidence in plenty, from Shurrupak, Nippur, Assur, and other Sumeric cities whose ruins have been investigated, of the existence of schools in later periods. School texts have been found that contain lists of gods, names, professions, and objects of daily life. Presumably these lists constituted a part of the lesson of the pupil. Large numbers of students' exercise tablets have also been found. These tablets contain both lists of names and copies of hymns with the numbers and kinds of scribal errors that would be expected of elementary pupils. There is not sufficient evidence to answer questions about how the instruction was managed, the content of the curriculum, or the length of the course.

It appears, however, that in the period of the universal state and perhaps also during the time of troubles schools were frequently if not normally connected with the temples, for the same ideogram designates both priest and scribe. In addition to the general courses there were also special courses, or special schools, in divination, astronomy, and medicine.

The schoolrooms that have been excavated at Sippur measure only about twelve by fifteen feet, so that the pupils must literally have sat at the feet of the teacher. Probably in good weather the classes were conducted out-of-doors in the yard of the school.[2]

According to Landersdorfer, education was predominantly scribal, and began with the study of writing.[3] The pupil learned to make tablets of clay and styluses of bamboo, and then to make the individual strokes of cuneiform writing, horizontal, vertical, diagonal, at first singly and then in combination. He then progressed to the use of the simple syllable signs and learned how to use the syllabaries and ideograms.

Having learned to make the cuneiform signs and to use the ideograms, the student then progressed to the study of linguistic texts and to learn the Sumerian language. Sumeric, although a dead language by 2000 b.c., was still assiduously cultivated because Akkadian and the cuneiform script were instruments that could not be used without a grasp of the Sumerian classical background. For this purpose syllabaries were used. Such a syllabary might contain in parallel columns the graphic sign, the Akkadian meaning, and the corresponding Sumerian word. Lists of synonyms and bilingual lists of names of material objects, professions, animals were also employed.

Hymns and odes from the religious literature were used as practical material for writing and for language study. Prayers, conjurations, magic texts, and hymns were repeatedly translated back and forth, and the texts were copied again and again.

Great stress was laid on memorization. The pupil got by heart large portions of the religious literature. There were line-by-line commentaries with factual and linguistic explanations. The teacher put oral questions and received the pupil's answers.

From the scanty evidence, it thus appears that education throughout the history of the Sumeric Civilization was predominantly scribal and connected with the priestly foundations, that it was not state controlled except so far as the temples were also politically controlled, that the curriculum was, in the main, general or "classical" rather than specialized or vocational. We must suppose that all specialized education was by the apprenticeship method.

5. The Shang Culture

The Shang culture, which was in existence in "the Land within the Passes" in the middle basin of the valley of the Yellow River in north China in the second millenium b.c., was an advanced, indigenous, autonomous civilization that was the predecessor of the Sinic Civilization. It arose, as did all other primary civilizations, out of a mutation of some primitive society in response to the challenge of the great alluvial plain of the river. It must have required centuries for the Shang peoples to harness the waters of the river and to raise themselves above the cultural level of their primitive neighbors. When they appear in the light of history during the second half of the second millenium they had already attained that high level.

In common with other late Neolithic peoples, the Shang people had the potter's wheel, the horse-drawn chariot, and the art of casting bronze—and they had also the art of writing.

The best present evidence strongly suggests that there was more intercourse between these people and their neighbors to the west and south than has been commonly supposed,[1] and that they did borrow tools and arts from those neighbors. But, whether borrowed or invented, all the elements were thoroughly adapted and assimilated to the indigenous culture.

The date of the beginnings of writing in the Shang society is not known, but the quite readable oracle bone inscriptions are not later than the fourteenth century B.C. The invention of writing was indigenous with the Shang and probably originated in the desire to communicate with the dead or with certain deities. The basis of the writing was ideograms, but some ideographic characters were used only for the sounds of the words designating the objects they represented and thus served to write other words homophonic to the first.[3] Creel[4] holds that the writing-brush was used, that wood or bamboo books were "not uncommon," and that there was a considerable literature, especially in history. Galt even conjectures that "systematic teaching in schools, or among certain social groups, was beginning to take shape."[5]

Whether these conjectures be accepted or not, it can be taken as established that the Shang culture did bequeath to its successor not only the other arts mentioned above, but also the arts of writing and of bookmaking.

Of the means of education employed in the society we can only conjecture that it must have used, as do all peoples, the apprenticeship method, and that it is likely that there was some sort of training given in the art of writing to selected individuals.

The society was probably divided into two classes, an aristocracy of noble clans, and the peasants. In this society the king presided over both religious and secular affairs and held the top rank.[6] After the king came the prime minister, then the grand domestic, the grand scribe—the head of the scribes, who wrote on bamboo the royal orders, and keeper of the archives—and the grand treasurer. Next in line was a whole series of functionaries and bureau heads, including inspectors and overseers of sowing and harvest.

Appendix II The Babylonic Civilization—With a Note on Jewish Education

The Babylonic Civilization was so closely related to the antecedent Sumeric that it may, in several aspects, be considered as a continuation thereof. In other respects, however, it may fruitfully be considered a distinct civilization. As such, it had its time of origin in about the first quarter of the fourteenth century B.C. The growth period continued until the breakdown at some date which can not be fixed, but was perhaps about the year 1000 B.C. The time of troubles lasted from the breakdown to 610 B.C., the date of the establishment of the Neo-Babylonian Empire as universal state. The empire endured only to 539 B.C., when it was absorbed by the Achaemenian Empire, the universal state of the Syriac Civilization.

The Sumeric Civilization had bequeathed its culture and languages to the Babylonic in a way similar to the way in which Rome was later to bequeath its culture and language to the younger Western Civilization. In the Babylonic society, the classical Sumerian language played about the same role that classical Latin played in the medieval West.

The data about education in this civilization are so scanty that it is not possible to give separate accounts thereof for the three main historical periods. The data that are available refer to education under the universal state, so that the following fragments are about education during the last historical phase.

For those Babylonic children who attended schools the period of schooling was long: it appears to have lasted from early youth to manhood. Instruction was not limited to boys; girls studied writing and music and, presumably, other subjects as well. One could not, as Daniel says[1] "master the writing and the language of the Chaldees in three years." Three years may, it appears, have been sufficient for the course in music, but clearly not for the total course. At the end of the course, candidates for the priesthood were required to stand an examination, and this may have been a requirement also for the lay students.[2]

An idea of the general curriculum at about 650 B.C. is suggested by what Assurbanipal says of his own education. He reports that besides physical training, he studied language. He could read "stones of the time before the flood" and understand "the difficult tablets with the dark Sumerian and the Akkadian hard to master." He adds that he studied divination, geometry, and arithmetic, and there is a suggestion that extensive memorization of texts was required.[3]

Such training led to the career of scribe. After the young graduates, who usually came from the families of scribes, had proved themselves as apprentice scribes or priests, and had shown their capabilities by copying many times the literary documents, they became full-fledged scribes, and an auspicious career lay ahead of them. Some became head or chief scribes and could aspire to the favored positions at court.[4]

Beyond the general schools, there were special schools for training in theology, law, medicine, and astronomy. The elite of the scholars and technicians were taken into a sort of academy, where they received this further training.

Closely connected with the temple schools were two other institutions: the archive and the library. The large temples needed for their extensive activities lists, indices, and copies of documents and texts. The adjustment of weights and measures seems to have been done in the archive. All sorts of state documents were also deposited there. The libraries preserved permanent documents by putting them in boxes made of reeds or clay. In Babylon these libraries were all temple libraries, and many sacred places had libraries as repositories for valuable business books and literary treasures.

State archives, as opposed to temple archives, existed from the oldest times, but not state libraries. Assurbanipal established the first such library at Niniveh, and had many works in various cities copied and the copies deposited in the state library. Nineveh thus became in the time of Assurbanipal a center of scholarship.[5]

During the time of troubles and the universal state period of the Babylonic Civilization, a people of the Syriac society had been forcibly incorporated into the Babylonic internal proletariat. These people were the Hebrews of Israel and Judah. With the fall of the Neo-Babylonic Empire and the absorption of the Babylonic by the Achaemenian Empire, the Hebrews were gradually—as Babylonia itself was gradually—reincorporated in the Syriac Civilization. But it was during the ninth and eighth and seventh centuries that Judaism as a higher religion, distinct from primitive Jahvism, appeared; it was during these centuries that the great prophets proclaimed their messages; it was during the period after the return from the exile that the Old Testament was fixed in written form. It was thus under the Babylonic Civilization and as members of the internal proletariat thereof that the Hebrew people made their great contribution of Judaism. It is therefore appropriate that a note on Hebrew education be given in connection with this civilization.

A Note On Jewish Education

For the Hebrew people throughout their early history up to the Exile in 586 B.C. education was by the apprenticeship method: the tribe and the family were the educational institutions; parents and relatives were the teachers. The priests and prophets of the ninth to the seventh centuries were the creators of the early Hebrew national literature. This literature was created, and transmitted from generation to generation, only orally during the long period before it was finally written down. Before the Exile a part of this literature existed in fixed written form, but it seems certain that the Old Testament as written may be ascribed to the period between the Exile and the rise of the Maccabees in the second quarter of the second century B.C.[6]

While it was still being learned and transmitted orally it had become the "national book of instruction,"[7] although many Old Testament references show that writing was known and used. Among these is the prescription[8] that the Law was to be written clearly on large stones along the highway that every one might read it. Further, each king or leader was to read in the Law, or recite parts of it, every day; all the people—men, women, and children—were to assemble every seventh year to hear a reading or recitation of the Law and to learn it. From this Biblical ordinance derived the custom of completing one consecutive reading of the Pentateuch at the Sabbath services every three years. This custom of reading the Law every Sabbath is so ancient that Josephus and Philo assign its origin to Moses.[9]

In course of time the Torah, which originally meant the "Law," came to mean "religious teaching." Thus religion to the Jew became a synonym for common instruction. However, there were no schools as such in the pre-Exilic period. The priests and prophets aimed at the adults in their efforts to teach a knowledge of the Law. The responsibility for training the child in the way that he should grow rested squarely upon the father, and it remained the father's until the first century B.C.

Thus family and tribal education during this period was basically religious: the purpose was to develop in the child a consciousness of his personal responsibility to the Lord his God, and of his obligation and duty to keep the Law through which God had covenanted with His people. It seems clear that the child learned by heart large parts of the Law and probably also much of the other literature as well, especially the Psalms.

In the last years before the Exile, and then especially under the severe discipline of the Exile, during which the Hebrews encountered a people of more advanced culture, the religious and moral principles of the Law assumed definite shape and form as the belief and religion of the Jewish people. After the end of the Exile it became vital to preserve these teachings, and slowly the literature was codified and written down. The Jews thus became a people of the Book. From the practice of transcribing and commenting on the books of the Law, the Prophets and the Writings, there arose a class of learned men, the scribes, into whose hands the education of the people now passed. The scribe replaced the prophet as teacher. This period was introduced by Ezra the Scribe, who was extolled as the restorer of the Torah. Ezra gathered about him important men and read and expounded the Law to them; he was a member of the priestly caste and from his time (fifth century, B.C.) onward, the teachers and scribes were of the tribe of Levi.

Now, for the first time in Jewish history, there was an organized body of teachers. The prophets were succeeded by the priests from whom came the scribes, i.e., the "learned," the "wise." The study of the Scriptures came to be the central point of the life of the people, and there arose a division of the people into two classes: the class of erudite scribes, and the much larger class of the unlettered.[9]

At first the scribes restricted their educational activities to adults. They gave lectures in synagogues and public places. The responsibility for the education of children still remained with the father.

Schools for children were first established in Jerusalem in the first quarter of the last century B.C. under the Maccabbees. This step was taken by the Rabbi Simon ben Shatach, the head of the Sanhedrin, who had observed the imperfection of the system in which the parent was the sole instructor of the child, and in which fatherless children were deprived of all means of education. The clause insisting upon general compulsory schooling for children reads as follows: ". . . that the children of the community should receive instruction in common in institutions specially appointed for this purpose."[10]

During the period of confusion following the fall of the Maccabbees the requirement was not always met, and the true founder of Jewish elementary education was the high priest Joshua ben Gamla. Whereas before there had been elementary teachers in Jerusalem and in most of the districts of Palestine, Joshua established, shortly after the middle of the first century A.D., elementary schools in each town. Statements in the Talmud indicate that these schools were enthusiastically hailed, but the system appears not to have taken deep root, for about A.D. 232 Yehuda II found it necessary to punish several congregations that had failed to provide adequate and proper means of instructing children in the schools. Yehuda himself puts his conception of the importance of schools as follows: "A community that neglects to establish schools for children is bound to perish; its well-being, its moral and social life, must needs be endangered, and it falls a prey to the enemy, when men of constant faith cease to exist therein."[11]

The example of the Jews in Palestine in promoting education for the young was followed by the Jews in Babylon. In Babylon, systematic provision for higher religious education was made and the two academies that were founded there became famous.[12] Once the Jewish elementary school was placed on a firm basis in Palestine and Babylon, it spread to other lands through which Jews were scattered; and it continued through later generations. There were such elementary schools in the Jewish communities in Arabia, Egypt, Italy and, later, in Spain and Western Europe.

The methods, plan and details of the elementary education are covered by various sentences in the Talmud. The core of the curriculum was religion: it was the center around which all other subjects of study revolved. The course of study was divided into three age periods of five years each. At the age of five the child began the study of the language and substance of the twenty-four books of the Old Testament; at ten he studied the oral Law, the tradition, that interprets the written Law and prescribes practical observances and duties; at fifteen he began the study of the science of religion as based on the Talmud. This latter and higher study enabled him to make deductions, to compare and analyze, and to make decisions according to the traditional rules about matters of faith in all aspects.[13]

This curriculum presupposed a knowledge of reading and writing. As soon as a child in the first period was able to read the texts he was introduced to the exegesis thereof. In the process of his learning to read, the letters were written on a large slate which was used as a sort of blackboard for common instruction, or on smaller slates or tablets for each child. When the child had learned to read he received scrolls or tablets and then had to memorize the texts that were written thereon; finally he was given a scroll on which was written only the initial letter alone of each word in the entire text, and he was to repeat from memory the entire text. Great emphasis was laid on faultless copying and on correct texts, and almost equal emphasis on memory work.[13]

There seems to have been no systematic instruction in history, geography, or mathematics in the schools, but some knowledge of these subjects seems to have been given, insofar as such knowledge had a bearing on the teaching of the Law. And although foreign languages were not included in the curriculum, a knowledge of them appears to have been highly esteemed.

The schools were at first located in teachers' homes or in synagogues, but later separate school buildings were erected in the uncrowded sections of the towns. Overcrowding of classrooms did not exist, for a teacher to pupil ratio was prescribed in the Babylonic Talmud: "One teacher is to have twenty-five pupils; if there be fifty, then two teachers must be appointed; if there be forty, the teacher is to have an assistant master."[14] The teacher enjoyed high social status and esteem; he wielded great influence in the community and the rabbis seem to have held him in as high esteem as did the rest of the community. According to the Talmud, the ideal teacher led a pure and unsullied religious life, was moderate in food and drink, loved his profession, was patient, conscientious, modest, bright, and cheerful; the appointment of young men and of older men who were still bachelors was not favored.

In the early period the teachers received no pay and expected none, regarding their teaching duties as the fulfillment of a divine command or calling; by the second and third centuries after Christ, however, it became necessary to give wages to those teachers who taught the Scriptures, but only to those—the teachers of exegesis still got no wages. A little later still, when the support of the schools fell to the congregations, the voluntary payments and presentation of gifts to all teachers ceased and they were paid regular and fixed salaries. In addition, they were exempted from all public burdens and from payment of taxes.[15]

Teachers had the right to terminate their engagements, but could be dismissed only on the grounds of ignorance, or incompetence, or the dissemination of false doctrine. The teacher could not be dismissed on the ground of undue severity in the treatment of the children under his care if he was otherwise proficient in his work.

The Talmud contains many practical pedagogic prescriptions: teaching was to be commensurate with the age and competence of the child, student interest was to be stimulated, instruction was to be graduated in difficulty so as to proceed from the near to the distant, from the known to the unknown. The teacher was to go over and explain the lesson at least four times and, if this were not sufficient, he should repeat again and again until all pupils knew it thoroughly. Pupils were to learn by heart as much material as they were capable of; as an aid to the memorization they were to be given various mnemonic devices, and were to learn audibly, reciting in sing-song the passage to be learned. Strict discipline was prescribed with regard to regularity of attendance, classroom order, and politeness and decorum. Where necessary, correction and chastisement were to be administered, but there was to be no coercion through fear and punishment. The teacher was enjoined to try to win the affection of his pupils and to be patient with the slow learners. If he had to resort to whipping— and it is clear that he often did—he was to use a small strap rather than a stick.[15]

As regards the theoretical higher education of women, opinion among the Jews seems to have been divided. In general it was not recommended that women be introduced to the more abstruse Talmudic learning. There were some exceptions, and a few women went as far with their learning and scholarship as did any man; but most educated women learned only the written Law—that is, advanced only through the elementary stage of schooling.

Even after the schools had been established and elementary education made compulsory, it was still the responsibility of the father to teach his sons a trade—and how to swim![12] It was considered that to have only a knowledge of the Law was to be developed in a one-sided way and that to have intellectual knowledge without also a knowledge of a trade was both impractical and incomplete.

Appendix III   Languages, Scripts, Literatures

In China

We have seen above[1] that at the very beginning of the Sinic universal state, the written language was standardized and that this standardization established an effective bond of unity among the Chinese peoples. During the preceding time of troubles each of the several contending states had begun to develop its own variants of the script, so that each local script was in process of becoming less intelligible to the scholars who had learned another local script with other variants. This process towards mutual unintelligibility was arrested when Shih Huang Ti decreed[2] that the script of Chi'in, his own state, was to be the sole official written language of his empire, which now united under one rule all the several states in the Sinic society.

The Chinese characters were not phonetic symbols,[3] but conveyed meanings independently of whatever sounds might be assigned to the characters, as the "Arabic" numerals convey the same meaning in all European languages independently of the sounds assigned to them. This single, uniform, official script thus gave to the Chinese scholar-officials a visual language which could serve as a means of communication even if the spoken language should develop into a number of mutually unintelligible vernaculars. There were also other factors[4] at work that made for uniformity. All the Chinese peoples of the time were linguistically homogeneous to an unusual degree, since all spoke some variety of the Chinese-Siamese languages; the corps of civil servants, who now all learned the common script, also all learned a common and standardized vocalization of the characters—as if all Europeans were to learn to pronounce the characters "1" and "2" as "one" and "two" and no longer as "ein" and "zwei," "un" and "deux," "uno" and "due," and so on. And these civil servants—who now had a common spoken, as well as a common written, language— were, under the Han, posted in any province of the empire except that of their birth and so were carriers and disseminators of the common language.

The standardized official pronunciation of the characters became the so-called Mandarin dialect or language which by the twentieth century still prevailed over a vast area of China: over some twenty provinces from Yunnan in the southwest to the River Amur in the north. In some five provinces on the southern and southeastern sea-board the local dialects were so differentiated from Mandarin and from each other that the areas of mutual intelligibility rarely exceeded the limits of a single province. In the twentieth century, however, Mandarin has made such great gains among the intelligentsia of the southern provinces that its victory as the *lingua franca* for the whole of China may be complete before the century has run its course.

Although the uniform visual means of communication and the standardized vocalization of the characters performed the great service of preventing a babel of tongues in China and so contributing to the rise of nationalism, yet the script placed a heavy burden on Chinese culture and education. The reasons for this lie in the nature of the script itself. For each simple word there is a separate and distinct character—at the present time there are some fifty thousand characters. These characters are drawn with a brush[5] and are complicated. The difficulties of such a system are obvious. Learning to read and write in Chinese is a feat requiring memorization of the form and meaning of thousands of characters and the acquisition of a great manual skill and dexterity. The time and energy required to master the language have been among the factors that limited the number of literates throughout the history of China in both civilizations.

We have seen[6] that the Five Classics, written in a language already different from the colloquial language, became, in the second century B.C., the basis of education, and remained so. Thus the hold of the

Sinic classical literature on Chinese thought and culture, and the role of the official literati and of literary officialdom, were not broken until the twentieth century. Yet, under the shadow of this literature and culture, there had arisen[7] a popular literature in the living vernacular, which was the Mandarin *lingua franca*.

In India

In India, the original language of the founders of the Indic Civilization was the Sanskrit of the Vedas.[8] By the time of the Buddha in the sixth century this language had ceased to be that of daily intercourse and had become a "classical" language. As such, it continued to be studied for the great religious literature enshrined in it. As the language of daily intercourse, its place was taken by a number of local vernaculars, called prakrits, all of which derived from it—as the European "Romance" languages are derived from Vulgar Latin. One of the more important of the prakrits was that called Pali; it was the language of the Hinayanian Buddhist scriptures.

The great Mauryan Emperor Asoka, in the third century B.C., did not designate any one of the prakrits as an official language. The edicts which he caused to be inscribed at very many places in his extensive empire were written in several different prakrits in two different scripts. Probably the reason for this impartial use of different vernaculars and scripts was that intelligibility seemed more important than the convenience of establishing as official a single script and language. Further, as we have seen, the state in India never at any time had the interest in education and its apparatus that was characteristic of the several Chinese governments and of the later Roman Empire. However, before the end of the third century B.C., an artificial revival of Sanskrit began just inside the northern frontier of Asoka's empire and continued and grew until, by the sixth century after Christ, the revived Sanskrit had triumphed over all the prakrits on the Indian sub-continent and had left Pali stranded on Ceylon.

The body of extant Sanskrit literature consequently falls into two parts, the older, original portion prior to the third century B.C., and the later portion which is marked by stylistic and linguistic innovations. The reason for the revival of Sanskrit, and one large use to which it was put, was that it might serve as the vehicle for the two then newly born higher religions, Mahayana Buddhism and Hinduism. In the Hindu Civilization[9] there was no renaissance of Sanskrit because the language and its literature, in both the earlier and later portions, continued to flourish throughout the interregnum and was continued into the growth period of the society. Sanskrit, as the language of the sacred writings of Hinduism, was itself a sacred or quasi-sacred language, and the Brahmans had incorporated the two great popular epics, the *Mahabharata* and the *Ramayana*,[10] into the canon of accepted writings. Both epics were the result of a long and slow growth, both had had theological and moral and didactic material inserted into them during their long growths, and both had an enormous popular appeal as well as a confirmed place in the "classical" literature. Thus these epics were cherished by people and pundits alike and their episodes, stories, language, and style were living elements in popular consciousness and speech as well as among the learned.

This is perhaps the reason that the Sanskrit language and literature did not act as an incubus and a blight upon the development of a popular literature in the vernaculars of the Hindu world but acted, instead, as stimuli. The poetry that was composed, between the ninth and thirteenth centuries, at the courts of the Rajput princes,[12] was composed in the Hindi vernacular; the *Ramcharit Manas* of the great Tulsi Das, who wrote at the turn of the sixteenth century, was composed in Hindi. This poem, which Sir Charles Eliot calls[13] "one of the great religious poems of the World and not unworthy to be set beside *Paradise Lost*," and which is a kind of bible to millions, certainly achieved some of its popularity because the minds and hearts of its possible audience had been prepared for it by their knowledge and appreciation of the ancient Sanskrit epics.

Tulsi Das lived under the Mughal Empire. Under the Mughals the official language had been Persian and the *lingua franca* among the Muslim Indians a Persianized form of Hindi known as Urdu.

With the coming of the British to India, English displaced Persian as the official language, for diplomatic correspondence and, A.D. 1835, as the medium of higher education. English was not, however, substituted for Persian in other uses: in all judicial and fiscal affairs Persian was replaced by local vernaculars which varied from province to province. And British Protestant missionaries devised a Sanskritized

Hindi vernacular called Hindustani to give the Hindus of northern India a counterpart of Urdu. When, A.D. 1947, the British abdicated their power in India it was taken almost as a matter of course in both India and Pakistan that English would remain the language of diplomatic correspondence and of higher education. Since then, however, the government of India has ordered that by the year 1965 all instruction must be in Hindi.[14] At the time of writing, 1957, educators agree that this goal is impossible of achievement; the effect of the announcement of the government's order has been to diminish student interest in learning English and, similarly, student proficiency in the language. This linguistic problem, a heritage from India's varied past and aggravated by the importation of nationalism from the West, is only one among the several grievous problems confronting higher education in India today.

In Greece and Rome

In the Hellenic world throughout the growth period there was a variety of Greek dialects and languages as well as the non-Greek Carian and Lycian. Among the speakers of the several Greek dialects there was a diversity not only in language but also in script between one district and another and even between one city-state and another in the same district. These differences were, in many districts and city-states, preserved as the marks of local distinctiveness of character. However, one dialect, that of the tiny region of Attica, had by the end of the Hellenic time of troubles gained currency throughout the whole Hellenic world.

The first step in the spread of Attic Greek was taken when the chief city in which it was used, Athens, made herself the mistress of the Aegean and, through her political supremacy, diverted the trade that had formerly gone to Aegina and Miletus to her own port of Peiraeus. Concurrently with the rise of Athens to political and commercial supremacy, there came the great burst of creative activity in philosophy and art and literature so that while the Attic Greek was being spread through commerce and diplomacy it was serving as the vehicle for a brilliant literature. It was adopted as the official language of Macedonia by Philip; it was carried by Philip's son Alexander as far abroad as India and Egypt, and became the official language of

Alexander's vast empire. It continued to be the official language of the successor states to that empire.

Rome early adopted Greek education and literature—and the Attic Greek language. With the imposition of the Roman power on Greek lands, the Attic Greek continued in use as the official language in those lands.[15]

This widespread currency of Attic Greek had not been achieved without compensating losses: the elegant and exquisite language of the Athens of the fifth century had become more and more changed and vulgarized until, by the first century, the gradual transformation had resulted in an obviously different language: the Attic *koine* or common language. The koine was a language stripped of its niceties and nuances, a language vulgarized to such an extent that it scarcely bears comparison with that of Sophocles and Plato. The non-Attic Greek dialects—partly under the influence of the Attic koine—had gradually fused and were gradually vulgarized and Atticized until, finally, they became indistinguishable from and merged with the Attic koine. Thus the Attic koine became the living spoken language.

This living language was the vehicle for a considerable and important literature, but of this literature only the New Testament, the Septuagint, and a part of the histories of Polybius have survived: the great works of the third and second centuries before the Christian era are lost. A part of the reason for this is that in the last century B.C., which was also the last of the four centuries of troubles from the breakdown to the universal state, the Greeks looked away from their own war-weary present back to the glories of the greater past when Attic art and literature were at their height. In so doing, they scorned the living koine and aspired to recapture the glorious past by servile and meticulous imitation of the vocabulary and syntax, of the form and style of the Attic Greek of the great creative period. This archaizing movement embraced writers from all parts of the Hellenistic-Roman world and continued into the fifth and even the sixth centuries of the Christian era. During the centuries when the archaizing tendencies were strongest, the criterion according to which it was decided whether or not a text or an author was to be copied and so transmitted and preserved was the purity of the Attic Greek of that text or author. The result was that many Neo-Attic works of little merit were preserved and many works of greater literary merit were preserved and many works of greater literary merit have been lost. The purpose of the whole archaizing Neo-Attic movement is judged by Toynbee[16] to have been that of escaping the well-nigh intolerable present by a flight to the magnificent past.

While Rome was still only the chief among a small group of Italian towns[17] her language was only one among several Italic dialects, which included Oscan and Umbrian, and the non-Italic Etruscan, Illyrian, and Punic. Latin, the dialect of the district of Latium and of the city of Rome, gradually replaced the other dialects as Rome rose to become the first of the cities of Italy. When Rome imposed her sovereignty on Greece she allowed the Attic koine, as has been seen,[18] to continue as the *lingua franca* of those areas in which it was already established, and she employed it as the official language in the Greek speaking lands.

After they had ceased to be truly living languages, both Latin and Greek had long careers. Vulgar Latin remained the intellectual *lingua franca* of the West until the seventeenth century, and Greek continued to be the vehicle for learned literature in the Orthodox Christian society until the fifteenth century. Latin still survives as the ritual language of the Roman Catholic Church, and Greek as that of the Greek Orthodox Christian Church.

The careers of the Greek and Latin alphabets have been even more successful than those of the languages. The Greek alphabet has been adopted and adapted to serve as the vehicle for Bulgarian, Serbian, Russian, Armenian, Georgian, and Coptic; the Latin has been used to convey not only all the Romance languages but also Irish, English, German, and the Scandinavian tongues, Polish and Czech and many non-European languages.

In the Orthodox Christian Society

The Attic koine had been the living, as well as the official, language of the East Roman Empire. As the living language of the emerging Orthodox Christian Civilization it continued to develop and change, as all living languages do. By the twelfth century the differences, in morphology, syntax, and vocabulary, between the living language and the earlier koine were so great that the latter was intelligible only to those who had studied it as another language. This now different living language was modern Greek, or, rather, the earliest stage in the development of modern Greek.

We have seen above[19] that there had been a revival of Hellenism in the eighth and ninth centuries. In the tenth century there had appeared an epic poem, in modern Greek, celebrating the exploits of Greek frontiersmen in Eastern Anatolia. This poem was, on the literary and social plane, the counterpart to the Old French *Chanson de Roland* but, as Toynbee remarks,[20] whereas the French poem became the parent of a vernacular literature, the modern Greek poem did not. And it did not because the Orthodox Christian writers, under the influence of the Hellenic renaissance, turned away from the literary use of the modern Greek vernacular to the imitation of the ancient models. Thus the literature which in the tenth century had begun to be written in the modern Greek vernacular could gain no prestige in competition with the resuscitated language and literature of the earlier society. The Orthodox Christian scholars and authors could not forget that they were the lineal descendants of the earlier Greeks and the heirs to their culture, and so the mighty cultural heritage acted as an incubus upon a literature composed in a vernacular offspring of the Attic koine and the classical Attic Greek.

In Sumeria and Babylonia

During the first half of the third millenium before Christ, the Sumeric Civilization had achieved a significant culture.[21] By about the year 3000 the society had invented writing, using a cuneiform, syllabic script, and this script had then become the vehicle of a cultic and religious literature. The heirs of this culture were the Akkadians, who were Semites, and other Semitic invaders who had been attracted out of the Arabian Steppe by the Sumeric Civilization. By the end of the third millenium Akkadian had supplanted Sumerian as the spoken language[21] and had been given equal status with it as the second official language of the universal state of the civilization. Although Akkadian was radically different in structure and vocabulary from the language it supplanted, yet the cuneiform script—the only script known to the society—was used as the vehicle for it. This script was ill adapted for such a different language, and learning to read and write it was a difficult and long process that involved learning also some Sumerian.

For this reason, and also because Sumerian continued to enjoy high prestige as the religious and cultic language, it was studied in the schools throughout the life span of the Sumeric society and, later, throughout that of the Babylonic Civilization.

Even after the dissolution of the Sumeric Civilization, Akkadian continued in use as the living *lingua franca* among the several successor states and during the beginnings of the Babylonic Civilization. It was the language of diplomacy and commerce for the whole of Southwestern Asia and was even used by the Egyptian New Empire in correspondence with its client states in Syria. By the eighth and seventh centuries, however, Akkadian was on the wane as a living language: it was being supplanted by Aramaic, another Semitic language. Aramaic had arisen in eastern Syria and western Mesopotamia and had spread rapidly, from the last century of the second millenium, over the territories of the Babylonic and Syriac civilizations.

Akkadian was the language of the militaristic Assyrians; Aramaic that of the Chaldeans who led the resistance movement against Assyria and succeeded, 610 B.C., in establishing the Neo-Babylonian Empire. Yet so great was the prestige of Babylon and its culture that the founders of the Neo-Babylonian Empire made Akkadian the official language of the empire and used the Akkadian cuneiform script in writing. Aramaic, however, continued to wax as the living *lingua franca* and its importance was finally recognized when it was made the official language for the provinces west of Babylon. By the first century of the Christian era, Aramaic had become the living language of the entire Semitic speaking population of the "Fertile Crescent," and this despite the fact that it had been deposed from its official position by Alexander the Great and his successors in favor of the Greek koine.

In Egypt

The classical Egyptian, written in hieroglyphic characters, had been the living language of the Old Kingdom[22] and continued as the medium of literary expression and as the official language down into the New Empire. The language seems to have been carefully cultivated even during the early period of the Old Kingdom. After the interregnum of the Hyksos invaders and the establishment of the New Empire, the old language and its script continued as official. But during the centuries the spoken language had changed until by this time it was so different from the official language that the latter could not be understood by ordinary people.

In the great revolution of the fourteenth century in which Ikhnaton was the chief actor, a break was made with the "dead" language of the past: poetry was written in the living vernacular, and Ikhnaton established it as the official language.[23] It continued as the vehicle for literature and as the living language for perhaps five centuries, after which it became a "dead" language that school boys had to learn as another tongue. By the eighth century a new vernacular—Demotic—written in a new cursive script, had almost completely supplanted New Egyptian. Demotic continued in use in Egypt through the Graeco-Roman era and down to about the fifth Christian century.

Thus Egypt, in its long history, twice preserved a language until it had become unintelligible to the masses, and this not merely in a liturgy or cultic literature, but in a secular literature.

CHART I.

Civilization	*Relations*	*Time and Place of Origin*	*Challenge*	*Time of Troubles*	*Universal State*	*Universal Peace*	*Philosophies*	*Religion*	*Source of Inspiration of Religion*
Egyptiac	wholly unrelated	Nile River Valley; before 4000 B.C.	physical: desiccation	*c.* 2424–2070/60 B.C.	Middle Empire New Empire	*c.* 2070/60–1660 B.C. *c.* 1580–1175 B.C.	Atonism (abortive)	Osiris-worship Atonism	alien ?—Sumeric ?
Andean	wholly unrelated	Andean coast and plateau; *c.* beginning of Christian Era	physical: coastal desert; bleak climate on almost soilless plateau	?–*c.* A.D. 1430	Incaic Empire (followed by Spanish Viceroyalty of Peru)	A.D. 1430–1533	Viracochaism (abortive)		
Sinic	unrelated to earlier; apparented to the Far Eastern	lower valley of the Yellow River; *c.* 1500 B.C.	physical: marsh and floods and extremes of temperature	634–221 B.C.	Ts'in and Han Empire	221 B.C.–A.D. 172	Moism; Taoism; Confucianism	Mahāyāna Buddhism Neotaoism	alien (Indo-Helleno-Syriac) indigenous but imitative
Minoan	unrelated to earlier; apparented (loosely) to the Hellenic and the Syriac	Aegean Islands before 3000 B.C.	physical: the sea	?–1750 B.C.	'Thalassocracy of Minos'	*c.* 1750–1400 B.C.			
Sumeric	unrelated to earlier; ? apparented to the Babylonic and ? the Hittite	lower Tigris-Euphrates valley; before *c.* 3500 B.C.	physical: desiccation	*c.* 2677–2298 B.C.	Empire of Sumer and Akkad	*c.* 2298–1905 B.C.	Tammuz-worship—but there is nothing created by the Sumeric Society that can be called a new religion.		
Mayan	unrelated to earlier; apparented to the Yucatec and the Mexic	Central American tropical forest; before *c.* 500 B.C.	physical: the luxuriance of the tropical forest	?–*c.* A.D. 300	'First Empire' of the Mayas	*c.* A.D. 300–690	The Mayan, Hittite, Babylonic and Indic societies all seem, as they disintegrate, to be reverting to the ethos of primitive man in their apparent insensibility to the gulf between the abandoned sexualism of their religion and the exaggerated asceticism of their philosophy; they show an awakening to a sense of sin through the shock of seeing an ancient social structure collapse.		
Yucatec } fused to produce: Mexic } Central American	both affiliated to the Mayan	waterless, treeless limestone shelf of Yucatan peninsula; after A.D. 629	physical: barren peninsula; social: the disintegrating Mayan Society	?–A.D. 1521	Spanish Viceroyalty of New Spain (the Aztecs were on the verge of founding a universal state when the Spaniards came)	A.D. 1521–1821			
Hittite	possibly loosely affiliated to the Sumeric but with a non-Sumeric religion	Cappadocia just beyond Sumeric frontiers; before 1500 B.C.	social: the disintegrating Sumeric Society	predominant in its own world by 15th century B.C.; wars with Egypt after 1352 until peace in 1278 B.C.; overwhelmed by a wave of migration *c.* 1200–1190 B.C.					
Syriac	loosely affiliated to the Minoan; apparented to the Iranic and the Arabic	Syria; before 1100 B.C.	social: the disintegrating Minoan Society	*c.* 937–525 B.C.	Achaemenian Empire Arab Caliphate	*c.* 525–332 B.C. *c.* A.D. 640–969	Zervanism (abortive)	Islam	indigenous indigenous
Babylonic	closely affiliated to the Sumeric	'Iraq; before 1500 B.C.	social: the disintegrating Sumeric Society	?–610 B.C.	Neo-Babylonic Empire	610–539 B.C.	Astrology	Judaism Zoroastrianism	alien—Syriac alien—Syriac
Iranic } fused to produce: Arabic } Islamic	both affiliated to the Syriac and, after A.D. 1516, fused to form the Islamic Society	Anatolia, Iran, Oxus-Jaxartes; before A.D. 1300 Arabia, 'Iraq, Syria, North Africa; before A.D. 1300	social: the disintegrating Syriac Society social: the disintegrating Syriac Society						
Far Eastern—Main Body	affiliated to the Sinic with an offshoot in Japan	China; before A.D. 500	social: the disintegrating Sinic Society	A.D. 878–1280	Mongol Empire Manchu Empire	A.D. 1280–1351 A.D. 1644–1853		Catholicism T'aip'ing	alien—Western semi-alien—Western tincture
Far Eastern—Japanese Offshoot	offshoot of the main body of the Far Eastern	Japanese Archipelago; after A.D. 500	physical: new ground; social: contact with the main body	A.D. 1185–1597	Hideyoshi's dictatorship and Tokugawa Shogunate	A.D. 1597–1863		Jōdo Jōdo Shinshū Nichirenism Zen	semi-alien—from main body indigenous indigenous semi-alien—from main body
Indic	unrelated to earlier; apparented to the Hindu	Indus and Ganges River Valleys; *c.* 1500 B.C.	physical: the luxuriance of the tropical forest	?–322 B.C.	Mauryan Empire Guptan Empire	322–185 B.C. A.D. 390–*c.* 475	Hīnayāna Buddhism; Jainism	Hinduism	indigenous indigenous
Hindu	affiliated to the Indic	North India; before A.D. 800	social: the disintegrating Indic Society	*c.* A.D. 1175–1572	Mughal Rāj British Rāj	*c.* A.D. 1572–1707 *c.* A.D. 1818–		Kabirism; Sikhism Brahmō Samāj	semi-alien—Islamic semi-alien—Western tincture
Hellenic	loosely affiliated to the Minoan; apparented to the Western and to the Orthodox Christian	coasts and islands of the Aegean; before 1100 B.C.	physical: barren land and the sea; social: the disintegrating Minoan Society	431–31 B.C.	Roman Empire	31 B.C.–A.D. 378	Platonism Stoicism Epicureanism Pyrrhonism	Christianity Mithraism Manichaeism Isis-worship Mahāyāna Buddhism Cybele-worship Neoplatonism	alien—Syriac alien—Syriac alien—Syriac alien—Egyptiac alien—Indic alien—Hittite indigenous
Orthodox Christian—Main Body	affiliated to the Hellenic with an offshoot in Russia	Anatolia; before A.D. 700 (final rupture with the West in 11th century)	social: the disintegrating Hellenic Society	A.D. 977–1372	Ottoman Empire	A.D. 1372–1768		Imāmī Sh'ism Bedreddinism	alien—Iranic semi-alien—Iranic tincture
Orthodox Christian—Russian Offshoot	offshoot of the main body of the Orthodox Christian	Russia; 10th century of the Christian Era	physical: new ground; social: contact with the main body	A.D. 1075–1478	Muscovite Empire	A.D. 1478–1881		Sectarianism Revivalistic Protestantism	indigenous alien—Western
Western	affiliated to the Hellenic	Western Europe; before A.D. 700	physical: new ground; social: the disintegrating Hellenic Society						

The *ABORTIVE CIVILIZATIONS*: The embryos of these civilizations were rendered abortive by the strain of having to respond to a series of challenges which were excessive in their severity. The Abortive Civilizations are: the *FAR WESTERN CHRISTIAN*, the *FAR EASTERN CHRISTIAN* and the *SCANDINAVIAN*.

The *FAR WESTERN CHRISTIAN CIVILIZATION* arose in the 'Celtic Fringe', mainly in Ireland, after *c.* A.D. 375, as a response to the physical challenge of new ground and the double social challenge of the disintegrating Hellenic Society and the nascent Western Society. The period of segregation was from *c.* 450 to *c.* 600. The Celts moulded Christianity to fit their own barbarian social heritage; by the sixth century Ireland was definitely the centre of gravity of Christianity in the West; its originality is manifested in church organization and in literature and art. The final blows against this civilization were delivered by the Vikings in the ninth to the eleventh centuries and by the ecclesiastical authority of Rome and the political authority of England in the twelfth century.

The *FAR EASTERN CHRISTIAN CIVILIZATION* arose within the chrysalis of Nestorian Christianity in the Oxus-Jaxartes Basin and perished when this region was annexed to the Arab Empire in A.D. 737–41 after it had been politically and culturally divorced from the rest of the Syriac World for the better part of nine centuries. This embryonic civilization was the product of nine centuries of Central Asian history in which this basin had been living a life of its own with special functions resulting from its place athwart the great trade routes and its large number of Greek colonists.

The *SCANDINAVIAN CIVILIZATION* emerged within the ambit of the Hellenic External Proletariat after the break-up of the Roman Empire; the Scandinavians were isolated from Roman Christendom before the end of the sixth century by the interposition of the pagan Slavs. They began to develop their own civilization only after contact with the West had been re-established, and this civilization was eventually annihilated as a result of the conversion of the Icelanders to Christianity. The ethos of the civilization was each remarkable resemblance to the Greek culture.

The *ARRESTED CIVILIZATIONS* include the *POLYNESIANS*, the *ESKIMOS*, the *NOMADS*, the *SPARTANS*, the *'OSMANLIS*. These were all immobilized in consequence of having attempted and achieved a *tour de force*: they were all responses to challenges on the very border-line between a degree that still affords some stimulus and a degree that brings into operation the law of diminishing returns. With the Spartans and the 'Osmanlis the superlative challenge was human, with the others it was physical. The two characteristics common to them all are caste and specialization. They all performed miracles of human will-power and ingenuity but at the price of a systematic repudiation of the characteristically human quality of versatile adaptability. They all set their feet on the path of retrogression from humanity to animality.

The *ESKIMOS*: the stimulus of economic advantage impelled them to the *tour de force* of staying at or on the sea ice during the winter and hunting seals; this demands so much of their energies that none is left over to apply to further advances. They pay the penalty of the rigid conformation of their life to the Arctic climatic cycle.

The *'OSMANLIS*: their superlative challenge was the geographical transference of a nomadic community to an alien environment where the novel problem was to exercise dominion over alien communities of human beings instead of over animals. Their *tour de force* was the Ottoman slave-household: i.e. the picking and training of human watch-dogs to keep the Pādishāh's human cattle in order. They achieved their astonishing triumphs by putting off their human nature as far as possible and assuming an animal nature instead by limiting their minds to the 'single-track' action of instinct.

The *NOMADS*: the physical challenge of the Steppe was brought on by the same desiccation that evoked the Egyptiac and Sumeric civilizations. The mastery of the Steppe demands so much of the Nomads' energies that none is left over. Nomadism is superior to agriculture in several ways: in the domestication of animals and in the development of economic techniques, in which it is comparable with industrialism rather than with agriculture. Thus nomadism demands a rigorously high standard of character and behaviour: the 'good shepherd' is the symbol of the highest Christian ideal.

The *SPARTANS*: the physical challenge of over-population confronted the whole Hellenic World in the eighth century B.C., and the Spartans met it by the great *tour de force* of forcing all their energies into a rigid and 'single-track' military training with—as in the Ottoman system—a total disregard for human nature. There are many striking similarities between the Spartan and the Ottoman systems, and these are attributable to a natural conformity between the responses which were made to a virtually identic challenge by two different communities acting independently of and unknown to one another.

The *POLYNESIANS*: to the physical challenge of the sea they responded with the *tour de force* of Oceanic voyaging; their skill was to perform these stupendous voyages in frail open canoes and their penalty has been to remain in exact equilibrium with the Pacific—they were just able to cross its vast open spaces, but never with any margin of security or ease, until at last the intolerable tension has found its own relief by going slack. The megalithic statues on Easter Island are witnesses to the great past of their makers, for the art of sculpture must have been brought there by the pioneers and lost by their descendants, as the latter lost also the art of navigation.

CHART II

1. PRIMITIVE SOCIETIES

2. PRIMARY CIVILIZATIONS

(all derived direct from primitive societies)

Egyptiac   Andean   Mayan   Sumeric   Indus Culture   Minoan   Shang Culture

RUDIMENTARY HIGHER RELIGIONS

(created, adapted, or adopted by internal proletariats of primary civilizations)

The Worship of Osiris and Isis

(? adopted by the internal proletariat of the Egyptiac Civilization from the internal proletariat of the Sumeric)

The Worship of Tammuz and Ishtar

(? created by the internal proletariat of the Sumeric Civilization)

3. SECONDARY CIVILIZATIONS

(derived from the primary civilizations)

(a) through their dominant minorities   (b) through their external proletariats

Babylonic   Yucatec   Mexic   Abortive First Syriac Hittite   Indic   Syriac Hellenic   Sinic

(from Sumeric)   (from Mayan)   (from Mayan)   (from Sumeric)   (from Indus Culture)   (from Minoan)   (from Shang Culture)

4. HIGHER RELIGIONS

(created, adapted, or adopted by internal proletariats of secondary civilizations)

Judaism Zoroastrianism   *Hinduism*   *Islam*   *Isis-Worship* *Cybele-Worship* *Mithraism* *Christianity* *Manichaeism*   *Neoplatonism*   *The Mahāyāna*   *Neotaoism*

(created by the internal proletariat of the Babylonic Civilization)

(created by the internal proletariat of the Indic Civilization)

(created by the internal proletariat of the Syriac Civilization)

(created by the internal proletariat of the Hellenic Civilization)

(adapted by the Hellenic internal proletariat from one of the philosophies of the Hellenic dominant minority)

(adapted by the Hellenic internal proletariat from one of the philosophies of the Indic dominant minority, and adopted by the Sinic internal proletariat)

(adapted by the Sinic internal proletariat from one of the philosophies of the Sinic dominant minority)

5. TERTIARY CIVILIZATIONS

(derived from secondary civilizations through chrysalis churches constructed by their internal proletariats)

Hindu   *Iranic* *Arabic*   *Abortive Far Eastern Christian*   *Western Christian* *Orthodox Christian* *Orthodox Christian in Russia*   *Abortive Far Western Christian*   *Abortive Scandinavian*   *Far Eastern* *Far Eastern in Korea and Japan*

(derived from Indic through Hinduism)

(derived from Syriac through Islam)

(derived from Hellenic and Syriac through Christianity)

(derived from Hellenic through Christianity)

(derived from Hellenic through its external proletariat and through Christianity)

(derived from Hellenic through its external proletariat)

(derived from Sinic through the Mahāyāna)

6. SECONDARY HIGHER RELIGIONS

Kabirism *Sikhism* *Brahmō Samaj*   *Baha'ism* *The Ahmadīyah*   *Beddreddinism*   *Russian Orthodox Christian Sects*   *The T'ai p'ing*   *Jōdo* *Zen*   *Jōdo Shinshū* *Hokke (alias Nichirenism)*

(created by the internal proletariat of the Hindu Civilization)

(created by the Iranic wing of the internal proletariat of the Western Civilization)

(created by the internal proletariat of the main body of the Orthodox Christian Civilization)

(created by the internal proletariat of the Orthodox Christian Civilization in Russia)

(created by the internal proletariat of the Far Eastern Civilization in China)

(adapted by the internal proletariat of the Far Eastern Civilization in Japan from the Mahāyāna)

(created by the internal proletariat of the Far Eastern Civilization in Japan)

Bibliography and Notes

General Bibliography

Some general books that have been found useful are: First and foremost: Arnold J. Toynbee, *A Study of History*, London, Oxford University Press; vols. i-iii, 1934; iv-vi, 1939; vii-x, 1954; xi, 1959. The ten volumes have been summarized by D. C. Somervell in a two volume abridgement, also published by the Oxford University Press: vol. i, vol. ii, 1957.

CONANT, JAMES BRYANT, *The Citadel of Learning*. London 1956, Oxford University Press.

HANS, NICHOLAS, *Comparative Education*. London 1949, Routledge & Kegan Paul.

HOFFMAN, ERNST, *Pädagogischer Humanismus*. Zurich 1956, Artemis.

JEFFREYS, M. V. C., *Beyond Neutrality*. London 1955, Pitman.

JEFFREYS, M. V. C., *Glaucon: An Enquiry into the Aims of Education*, rev. ed. London 1955 (1st ed. 1950), Pitman.

MAYER, MAX, *Geschichte der Abendländischen Erziehung und Bildung: ein Grundriss*. Freiburg 1955, Herder.

MOORE, ERNEST C., *The Story of Instruction*. (2 vols.), New York 1936-38, Macmillan.

SMITH, W. O. LESTER, *Education in Great Britain*. London 1956, Oxford University Press.

TURNER, RALPH, *The Great Cultural Traditions*. New York 1941, McGraw-Hill. (2 vols.).

Part One   Introduction

1. The Toynbee Background

1. Oxford University Press; vols. i-iii, 1934; iv-vi, 1939; vii-x, 1954; vol. xi, an atlas and gazetteer, 1959. References to this work will be given in the form, "i, 46," signifying page 46 of volume i.

2. i, 46.

3. iii, 217.

4. iii, 230-231.

5. For the Civilizations, see Chart I, above. This chart is a summary of the facts about the several civilizations and is intended to be both a help to the reader and a device for saving space in the text.

6. i, 192.

7. i, 195.

8. i, 245.

9. i, 300.

10. The challenges that have produced the several civilizations are given in Chart I.

11. ii, 259.

12. The Arrested and Abortive Civilizations are listed in Chart I.

13. iii, 119.

14. iii, 183.

15. iii, 192.

16. iii, 196.

17. v, 17.

18. i, 41, n.

19. v, 63.

20. v, 25.

21. The philosophies and religions are listed in Chart I.

22. i, 56 ff.
23. v, 23.
24. vii, 1.
25. viii, 97.
26. The arrangement of the civilizations in the several generations and their relations to the higher religions are given in Chart II.
27. vii, 423.
28. vii, 4.
29. vii, 54.
30. vii, 381.
31. Toynbee had suggested this other sense in the essay on "History" in *The Legacy of Greece* (Oxford 1921, Clarendon Press); he had stated it in the essay entitled "My View of History," which was reprinted as the first chapter of *Civilization on Trial* (New York 1948, Oxford University Press). The quotation is from pp. 7-8 of *Civilization on Trial*.

2. The Apprenticeship Method and Oral Tradition

1. See below, under "Indic Civilization."
2. Cf. Piggott and Stuart, *Prehistoric India* (Penguin Books, 1950), p. 253.
3. *Phaedrus,* 274 E—275 E; trans. H. N. Fowler (London 1927, Heinemann).
4. Nielsen, Eduard, *Oral Tradition* (London 1954, SCM Press), p. 33; for a discussion of the whole subject, see this book.
5. Cf. the titles on the subject listed in the bibliography under "Babylonic Civilization."
6. Widengren, G., *Literary and Psychological Aspects of the Hebrew Prophets* (Uppsala 1948, Uppsala Universitets Arsskrift 1948): 10, p. 93.

Part Two Education in Thirteen Civilizations

3. The Sinic Civilization

CARTER, T. F., *The Invention of Printing in China and Its Spread Westward,* 2nd ed. New York 1931, Columbia University Press.

CHIANG, MOULIN, *A Study of Chinese Principles of Education.* Shanghai 1924, Commercial Press.

CHU, K., "Education," Ch. XIII in Zen's *Symposium,* q.v.

CREEL, H. G., *The Birth of China.* New York 1937, Reynal & Hitchcock; London 1936, Jonathan Cape.

CREEL, H. G., *Studies in Early Chinese Culture.* Washington 1938, American Council of Learned Societies.

FITZGERALD, C. P., *China: A Short Cultural History.* London 1935, Crescent Press.

FORKE, A., *Geschichte der chinesischen Philosophie.* 3 vols., Hamburg 1927-38.

FRANKE, H., *Forschungsbericht Sinologie.* Bern 1953, Verlag a. Francke.

FRANKE, O., *Geschichte des chinesischen Reiches.* 5 vols., Berlin and Leipzig 1930, de Gruyter.

FUNG YU-LAN (trans. Derk Bodde), *A History of Chinese Philosophy.* Vol. I, *The Period of the Philosophers.* Princeton 1952, Princeton University Press. Vol. II, *The Period of Classical Learning.* Leiden 1953, Brill.

GALT, H. S., *A History of Chinese Educational Institutions.* London 1951, Probsthain.

GARDNER, C. S., *Chinese Traditional Historiography.* Cambridge 1938, Harvard University Press.

GOODRICH, L. C., *A Short History of the Chinese People.* London 1948, Allen & Unwin.

HU SHIH, *The Development of Logical Method in Ancient China.* Shanghai 1922, Oriental Book Co.

MASPERO, H., *La Chine Antique,* rev. ed. Paris 1956, Boccard.

NEEDHAM, JOSEPH, *Science and Civilization in China.* Vol. I, *Introductory Orientations.* Cambridge 1954, Cambridge University Press.

QUISTORP, M., *Männergesellschaft und Altersklassen im alten China,* in *Mitteilungen des Seminars für Orientalische Sprachen,* Bd. 18, Berlin 1915.

TING, V. K., "How China Acquired her Civilization," Ch. I in Zen's *Symposium,* q.v.

WILHELM, R., *Geschichte der chinesischen Kultur.* Munich 1928, Bruckmann.

WRIGHT, ARTHUR F. (ed.), *Studies in Chinese Thought.* Chicago 1953, University of Chicago Press.

ZEN, S. H. (ed.), *Symposium on Chinese Culture.* Shanghai 1931, China Institute of Pacific Relations.

1. Cf. below, pp. 312 ff.
2. Creel, *Birth,* p. 278.
3. The two classes may be subdivided as follows: 1. The nobility and scholars and officials, 2. The great mass of uneducated common people included the farmers, the laborers, and the merchants.
4. Fitzgerald, p. 44.
5. *Ibid.,* p. 61.
6. Cf. Ting, p. 12; Creel, *Birth,* p. 257; Fitzgerald, p. 61.
7. Cf. Creel, *Birth,* p. 257.
8. *Ibid.,* pp. 314, 358.
9. *Ibid.,* p. 257.
10. *Ibid.,* p. 358.
11. Fitzgerald, p. 76.
12. *Ibid.,* p. 35.
13. *Ibid.,* p. 42.
14. Cf. Maspero, pp. 109 ff.
15. *Ibid.,* pp. 113 ff.
16. Quoted by Fitzgerald, p. 89.
17. Cf. Fung Yu-Lan, I, p. 48.
18. Cf. Maspero, pp. 113 ff.
19. Galt, p. 79.

20. Cf. Kant's dictum that concepts without percepts are empty, and percepts without concepts are blind.

21. Cf. Fung Yu-Lan, I, p. 3; Wright, pp. 4, 20. One result of the failure to draw the distinction is that, in Chinese thought, the question about how the self gets knowledge of what is not the self, that is, the "epistemological" question, which has engaged so much of the attention of Western philosophers, does not arise.

22. By Fung Yu-Lan, I, p. 129.

23. *Ibid.*, p. 130.

24. Cf. Fitzgerald, p. 139.

25. See also below, pp. 323 ff. (Lang, Scripts, etc., p. 1).

26. Vol. I, p. 15.

27. Cf. Fitzgerald, pp. 104, 142, 146.

28. Cf. Fitzgerald, p. 202.

29. Vol. I, p. 405.

30. Cf. Fitzgerald, p. 104.

31. *Ibid.*, p. 105.

32. Cf. Franke, I, pp. 274 ff.

33. Cf. Franke, *ibid.*, and Galt, p. 197.

34. Cf. Galt, pp. 197 ff.

35. Cf. Goodrich, p. 51, n. 18.

36. *Ibid.*, p. 31.

37. Cf. Franke, I, pp. 301 ff.

38. Cf. Gardner, p. 37.

39. *Ibid.*, p. 61.

40. The earliest extant paper dates from the middle of this century; cf. Carter, *Printing*.

41. Cf. Gardner, Ch. III.

42. *Ibid.*, p. 18.

43. In Zen's *Symposium*, pp. 132 ff.

44. Cf. Chiang, pp. 1 ff.

4. The Indic Civilization

ALTEKAR, A. S., *Education in Ancient India*. Benares 1934, The Indian Bookshop.

DAS, S. K., *The Educational System of the Ancient Hindus*. Calcutta 1930, Mitra Press.

ELIOT, SIR CHARLES, *Hinduism and Buddhism*, 3 vols., London 1921, Edward Arnold.

MAJUNDAR, R. C., *An Advanced History of India.* London 1950, Macmillan.

MAJUNDAR, R. C. (ed.), *The History and Culture of the Indian People,* as follows: Vol. I, *The Vedic Age.* London 1951, Allen & Unwin. Vol. II, *The Age of Imperial Unity.* Bombay 1951, Bharatiya Vidya Bhavan. Vol. III, *The Classical Age.* Bombay 1954, B.V.B. Vol. IV, *The Age of Imperial Kanauj.* Bombay 1955, B.V.B.

SMITH, V. A., *The Early History of India,* 3rd ed. Oxford 1914, Clarendon Press.

VENKATESWARA, S. V., *Indian Culture Through the Ages.* Vol. I, *Education and the Propagation of Culture.* London 1928, Longmans, Green and Co. Vol. II, *Public Life and Political Institutions.* London 1932, Longmans, Green and Co.

1. Cf. below, pp. 307 ff.
2. Majundar, *Vedic Age,* p. 225.
3. Majundar, *Advanced History,* p. 41.
4. Venkateswara, Vol. I, p. 9.
5. Das, p. 13.
6. Venkateswara, Vol. I, pp. 75 ff.; Majundar, *Vedic Age,* p. 515.
7. Majundar, *Vedic Age,* p. 455.
8. *Ibid.,* p. 515.
9. Cf. Majundar, *Vedic Age,* p. 514. This point is emphasized by every writer on early Indic education.
10. Cf. Das, pp. 14 ff.
11. Cf. Das, p. 32.
12. Cf. Das, pp. 7 ff.; Venkateswara, pp. 31 ff.
13. Cf. Majundar, *Age of Imperial Unity,* p. xxvii.
14. Majundar (*Vedic Age,* p. 420) points out that they were, literally, the end of the Vedas in at least three senses, and that all three senses entered into the meaning of the term. They were composed and compiled after, or at the end of, the time when the Vedas were composed; as the most difficult of all, they were taught only towards the end of the pupil's time with the guru; they came at the end of the daily Vedic-ritual.
15. From "upa-ni-sad," "to sit down near" some one; also, "upa" suggests "approaching" the teacher with the request that he impart his doctrine.
16. Cf. Venkateswara, p. 24; Majundar, *Age of Imperial Unity,* p. 584.
17. *Ibid.,* p. 585.
18. Cf. above, on Oral Tradition, pp. 24-28.
19. Cf. Das, Chs. I-III.

20. Das, p. 30.
21. Venkateswara, Vol. I, pp. 148 ff.
22. Majundar, *Age of Imperial Unity,* p. 582.
23. *Ibid.,* pp. 583 ff.
24. Cf. Majundar, *Classical Age,* p. 583.
25. *Ibid.*
26. Cf. above, pp. 40 ff.
27. Cf. below, pp. 299 ff.
28. In *The Varieties of Religious Experience* (London 1902, Longmans, Green & Co.), p. 392.
29. For other examples, and a tentative attempt to account for them, see R. C. Johnson, *The Imprisoned Splendour* (London 1953, Hodder and Stoughton).
30. This was Arnold Toynbee's way of putting the assumption in a letter dated 3rd February 1954.
31. Broad, C. D., *Religion, Philosophy and Psychical Research* (London 1953, Routledge and Kegan Paul), pp. 9 ff.
32. For the evidences, see Broad, *op. cit.,* and Johnson, *op. cit.*
33. Reported in the *Proceedings* of the Society for Psychical Research, Vol. 29, p. 46, and Vol. 34, p. 212.
34. The figure is Housman's.
35. Bhagavadgita, vi, 29-30.
36. First Ep. John, iv, 13.
37. In the order in which the quotations are given, they are from *John,* xiv, 11; *John,* xiv, 20; *Matthew,* xxv, 45; *John,* x, 30; the writer is aware that this is not the orthodox interpretation of these verses.
38. See, e.g., the anthology in Aldous Huxley's *The Perennial Philosophy* (New York 1945, Harpers).
39. For an excellent brief summary on this point see Kuhn, Herbert, *Das Erwachen der Menschheit* (Frankfurt and Hamburg 1954, Fisher), pp. 168 ff.; for a more elaborate analysis, see Northrop, F.S.C., *The Meeting of East and West* (New York 1947, Macmillan).
40. Among physicists: Schrödinger, Erwin, *What is Life?* (Cambridge, 1944, Cambridge University Press), and Johnson, R. C., *The Imprisoned Splendour;* among biologists: those cited by Johnson in *op. cit.;* among historians: Kuhn, Herbert, *op. cit.* and *Der Aufstieg der Menschheit* (Frankfurt and Hamburg 1955, Fischer); among philosophers and theologians: Watts, Alan W., *The Supreme Identity* (New York 1950, Pantheon Books), and *Behold the Spirit* (New York 1947, Pantheon); Schuon, Frithjof, *The Transcendent Unity of Religions* (London 1953, Faber); Huxley, A., *op. cit.* These are only a very few of those authors and books

in the several fields that might have been mentioned; further bibliographies are listed in these that are.

41. Kuhn, Herbert, *Das Erwachen der Menschheit* (Frankfurt and Hamburg 1954, Fischer), p. 169.
42. Cf. Kuhn, *op. cit.*
43. Eliot, Vol I, p. xci.
44. Eliot, Vol. I, p. x.
45. Das, Ch. XV.

5. The Hellenic Civilization

CAPES, WILLIAM WOLFE, *University Life in Ancient Athens*. London 1877, Longmans, Green & Co.

CLARKE, M. L., *The Roman Mind*. London 1956, Cohen & West.

COLE, P. R., *Later Roman Education in Ausonius, Capella, and the Theodosian Code*. New York 1909, Columbia University Press.

DOBSON, J. F., *Ancient Education and Its Meaning to Us*. New York 1932, Longmans, Green & Co.

GWYNN, A., *Roman Education from Cicero to Quintilian*. Oxford 1926, Clarendon Press.

JAEGER, WERNER, *Paideia: The Ideals of Greek Culture*, trans. from the 2nd German ed. by Gilbert Highet. New York 1939, Oxford University Press; vols. II and III, Oxford 1947, Blackwell.

KENYON, F. G., *Books and Readers in Ancient Greece and Rome*. Oxford 1932, Clarendon Press.

MARROU, H. I., *Histoire de l'éducation dans l'antiquité*, revised ed. Paris 1950 (first ed., 1948), Editions du Seuil. English translation by George Lamb, *A History of Education in Antiquity*. London 1956, Sheed and Ward. This is by far the best book on the subject.

NILSSON, MARTIN P., *Die hellenistische Schule*. München 1955, Beck.

RAUSCHEN, G., *Das griechische-römische Schulwesen zur Zeit des ausgehenden antiken Heidentums*. Bonn 1900, Georgi.

ROSTOVTZEFF, M., *The Social and Economic History of the Hellenistic World*, 3 vols. Oxford 1942, University Press.

ROSTOVTZEFF, M., *The Social and Economic History of the Roman Empire*. Oxford 1926, Clarendon Press.

SANDYS, JOHN EDWIN, *A History of Classical Scholarship*. Cambridge, 2nd ed. 1906 (1st. ed. 1903), University Press.

SEECK, O., *Geschichte des Untergangs der Antiken Welt*. Stuttgart 1920-21, Metzler.

ZIEBARTH, ERICH, *Aus dem griechischen Schulwesen, Eudemos von Milet und Verwandtes.* Leipzig 1909, Teubner.

1. Marrou, Eng. Trans., p. 11.
2. Jaeger, p. 2.
3. Marrou, p. 11.
4. *Ibid.,* p. 12.
5. Cf. Jaeger, pp. 20-21.
6. Cf. Marrou, p. 3.
7. *Ibid.,* pp. 32 f.
8. Cf. above, p. 26 f.
9. Kenyon, p. 14.
10. These may be seen in the Museum at the American School of Archaeology in Athens.
11. Jaeger, I, xix ff.
12. *Ibid.,* I, xxiv.
13. From Thucydides, Bk. II, chs. 31-36.
14. Cf. Hoffman, Ernst, *Pädagogischer Humanismus* (Zürich 1956), Artemis, pp. 125 ff., and Jaeger, I, 96 ff.
15. Cf. Hoffman, pp. 119 f.
16. In *The Clouds,* 961.
17. Bk. I, ch. 6.
18. p. 41.
19. *Laws,* II, 654 ab.
20. The incident is reported by Plato in the *Phaedo,* 97 b f.
21. This type of explanation has reappeared in Western thought from time to time and, recently, in the so-called "Behaviorist" psychology of the third decade of the twentieth century. It is still possible in 1957 to find high scientific authority for the view that human beings are just chemical mechanisms: cf. Butler, J. A. V., *Science and Human Life* (London 1957, Pergamon Press). It is also possible to find high scientific authority for the view that the ground of the universe is thought.
22. In any account of Greek philosophy or education or thought it is impossible to avoid a section on the sophists, and it is equally impossible to make the section wholly satisfactory: the evidence is too scanty and too ambiguous. The traditional picture of them in philosophy is derived from Plato, who was hostile. This is offset to some extent by Grote's powerful rehabilitation of them. Marrou holds that they do not properly belong either to philosophy or to science; but this is not the impression received from reading a chapter on them in any of the standard histories. It may perhaps be sufficient for our purpose to accent Marrou's position that they

were primarily educators and to add that several of them, at least, did hold definable philosophical views.

23. I, Ch. 3, pp. 284 f.

24. Protagoras is said by Diogenes Laertius to have received ten thousand drachmas, and Marrou reckons that one drachma was, at the time, a qualified worker's daily wage. (By the middle of the fourth century, however, Isocrates was getting only one thousand drachmas for the course.)

25. I, 299. The quotation continues: "Education always needs a standard; and at that period, when the traditional standards were dissolving and passing away, it chose as its standard the *form* of man: it became formal. Situations of that kind have recurred at various periods in history, and the appearance of humanism is always closely connected with them. But it is quite as essential a feature of humanism that, formal as it may be at any moment, it always looks forwards and backwards, beyond itself—backwards to the rich religious and moral forces of historical tradition, as the true 'spirit' from which the intellectual concept of rationalism, empty to the point of abstraction, must derive its concrete and living content; and forwards to the religious and philosophical problem of a concept of life which surrounds and protects humanity like a tender root, but also gives it back the fertile soil in which to grow. This is the fundamental problem of all education: our answer to it will determine our judgment of the importance of the sophists. In historical terms, the main question is whether the humanism of the sophists . . . was destroyed or perfected by Plato. . . . Plato, by going behind the ideal of the sophists, went beyond it."

26. *Ibid.*, pp. 311 ff.

27. Marrou, p. 57.

28. Cf. More, Paul Elmer, *Platonism* (Princeton 1917, Princeton University Press).

29. As reported by Plato in *The Apology*.

30. Cf, above, pp. 61 ff. The following comments on the doctrine may perhaps be helpful.

The Greek words used to refer to these entities have been variously translated, and no translation is quite satisfactory. The word "idea" inevitably suggests a conception in the mind of an individual human being and, whatever else Plato meant, he certainly did not mean this—the entities are quite independent of human thought. The word "form" suggests determinate structure and is perhaps less misleading as a translation than is "idea," but Plato nowhere suggests that the ethical entities have determinate structures. "Archetype" is perhaps an adequate translation when referring to the archetypes of biological classes and natural kinds and of artifacts but, again, not when referring to the ethical entities. We shall use the term "Idea" because it is the familiar term.

If we suppose that the general propositions about triangles, for example, are eternally true in the sense that they would still be true whether any human mind had ever discovered and formulated them or not, then it is intelligible to say that the Idea triangle is eternal, perfect, independent, and immutable. And similarly with all other mathematical Ideas. It is correct to say, further, that the mathematical point or line or triangle cannot, by its nature, be perfectly embodied in any material representation of it and, conversely, that all material representations are only approximations to the Idea. When one has genuine mathematical knowledge, therefore, it is knowledge of the mathematical Ideas, not mere acquaintance with empirical facts such as the Egyptians seem to have discovered in their measurements of plots of ground. Or, to use a more trifling example: the child may discover empirically that when his pile of four marbles is added to his playmate's pile of six marbles the resultant pile has ten marbles; it is quite another thing to discover that the abstract number four added to the abstract number six *is* ten, quite independently of empirical representations.

In Plato's view, genuine knowledge is an immediate, rational knowledge of the unchanging Ideas. One may have, to be sure, a kind of so-called knowledge of things, but things are always changing: the marbles may get lost or destroyed, the plot of ground may get washed away by a flood or buried by an earthquake or obliterated by a volcanic eruption. Indeed, all material things are in process of change—sometimes rapidly, sometimes slowly—so that any so-called knowledge of *things* is and must be impermanent and unstable. Plato therefore reserves the term knowledge for the immediate, rational awareness of the Ideas as they are in themselves, and uses the term "opinion" for whatever we "know," or think we know, about the unstable flux of material things, the realm of becoming.

As there are mathematical Ideas, so also are there Ideas of natural kinds and of artifacts: there is an Idea tree, an Idea horse, an Idea man, an Idea table and chair, and so on. The actual living horse is excellent to the degree to which it approximates the Idea horse, and so with other things.

The third general class of Ideas includes the aesthetic and the ethical. In it are the Ideas of the particular virtues—temperance and courage and the others, truth, justice and, finally, the Idea Good. The Good somehow both includes and is the source of all the other ethical Ideas and, in the great myth in the seventh book of the *Republic,* is the source or ground of all.

There is a kind of progression in knowledge: one may arrive at "right opinion" from a study of particular things, just as the child may correctly count the number of marbles in a heap; and one may arrive at a right opinion about right and wrong and some of the particular virtues from poetry, but in neither case is the principle involved grasped or understood. To have knowledge of number, or of right or wrong, or of virtue, one must grasp the universal principle involved, that is, must know the Idea of number or of the virtue. And so the progression is from right opinion to an understanding of the universal principles or Ideas. The prototype of this first grasp of the Idea is in mathematics, in the study of which the mind gets directly at the intelligibles freed of the bonds of merely sensory knowledge of (that is, in Plato's language, opinion about) particulars. But although this knowledge of "pure" mathematics is genuine knowledge, it is not the highest knowledge. Beyond or above it is knowledge of the ethical Ideas and, at the apex of the whole progression, knowledge of the Good itself.

The account given here is of course based on Plato's dialogues, but the order of presentation follows, with modifications, that of Paul Elmer More in his *Platonism*. The bibliography on Plato's doctrine is enormous: any standard history or library catalogue will list the more important works.

31. In the Seventh Letter.

32. pp. 26 f.

33. It is perhaps worth mentioning in this connection that his works were thought well enough of so that care was taken throughout the long history of the Academy and, after it was closed by Justinian A.D. 529, by later generations, to preserve a remarkably uncorrupted text of them. The text of Plato's works has, on the whole, fewer doubtful readings than that of either Shakespeare or the Bible.

34. Cf. *Rep.*, Bks. I, III, X; *Laws*, Bk. VII. In these places Plato stated his famous condemnation of the poets: they should be censored or rewritten or omitted from the curriculum altogether because their accounts give a false picture of the gods and heroes and this is inconsistent with Truth, which is both the basis and goal of all education. Marrou's comment (p. 72) here is pertinent: "By his vigorous contrast between philosophy and poetry, and by breaking with the settled tradition that Homer was the basis of all education, Plato put the Greek soul in a dilemma: should education remain fundamentally artistic and poetical, or become scientific? Every educator since has had to face this problem, and it has never received any final solution, our own education still being divided between the opposing claims of 'science' and 'the arts.' " Greek civilization did not accept these suggestions, and Plato was himself a first-rate poet.

This condemnation of the poets by Plato the poet is parallel to the distrust of the written word by Plato the writer. In the first he is basing his objection on the prior claim of Truth, rationally or logically arrived at, and, in the second, on the priority of direct inspiration—transmitted "as a light from a leaping flame"—from the teacher to the disciple. The second is a counsel of perfection not practicable except for small groups in relatively simple social organizations and, indeed, not practicable in any case until the masses of men become as creative as the minority. The first is also a counsel of perfection and appears to overlook the possibility that there is more than one road to Truth, more than one way of apprehending it and of formulating the apprehension and, perhaps above all, that since no formulation can be final or definitive, the poetic, ambiguous, mythological presentation is less misleading than the logical and ostensibly demonstrative. Jesus always taught in parables, the Buddha always refused to formulate propositions about ultimate truths, Plato himself almost invariably resorted to myth when presenting the heart of his doctrine—and the heart of his doctrine, as with other great philosophers, is indistinguishable from religion.

35. Marrou sums up the half-dozen relevant passages from the *Republic* and *Laws* as follows: "Plato believed that mathematics provided the test for the 'best minds,' the people who would one day be ready to study philosophy: mathematics would discover their learning ability, their perceptiveness, their powers of memory, their capacity for hard work despite the aridity of such gruelling study. And in the very process of being selected, the future philosophers would at the same time be undergoing training and preparation for their future work. The essential element in this 'preparatory education' was mathematics. . . . Rising above all utilitarian considerations, Plato assigned to mathematics a role which was above all propaedeutic: its purpose was . . . to create a 'well-developed head,' i.e. a mind capable of receiving intelligible truth. . . . It is impossible to overestimate the immense historical importance of this doctrine, which marks a decisive step in the history of education; for Plato here introduces nothing less than the actual theory, and indeed the specific syllabus, of what can only be called secondary education." (pp. 74-75).

36. In respect of the three main stages of early studentship, practical experience in affairs, and contemplation, this program presents an interesting parallel to the Indic and Hindu stages of studentship, life of the householder, and contemplation. In respect of the successive screenings of students until only the most able are left in the course, this Platonic ideal program was perhaps most nearly put into practice by the actual system of education employed by the Osmanlis. This will be examined below. In respect of its extreme thorough-going character, it ran completely

counter to the Thucydidean-Periclean ideal of "not going to excess" in any study. In respect of its primary concern for the intellectual elite, the "philosopher-kings," it was no sort of answer to the educational problem either of fourth century Hellenic society or of twentieth century Western society: the problem of how and in what way to raise the educational level of all the different groups of people in the state. But in respect of its primary concern for the leaders of the people it does offer a fully developed educational program.

But was it practicable? It is more than doubtful that Plato believed that the "philosopher-king" could, or even should try to, take over the actual government of any actual state. He was well aware—having had personal experience of many of them—of the pitfalls that lay in the path of any one who would attempt to. Towards the end of the *Republic* (IX, 591e) he wrote that the philosopher should have care "for the city he bears within himself" and so seems to be reasserting, in essence, the teaching of his master Socrates that the sole concern of a serious man is not fame, nor wealth, nor honor, but only "the tendance of the soul."

37. The following account is based on that of Marrou.

38. p. 61.

39. We have noticed Isocrates's criticism of Plato's doctrine—the criticism that ultimate philosophical principles can never be formulated precisely enough, nor their logical implications be developed far enough, to enable them to be applied to concrete situations in actual affairs. This criticism seems to be valid. In both public and private affairs, the choice often seems to be not between the absolutely good and the absolutely evil, but between the relatively better and worse, or sometimes, the greater and the lesser evil. And concrete situations do occur in which men must act, not philosophize. Yet a case can be made for Plato's belief that a man can not know which is the good action, or the better one, or even the lesser evil of two, unless he has knowledge of the principle involved. In the little dialogue, the *Euthyphro,* Plato makes such a case in connection with an actual situation.

In this dialogue Socrates, who is the spokesman for Plato, meets a young man named Euthyphro. Euthyphro is on the way to the magistrates to lay a charge against his own father. This is a drastic and, to Socrates, surprising thing for a man to do, so he asks the young man what it is that the father has done. Euthyphro tells him, and then says that the real offense is that his father has acted impiously. Socrates comments that Euthyphro must be very sure that he knows what piety is, in order to be able to lay such a charge against his own father. O yes, replies Euthyphro, to be sure I know what piety is.

Socrates then, with his accustomed irony, confesses that he does not know what piety is, that he is anxious to learn, and rejoices that now he has found someone who can tell him. Would Euthyphro be willing to? Yes, gladly, replies the young man, and proceeds to define piety. Socrates, after expressing admiration for the definition, again confesses that there are one or two points about the definition that are not clear to him, and begins to question Euthyphro. The questioning elicits insuperable difficulties with the first definition—and with the second and third and fourth. The outcome is that the young man confesses that he cannot give a definition of piety—he does not know what it is. Yet he is still sure that his father had acted impiously—or, rather, that he is acting rightly in laying the charge against his father. How can this be?

Similar procedures in other dialogues show that persons who profess to know what justice is, and temperance, and courage, and other virtues, do not know, but only think they know. Yet, if one does not know what justice is, how can he say that this or that act, this or that law, is just? And if he does not know what the good is, how can he say that this act or law is good, or even better than some possible alternative? These are hard questions to answer: Plato believed that there were no answers, and that therefore the man who would advise and lead the state as well as every man who would care for "the city he bears within himself" must learn the essential nature of the principles of justice and of the good. Hence the necessity for the "philosophical" education.

40. Cf. Kenyon, pp. 24 f.

41. *Politics,* Bk. VIII, 1338 a.

42. Cf. Kenyon, *Ibid.*

43. The Greek world, with the conquests of Aristotle's pupil, had suddenly expanded to an extent wholly unimagined by his predecessors: eastwards the frontier had retreated two thousand miles to India, southwards to include Syria and Egypt. In expanding the geographical frontiers the Greeks had encountered many peoples who did not speak Greek but some other tongue that sounded to them like "bar-bar" and these peoples were therefore "bar-barians." The terms did not mean that the other peoples were naked savages who ate raw meat, but only that they were not speakers of Greek. And, as they did not speak Greek, neither did they think Greek. Hence one of the main purposes of Greek education in the distant districts—districts that stretched from the Libyan desert to the Oxus-Jaxartes Basin—was to perpetuate and to make secure the "Greek Way."

44. Cf. Kitto, H. D. F., *The Greeks* (Penguin Books, 1951).

45. Cf. Rostovtzeff, *The Social and Economic History of the Hellenistic World*.

46. These and the following details are from Marrou and Capes.

47. In Miletus, as an example, in the first half of the second century, a private citizen gave to the city a capital fund the income from which was used to support the school. The amount of income to be used for teacher's salaries was fixed in the charter, as were many other details. The teachers were elected annually by the citizens' assembly from a list of candidates presented by the school inspector; the military instructors were appointed by the magistrate for schools, but the appointment was confirmed by the assembly; the benefactor held a sort of honorary position in the school (he marched in the processions) but did not interfere in the administration. The school was administered entirely by the city itself and existed solely for the citizens. But these foundation schools were not prominent in Hellenistic education: all four of the known examples were founded during the first half of the second century and Marrou conjectures (p. 113) that they all probably "faded away into insignificance" after an unspecified period of time.

48. These details are from Marrou, Eng. trans., pp. 145 ff.

49. Eng. trans., p. 160.

50. One incidental consequence of the anthologizing and selecting for teaching purposes is that we now have copies of the plays of Aeschylus and Sophocles and others—those plays that were selected, out of the great number that the dramatists produced, for school use. The anthologies included selections from all the best writers and from a good many second-rate ones—poets, tragedians, orators, historians—but the chief of all was Homer. After Homer came Euripedes and Menander and Demosthenes and Thucydides, but other writers were studied too.

51. The museums as at Ephesus, Smyrna, and Alexandria were centers of advanced research, mainly in the natural sciences but also in other subjects, and were at the same time universities with students. The scholars at Alexandria were crown pensioners and had very considerable facilities for their work: the greatest library of the time (at the end of the third century, about one hundred twenty thousand volumes), a zoo, and botanical gardens. Advanced instruction was given, while advanced research was being carried on, in all the usual subjects, including medicine.

The teaching of medicine was by now a genuine art or skill, and there was a system that had been developed out of the practical rules that had been found to be effective. There were "competitions" for advanced students; in several cities there were "medical schools" in the sense that there were a few teachers with a number of pupils. But the only really important training for the would-be physician was by the apprenticeship method.

A third type of higher school was the school of philosophy. After Plato and Aristotle had founded their schools and the schools had produced a generation or two of students, some of the students departed from the teaching of their masters and founded schools of their own. The schools proper were organized more or less as that of Plato had been: a sort of confraternity with the master, the one teacher, as head of the school. He was usually succeeded by his most able pupil, and so on for generations. In addition to these "regular" schools, there were wandering philosophers who, like the earlier sophists, would go from place to place, give one or a few or several lectures, and then move on.

Most of the schools of philosophy required that the applicant for admission should have completed his secondary education. Some exceptional women were admitted. One of the striking features is that, in very many cases, when the student "turned" from the ordinary life or from study in some other field to philosophy, the experience seems to have been very like a religious conversion. The different "schools" of philosophy might, almost equally appropriately, be called sects.

In almost all these schools the instruction began with the history of philosophy—as it does today, with Thales and Anaximader and Anaximenes,—went on to instruction in logic, physics, and ethics, and then to instruction in the particular doctrine of the school. After all this, the student was initiated, so to speak, into the deeper and more personal doctrines of the head of the school—one might almost say, into the esoteric doctrines. This teaching was still done in the way that Plato had done it: by private, or in a very small company, conversation between the teacher and the pupil. And in this we can see the older tutorial method still in use. The philosophers of the time were searching for the Good for man and the way to lead students to a realization of it.

The fourth type of advanced school was the school of rhetoric, and these drew the great majority of students who did any advanced work at all. In Greek culture and Greek education as a whole, and in respect of the number of persons influenced, both then and later, it was Isocrates rather than Plato who was the victor in the earlier struggle between philosophy and rhetoric. Eloquence was the main cultural objective and was regarded as the completion of liberal education. The eloquent man was still the man who could influence kings, was chosen by them as representative and ambassador, as spokesman at public ceremonies.

There were teachers of rhetoric nearly everywhere in the Greek world, and the content of the teaching was about what it had been under Isocrates, with one important exception. The exception was the development of the theoretical content, which Isocrates had kept to a minimum. Now there were classifications and definitions, divisions and subdivisions, systematizations and analyses almost without end. A whole new technical vocabulary had grown up within the subject so that, in its advanced form, it was a subject for the specialist and the most advanced student. To give a single illustration: if a eulogistic speech on a person were to be written and delivered, there were thirty-six definite stages to the speech that were regarded as basic—and others might be added (cf. Marrou, pp. 198-199). The arrangement, and all the techniques with the writing of the speech, had become systematized and perfected and, in the process, had come to be regarded as almost infallible.

52. This section follows Gwynne.

53. Eng. trans., p. xiv.

54. For an account of Jewish education see Appendix II, pp. 316 ff.

55. It did not, that is, in the geographical area served by the Graeco-Roman schools. In other areas it did, and it created a written, Christian culture in lands that had not had one before the Christian missionaries arrived. It did this, for example, for Ethiopia in the fifth century, for East Gothic under Ulfilas, for Armenian and Georgian and, as we shall see, for the Slavic languages in the ninth century.

6. The Main Body of the Far Eastern Civilization

(See also the books listed in the Bibliography for the Sinic Civilization.)

EBERHARD, W., *Das Toba-Reich Nord Chinas.* Leiden 1949, Brill.

HU SHIH, "The Literary Renaissance," Ch. VII in Zen's *Symposium,* q.v.

KUO, PING WEN, *The Chinese System of Public Education.* New York 1915, Teachers College, Columbia University.

MICHAEL, F., *The Origin of Manchu Rule in China.* Baltimore 1942, John Hopkins University Press.

TENG SSU-YU, "Chinese Influence on the Western Examination System," in *The Harvard Journal of Asiatic Studies,* Vol. 7 (1943), pp. 267-312.

WITTFOGEL, KARL A., and FENG, CHIA-SHENG, *History of Chinese Society: Liao (907-1125).* New York 1949, Macmillan, Vol. 36 (1946) of "Transactions of the American Philosophical Society."

1. Fitzgerald, p. 280.

2. p. 274.

3. Carter, pp. 12 ff.

4. Cf. Fung Yu-Lan, II, p. 239.

5. Goodrich, 71 ff.; Franke, II, pp. 260 f.

6. pp. 294 f.

7. See under Jewish education, pp. 316, above.

8. Cf. Fitzgerald, p. 290.

9. According to a T'ang encyclopedia, quoted by Goodrich, p. 135, n. 18.

10. Cf. Franke, II, p. 604.

11. Goodrich, p. 135.

12. Franke, II, p. 605.

13. Cf. above, pp. 44 ff.

14. Franke, II, p. 604.

15. This is the title of Chapter IV of his *Invention of Printing.* For the details in the paragraph see this book.

16. The reasons for the persecutions were utilitarian or economic, not religious. Buddhism was persecuted because the monks were celibate and thus to avoid family responsibilities was deemed unpatriotic, even wicked; the monks did no work and so failed to contribute to the economy; the monasteries, with their wealth, accumulated copper which was needed for coins; and, finally, Buddhism and the other religious were alien.

17. Fitzgerald, p. 340. The details in this paragraph follow those given by Fitzgerald, pp. 325-40.

18. Fitzgerald; this is the title of his Chap. XVI.

19. Cf. Hu Shih, "The Literary Renaissance," Chap. VII in Zen's *Symposium.*

20. Wittfogel and Feng, p. 15.

21. *Ibid.,* p. 297.

22. Cf. Munsterberg, O., *Chinesische Kunstgeschichte* (Esslingen 1910, Neff), Vol. I, p. 204.

23. Carter, *Printing,* Ch. 10.

24. The parallel is stated by Toynbee, vi, 306.

25. Cf. Fitzgerald, p. 409.

26. Cf. Fitzgerald, Ch. XIX: Williamson, H. R., *Wang An Shih* (London 1935-1937, Probsthain), 2 vols.; Hackmann, H., *Chinesische Philosophie* (Munich 1927, Reinhardt), pp. 313-315; Goodrich, *op. cit.,* pp. 155 ff.

He seems to have aimed chiefly—as a proper minister should—at increasing the prosperity of the state by lightening the burden of the peasantry on whose shoulders rested the greater part of the economic structure. He sought to do this by alleviating the two particular burdens imposed by the tax-collector and the money-lender. His particular measures included a system of state loans to farmers—a kind of rude land

and credit bank—to lower the exorbitant interest charged by the money-lenders; an arrangement whereby the produce of one province could be exchanged against that of another; a graduated tax on five grades of wealth; fixed prices and limitation of profits. These admirable laws were bitterly opposed by the Neo-Confucians and chiefly by the historian Ssu-ma Kuang, not on the ground that they might not be beneficial and actually increase state revenues, but on the ground that they were innovations that departed from the way of the ancestors. Since the new proposals broke with tradition, it was argued, they must therefore be wrong. And since they were wrong, there would be mass revolts by the people against them. But the new laws remained laws from 1068 to 1085 or 1086 and then after a time of being in abeyance, again under a disciple of Wang An-Shih's from 1094 to about 1124. The revolts did not materialize.

Fitzgerald says (p. 405) that "it is difficult to discover the real effects of the new laws" but perhaps the census figures are relevant to questions about their success: A.D. 1083 the population was estimated at about ninety millions, A.D. 1124, at about one hundred millions.

27. Quoted by Goodrich, p. 155.

28. Fitzgerald, p. 409.

29. Franke, IV, pp. 392, 396 ff.

30. Cf. Goodrich, p. 155.

31. Cf. Bodde, D., in Wright's *Chinese Thought,* pp. 44 ff.

32. Franke, IV, pp. 581 f.

33. Wittfogel and Feng, p. 463.

34. Goodrich, p. 185.

35. Cf. *The Encyclopedia Britannica,* 1929, vol. v., p. 573; *Der Grosse Brockhaus* (Leipzig 1929, Brockhaus), vol. iv, p. 54.

36. Goodrich, pp. 197-198.

37. Quoted by Goodrich, p. 200.

38. As put by Michael, p. 111.

39. The only Chinese leader that showed strength was the war lord Li Tse-cheng. But Li had persecuted the official class and so could not win their allegiance, which was indispensable to any successful effort to establish a new dynasty.

40. The succession of dynasties in the civilization and, earlier, in the latter end of the preceding Sinic society from the Han regime, is a phenomenon that calls for some explanation. In very brief, and with certain modifications, the explanation accepted by Michael, following Wittfogel and Lattimore, (Lattimore, Owen, *Inner Asian Frontiers of China,* New York 1940, American Geographical Society), is as follows. Chinese society has been, from a very early period, chiefly agrarian and under the

control, both financially and politically, of the landed gentry. It was chiefly from this class that the state officials were drawn and this was so to an increasing degree after the early institution of the examination system for candidates for office. It was so because, as we have seen, it was only the sons of the gentry that could afford the time and money for the long course of studies preparatory for the examination. These officials were responsible to the central government and so in theory worked the agrarian taxation system for its benefit; being human, they worked the system for their own benefit also—they could, for example and among other possibilities, exempt their own property from taxation. These two interests—that of the government and that of the individual officeholder— often conflicted, so that any weakness in the central control served to strengthen the wealth and power of the local official as an individual. As he exempted his own land from taxation, the burden on the small land-owner was increased, who often had to borrow in order to pay his taxes. The lender was often or usually the official who had land and so he could increase his interest rates—and foreclose on mortgages—so that his holdings tended to increase. Thus, more and more land came into the ownership of those who could exempt it, or get it exempted, from taxation. And the burden of the peasant and small land owner increased still more. And as the power of the officials increased, the control that could be exercised by the central government decreased, and, simultaneously, public services and enterprises. All this led to widespread unrest and, sooner or later, to rebellion. Finally, one rebel or another was successful or, during the period of weakness and rebellion, one or another foreign power could successfully impose its rule. Then the new dynasty would establish a strong central government, impose order on the provinces, and control the officials. But each new dynasty needed the services of the scholarly officials, the examination system would be re-established and strengthened, only the sons of the relatively well-to-do could pursue the studies that would enable them to pass the examinations, and the cycle would begin again.

With none of the alien rules established over the Far Eastern society was it a case of a completely un-Sinified people coming into a completely strange environment and establishing a radically new and different government on the Chinese people. All the foreign peoples—the T'o-pa, Ch'i-tan, Kin, Mongol and Manchu—had served an apprenticeship, so to speak, on the northern marches of China proper, had learned Chinese ways and languages and theories, and had, in some part and to some extent, adopted (and adapted) Chinese religions and philosophies. They had all developed a mixed culture and had, as it were, "grown" into China to some extent before they finally overran and conquered her. All this was conspicuously true of the Manchus.

41. Michael, p. 79.
42. Wittfogel and Feng, p. 14.
43. Hu Shih, in Chap. VII in Zen's *Symposium,* p. 124.
44. This account follows chiefly Eberhard, Wolfram, *Die Chinesische Novelle des 17.-19. Jahrhunderts* (Ascona 1948, Artibus Asiae), but draws also on Hu Shih, *The Chinese Renaissance* (Chicago 1934, University of Chicago Press). The quotation is from Eberhard, p. 17.

7. The Japanese Offshoot of the Far Eastern Civilization

BARTH, JOH., *Literatur und Drama im Dienste der nationalen Erziehung Japans.* In MOAG XXVIII c, Tokyo 1935.

BOLLJAHN, J., *Japanisches Schulwesen: seine Entwicklung und sein gegenwärtiger Stand.* Berlin 1896, Haack.

BURTON, M. E., *The Education of Women in Japan.* New York 1914, Revell.

GRAF, OLAF, *Kaibara Ekiken—Ein Beitrag zur japanischen Geistesgeschichte des 17. Jahrhunderts und zur chinesischen Sung-Philosophie.* Leiden 1942, Brill.

HALL, ROBERT KING, *Kokutai no hongi.* Cambridge 1949, Harvard University Press.

HAMMITZSCH, HORST, *Kamishibai—das japanische Bildertheater. Ein Mittel zur Volkserziehung.* In Nippon IX/3, Berlin, 1943.

HAMMITZSCH, HORST, *Die Mito-Schule und ihre programmatischen Schriften.* In MOAG XXXI/B, Tokyo 1939.

KEENLEYSIDE, HUGH L., and THOMAS, A. F., *History of Japanese Education and Present Educational System.* Tokyo 1937, Hokuseido Press.

KIKUCHI, DAIROKU, *Japanese Education.* London 1909, John Murray.

KOIKE, KENJI, *Nisshinkan, eine Daimyatsschule der Tokugawazeit.* In *Monumenta Nipponica* III/2, Tokyo 1940.

KOIKE, KENJI, *Onna Daigaku. Ein Frauenspiegel der Tokugawazeit.* In *Monumenta Nipponica* II/2, Tokyo 1939.

LOMBARD, FRANK A., *Pre-Meiji Education in Japan.* Tokyo 1914, Kyo Bun Kwan.

MEISSNER, KURT, *Grundlagen der nationalen Erziehung in Japan.* In Mittig. d. Deutsch. Gesellsch. f. Natur-und Völkerqunde (MOAG), XXVIII/2, Tokyo 1934.

MURAKAME, KOMAO, *Das japanische Erziehungswesen.* Tokyo 1934, Fuzambo.

NITOBE, INAZO, *Bushido: The Soul of Japan.* Tokyo 1908, Teibi.

SANSOM, G. B., *Japan: A Short Cultural History.* London 1943, Cresset Press. (1st Ed., 1921.)

SCHMIDT, E. A., *Die ersten Hoch— und Privatschulen Japans im Lichte zeitgenössischer Gesetze und Verfügungen.* München 1956. (Unpublished doctoral dissertation, courtesy Prof. Dr. Horst Hammitzsch.)

SCHWAGER, L. H., *Die nationalpolitische Auswertung historischer Gestalten in der Schulerziehung Japans.* In MOAG, XXVIII/B, Tokyo 1934.

VON WEEGMANN, CARL, *Die vaterländische Erziehung in der Japanischen Volksschule: Tokuhon und Shushinsho.* In MOAG, XXVIII/D, Tokyo 1935.

YOSHIDA, T., and KAIGO, T., *Japanese Education.* Tourist Library No. 19, Tokyo 1937, Board of Tourist Industry, Japanese Government Railways.

1. Sansom, p. 54.
2. Lombard, pp. 24-34.
3. Lombard, pp. 49 ff.; Schmidt, pp. 7 ff.
4. Schmidt, p. 70.
5. Lombard, pp. 44 ff.
6. Sansom, p. 111 f.
7. These details are from Lombard, pp. 54 ff.
8. Schmidt, pp. 57 ff.
9. Schmidt, pp. 62 ff.
10. These symptoms are all recorded by Murdoch, J., *History of Japan* (London 1910, Kegan Paul), Vol. I, and are collected by Toynbee, iv, p. 94, n. 2.
11. This account follows Nitobe.
12. Nitobe, p. 146.
13. Schmidt, pp. 67-71.
14. Quoted by von Weegmann, p. 6.
15. Bolljahn, pp. 28-30; Kikuchi, p. 34.
16. Murdoch, III, pp. 616-617.
17. Von Weegmann, p. 7.
18. Lombard, pp. 73 ff.
19. The account follows Koike, pp. 414 ff.
20. Lombard, pp. 86-87.
21. Von Weegmann, p. 7.
22. Lombard, p. 182.
23. Lombard, p. 182.

24. Cf. Professor Dr. Hammitzsch's excellent article, *Die Mito-Schule,* which this account follows.
25. Hammitzsch, *op. cit.,* pp. 2-4.
26. Yoshida, pp. 15 ff.
27. Yoshida, p. 19.
28. Yoshida, p. 25.
29. Cf. Hall, *Kokutai.*
30. This account follows Hall.
31. The calligraphy was Chinese calligraphy. There was no indigenous system of writing in Japan. The Chinese symbol is only a visual representation that stands for one, and only one, word, without inflections, and has no reference to whatever phonetic value it may be given—much as the symbols "1" and "2" stand for an idea which is the same regardless of the difference in sounds with which it is associated in different European languages: "one" and "two," "ein" and "zwei," "un" and "deux," "uno" and "due," and so on. The first Japanese who learned and read Chinese characters learned them purely visually, that is, by associating only an idea, not a sound, with the character. But this put an enormous burden on the visual memory and it was easier by far to associate a sound as well as an idea with the symbol, and so sounds were associated with the characters. The sound that was assigned to a given character was either the Chinese sound or the sound of the Japanese word that had approximately the same meaning. But to use the Chinese sound was ambiguous and therefore unfeasible, because of the large number of homophones in Chinese and because the entire grammatical structure of Chinese was different from that of Japanese. Hence, as more and more Japanese took to the study of Chinese, there was an increasing need for some device whereby a Japanese pronunciation could be given to the Chinese character.

The system that was devised was awkward, cumbrous, ambiguous, and difficult. It gave to some Chinese characters the Chinese sounds, to others Japanese sounds; it arranged the symbols, as far as possible, in Japanese word order; it supplied orally inflections and particles needed in Japanese to show the relations between words in the sentence; and it used diacritical marks to show the same relations in the written sentence and to indicate the inflectional endings to be supplied to the Japanese equivalent of the Chinese word. This system, awkward as it was, survived because the Japanese language was extraordinarily poor in vocabulary and had to borrow from Chinese, the only source open to it, words to stand for the multitudes of new ideas and things it now possessed as a result of its acquaintance with the Far Eastern thought and culture. These new words were simply borrowed, with an approximation of their original pronunciation. This borrowing from Chinese continued through the centuries until now the majority of words in the Japanese vocabulary are of Chinese origin. A second reason the system survived was that the very difficulty and esoteric character were, in the view of those early scholars who used it, merits. Different schools of Confucian scholars and different sects of Buddhist scholars each had its own system of diacritical marks; each kept its own secret, imparting the secret only to its own disciples.

During the course of the fifth century another system of writing Japanese words was devised. This was phonetic. The system used combinations of Chinese characters to stand for the sounds of polysyllabic Japanese names. During the fifth and sixth centuries most official records were written in Chinese but contained these phonetic representations of Japanese names.

The *Kojiki* is written basically in the Chinese ideographic characters but is interlarded with the phonetic representation of Japanese names, and with about a hundred Japanese poems and songs. A later chronicle of the eighth century is written also in Chinese characters with phonetic insertions. Other eighth century works were written also in part phonetically; so it seems that by the end of the century, the Japanese were on the way to establishing a system of representing Japanese words by the *kanamajiri* —the Mixed Phonetic Script. In this, the main words in a sentence were represented by Chinese characters used ideographically and the particles, modals, inflections, and so on represented by Chinese characters used phonetically.

The syllabary invented or perfected by Kobo Daishu in the beginning of the ninth century used forty-seven selected Chinese symbols as the arbitrary conventional equivalents of forty-seven syllables to which the sounds of Japanese had been reduced. Another syllabary came into use at about the same time. The convenience of these syllabaries encouraged the wider use of the Mixed Phonetic Script, which is now the normal script for writing Japanese in manuscripts and printed matter.

The mixture of phonetic and semantic symbols varies according to the writer and the degree of literacy that he expects from his readers. The method, very roughly, is as follows: words of Chinese origin—that is, over half of the total Japanese vocabulary, uninflected Japanese words and the stems of inflected Japanese words, are represented by Chinese characters according to meaning; grammatical endings and particles are represented by symbols derived from the Chinese and used according to sound; the syllabary symbols are used mainly for representing foreign words or colloquialisms or as a typographical device for italics and, chiefly, as diacritical marks indicating the pronunciation of ideographic characters in popular publications. Sansom remarks that the system is "a practical instrument without inferiors," and that absolute certainty in reading any Japanese text is almost unattainable.

When, after the Meiji Revolution, Japan began to adopt Western culture and ways, it was necessary to turn again to Chinese for new words for the new things and ideas. This was because the English and German and other words which were borrowed could not be written in Japanese with Chinese characters nor with syllabary, and it was therefore easier to borrow the recently invented Chinese compounds for the new things: e.g., "lightning-spirit" for electricity and "iron-road" for railway. Recently, however, new compounds have been formed without reference to Chinese practice.

The obvious advantages of devising an alphabet outright and introducing it as the medium of all Japanese writing are many: clarity, simplicity, and above all, the enormous saving in time and energy required to learn to read and write. On the other hand, to abolish the old system would make all Chinese and Japanese literature inaccessible and would require a complete revolution in the style and content of the written language; it would also, in the period of transition, disorganize or disrupt all public and private affairs that require the use of writing. At present, to the Japanese, the disadvantages of a change seem to outweigh the advantages. (This note is based on Sansom, George, *An Historical Grammar of Japanese* (Oxford 1928, Clarendon Press), pp. 1-72.)

8. The Main Body of the Orthodox Christian Civilization

BAYNES, NORMAN H., and MOSS, H. ST. L. B. (eds.), *Byzantium: An Intro-duction to East Roman Civilization*. Oxford 1948, Clarendon Press.

BRÉHIER, L., *L'Enseignement classique et l'enseignement religieux a Byzance*. In *Revue d'Histoire et de Philosophie religieuses*, XXI, 1 (1941), 34-36.

FUCHS, F., *Die höheren Schulen von Konstantinopel im Mittelalter*. In *Byzantinisches Archiv—Byzantinische Zeitschrift*, VIII, Leipzig, 1926.

HUSSEY, J. M., *Church and Learning in the Byzantine Empire, 867-1185*. London 1937, Milford.

MARROU, H. I., *A History of Education in Antiquity*. London 1956, Sheed and Ward.

1. p. 116.
2. Cf. Moss, in Baynes and Moss, pp. 3-4.
3. Cf. above, p. 238.

4. Cf. Hussey, p. 7.

5. Cf. Gregoire, in Baynes and Moss, p. 86; and Baynes, p. xviii.

6. Hussey, p. vii.

7. Marrou, p. 340.

8. Cf. above, p. 111; and Brehier, pp. 34-5.

9. Marrou, p. 341.

10. Cf. Buckler, in Baynes and Moss, p. 201.

11. Cf. Buckler, p. 215; Marrou, p. 341.

12. Cf. Buckler, pp. 201 ff.

13. Cf. above, pp. 111 ff.

14. Cf. Buckler, p. 216.

15. Cf. Bury, J. B., Editio Minor of Gibbon's *The History of the Decline and Fall of the Roman Empire* (London 1901, Methuen), vol. v, p. 499; quoted by Toynbee, iv, 345, n. 3.

16. Toynbee in iv, 345 calls this an academy for the training of civil servants and A.D. 864 the date of its establishment, and distinguishes this academy for "the foundation of the university, A.D. 1045"; Buckler, p. 217, writes of the "reorganization of the university" A.D. 864 and of the "re-foundation" thereof A.D. 1045. It seems clear that the evidence for the continuity of the ninth century school with that of the eleventh is incomplete.

17. Cf. Toynbee, iv, 345 and n. 1.

18. Cf. Buckler, p. 217 f.

19. Dvornik, F., *Les Slaves, Byzance et Rome au ix Siecle* (Paris 1926, Champion); quoted by Toynbee, iv, 345, n. 3.

20. Brehier, pp. 36 ff.

21. Toynbee, iv, 346.

22. Buckler, p. 215, says the ban was "consistently observed" and Brehier, 59-67, seems to be of the same opinion; Marrou, p. 341, on the other hand, thinks that the several renewals of the ban suggest that there was a tendency to infringe it.

23. Buckler, p. 218, writes that "of the School of the Patriarch no history can be written, for our sources are totally inadequate . . . There may have been several schools under the control of the Church"; Marrou, p. 341, writes, "The origin of this type of school is still not clear; it may go back to the seventh century but it certainly appears quite clearly and quite fully developed in the eleventh"; Brehier, pp. 41 ff., writes that the history of the school is fairly well known and that its organization in the ninth century is well known;—surely Brehier is using these adjectives only by contrast with what is known of the monastic schools. For accounts

of these schools see Buckler, pp. 218 f., Brehier, pp. 41 f., and Marrou, pp. 341 f.

24. Marrou, p. 342.
25. Mavrogordato, in Baynes and Moss, pp. 221-249.
26. Cf. above, pp. 124 and 134.
27. Hussey, pp. 158 ff.
28. The quotation is Toynbee's summary in vii, 389-390 of the English translation of the Greek text of the story in Dawes, E. and Baynes, N. H., *Three Byzantine Saints* (Oxford 1948, Blackwell), pp. 49-59.
29. Cf. Runciman, in Baynes and Moss, pp. 338-368.

9. The Russian Offshoot of the Orthodox Christian Civilization

BAYNES, NORMAN H. and MOSS, H. ST. L. B. (eds.), *Byzantium: An Introduction to East Roman Civilization*. Oxford 1948, Clarendon Press.

DVORNIK, FRANCIS, *The Making of Central and Eastern Europe*. London 1949, Polish Research Centre.

FALBORK, H. and TCHARNOLONSKY, *Enseignement primaire populaire en Russie*. St. Petersburg 1900 (in Russian).

FUDEL, C. I., *Volksbildung und Schule in Russland*. Moskau 1897 (in Russian).

HANS, N. A., *History of Russian Educational Policy 1701-1917*. London 1931, King.

KNYASKOV, S. A. and SERBOV, N. I., *A Sketch of the History of National Popular Education in Russia to the Epoch of the Reforms of Alexander II*. Moscow 1910 (in Russian).

LEARY, DANIEL BELL, *Education and Autocracy in Russia from the Origins to the Bolshiviki*. Buffalo 1919, the University of Buffalo Press.

MILIOUKOV, PAUL, *Histoire de Russie*. 3 vols. Paris 1932, Leroux.

NOVIKOV, A., *Aus der Geschichte der russischen Schule*. Moskau 1917.

ROZDESTVENSKII, S. V., *Skizzen zur Gerschichte des Systems der Volksaufklärung in Russland im 18.-19. Jahrhundert*. St. Petersburg 1912 (in Russian).

STAHLIN, KARL, *Geschichte Russlands*. 4 vols., Berlin 1930-39, Ost-Europa Verlag.

SUMNER, B. H., *Peter the Great and the Emergence of Russia*. London 1950, English Universities Press.

TOLSTOI, D. A., *Das akademische Gymnasium und die akademische Universität im 18. Jahrhundert*. St. Petersburg 1886 (in Russian).

VERNADSKY, GEORGE and KARPOVICH, MICHAEL, *A History of Russia*. Vol. I, *Ancient Russia*. G. Vernadsky, New Haven 1943, Yale Uni-

versity Press. Vol. II, *Kievan Russia*. G. Vernadsky, New Haven 1948.
Vol. III, *The Mongols and Russia*. G. Vernadsky, 1953.
VERNADSKY, G., *A History of Russia*. 4th ed. New Haven 1954 (1st ed.
1929), Yale University Press.

1. Runciman, in Baynes and Moss, p. 356.
2. Cf. Baron Meyendorff and Baynes, in Baynes and Moss, pp. 373 f.
3. Milioukov, pp. 89 f.
4. Meyendorff and Baynes, in Baynes and Moss, p. 375.
5. Vernadsky, *Kievan Russia*, pp. 80, 277 ff., calls it Russia's "first
learned academy."
6. Cf. Dvornik, pp. 236 f.; Vernadsky, *Kievan Russia*, pp. 277 ff.
7. Vernadsky, *Kievan Russia*, pp. 280 f.
8. Dvornik, p. 240.
9. Cf. Milioukov, p. 142 f.; Meyendorff and Baynes, in Baynes and
Moss, pp. 383 f.
10. Meyendorff and Baynes, in Baynes and Moss, pp. 384-385.
11. Mikioukov, pp. 142 f.
12. Cf. Leary, p. 28; Toynbee, viii, 555, n. 10.
13. Leary, p. 28.
14. Milioukov, pp. 243-244.
15. Cf. Vernadsky, one-vol. *History,* pp. 145 f.
16. Toynbee, iii, 278 ff.; the account follows Bruckner, A., *Peter der
Grosse* (Berlin 1879, Grote).
17. Cf. the note from Prince D. Obolensky quoted by Toynbee, viii,
674.
18. Cf. Sumner, p. 34; Milioukov, p. 397.
19. Cf. Sumner, pp. 35, 152.
20. Cf. Sumner, p. 153.
21. Sumner, p. 206.
22. Vernadsky, one-vol. *History,* p. 183.
23. Sumner, pp. 152, 205.
24. Toynbee, viii, 542 ff.
25. Sumner, pp. 152, 205; quoted by Toynbee, viii, 557.
26. Sumner, p. 207.
27. Cf. Milioukov, pp. 402-403.
28. Cf. Vernadsky, one-vol. *History,* p. 183; Milioukov, p. 597; Hans,
p. 24.
29. Vernadsky and Milioukov give the number of schools as 315; Hans
gives 254.
30. Vernadsky, p. 183; Milioukov, pp. 777 f.

31. Hans, p. 222.
32. Milioukov, pp. 404 f.
33. Milioukov, pp. 784 and 876 ff.
34. Cf. Toynbee, v, 154 ff. and viii, 339 ff.
35. Toynbee, v, 154 ff.
36. Cf. above, p. 15.
37. Cf. Milioukov, pp. 1006 ff.

10. The Hindu Civilization
(See also the titles listed for the Indic Civilization.)

ELIOT, SIR CHARLES, *Hinduism and Buddhism*. 3 vols., London 1921, Edward Arnold.

RAWLINSON, H. G., *India: A Short Cultural History*. London 1948, Cresset Press.

SMITH, V. A., *Akbar the Great Mogul, 1542-1605*. Oxford 1917, Clarendon Press.

SPEAR, PERCIVAL, *Twilight of the Mughals*. Cambridge 1951, University Press.

VAIDYA, C. V., *The History of Medieval India*. 2 vols., Poona 1924, Oriental Book Supplying Agency.

1. Cf. above, p. 70.
2. Cf. Vaidya, ii, pp. 1-3; Smith, p. 408; Toynbee, i, 85 and n.; Majundar, Vol. IV, p. vii.
3. Rawlinson, pp. 199 ff.
4. Cf. above, pp. 49 ff. and 56 ff.
5. Cf. above, p. 60.
6. Majundar, AIK, pp. 366 ff.
7. Cf. above, pp. 59.
8. Rawlinson, p. 372.
9. Cf. above, pp. 193 ff.
10. Majundar, *Advanced History,* p. 578 f.

11. The Islamic Civilization

ARNOLD, T. W., *The Caliphate*. Oxford 1924, Clarendon Press.

BROWNE, E. G., *Literary History of Persia*. 2 vols., London 1902-06, Fisher Unwin.

CARTER, T. F., *The Invention of Printing in China and Its Spread Westward,* 2nd ed. New York 1931, Columbia University Press.

HITTI, PHILIP K., *History of the Arabs*. London 1937, Macmillan.

LECLERC, LUCIEN, *Histoire de la médécine arabe*. Paris 1876.

LYBYER, A. H., *The Government of the Ottoman Empire in the Time of Suleiman the Magnificent*. Cambridge 1913, Harvard University Press.

MILLER, B., *The Palace School of Muhammad the Conqueror*. Cambridge 1941, Harvard University Press.

TALAS, ASAD, *L'Enseignement chez les Arabes: La Madrasa Nisamiyya et son histoire*. Paris 1939, Geuthner.

TOTAH, KHALIL A., *The Contributions of the Arabs to Education*. New York 1926, Columbia University Press.

TRITTON, A. S., *The Caliphs and their Non-Muslim Subjects*. London 1930, Milford.

1. Arnold, pp. 23-24; Hitti, pp. 10-11. The other great emigrations had been: (1) c. 3500 B.C. across the Sinaitic Peninsula to the Nile and into Sumeria, the latter wing producing the Baylonians; (2) c. 2500 B.C. into Syria and the Fertile Crescent, producing the Canaanites and Phoenicians; (3) c. 1500-1200 B.C., into southern Syria and Palestine—these were the Hebrews and Aramaeans; (4) c. 500 B.C. into the Sinaitic Peninsula— these were the Nabataeans. It will be seen that these waves of emigrations were roughly one millenium apart.

2. i, 68-72, 347 ff.

3. Toynbee analyzes the causes of this successful attempt in i, 347 ff.

4. Hitti, pp. 87 ff.

5. Hitti, p. 108.

6. Totah, p. 34.

7. Hitti, pp. 123 ff.

8. Arnold, pp. 11 ff.

9. Hitti, p. 408; Totah, p. 49.

10. The Arabic, like other Semitic alphabets, is wholly consonantal; the vowel signs or "points" are written in above or below the letters, if they are written at all.

11. Hitti, pp. 410 ff.

12. Leclerc, Tome I, p. 92.

13. Hitti, pp. 413 f.

14. Until the beginning of the tenth century, books and the writing material of students were of parchment or papyrus. As has been seen, paper had been invented in China at the beginning of the first century A.D., and it may be of some interest to note the stages of advance in its long journey to the West. According to Carter, paper was in use in

Turkestan about the middle of the second century, imported and used in Samarkand the middle of the seventh century, imported into Mecca at the beginning of the eighth, manufactured in Samarkand the middle of the eighth and imported into Baghdad a little earlier, manufactured in Baghdad and used in Egypt at the beginning of the ninth century, manufactured in Egypt and used in Spain the first half of the tenth century. The dates and places are perhaps sufficient to indicate the march westward first of the importation and then, a century or so later, of the indigenous manufacture and use of paper. By the end of the tenth century, according to Hitti (p. 414), paper had wholly replaced parchment and papyrus in the Muslim world, although this date is perhaps a little early for western North Africa and Spain.

15. Cf. Toynbee, i, 354.
16. Cf. Arnold, pp. 19 ff.
17. Cf. Toynbee, i, 393.
18. Cf. Toynbee, i, 104 f.
19. Cf. Hitti, p. 410.
20. Cf. Miller, pp. 12 ff. and Totah, p. 20 F., and Hitti, p. 410.
21. Hitti, p. 410.
22. Totah, pp. 19 ff.
23. Miller, p. 188; Totah, p. 20.
24. Miller, p. 31.
25. Totah, p. 25.
26. Miller, pp. 19 ff.
27. Hitti, p. 411; Miller, pp. 19 f.
28. Lybyer, p. 203 f.
29. Arnold, pp. 25 f.
30. Hitti, pp. 562 ff.
31. Lybyer, p. 204.
32. Carter, pp. 112 f.

12. The Early Period of the Western Civilization

(Since any library catalogue lists more books on education in the Western Civilization than anyone can read, it was not thought necessary to give a bibliography. Books referred to in the text are listed below.)

MARROU, H. I., *A History of Education in Antiquity*. London 1956, Sheed and Ward.

RASHDALL, HASTINGS, *Universities of Europe in the Middle Ages*. 2 vols., Oxford 1895, Oxford University Press.

TAYLOR, HENRY OSBORN, *The Medieval Mind,* 4th ed. London 1925 (1st ed., 1911), Macmillan.

1. Cf. above, pp. 115.
2. Cf. Marrou, pp. 333 ff.
3. Cf. Marrou, p. 336.
4. Our modern words "grammar" and "glamor" are etymologically identical: the "glamorous" is (or was, until the word was taken up by advertising copywriters and Hollywood) that which is somehow secret and mysterious and esoteric; "grammar" as a knowledge of writing was secret and mysterious and known only to initiates.
5. Cf. Taylor, p. 250.
6. Cf. above, pp. 226.
7. Cf. Rashdall, p. 28.
8. Cf. Rashdall, pp. 33 ff., Taylor, pp. 300 ff.
9. Cf. above, pp. 78 f. and 92 ff.
10. Cf. Rashdall, pp. 36 ff.
11. Cf. above, p. 226.
12. Rashdall, p. 38; cf. above, pp. 92 ff. and n. 30.
13. Rashdall, p. 47.
14. Cf. Rashdall, Ch. III.
15. The sketch of the rise of the University of Bologna follows Rashdall, Ch. IV.
16. Rashdall, p. 21.
17. Rashdall, p. 19.
18. Cf. Taylor, pp. 3000 f.
19. Cf. Rashdall, pp. 277, 345; the sketch of the rise of the University of Paris follows Rashdall, Ch. V.
20. Cf. Rashdall, p. 15.
21. Rashdall, pp. 19-20.
22. Cf. Rashdall, pp. 68 ff.; Taylor, pp. 17 f.
23. Rashdall, p. 24.
24. Rashdall, pp. 700 ff.
25. Rashdall, p. 710.

13. The Abortive Far Western Christian Civilization
DUKE, J. A., *The Columban Church.* Oxford 1932, Oxford University Press.
GOUGAUD, L., *Christianity in Celtic Lands.* London 1931, Sheed and Ward.
GRAHAM, H., *The Early Irish Monastic Schools.* Dublin 1923, Talbot Press.

HANSON, W. G., *The Early Monastic Schools of Ireland.* Cambridge 1927.

LORCIN, A., *La Vie Scolaire dans les Monasteres d'Irlande aux V-VII siecles.* In *Revue du Moyen-Age latin,* I, 1945, pp. 221-236.

ROGER, M., *L'Enseignement des lettres classiques d'Ausone à Alcuin.* Paris 1905, Picard.

RYAN, J., *Irish Monasticism: Origins and Early Development.* London 1931, Longmans, Green & Co.

1. Toynbee, ii, 324.
2. Graham, pp. 52 ff.
3. Cf. Toynbee, ii, 325; Ryan, pp. 171 ff.; Gougaud, p. 83; Graham, pp. 52 ff.
4. Cf. Gougaud, p. 204.
5. Cf. Gougaud, p. 271-2.
6. Cf. Gougaud, pp. 247 ff.
7. Cf. Roger, pp. 247 ff.
8. Cf. Graham, pp. 14 f., 73 ff.
9. Cf. Lorcin, pp. 223 ff.
10. Cf. Graham, pp. 79 f.
11. Gougaud, p. 307.

14. The Arrested Spartan Civilization

CHRIMES, K. M. T., *Ancient Sparta.* Manchester 1949. Manchester University Press.

MARROU, H. I., *A History of Education in Antiquity.* London 1956, Sheed and Ward, Chapter II.

NILSSON, MARTIN, *Die Grundlagen des Spartanischen Lebens.* In *Klio,* B. XII, Leipzig 1912, Dieterich.

TOYNBEE, A. J., iii, espc. 50-78.

1. Cf. above, p. 12; cf. also Chart I.
2. Cf. Toynbee, iii, 1-21.
3. Cf. Toynbee, iii, 455.
4. In the *Hellenica,* III, iii, 4-11; quoted by Toynbee, iii, 456.
5. Cf. Toynbee, iii, 456.
6. Cf. Chrimes, 205.
7. Cf. above, p. 71.
8. It is possible, but not likely, that the Spartans established one overseas colony, Tarentum; cf. Toynbee, iii, 52.
9. Cf. Nilsson, pp. 308, 340.

10. Chrimes, p. vi.

11. Cf. Toynbee, iii, 57 and notes; Herodotus, IX, 28, 2, suggests that each allotment had seven serf families.

12. Chrimes, p. 39.

13. Cf. Toynbee, iii, 59 f.

14. Cf. above, p. 239.

15. Cf. Toynbee, iii, 60; Toynbee quotes Plutarch, *Life of Lycurcus*, Ch. xv, as follows: Lycurgus "saw nothing but vulgarity and vanity in the sexual conventions of the rest of Mankind, who take care to serve their bitches and their mares with the best sires that they can manage to borrow or hire, yet lock their women up and keep them under watch and ward in order to make sure that they shall bear children exclusively to their husbands—as though this were a husband's sacred right even if he happens to be feeble minded or senile or diseased. This convention ignores the two obvious truths that bad parents produce bad children and good parents good children, and that the first people to feel the difference will be those who possess the children and who have to bring them up."

16. Chrimes, p. 116.

17. Cf. Toynbee, iii, 61, n. 1; Marrou, pp. 18-19.

18. Cf. Toynbee, iii, 61 and n. 3, on the evidence of Plutarch.

19. Cf. Chrimes, pp. 119 ff., espc. p. 125.

20. Plutarch, *Life of Lycurgus*, xviii; quoted by Toynbee, iii, 65, n. 1.

21. Toynbee, iii, 65-66.

22. Thucydides, IV, 80; quoted by Toynbee, iii, 66, n. 1.

23. Plutarch, *Apophthegmata Laconica:* Lycurgus, No. 6; quoted by Toynbee, iii, 62-63.

24. Xenophon, *Respublica Lacedaemoniorum*, Ch. ix; quoted by Toynbee, iii, 63.

25. Herodotus, Bk. VII, Ch. 105.

26. Marrou, p. 25.

27. Cf. Toynbee, iii, 74 ff.

28. Toynbee, iii, 72.

29. Plutarch, *Life of Agis*, Ch. v; quoted by Toynbee, iii, 74.

30. Chrimes, p. 43.

15. The Arrested Osmanli Civilization

LYBYER, A. H. *The Government of the Ottoman Empire in the Time of Suleiman the Magnificent.* Cambridge 1913, Harvard University Press.

MILLER, B., *The Palace School of Muhammad the Conqueror.* Cambridge 1941, Harvard University Press.

Penzer, N. M., *The Harem*. London 1936, Harrap.
Toynbee, A. J., iii, espc. pp. 22-49.

1. Cf. above, p. 202.
2. Toynbee, iii, 29, n. 3 reads: "The Abbasid's Turkish bodyguard . . . had its counterpart . . . in a bodyguard of European barbarians who were purchased by the Spanish Caliphs from their Frankish neighbours. The Franks supplied the Cordovan slave-markets by making slave-raids across the opposite frontier of the Frankish dominions. The barbarians who were thus captured by the Franks in order to be sold to the Spanish Umayyads happened to be Slavs; and this is the origin of the word 'slave' in the English language."
3. Cf. Toynbee, iii, 28 ff., and Miller, p. 14.
4. Lybyer, pp. 47 ff.
5. Toynbee, iii, 35, n. 3, following Sir Paul Rycaut, *The Present State of the Ottoman Empire* (London 1668, Starkey and Brome).
6. Lybyer, p. 58.
7. Toynbee, iii, 33, n. 1.
8. Lybyer, pp. 45 f., quoted by Toynbee, iii, 33-34.
9. Toynbee, iii, 34-35.
10. Miller, pp. 71 ff.
11. Rycaut, *op. cit.*, p. 205, quoted by Toynbee, iii, 46, n. 6.
12. O. G. Busbecq, Ambassador from the Hapsburg Court to Suleiman the Magnificent, A.D. 1555-1562; Cf. *A Gislenii Busbecquii Omnia quae Extant* (Leyden 1633, Elzevir), quoted by Toynbee, iii, 36 ff.
13. Miller, pp. 30 ff.
14. This sketch follows Miller, pp. 80 ff.
15. Miller, pp. 163.
16. Lybyer, p. 114.
17. Lybyer, pp. 83-84.
18. Cf. above, pp. 92 ff.
19. Cf. Miller, pp. 171 ff.; Toynbee, iii, 44; Lybyer, pp. 120, 69. The phrase "psychological impossibility" is Toynbee's.
20. So in the Peace Treaty of Kuchuk Kainarji which ended the 1768-1774 Russo-Turkish War; quoted by Miller, p. 174.
21. Cf. above, pp. 207 f.
22. Toynbee, iii, 48-49.

Appendix I Education in Five Primary Civilizations

1. The Andean Civilization

BAUDIN, L., *L'Empire Socialiste des Inka*. Paris 1928, Institut d'Ethnologie.

BUSHNELL, G. H. S., *Peru*. London 1956, Thames and Hudson.

HARING, C. H., *The Spanish Empire in America*. New York 1947, Oxford University Press.

MARKHAM, SIR C., *The Incas of Peru*. London 1910, Smith Elder.

MEANS, P. A., *Ancient Civilizations of the Andes*. New York 1931, Scribners.

NORDENSKIOLD, ERLAND, *Origin of the Indian Civilisations in South America*. Göteborg 1931, Elander. (Vol. 9 of *Comparative Ethnographical Studies*.)

WHITAKER, ARTHUR P. (ed.), *Latin America and the Enlightenment*. New York 1942, Appleton-Century.

1. Cf. Means.
2. Baudin, pp. 119 ff.
3. *Ibid.*, p. 68.
4. *Ibid.*, p. 69.
5. *Ibid.*, p. 70.
6. Means, p. 262.

2. The Egyptiac Civilization

BREASTED, J. H., *The Development of Religion and Thought in Ancient Egypt*. London 1912, Hodder & Stoughton.

BRUNNER, HELLMUT, *Altaegyptische Erziehung.* Wiesbaden 1957, Harras-sowitz.

DÜRR, L., see title listed under "Babylonic Civilization," appendix II, p. 314.

ERMAN, A., *Die Ägyptischen Schülerhandschriften.* Berlin 1926, (Abhand-lung der Akademie der Wissenschaftern von Berlin, Phil.-Hist. Klasse, 1925, 2, 1-32).

FRANKFORT, H. *et al, Before Philosophy.* See under "Sumeric."

MEYER, EDUARD, *Geschichte des alten Ägyptens.* Berlin 1887, Grote.

WILSON, J. A., *The Burden of Egypt.* Chicago 1951, University Press.

1. Cf. above, pp. 11 ff.
2. Wilson, p. 35.
3. Cf. above, pp. 9 ff.
4. Wilson, pp. 37 ff.
5. Cf. Wilson, p. vii.
6. Cf. x, 167 ff., espc. p. 212.
7. Wilson, p. 32, n. 12.
8. Both in *The Burden of Egypt* and in his chapter on Egypt in *Before Philosophy.*
9. In the Introductory Chapter in *Before Philosophy.*
10. Frankfort, p. 12.
11. Wilson, *Burden,* p. 59.
12. *Ibid.,* p. 104.
13. Anthes, Rudolph, *Lebensregeln und Lebensweisheit der alten Ägypter* (Leipzig 1933), pp. 12-13; quoted by Wilson in *Before Philos-ophy,* 109.
14. Wilson, *Burden,* p. 63.
15. Cf. Brunner.
16. Quoted by Wilson, *Before Phil.,* p. 115.
17. Wilson, *Burden,* p. 114.
18. Cf. Burden, pp. 143 f.; *Before Phil.,* pp. 116 ff. A single passage, in which the supreme god states the purpose of creation, expresses the idea: "I relate to you the four good deeds which my own heart did for me . . . in order to silence evil. I did four good deeds within the portal of the horizon. I made the four winds that every man might breathe thereof like his fellow in his time. That is (the first) of the deeds. I made the great flood waters that the poor man might have rights in them like the great man. That is (the second) of the deeds. I made every man like his fellow. I did not command that they might do evil, (but) it was their hearts that violated what I had said. That is (the third) of the deeds. I

made that their hearts should cease from forgetting the west, in order that divine offerings might be made to the gods of the provinces. That is (the fourth) of the deeds." (*Ibid.,* 117 f.)

Other passages suggest that the value of right social and personal relations was replacing the earlier materialistic values of social position and material prosperity.

19. Cf. Brunner.
20. Dürr, pp. 7-13, 16 f.
21. Erman, pp. 23 ff.
22. Wilson, *Burden,* pp. 154 f.
23. Toynbee, i, 139.

4. The Sumeric Civilization

Bibliography: See books listed for the Babylonic Civilization.

1. Toynbee, i, 116.
2. Meissner, pp. 325 ff.
3. Landersdorfer, pp. 587 ff.

5. The Shang Culture

Bibliography: See books listed for Sinic Civilization.

1. Cf. Needham, Vol. I, p. 157; Creel, *Studies,* p. 254.
2. Cf. Creel, *op. cit.,* p. 33; Fitzgerald, p. 26.
3. Maspero, p. 32.
4. Creel, *op. cit.,* p. 46.
5. Aalt, p. 59.
6. Maspero, p. 33.

Appendix II   The Babylonic Civilization

DÜRR, L., *Das Erziehungswesen im Alten Testament und im antiken Orient*. Leipzig 1932 (Mitteilungen der Vorderasiatisch-Aegyptischen Gesellschaft, 36, Bd., 2. Heft.).

Encyclopaedia Judaica. Berlin 1930; Bd. VI, Art. *Erziehung*.

Encyclopedia of Religion and Ethics (ed. James Hastings). Edinburgh 1917, T. and T. Clark, Vol. V, Art. Education (Jewish). Abbreviated as ERE.

GOLLANCZ, H., *Pedagogics of the Talmud and That of Modern Times*. Oxford 1924, Clarendon Press.

GUNKEL, HERMANN, *The Legends of Genesis*. Chicago 1901, Open Court Pub. Co. (transl, W. H. Carruth).

The Jewish Encyclopedia. New York 1903, Funk and Wagnalls, Vol. V, Art. *Education*. Abbreviated as JE.

KÖNIG, F. W., *Älteste Geschichte der Meder und Perser*. Leipzig 1934, Heinrichs.

LANDESDORFER, S., *Schule und Unterricht im alten Babylonien*. München 1909, (Blätter für d. Gym.-Schulwesen, XLV, 577-624).

MARCUS, SAMUEL, *Die Pädagogik des israelitischen Volkes*. Wien 1877.

MEISSNER, B., *Babylonien und Assyrien*. 2 Bde., Heidelberg 1920 (Kulturgeschichtliche Bibliothek, herausgegeben von W. Foy).

MOWINCKEL, SIGMUND, *Prophecy and Tradition*. Oslo 1946, Jacob Dybwad (Avhandlingen utgitt av Det Norske Videnskaps-Akademi i Oslo; 11. Hist.-Fiols. Klasse, 1946, 3).

NIELSEN, EDUARD, *Oral Tradition*. London 1954, SCM Press (Studies in Biblical Theology No. 11).

NOTH, MARTIN, *Überlieferungsgeschichtliche Studien.* Halle 1943, Niemeyer.

NYBERG, H. S., *Die Religionen des alten Iran.* Leipzig 1938 (Mitteilungen der vorderasiatisch-ägyptischen Gesellschaft, vol. 43).

PARROT, ANDRE, *Les Fouilles de Mari.* In *Syria,* XVII, Paris 1936, Geuthner, p. 21, pl. III, 3-4.

ROBERTS, BLEDDYN J., *Old Testament Texts and Versions.* Cardiff 1951, University of Wales Press.

STRASSBURGER, B., *Geschichte der Erziehung und des Unterrichts bei den Israeliten.* Stuttgart 1885.

SWIFT, FLETCHER H., *Education in Ancient Israel to 70 A.D.* Chicago 1919, Open Court Pub. Co.

WEBER, OTTO, *Die Literatur der Babylonier und Assyrer.* Leipzig 1907, Hinrich.

WIDENGREN, GEO., *Literary and Psychological Aspects of the Hebrew Prophets.* Uppsala 1948, Uppsala Universitets Arsskrift 1948: 10.

1. Daniel, I, 4.
2. Meissner, pp. 327 ff.
3. *Ibid.*
4. *Ibid.*
5. *Ibid.*
6. Nielsen, p. 39; Nyberg, p. 11.
7. Cf. Swift, p. 19.
8. Deuteronomy, xxvii, 1-8.
9. JE, pp. 42 ff.
10. Jerusalem Talmud, Ket. VIII end; Quoted by Gollancz, pp. 10 f.
11. Cf. Gollancz, pp. 12 f.
12. ERE, V, pp. 194 ff.
13. Gollancz, pp. 54 f., pp. 60 ff.
14. Baba Bathra, p. 21 a; quoted by Gollancz, p. 81; quoted by Dr. Alvin C. Eurich of the Fund for the Advancement of Education in an address at the Eleventh National Conference on Higher Education at Chicago, 6 March 1956, p. 7. Dr. Eurich suggests that the modern American academic superstition that there must be one teacher for every 25 students derives, at least in part, from this source.
15. Gollancz, pp. 88 ff.

Appendix III   Languages, Scripts, Literatures

1. Cf. above, p. 32 ff.
2. Toynbee points out, vii, 240, n. 3, the parallel between this official act on the part of Shih Huang Ti and that on the part of President Mustafa Kemal Ataturk in making, A.D. 1928, the use of the Perso-Arabic alphabet illegal and the use of the Latin alphabet obligatory in the Turkish Republic.
3. Cf. below, p. 360, note 31.
4. These are given by Toynbee, vii, 241 f.
5. Cf. above, 313.
6. Cf. above, 46.
7. Cf. above, 137 ff.
8. Cf. above, 49; for a discussion of linguistic archaism in the Indic Civilization cf. Toynbee, vi, 75 ff.
9. Cf. above, 190 ff.
10. Cf. Toynbee, v, 596 ff.
11. Toynbee, ix, 80.
12. Cf. above, 191; and Rawlinson, H. G., India, *A Short Cultural History* (London 1948, Cresset Press), 214 f.
13. Eliot, Sir Charles, *Hinduism and Buddhism*, 3 vols. (London 1921, Arnold), II, 246.
14. I am indebted for this note to Dr. O. C. Carmichael, who, in 1956-1957, made a study of higher education in India and Pakistan. See his *Universities: Commonwealth and American* (New York 1959, Harpers).

15. Cf. above, 109.
16. Cf. Toynbee, vi, 78.
17. Cf. above, 108.
18. Cf. above, 109 ff.
19. Cf. above, 164 ff.
20. Toynbee, ix, 73.
21. Cf. below, 309 ff.
22. Cf. below, 298 ff.
23. Cf. Erman, A., *The Literature of the Ancient Egyptians,* Eng. trans. (London 1927, Methuen).

Index

Index